Palgrave Studies in Prisons and Penology

Series Editors
Ben Crewe
Institute of Criminology
University of Cambridge
Cambridge, UK

Yvonne Jewkes
School of Social Policy, Sociology
and Social Research
University of Kent
Canterbury, UK

Thomas Ugelvik
Criminology and Sociology of Law
University of Oslo
Oslo, Norway

This is a unique and innovative series, the first of its kind dedicated entirely to prison scholarship. At a historical point in which the prison population has reached an all-time high, the series seeks to analyse the form, nature and consequences of incarceration and related forms of punishment. Palgrave Studies in Prisons and Penology provides an important forum for burgeoning prison research across the world. Series Advisory Board: Anna Eriksson (Monash University), Andrew M. Jefferson (DIGNITY - Danish Institute Against Torture), Shadd Maruna (Rutgers University), Jonathon Simon (Berkeley Law, University of California) and Michael Welch (Rutgers University).

More information about this series at
http://www.palgrave.com/gp/series/14596

Sacha Darke

Conviviality and Survival

Co-Producing Brazilian Prison Order

Sacha Darke
University of Westminster
London, UK

Palgrave Studies in Prisons and Penology
ISBN 978-3-319-92209-6   ISBN 978-3-319-92210-2   (eBook)
https://doi.org/10.1007/978-3-319-92210-2

Library of Congress Control Number: 2018942884

© The Editor(s) (if applicable) and The Author(s) 2018
This work is subject to copyright. All rights are solely and exclusively licensed by the Publisher, whether the whole or part of the material is concerned, specifically the rights of translation, reprinting, reuse of illustrations, recitation, broadcasting, reproduction on microfilms or in any other physical way, and transmission or information storage and retrieval, electronic adaptation, computer software, or by similar or dissimilar methodology now known or hereafter developed.
The use of general descriptive names, registered names, trademarks, service marks, etc. in this publication does not imply, even in the absence of a specific statement, that such names are exempt from the relevant protective laws and regulations and therefore free for general use.
The publisher, the authors and the editors are safe to assume that the advice and information in this book are believed to be true and accurate at the date of publication. Neither the publisher nor the authors or the editors give a warranty, express or implied, with respect to the material contained herein or for any errors or omissions that may have been made. The publisher remains neutral with regard to jurisdictional claims in published maps and institutional affiliations.

Cover credit: © Stefano Paterna/Alamy Stock Photo

Printed on acid-free paper

This Palgrave Macmillan imprint is published by the registered company Springer International Publishing AG part of Springer Nature
The registered company address is: Gewerbestrasse 11, 6330 Cham, Switzerland

Acknowledgements

This book would not have been written if it wasn't for two chance events. The journey began one sunny late summer day in 2005 in São Paulo, when my brother-in-law, Rogério Galvão, suggested we break the monotony of the afternoon by visiting the ruins of the infamous Carandiru prison, Latin America's largest ever prison and arguably the birthplace of Latin America's largest prison gang, the equally infamous First Command of the Capital. A few months later the last standing cell blocks were destroyed. Today all that left is the steel and concrete walkway that surrounded parts of the prison complex and from which I caught my first glimpse of the compound. The imagine is etched on my memory. The photographs we took inside cellblocks two and five, and the rubble I kept from the remains of cell blocks eight and nine, serve to remind me of the hundreds that lived and died there, and in whose memory this book is dedicated.

Four years later, I met judge Maria Lúcia Karam on a drizzly late summer day in Preston, England. Over the next year, I made three trips to Rio de Janeiro, where Maria Lúcia put me in contact with a number of people without who my research might have taken a quite different path. Renata Tavares, who accompanied me to the Bangu prison complex and introduced me to the People of Israel, Rio de Janeiro's largest yet still barely mentioned prison gang. Orlando Zaccone, who granted me unlimited access to my first site of prison fieldwork, an illegal police lock-up he later succeeded in closing down. Virgílio de Mattos and Andreza Lima de Menezes, who introduced me to the former prisoner led, voluntary sector APAC prison system in Minas Gerais, where I returned to complete my second fieldwork study. Maria Lúcia continues to support my research. She generously insists on translated my published work.

There are several other people whose contribution to my research journey I take this opportunity to mention. My former boss, Maggie Sumner, who gave me the support and encouragement I needed as an early career researcher to undertake my first research trips and write my first academic papers. Penny Green, who gave me the invaluable though daunting advice to 'make Brazil my own' in the English speaking prisons research world. Fiona Macaulay, who I soon discovered to be years ahead of me, and who I have since had the privilege to present alongside at a number of conferences and workshops.

Finally, Susanna Darke, who accompanied me on my visit to Carandiru as a ten year old, and eight years later trekked for three hours in the blistering heat of Ilha Grande, Rio de Janeiro, along the path once taken by thousands of prisoners to reach another prison ruin, Cândido Mendes, the birthplace of the Red Command. Sylvia Darke, too young to join her sister on her father's adventures, but equipped with a sense of empathy and understanding of the contradictions of prison far beyond her years. Cristiane Darke, for her unrelenting support, and for putting up with my efforts to keep up my Portuguese over the past 25 years. My mum and dad, Wendy Darke and Jim Darke, and my brother, Nat Darke, for the interest they have always shown in my research and for all the constructive insights they have shared.

Contents

1	Self-Governing Prison Communities	1
2	Law and Repression	45
3	The Northern Massacres	101
4	Surviving through the *Convívio*	139
5	Managing without Guards	199
6	Prison Gangs	235
7	Co-producing Prison Order	279
References		321

List of Figures

Fig. 1.1 The remains of cell blocks eight and nine of the deactivated Carandiru prison, São Paulo, Brazil. In the background, cell block five to the viewer's left, cell block two to the viewer's right. Photograph taken by the author 8 April 2005   6

Fig. 1.2 The entrance to the police *carceragem* "Polinter", Rio de Janeiro, Brazil. Real name blacked out. At the top of the gate is written *carceragem cidadã* (citizen police lock-up), a title Zaccone first introduced in 2008 when had inaugurated an award-winning civil police initiative, Projeto Carceragem Cidadã (Citizen Police Lock-up Project), while governor of a second *carceragem* in the city, Nova Iguaçu. Photograph taken by the author, 17 September 2010   15

Fig. 1.3 The entrance to the cell block at an APAC prison in Minas Gerais, Brazil. To the viewer's left, a portrait of Franz de Castro. To the right, a portrait of Mário Ottoboni. Photograph taken by the author, 10 July 2012   28

Fig. 4.1 A cell block *pátio* at the deactivated Carandiru prison, São Paulo, Brazil. Photograph taken by the author, 8 April 2005   146

Fig. 4.2 A wooden model of a modern remand prison in São Paulo, showing the main cell block with the roof removed from the central corridor and cells on four of the prison's ten wings.

	The first two wings, to the forefront of the picture, contain the *seguro* to the viewer's left and the *isolamento* to the viewer's right. The other wings all house gang-affiliated prisoners	147
Fig. 4.3	A wooden model of a modern remand prison in São Paulo, showing the entrances to the four cells on one of the gang wings, and the *pátio* that prisoners have access to during the day	148
Fig. 6.1	Replica prisoner uniforms on display at the Museu do Cárcere (Prison Museum), Ilha Grande, Rio de Janeiro, Brazil. To the viewer's left, a replica of the stripy uniform used by trusty *faxinas* in Rio de Janeiro's prisons up to the 1940s. Photograph taken by the author, 19 April 2013	240

1

Self-Governing Prison Communities

Things were clearly going wrong in *pavilhão cinco* (pavilion five or cell block five) of Carandiru. When Jocimar, who headed the cell block *faxina* (literally, cleaning, in Brazilian prison slang also meaning cleaning team or, as in the context here, cell block housekeepers), was confronted by the head of security, Luis, over rumours members of his team were abusing their position and collecting drugs debts and protection money directly from prisoners' families, the best explanation he could provide was that it was not possible for him to control everything that happened under his command. By refusing to take responsibility for a matter that went to the heart of inmate relations at the men's prison[1]—"*só pode se dirigir a um familiar do outro se convidado a fazê-lo*" ("never approach another prisoner's family/acquaintance unless he asks you") (Varella 2008: 128)—Jocimar must have known he was treading on thin ground. Luis had every right to warn him of the consequences of not restoring order as quickly as possible. A few evenings later the status quo in the cell block was completely shattered, when the six guards on duty were taken hostage by the occupants of one of the cells set aside for members of the *faxina* on the second floor.[2] Landing staff had been held hostage many times before, but what was unusual this time was that the inmates assaulted one of the officers in a bid to hasten their transfer out of the prison. Luis resisted demands from other guards to allow them to retaliate to such a clear breach of trust by beating up the hostage takers once they had reached the apparent safety of the police van and released their captives. Fortunately for the outraged prison officers, any informal agreements they had with prisoners not to *reagir* (react) in hostage situations did not apply to the police that transported them.

Luis was faced with a dilemma. Transferring Jocimar was the easy part. Having overseen the extortion of prisoners' families and the humiliation of guards, Jocimar was also guilty of failing to enforce codes relating to inmate solidarity and dealings with prison staff. He would not be missed on the *galerias* (galleries or wings[3]). Removing the other 200 inmates that made up the current cell block hierarchy would be far more risky and certainly controversial. Running a leaderless cell block of 1500 inmates was not an option with the handful of guards Luis had at his disposal; and a cell block *faxina* seen to be put in place by the prison management would never gain the confidence of other inmates. In a successful Machiavellian manoeuvre, Luis approached Pirulão, a powerful prisoner he knew he could trust on pain of exposing him to other inmates as a previous police informant and now prison snitch. Within a few days, Pirulão had gathered a group of more than 300 disgruntled prisoners. Shortly after lockdown they removed the old cell block *faxina xadrez* (literally, chess here meaning shared cell) by *xadrez*,[4] masked and armed with sticks and knives, before beating them and handing them over to officers to distribute them to the *masmorra* (dungeon or segregation unit) in cell block four.

I return to the significance of this episode, narrated by Drauzio Varella (2008) in the book Estação Carandiru (Carandiru Station), in a moment. Varella worked voluntarily as a doctor at the prison for more than 10 years, from 1989 to 2001. Estação Carandiru was originally published in 1999. It was later adapted for the award-winning film Carandiru (Babenco and Kramer 2003).

Managing in Prison

When I visited the by then deactivated and part demolished Carandiru prison, in the Brazilian city of São Paulo, with my brother-in-law in April 2005, I had just submitted a doctoral thesis and was in search of a new research project. Carandiru made international headlines on 2 October 1992, when 300 shock troops, many armed with machine guns, entered cell block nine in response to a dispute among rival groups of prisoners. Within 30 minutes, at least 111 prisoners were dead or mortally injured (Veja, 14 October 1992).[5] Most prisoners died at the hands of the equally infamous military police unit Rondas Ostensivas Tobias de Aguiar (ROTA) (Folha de São Paulo, 21 June 2001), whose 700 officers were responsible for a large proportion of the 1470 citizens killed by São Paulo state police that year (Caldeira 2000), and continued to be responsible for up to one in five police killings in the state in the 2000s and into the 2010s (Veja São Paulo, 11 August 2010; Folha de São Paulo, 28 January 2012). As the police entered the cell block, television reporters read out the names and death records of their commanders, including Captain Wanderley Mascarenhas, five of whose 34 previous victims had died at the same prison 10 years earlier (Ramos 2003). Guards, prisoners and police that witnessed the killings give varying descriptions of the source of the dispute that led to the tragic police incursion, from unpaid debts, the results of a game of football, an accusation of sleeping with a sex offender, to someone's space being taken on a washing line. What is clear is that the *faxina* running the cell block failed to prevent what had started out as a relatively minor, everyday dispute from escalating out of control. Varella depicts the riot as an illogical, chaotic affair, and is quick to point out that cell block nine was populated by first time prisoners, who not surprisingly were renowned for being undisciplined and volatile. They also made the mistake of allowing the guards on duty to leave the cell block rather than take them as hostages (Mendes 2009; Varella 2012). Tragically, and in complete contrast to the inexperience demonstrated by these prisoners, Varella (2008) laments, ROTA's response was unleashed with military precision.[6]

Aware inmates across the prison were in fear of their lives, the officer in charge of the neighbouring cell block eight convinced its 1700 prisoners to return with their weapons to their cells, with the promise he would leave the keys to the cells in the hands of the cell block *faxina* in case the shock troops did not stop at cell block nine (Varella 2012). Explanations for why the police took control of cell block nine with such deadly force also vary, from public expectation (ROTA, for instance, could count on the support of the majority of the São Paulo public, despite their reputation for summary executions), prisoners threatening to attack officers with knives covered in HIV contaminated blood, to a systematic attempt to rid the cell block of its inmate hierarchy. What is broadly agreed is that most of the killings occurred on the *faxina*-occupied second floor, and that by the time ROTA reached this floor prisoners had, like those in cell block eight, discarded their weapons and fled to the nearest cells. Survivors claim officers fired their machine guns into many cells, in some cases through the service hatches (e.g. Ramos 2003; Rap and Zeni 2002). The police forensics team that examined the crime scene concluded a number of prisoners had also been shot while kneeling or lying down. Of the 397 bullets that reached their target, 126 were to the head (Justiça Global 2001; see also Pereira 2015; Willys 2015). Carandiru did not recover from the controversy surrounding the operation and was eventually deactivated in September 2002. Two months later three cell blocks, including cell blocks eight and nine, were imploded live on television. The remaining cell blocks were demolished just a short while after I was there in 2005. Paradoxically, the final victims of the Carandiru massacre, as the event came to be known, were the governor[7] of the prison, José Ismael Pedrosa, and the head of the São Paulo state military police, who commanded the operation, Ubiratan Guimarães. Pedrosa was assassinated in 2005 on the orders of the Primeiro Comando da Capital (First Command of the Capital: PCC), a gang formed in the aftermath of the massacre with the explicit aim to protect prisoners from such a tragedy being repeated. Today the PCC operates in over 90% of São Paulo prisons and is Latin America's largest criminal organisation. Guimarães was sentenced to 632 years imprisonment in 2001, only to escape punishment by being elected onto the São Paulo state legislature before winning an appeal against his conviction in 2006. Seven months later he was shot dead in as yet unexplained circumstances.

On the day of my visit I was aware of the massacre, but not the depth inmates participated in governing the prison. Nor did I have any idea of the symbolic significance the prison would have on my next 10 years of research, or the effect visiting it would have on my understanding of what it was about Brazilian prisons I would be drawn to study. Although 15 years have passed since Carandiru last received a prisoner, not only was it the largest ever prison in Latin America, at times holding as many as 9000 prisoners, but it also remains the most written about and filmed prison in Brazil. Equally important for the purposes of this book, first-hand accounts of the prison teach us as much about the daily lives of its inmates and staff as they do about prison conditions.

As I sifted through a pile of rubble just inside the outer wall of the prison compound that contained the remains of cell blocks eight and nine (see Fig. 1.1), I remained in my comfort zone. A law graduate versed in the language of human rights and prison abolition, I contemplated the degrading treatment Carandiru's prisoners must have experienced. The security guard on duty at a gap in the wall we had entered hesitated to allow us to go any further into the compound, but as Brazilians are fond of saying, *sempre tem um jeito* (there is always a way) or *a gente pode dar um jeito* (we can find a way). This was the first of many occasions when the word *jeito*, or the diminutive *jeitinho*, would come to the aid of my research and analysis. It is a word I find increasingly important to understanding the flexible and clientelistic characteristics of everyday political and social interactions in Brazil.

When the security guard eventually agreed to let us in, we walked through the compound to what I later discovered to have been cell block four. Wary of the security guard getting into trouble if anyone else showed up, we spent a few frantic minutes taking photographs of the yard, corridors and cells, before crossing over the ruins of cell block six to take more photographs in cell block two. On the way into and back out of the prison compound we passed by cell block five, scene of the breakdown of governance at the prison described above, and then in the early stages of preparation for the filming of the part fact, part fictional

Fig. 1.1 The remains of cell blocks eight and nine of the deactivated Carandiru prison, São Paulo, Brazil. In the background, cell block five to the viewer's left, cell block two to the viewer's right. Photograph taken by the author 8 April 2005

television series, Carandiru: Outras Histórias (Carandiru: Other Stories) (Babenco et al. 2005). Besides the utter physical disrepair of the prison, what caught our attention in each of the cell blocks were the murals and scribbled writing left behind by prisoners in almost every cell and communal area. A few of these referred to the PCC. Others depicted religious scenes or artefacts, most Christian, some spiritualist or demonic. The majority were more mundane—emblems of São Paulo's major football clubs; messages of love for those on the outside; and messages of support for those on the inside.

Opened in 1952, the Casa de Detenção de São Paulo (São Paulo House of Detention: Carandiru prison) remains the largest ever or at least most populous self-contained prison in Latin America. In 1992, it held 7000 prisoners, three times the number for which it had been built. Since the massacre numerous first-hand accounts of life in Carandiru have been published, including Luiz Alberto Mendes (2005, 2009, 2012, 2015), Drauzio Varella (2008, 2012), Luiz Wolfmann (2000), and (Rap and Zeni 2002), and also a quite remarkable documentary film, O Prisioneiro da Grade de Ferro (The Prisoner of the Iron Bars) (Steinberg and Sacramento 2004), shot by prisoners over seven months the year before the prison was deactivated.

The Carandiru massacre highlighted two aspects of life behind bars in Brazil. The first, and the basis of most academic and governmental literature, concerns the appalling conditions in which prisoners find themselves, from severe staff shortage and overcrowding to wholly inadequate facilities, legal and medical cover. Varella (2008) devotes several chapters to prisoners' health, outlining among other things the devastatingly high levels of drug abuse and serious illness such as tuberculosis, leprosy and HIV Aids. I briefly explore such matters in Chapter 2. The second aspect of Brazilian prison life highlighted by the massacre, and the main focus of my research, concerns the means by which Brazilian prison managers, staff and inmates manage to get by in spite of such adversity and state neglect. This, we will see, is due in part to the amount of time the majority of inmates spent outside their cells, often from sunrise to sunset, mixing freely in the cell block corridors and *pátios* (courtyards or exercise yards). It is also part due to prison work. At Carandiru, most prisoners had some form of paid activity to occupy their time. Some were employed by private contractors, not always officially, manufacturing items such as toys, umbrellas, footballs or greetings cards. The prison even had a bakery and ice-cream factory. As in other prisons in the country, these inmates gained up to—although usually far less than—three-quarters of the national minimum wage. Inmates also got by through participating in the prison's thriving informal economy in drugs, alcohol, pornography, sex, even clothing repairs. A further 1000 inmates affiliated to the prison's Assembléia de Deus (Assembly of God) spent five to six hours a day in prayer or religious learning. As many as 3000 family visitors filled the cell block yards each weekend, 20,000–25,000 at Christmas, Easter or on mothers' day (Varella 2012). 2000 prisoners' wives or girlfriends were registered for intimate visits. Sexual services were also provided by prisoners housed on the Rua das Flores (Street of Flowers) or Paris, a corridor that in the past had housed female prisoners and by the 1970s had become perhaps one of the first spaces in a prison anywhere in the world to be reserved for transvestites.

I explore aspects of what I have come to understand as the collective nature of life at Carandiru and other Brazilian prisons I have visited in Chapter 4. What continues to fascinate me most about Carandiru, like Varella (2004),[8] is how the prison operated despite employing very few staff, in particular the roles played by inmates in running the prison, and the formal and (mostly) informal relations they maintained with prison staff. At the time of the massacre, Carandiru's main cell blocks (five, eight and nine) each held up to 2000 prisoners, guarded by five or six officers during the day, even fewer during the night time (Varella 2012). In order to govern the prison, staff relied on its inmates.

Varella's (2008) interest in inmate participation is made clear from the first few pages, where he describes the work carried out by prisoners loading and unloading vans used to transport prisoners, food and building materials. He goes on to explain that some 1700 of the prison's 7000 inmates worked alongside or in the place of staff in the 1990s, up to 1000 officially as trusty prisoners, for instance as porters, couriers, cooks, cleaners, laundry washers, tailors, hairdressers or clerks. Like other prisoners formally employed by private contractors, trusty prisoners gained a day's remission of sentence for every three days worked. Most were held separately in cell block two, but carried passes that allowed them access to other parts of the prison. It is Varella's first impression of the prison that sets the central theme and my interest in the book: how inmates are formally recruited to work as janitors and administrators, and how prisoners organise themselves to provide security, discipline and material support on the wings. In chapters four to six, we will see that, while much has been written about the rise of major gangs like the PCC since the 1980s and 1990s, few studies have provided more than a partial picture of the nature of inmate involvement in running Brazilian prisons, or the complexity of relations between inmates and prison staff.

Having outlined the functions played by trusty prisoners, whose work was restricted to the communal areas of the prison, Varella (2008) moves on to explore the work of prisoners who worked unofficially in the remaining cell blocks, 150–200 in each of cell blocks five, eight and nine, and 20–30 in cell blocks four, six and seven. In total around 700 prisoners were integrated into these cell block *faxina*, most of who we have seen accommodated in cells on the second floor.[9] Each cell block had its own inmate hierarchy. In addition to performing domestic tasks such as sweeping corridors, mopping, cooking and distributing meals, we will see that these *faxineiros* (cleaners)—or the grammatically incorrect but more commonly used word in Brazilian prison slang, *faxinas*, or as a collective noun, *faxina*—acted as cell block leaders and representatives, and maintained order through enforcing inmate codes and, as we saw in Varella's account of the changing of the *faxina* in cell block five, tacit agreements with prison staff. Through enforcing the decisions of ad hoc quasi-legal *debates* (debates) when prisoners are accused of breaking inmate codes (which at Carandiru, as elsewhere, included averting your eyes from others' visitors, remaining in your cell and not using the bathroom during mealtimes, maintaining silence during sleeping hours, not getting into debt, not resorting to violence without permission, and sharing food, toiletries and clothing brought in by your family), the cell block *faxina* set the *ritmo* (rhythm) of the prison. Carandiru guards did not interfere with the organisation of the *faxina*, nor with its management of the wings unless prisoners were severely beaten, though even an execution would more often than not be settled by a *laranja* (orange or scapegoat), typically an indebted crack addict, stepping forward to falsely confess to the crime. Moreover, guards would consult senior *faxina* before making their own decisions as to when and how to discipline wayward prisoners. Varella refers to the cell block *faxina* as essential to order at the prison:

> The *faxina* is the spine of the prison. Without understanding its structure, it is not possible to comprehend everyday life [in the prison], from ordinary moments to the most serious ones. Its function is to… distribute cell by cell the three daily meals and do the general cleaning […] Dialogue

between the administration is [also] fundamental for maintaining order…
for keeping violence in check. Without the agreement of the cell block
leader, nothing can be done. (Varella 2008: 99 and 100)

In focusing on the collective nature of Brazilian prison life, I do not intend to play down the desperate plight faced by many prisoners, or to question the need for criminologists to challenge political and media discourses that lend legitimacy to Brazil's apparently insatiable appetite for more and more imprisonment. Nor is my purpose to steer prison researchers away from lending support to the important work of international and local penal reform and human rights organisations in giving voice to the grievances of Brazilian prisoners, and exposing the appalling situation under which three quarters of a million people now find themselves incarcerated or working. Compared to the relatively well-resourced prisons of the post-industrial world, the average Brazilian prison is remarkably overcrowded and unhealthy. I deal with these matters in Chapter 2. My point is simply that to understand what it is like inside Brazilian prisons, it is also important to study the means and extent to which they continue to operate and the ordinary inmate and staff member get along in spite of their poor conditions of work and incarceration: to study everyday matters of prison management and situational adjustments as much as deprivations, staff shortages and the need for decarceration. In my experience, Brazilian prisons are as striking for the fact they continue to exhibit complex social orders as the fact they are effectively abandoned by state authorities. Central to my analysis is that the daily lives of front-line prison workers and inmates are entangled to an extent that would be hard to imagine in the west of Europe or north of America. Not only do prison inmates rely on each other as much as they do on prison staff, but prison staff also rely on the cooperation and support of prisoners. Prison staff also experience diminishing levels of everyday authority, as cell block, prison, city, state, even nationwide inmate collectives, including self-proclaimed criminal gangs such as the PCC, increasingly step in to occupy historical voids in state responsibility and governance. At the same time, prison staff rely on prisoners' families and local volunteers to make up for shortfalls in state provision, including bedding, clothing, pharmaceuticals, food, cigarettes, legal and medical services. As a result, the barriers between prison and community life are generally more permeable than they are in, for instance, the USA, the UK or Norway. Prison life in Brazil, therefore, is shaped as much by attachments as detachments, between inmates and staff, and also between prisons and the localities in which they are situated. Under such conditions, shared, or my preferred term, co-governance (for reasons I will explain later), is a social (or institutional) fact of increasing importance in Brazil. Human rights abuses tell one side of the story of what it means to live or work in a Brazilian prison; co-governance tells the other. Remarkably, at the time of the Carandiru massacre prison staffing levels were significantly higher than they are today. In São Paulo, for instance, the official number of inmates per member of prison staff has risen from around two to one in the early 1990s to eight to one today. Once shift patterns, staff roles and absence through sickness are taken into account, it is quite normal to find one officer on duty per 100, even 200 prisoners (Karam and Saraiva 2017; Salla 2006). To make up for staff shortages, not only are as many as one in ten prisoners officially employed by prison authorities in trusty positions (henceforth referred to as trusty *faxina*; I explain this in due course), but thousands more prisoners work informally on the wings, usually with the implicit or explicit support of prison staff, as was the case in Carandiru. As for situational adjustments to the deprivations of prison, at the weekends the number of visitors sometimes exceeds the number of inmates. Families start queuing up outside prisons with their *jumbos* (bags of food and other basic goods—toiletries, confectionaries, cigarettes, clothing and so on—they are allowed to take for those they are visiting) from well before dawn.

Indeed, accounts of prison life point towards an everyday reality in which inmates and staff are often able to create and maintain relationships of accommodation and trust in even the most despairing of settings. This, I have previously written, broadly applies to prisons across Latin American (Darke and Karam 2016; Darke and Garces 2017a). Similar to the ways in which alternative systems of governance have filled the gap left by ineffective state governance in the country's urban slums (see, inter alia, Biondi 2014; Feltran 2010; Santos 2002), most Brazilian prisons continue to operate under normative, if generally "thin and multilayered" (Darke 2014a: 65) and "forced" (Darke 2013b: 280) reciprocal and customary orders, based not upon the democratic rule of law or bureaucratic regulations, but on organically produced *regras de procedimento* (rules of procedure) (Varella 2008: 78) or *regras de convivência* (rules of conviviality or rules of coexistence) (Marques 2010b: 318). As Arruda (2015), Human Rights Watch (2015b), and Muñoz (2015) demonstrate in the case of the Curado complex in the North-eastern state of Pernambuco, in some prisons officers have gone so far as to delegate even their most basic of tasks—security and discipline—to inmates. Pernambuco has the highest level of prison overcrowding and lowest staff-inmate ratio of the 27 states in the country. A Brazilian parliamentary report I explore in some detail in chapters two and four found an average of just five guards on duty in the complex, which at the time was holding 4200 inmates (Câmara dos Deputados 2008). To make up for these shortfalls, prison governors rely on police to secure the spaces between the three prisons in the complex, and on *chaveiros* (key holders) to manage the spaces within its 17 cell blocks. At another prison highlighted in Câmara dos Deputados (2008), Penitenciária Lemos de Brito, in the central-eastern state of Bahia, the parliamentary investigators found the head inmate leader had a key to his own cell. When the discovery was reported to the press and police officers subsequently arrived to transfer the prisoner, the governor of the prison had to knock on his door (ibid.). Sensationalism aside, the fact is it is not so unusual in Brazil for prisoners to be entrusted with keys. In some cases, this may mean no more than having a key to a room in which they work, for instance a kitchen or library. In other cases, prisoners may be given keys to allow them access to individual prison wings, for instance to distribute meals. Besides the Curado complex, inmates are also employed and entrusted with keys to control access to and from the wings in at least two other major prisons in Brazil, Cadeia Pública de Porto Alegre (Porto Alegre Public Prison; more commonly referred to by its previous name, Central Prison) in the Southern state of Rio Grande do Sul (Bassani 2016; Sager and Beto 2016; França et al. 2016), and Alcaçuz prison complex in the Northern state of Rio Grande do Norte (Madeiro 2017), scene of a recent gang-related massacre that

I explore in Chapter 3. In Chapter 5, we will see a similar situation was to be found in Rio de Janeiro's[10] now deactivated police *carceragem* (lockup; units of holding cells) system. During my prison visits and communications with prison workers, I have heard of inmates being entrusted with keys to the cell blocks at police *carceragens* in São Paulo in the 2000s and at a remand prison in Rio de Janeiro today (I describe this latter prison in Chapter 3). Most recently, I learnt of a prison in Bahia where prison officers have resorted to passing keys to gang leaders to lock the cells on their wing at the end of the day. Inmates also control the wing entrances in dozens of community prisons across the country, nine of which I have visited in the states of Minas Gerais and São Paulo. I introduce Rio de Janeiro's pre-trial system, and Minas Gerais and São Paulo's community prison systems below.

Moreover, Brazilian prisons do not inevitably become violent and disorderly or their governance illegitimate when the power to maintain order and security is delegated to prisoners. In this book I describe many prisons, including Carandiru, where co-governance has arguably been to the benefit of inmates and staff. In doing so I endeavour to identify the possibilities and potential dangers of including inmates in administering the prisons in which they are incarcerated alongside and in place of staff. This does not signify that certain aspects of co-governance should be adopted as prison policy in Brazil or anywhere else, but that in many cases prison inmates and staff are simply better off with than without it. This book is concerned with realities more than ideals. I leave the latter to the judgement of the reader.

Getting By

Compare my reflections on my initial impressions of Carandiru, and Varella's description of the changing of the *faxina* in cell block five, with my field notes of my first visit to a *carceragem*, in Rio de Janeiro in 2010, where I returned in September the same year to complete the first of two fieldwork prison studies. I was accompanied on this initial visit by Judge Maria Lúcia Karam and Orlando Zaccone, a senior civil police officer and prison and drugs prohibition abolitionist.

Zaccone coordinated the state's 16 *carceragens* from 2009 until he succeeded in closing them down in the early 2010s:

Orlando picked us up soon after 1 p.m. As we drove to Polinter,[11] he explained that with a current population of around 650 inmates the *carceragem* was the largest in the state. Prisoners stayed on average six months while they waited for spaces to become available in remand prisons, when by law the police were only allowed to hold them for 24 hours.[12] Many chose to stay there until they were tried and sentenced, so as to stay closer to their families, who were treated with as much dignity as possible when they visited. The officers that worked there received no resources to run the *carceragem* apart from the delivery of prison meals. Converted from police horse stables, there were no outdoor spaces to allow prisoners their legal right to a minimum of two hours *banho de sol* (literally, sunbathe; here meaning access to exercise yards) a day, but the police had been able to open up a corridor that ran along across the front of the cells. Orlando assured us relations were good between officers and the Comando Vermelho (CV), Rio's largest and Brazil's second largest "criminal" gang after the PCC, that ran one of the two wings at the *carceragem,* and the Povo de Israel, made up of prisoners that were not accepted or not interested in gang membership, that ran the other, the *seguro* (literally, insurance: vulnerable persons unit). Importantly, Orlando had managed to put an end to police violence. He had also ended the strip-searching of prisoners' families and made sure the family of every prisoner was able to visit almost any day of the week. In response, the CV and Povo de Israel leadership assured the safety of the police and trusty prisoners, and discipline and order in the cell block. They had also agreed to ban weapons and hard drugs from entering.

When we arrived, it was immediately apparent that Polinter was far from large physically (see Fig. 1.2). With the use of Google satellite images, I later discovered the single-storey *carceragem* occupied a space of no more than 1200 m^2. A whiteboard in the office showed there to be currently 603 inmates, around 550 of which were being held across nine cells, or rather caged former animal stalls, which I subsequently estimated to be an average of 25 m^2. When I returned to the

1 Self-Governing Prison Communities 15

Fig. 1.2 The entrance to the police *carceragem* "Polinter", Rio de Janeiro, Brazil. Real name blacked out. At the top of the gate is written *carceragem cidadã* (citizen police lock-up), a title Zaccone first introduced in 2008 when had inaugurated an award-winning civil police initiative, Projeto Carceragem Cidadã (Citizen Police Lock-up Project), while governor of a second *carceragem* in the city, Nova Iguaçu. Photograph taken by the author, 17 September 2010

carceragem to conduct fieldwork six months later, a prisoner told me that a year earlier he had shared one of the cells with over 100 people.

Orlando took us straight to the office where, besides two of only three officers working that afternoon (the other was stationed at the entrance to the *carceragem*), we met the first of perhaps 50 *colaboradores* (collaborators: Rio de Janeiro prison worker's preferred term for trusty prisoners) at the *carceragem*, who worked as clerks. Alongside the police, they were dealing with a group of newly arrived prisoners, represented by a current prisoner who I was soon to realise to be the leader of the *carceragem*'s CV. Sitting down for coffee after the new prisoners had been registered and taken to the cell block, one of the officers explained the police could not run the *carceragem* without their *colaboradores*, and that at night there was sometimes only one officer on duty. (I later discovered it was actually unusual to have more than one officer on duty overnight.) At these times he slept with his mobile phone by his bed, not as I inquired because of the risk of escape or rebellion, but in case a prisoner was taken ill and had to be rushed to hospital. Clearly appreciating the effect this would have on me, he broke into a grin. It wouldn't look good if there were only prisoners left in charge, he added. I only understood the full irony of this otherwise throwaway comment when I returned to start research. When I arrived on the first day, the governor was away. While I waited for him to return, I was left in the hands of two former police officers, now prisoners and chief *colaboradores*. Together with the governor, these two *colaboradores* were referred to by other inmates as Polinter's *administração* (administration). Both carried mobile phones and keys. These included keys to an unstaffed back gate, which was used as a trade entrance, and also keys to the cell block.

After coffee, Orlando took Maria Lúcia and I onto the CV wing to explain my plans for research. Crossing the few metres of the yard to the cell block, a group of prisoners on the *seguro* shouted out to Orlando, *"tu vai ser o novo presidente!"* ("you're going to be the next president!"), in reference to nationwide elections that were due to take place later in the year. As *colaboradores* opened the gate to the CV wing, inmates on the other side noticed Maria Lúcia's presence and the word was spread that a woman was entering. In spite of the cramped conditions and searing heat (Orlando instructed me to put my hand up to a grill to the outside, where the 30 degree centigrade air coming through felt as cool as if it were emerging from an air conditioning unit), the 250 or so prisoners quickly put on immaculately clean and pressed white T-shirts (each of the cells had a stove, which allowed them to boil water for washing and filling two-litre plastic soft drinks bottles for ironing). We squeezed along the wing corridor to speak with the CV leader I had seen in the office, who greeted Orlando and, encircled by his entourage, agreed to my research schedule. On the way back to the town centre, Orlando remarked that he was quite sure he was the only police officer the CV shook hands with. I wondered whether I was the first prison researcher they had given permission to conduct ethnographic research on their organisation and structure.[13]

Polinter is the focus of Chapter 5. If Varella's accounts of disorder at Carandiru help introduce the reader to the realities of co-governance as a means of negotiating personal safety (of resolving conflicts, and allowing prison inmates to keep their heads down and do their time safe in the knowledge that to do so would not be interpreted as a sign of weakness), my intention in focusing on my first impressions of Polinter is to emphasise the broader importance of co-governance in enabling prison staff and inmates to get by. Without the support of prisoners and their survival "know how", it would not have been possible for the police to do any more at the *carceragem* than patrol the perimeter walls and deliver food to the entrances to the cell block, even had there always been two officers on duty. Not only would escapes have been more likely, and disputes between and among prisoners and staff more difficult to resolve, as already noted, but who for example would have distributed the food to the cells? Subsequently collected the empty food containers? Swept the floors? Organised cell rotas for the use of corridors during unlock, and in-cell rotas for the 40–50 prisoners who had to share each shower and toilet? Attended to prisoners with ailments? Regulated their medication? Registered and seen to the needs of visitors? Checked that the *jumbos* brought in by visitors did not contain weapons or drugs? Made sure prisoners stood out of the way and averted their eyes from each other's families during visiting hours, and kept their voices down in the evening so others could get to sleep? Dealt with lawyers, court and prison service officials? Represented the *coletivo* (collective or inmate body) in dealings with *colaboradores* and police? Mended the showers, water taps and fans that prevented the temperature from rising to life-threatening levels such as the 56.7 degrees centigrade recorded at the *carceragem* shortly after Zaccone took over (Globo, 11 February 2010)? Of course, all of this does not happen in every Brazilian prison. It is also true that under Zaccone's oversight, Polinter was also going through extraordinary times. But it is equally true that hunger and sickness are no more in the interest of those who live and work in any Brazilian prison as are conflict and disorder; nor the ill-treatment of prisoners' families, without whom prisoners would have to go without some of the most essential of items. To the extent prison staff and inmates want routines to run smoothly, and for neither to be damaged by their prison experience, they likewise have to negotiate. In most prisons, staff and inmates cobble together ways to co-produce everyday matters of survival as well as personal safety. In chapters three to six, we will see many of the practices I observed at Polinter are common to prisons of all types across Rio de Janeiro and the remainder of the country. The pertinent question is not why, but under what conditions they manage to do so.

More generally, I make use of this narrative of my first visit to the *carceragem* in order to highlight three areas in which my analysis departs from much of the existing literature on Brazilian prisons alluded to in this introduction.

First, Brazilian prisons are not necessarily as disorderly or violent as they are often depicted. In most Brazilian states, homicide rates are not significantly higher in prison than on the outside, and in many cases are lower than homicide rates among young men in the areas prisoners come from. This includes Pernambuco. It included Carandiru, and also Rio de Janeiro's police *carceragens*, where no prisoner was killed during Zaccone's three-year tenure. Similarly, while it is arguably mistaken to regard the gangs that increasingly monopolise networks of co-governance as having "pacified" the prison system (Dias 2013), it is equally important not to underestimate the role prison gangs play in supporting systems of mutual aid and protection. In a groundbreaking study of the unprecedented drop in violence in prisons in California and other parts of the USA over the past two decades, Skarbek (2014) demonstrates prison gangs have the potential to make the average prisoner safer and their lives more predictable. "Governance institutions", Skarbek (2014: 6) writes, "[are] necessary for people to live orderly, prosperous lives". In this book, I explore similar claims that have been made about understaffed prisons in other parts of the world, especially in Latin America and, my focus, Brazil.

Second, in Brazil prison governance is a largely temporal and localised matter that varies from one context to another. This remains the case despite the rise of prison gangs and is the main reason I have adopted the term prison communities in the title to this opening chapter (the other reason being entanglements between individual prisons and the localities in which they are situated). The examples of inmate trusty and inmate leader systems I cover in chapters four and six each vary in form and substance. Further, while many of these practices may have been absorbed and formalised by local prison authorities and prison gangs, in most places co-governance continues to be more fluid and customary than bureaucratic and prescriptive, and grounded as much in interpersonal and social interactions and everyday interdependencies and accommodations, what Garces, Martin and I refer to as informal prison dynamics (Darke and Garces 2017a; Garces et al. 2013), as hierarchies and impositions of formal rules. In this sense, prison governance is made up of informal practices that are not so much shared, as if they were the result of calculated policies, as co-produced from convergences in everyday practices of coexistence, which will be different in one context to another. Some prison researchers in Brazil argue, convincingly in my view, that co-governance is less hierarchical as habitual even in the PCC prisons of São Paulo. This can be noted in the position occupied by the PCC leadership. Important decisions are collectively made among affiliated gang members, and most roles are interchangeable (Dias 2013). Moreover, local gang members are typically chosen among those considered to have good skills of negotiation and control over their emotions and impulses (ibid.), *humilde* (humble) (Biondi 2010, 2014), and committed to *igualdade* (equality) and *paz entre ladrões* (peace among thieves) (cf. Marques 2014) rather than their depth of involvement in crime. (A former PCC member once told me inmates in the prison he was currently incarcerated, and I was researching, were willing to open up to me because I was *humilde*; hardly the attitude one would expect from a person familiar with top-down, bureaucratic structures). All prisoners participate in the PCC's quasi-legal processes of adjudication. In some prisons, PCC codes of conduct are enforced even in the complete absence of gang leaders. PCC affiliated prisoners do not feel obliged to take orders from gang members that vary from the codes to which they are accustomed. At the same time, inmate codes of conduct vary with the *ritmo* of one PCC prison to another:

> Even the most general of ideas, including 'peace', 'equality', and the PCC itself are inscribed by and with the local conditions of their emergence, in relation to which they vary. Thieves refer to these variations as 'rhythm'. (Biondi 2016: 157)

Finally, and closely related to this methodologically, is the importance, first and foremost, of studying places (in this case Brazilian prisons) in their own terms. To paraphrase Nelken (2010), a criminologist should only draw comparisons on issues of crime and justice between one place and another, or between one place and global averages, once they have an understanding of its history and culture. In a brutally honest account of the time she spent working at the University of West Indies in Trinidad and Tobago, Cain (2000) emphasises the difficulties she encountered as a British academic making sense of, among other things, relatively low levels of youth crime, and the importance attached by women's anti-violence movements to their male colleagues' experiences and standpoints. The social and criminological theories utilised by feminist and youth crime researchers in the UK, Cain demonstrates, are of limited use in the Caribbean context. An estimated 90% of articles published in social science journals were written by academics in Northern America or Western Europe (Aas 2012). As they are tested and revised over time, theories of crime and justice become academic common sense. Yet, as postcolonial theorists such as Said (1978) and more recently Comaroff and Comaroff (2006, 2012), Connell (2006, 2007), Coronil (2000, 2004), Karstedt (2001), Lee and Laidler (2013), de Souza Santos (2007; Santos et al. 2007), and Tuhiwai Smith (2012) observe in their analysis of the historical and continuing global dominance of Western thought, few social science theories have been adequately put to the test beyond the Global North, yet many are presented as if they are of universal application. At the same time, too many social scientists in the South continue to privilege the standpoints and knowledge of Northern experts, and to rely on utilising Northern concepts and theories in contexts that are often very different to those upon which they were developed.[14] This is certainly the case in Brazil (Dwyer 2012; Godoi 2016; Steinberg 2016) and in Latin America more widely (see, inter alia, Blaustein 2016; Bortoluci and Jansen 2013; Castro 1987, 2000; Codino 2014; Coronil 2004; Mascareño and Chernilo 2009; Olmo 1981, 1999; Rosa 2014; Santos 2010, 2012; Sozzo 2006, 2017; Supervielle 2012). This is not to say localities should not also be studied in the light of what happens elsewhere. Nor is it to say Latin American social scientists have failed to adapt imported theories to local situations. There exists a wealth of liberal and critical Latin American research that has focused on reinterpreting Northern theories on matters relating to order, liberty, marginalisation and authoritarianism, as well broader sociopolitical issues pertaining to race, social movements, colonisation and North-South relations (Santos 2012; Supervielle 2012). Still, it is not an exaggeration to say that Latin American social science scholarship, as Northern scholarship on Latin America, continues to be restrained by domestic colonisation (Supervielle 2012: 65) and corresponding tendencies either to adapt Northern theories in a way that serves to legitimise existing exclusionary and repressive policies (Olmo 1999; Salvatore and Aguirre 1996; Zaffaroni 1989) or to downplay the value of locally produced knowledge altogether. Both of these tendencies are likely to become further entrenched with the increasing importance attached to policy and international impact in global university rankings (Blaustein 2017). The strain towards Northern perspectives starts early in a Brazilian social scientist's career. PhD. students invariably depend on state funding bodies rather than university bursaries for research grants. They are required to have working knowledge of at least one European language besides Portuguese and Spanish, gain particular prestige if they do a sandwich or postgraduate year in a Northern America or Western European university, and are expected to publish in English and/or "international", that is American or British peer-reviewed journals (Dwyer 2012). Moreover, like researchers anywhere else in the world, Brazilian social scientists naturally tend to focus most attention on the Northern theories published in languages they understand or those that have been translated into their native language. Italian and German research is particularly well cited in Brazilian criminology. Many academics are second- or third-generation Italian or German immigrants. French and Spanish research is cited less. For example, Foucault's (1977) Discipline and Punish was barely cited in Brazilian prisons research before it was translated and published in Portuguese in 1985 (Salla 2017).

With this epistemological position in mind, a major aim of my research has been to question the extent to which our established (Northern) understanding of prisons is useful in Brazil. Throughout the research process, it has also been necessary for me to critically reflect on the presumed standpoints and knowledge I have developed through my own academic training in England, as well as the privileged position I have enjoyed in Brazil as a researcher from the North. In this book I draw on the work of scholars that are concerned with developing nuanced accounts of prison life beyond the West. Most of the works I cite are either written by Brazilians or by foreigners who conducted their research in Portuguese. Moreover, I am constantly reminded of the dangers highlighted by Blaustein (2016, 2017), Cain (2000), Cohen (1988), Fonseca (2018), Jefferson and Jensen (2009) and others that even the most benign transfer of criminal justice theories and practices developed in one part of the world to another may do more harm than good. This Northern occidentalist mindset (Cain 2000: 257) is at the centre of much that is wrong with international prison reform. After three weeks participant observation, I came to the conclusion it would have been potentially disastrous if prison staff were not allowed to co-govern Polinter with its prisoners on the assumption inmate and staff-inmate relations are inherently predatory and conflictual in overcrowded, under-resourced prisons. I could not help but be troubled by many of the practices I observed and outline in Chapter 5—prisoners handcuffing and strip-searching other prisoners; prisoners being entrusted with weapons; officers turning a blind eye to minor assaults; prisoners deciding who was allowed to talk with officers; prisoners being required to share food brought in by their families with their less fortunate cellmates—but I knew I had to set aside my cultural sensibilities and academic training to evaluate these practices objectively.

Equally concerning is the opposing tendency—emerging from an orientalist mindset (ibid.)—for criminal justice policies to be tainted by underlying assumptions that certain aspects of Southern cultures and everyday realities are quite different to those in the occidental North. In Brazil, perceived differences map on to a long colonial and postcolonial history of social and political divisions and take on radical class, gender and racial identities. We will see some of the discourses employed by advocates of penal reform in Brazil inadvertently shift attention beyond the toxic nature of poor prison conditions towards popularised notions of the dangerous, irrecoverable prisoner. If my work is to inform prisons policy in Brazil, and as a research activist my ultimate goal is indeed to make a positive difference, however small, to the lives of those caught up in prison, it is paramount I remain committed to exploring the local conditions under which international penal and human rights norms might be implemented. I outline the potential policy implications of my research in Chapter 7.

Mutual Aid

Counter-intuitively perhaps, Brazilian inmates do not leave prison any more harmed socially and psychologically than prisoners in the USA or England and Wales. Prison guards likewise appear to suffer no more than their Northern American or Western European counterparts. In Chapter 4, I cite studies that point to relatively low levels of both self-reported and diagnosed psychiatric illness. Where it is able to take root, it appears inmate conviviality provides support networks and a sense of togetherness that shield the average prison inmate from some of the most debilitating pains of imprisonment (Sykes 1958) and institutional processes of mortification (Goffman 1968). We will see the chances of a Brazilian prisoner dying or being maimed by accidents or preventable illnesses or disease are relatively high. Overcrowding also has negative psychological as well as physical effects (Inter-American Commission on Human Rights 2011). On the other hand, fewer experience the pains of isolation, and fewer live in fear of being humiliated or bullied by disciplinarian or sadistic prison guards. As previously stated, most enter a climate of violence that is little if any more intense than they experience outside. Finally, their families will have suffered, and they will face the stigma of having been imprisoned, but most former prisoners will soon find work, at least in the informal economy (see Madeira 2008). A survey of prisoners in São Paulo in the 1980s found only one in a hundred had never worked (Brant 1986, cited in Goifman 2002). Nor does prison have quite the same impact on people's social stability as it does in many Northern countries. 17 in 20 male prisoners maintain regular contact with their families throughout their sentence (Câmara dos Deputados 2008). In Chapter 4, I analyse inmate adjustments to the pains of imprisonment in the context of what at first sight might appear to Western, jaundiced eyes a quite surprising fact about Brazilian prisons: that prisoners are, if anything, less likely to suffer from anxiety, neurosis or depression as a result of their incarceration than their Northern American or Western European counterparts. Moreover, comparatively fewer Brazilian prisoners resort to self-inflicted harm or suicide.

None of this means people exactly flourish in Brazilian prison. To borrow again from Skarbek's (2014) analysis of North American prison gangs, it is simply to state that the more prison authorities fail in their responsibilities towards prisoners, the more they are replaced by alternative, informal systems of governance. As anyone else, most prisoners need systems of collective responsibility to help them cope with the uncertainties of their social/institutional selves, and to enable them to make better use of their time. It also means going to prison in Brazil may not interrupt the processes by which most young people eventually leave crime behind to the extent it does in the North. I will explain what I mean by this in a little more detail in a moment. First I present one more narrative of prison co-governance, this time taken from my field notes regarding an incident I witnessed during my second fieldwork study in 2012, at a faith-based, voluntary sector prison:

> When I arrived back at the semi-open unit of Franz de Castro prison,[15] after a day out visiting another prison in the area, a scuffle broke out in the workshop. A prisoner from the Conselho de Sinceridade e Solidariedade (Sincerity and Solidarity Council: the CSS) had just approached another prisoner to escort him back to the cell block after work as punishment for refusing to stand up during morning prayers earlier that day. Both had to be physically restrained by other prisoners. Once CSS members had taken the two culprits to their cells, the

president of the council immediately called for a disciplinary hearing, where it was informally agreed that the second prisoner, who had picked up a metal instrument, was mostly to blame. When the president told others on the council the governor's initial reaction to the incident had been to suggest both inmates return to the closed unit, they complained the governor was also partly to blame, having only that morning overridden a decision they had made following the first incident not to allow the second prisoner to lose both an evening's association and a day of work. While the CSS was solely responsible for dealing with breaches of low-level offences, the governor had been right to insist prison rules did not allow for the offender to lose his right to work. Nonetheless, some members of the council insisted it was still a decision that was theirs to make, and the governor had not understood the culprit, a known troublemaker from since their school days, was bound to use the fact he had worked all day as an excuse for argument. Since arriving at the prison two weeks earlier, I had already formed the opinion the governor exercised limited authority at the prison, and that this was partly due to him being the first governor in the prison's by then 17 year history not to have previously served time there himself. The last two governors had both risen through the CSS ranks at Franz de Castro to become governors of the prison on release. In a clear show of defiance, when it came to recording their testimonies, each witness, including several council members, downplayed the entire incident, now "officially" telling the president they had not seen any weapons being raised at all. Still, at the end of the meeting, the president explained to the governor the council would be recommending the second prisoner return to the closed unit, but that the first prisoners receive no more than a few days' loss of association. When the prison's disciplinary committee received the CSS's formal report on the incident, it agreed to their suggestion.

To enforce the second prisoner's punishment (I shall call him Robson), the CSS temporarily moved the tuck shop he ran in the evenings into the cell block. In the immediate days after he had completed his punishment, Robson was given the responsibility to sleep on a sofa in a corridor of the administrative block to care to the needs of Mário Ottoboni, the elderly founder of the APAC (Associação de Proteção e Assistência ao Condenado: Association for the Protection and Assistance of the Convict) movement, who was staying for a few days during the movement's 40th anniversary celebrations. I was also staying in the administrative block and was quite annoyed at having lost the sofa, which I had been sleeping on for two weeks due to sharing a room with another guest who snored profusely (I also found it difficult to take my mind off the fact the room had in the recent past been used for intimate visits). One late evening Robson told me he was ashamed of himself for rising to the provocation, and that he still had much to learn before he was released. Over breakfast one morning, Mário told me the story of one of the first APAC prisoners, a particularly troublesome young man who eventually went on to help develop the APAC methodology. Mário claimed to have finally turned him around following a similar violent incidence by giving him money and sending him to the shops to buy some prison supplies. Sometime after I finished my research at Franz de Castro Robson became president of the CSS on the prison's semi-open unit. Like many CSS presidents before him, after he is released he may return to the prison to work as a volunteer or paid guard. From the number of times he has appeared in news items on the Fraternidade Brasileira de Assistência aos Condenados (Brazilian Fraternity for the Assistance of Convicts: FBAC)'s website and Facebook page, I expect he has already been identified as a potential APAC prison governor.[16]

The title APAC is associated with a Catholic Cursillo group that in the early 1970s opened Brazil's first voluntary sector prison wing at Humaitá, São José dos Campos, São Paulo, before taking full control of the prison in 1984. In 1985, the group established a second non-profit legal entity to inaugurate a new APAC prison, Franz de Castro, in Itaúna, Minas Gerais, and a regulatory body, FBAC, to oversee the two. Only a handful of APAC prisons opened over the next 20 years. However, the movement advanced considerably from the mid-2000s, principally in Minas Gerais. In 2006, state legislation came into effect that authorised prison authorities to enter into formal agreements to fund the building and maintenance of APAC prisons irrespective of the fact they operated without state employees, including police or prison officers. In the past decade, the APAC movement has spread to other parts of Brazil, for instance Maranhão (which opened its first APAC prison in 2008), and Paraná (which opened its first APAC prison in

2013). 147 voluntary sector organisations had registered with FBAC by the time I visited Franz de Castro for the first time in 2012 (Fundação AVSI 2012), although the majority had not yet secured permission or funding to start building. 41 APAC prisons were in operation by the end of 2013, 35 of which in Minas Gerais. My introduction to this alternative prison system came in 2010 when I visited APAC de Nova Lima and encountered a prisoner working at the front gate. In 2012, I visited a further six APAC prisons, including Franz de Castro, where I stayed for the next three weeks. FBAC no longer regulates Humaitá (since renamed São José dos Campos) or other prisons in São Paulo. A further 21 voluntary sector prisons were eventually opened in São Paulo following the introduction of government funding in 1996, many by groups that were likewise originally constituted under the title APAC. However, in contrast to the situation in Minas Gerais, these CR (Centro de Ressocialização: Resocialisation Centre) prisons were administered in partnership with state authorities. While voluntary sector nongovernmental organisations managed the inside of the prisons, state penitentiary guards retained control over the outer walls. After a major rebellion across São Paulo's prison system in 2006 (covered in Chapter 6), guards were stationed inside CR prisons as well. Many CR prisons managed to retain their ethos of rehabilitation and regimes of full-time, purposeful activity (Macaulay 2014, 2015). Still, many voluntary sector services were replaced with private sector provision (Macaulay 2013).

APAC prisons operate strict but active regimes. They boast a reconviction rate of less than 10% (Ferreira 2016). However, it was not the religious or disciplinary elements of APAC regimes that originally drew me to study Franz de Castro, nor their broader focus on humanity and therapy, but the fact they are deliberately designed to operate with minimal interference from state authorities and prisoners deliberately put into positions of authority. APAC prisons are administered according to a methodology that takes state abandonment of prisoners and the failure of the prison system as its starting point (ibid.). The APAC vision, FBAC explains in its rules and regulations (Fraternidade Brasileira de Assistência aos Condenados 2014), is of community and peer-facilitated

Fig. 1.3 The entrance to the cell block at an APAC prison in Minas Gerais, Brazil. To the viewer's left, a portrait of Franz de Castro. To the right, a portrait of Mário Ottoboni. Photograph taken by the author, 10 July 2012

reintegration rather than state-led exclusion. At the entrance to every APAC prison is written the message, *aqui entra o homem, o delito fica lá fora* (here enters the man, his offence stays outside) (see Fig. 1.3). Under the headings of *aprendendo a viver em comunidade* (learning to live communally) and *aprendendo a servir* (learning to serve), inmates are required to be centrally involved in all aspects of prison community life, including religious services, group therapy, cleaning and (for women prisoners) cooking, representing their cellmates, participating in family days and local events, assisting guards, of which there is usually just one on duty, and through their participation in inmate councils, whose membership rotates every six months, adjudicating on breaches of APAC prison rules and implementing punishments. APAC prisoners also develop their own "house rules", much in the same way as (to use FBAC terminology) any responsible person living with others would do on the outside. One house rule I had explained to me by inmates at a women's APAC prison was not to leave your wet towel on your bed. Failure to do so could mean a day's loss of association, which in the APAC vision of rehabilitation is the equivalent of a child being grounded or sent to bed early.

As such, APAC prisons are relevant to my study of co-governed prison order for the extent they depart from certain aspects of the common Brazilian prison system (its abandoning of prisons and prisoners), but comply with others (its reliance on prisons and prisoners self-governing and collaborating with staff). In the words of Ottoboni (2006: 30), what the APAC methodology rejects is the view prisoners are "beyond recovery, social rubbish". What it embraces, though for very different reasons (rehabilitation rather than order), is the need to maintain prisoners' connections to their community, and for prisoners, as people who have lost sight of what it means to be part of the community, to learn to be responsible (to lead and care for) one another. APAC prisons are therefore co-governed in three ways. First and most obviously, like Carandiru, Polinter and prisons across the country, APAC prisons are co-governed in the sense staff run them in partnership with inmates, and with the local community. Here, the APAC methodology embraces the collective nature of Brazilian prison life, and the consequent entanglements between inmates and staff, prisons and communities, and on purpose, not by default. Second, in order for the APAC vision of staff-inmate-community co-governance to work in practice, FBAC rules require all inmates and staff come from within a short distance of the prison. Moreover, FBAC draws little distinction between prison staff and inmates, both of who are ultimately tasked with setting good examples to one another and behaving as mentors and substitute families. A special case is made for inmates' families, whose presence as volunteers is seen as the best means to prepare prisoners for release, and also for former APAC inmates, many of whom, as I noted in the narrative above, are encouraged to stay on at the prison in which they served their sentence. Indeed, most volunteers and FBAC employees, including prison guards and governors, are former APAC prisoners. One prison governor and one senior FBAC manager I met in 2012 were still on conditional release.

Finally, APAC prisons are co-governed in the sense prisoners and volunteers jointly administer them in order to promote a version of rehabilitation premised in philosophies of mutual aid and self-help. Similar to the methods utilised by therapeutic community prisons such as HMP Grendon in the UK, and peer-support groups like Alcoholic Anonymous and Narcotics Anonymous, APAC prisons treat desistance as a personal journey that is best undertaken with fellow recoverers. APAC prisons have clearly been instrumental in helping some people turn their backs on their criminal lifestyles, or perhaps more accurately, not damaging people as much as they might do. But in the refusal of some APAC prison managers not to go beyond FBAC prison rules and take seriously, for instance, issues of trauma, substance abuse, education and training, they have failed many others. In contrast to wider developments in the peer-support/therapeutic community movements, FBAC's methods are based less on the ideal of mutual aid as mutual control.

***

This book is the product of a decade of continuing research on Brazilian prisons and, more recently, prison systems in other parts of Latin America. In addition to Franz de Castro, Polinter and the deactivated Carandiru, my research in Brazil to date has included visits to more than 40 prisons or police *carceragens* in ten states (Bahia, Espírito Santo, Goiás, Mato Grosso do Sul, Minas Gerais, Paraná, Rio Grande do Sul, Rio de Janeiro, Rondônia and São Paulo), and ongoing contact with former prisoners, prison guards and governors, prison ethnographers, prisoner support groups, criminal lawyers and judges. All but one of my prison visits has included tours of the cell blocks and conversations with inmates as well as administrators and guards. I have visited six of the prisons on more than one occasion. Five of the prisons I have visited housed women offenders; two more (both in Goiás) had wings for female as well as male offenders. Over the following chapters, I provide illustrations from most of my prison visits. However, to the extent that I am able to generalise from my research on prison cultures, it is mostly on the experiences of men.

To summarise and conclude this introductory chapter, my intention in writing this book is to contribute to the existing academic literature on Brazilian prisons in five ways. First and foremost, the book is distinctive in its focus on the historically informal, self-governing aspects of prison life in Brazil, which I hope to have already demonstrated to be crucial to understanding everyday prison routines and relations among prisoners, and between prisoners and prison staff, prisons and communities.

Second, this is one of only a handful of books on prisons research anywhere to be written within a comparative research framework. By the end of the book, I aim to have left the reader in no doubt of the futility when undertaking comparative prisons research, at least prisons research beyond Western Europe and Northern America, of failing to pay equal attention to local and regional, cultural and historical specificities as global norms and trends. I argue that we can draw few concrete parallels between prisons in Brazil and prisons in the Global North, and that wherever possible researchers of Southern prisons should privilege Southern (in this case, Latin American and, more localised still, Brazilian) perspectives. As previously indicated, part of this analysis involves warning against misguided Northern occidentalist tendencies to pressure Southern countries into reforms that will not work in theory or in practice. It also involves turning the tables on mainstream criticism of the realities of the Brazilian prison experience and asking what can be taken from the models of co-governance explored in the book by those interested in prison reform in the North, including the roles played by imprisoned, former criminal justice practitioners, and former prisoners, turned prison workers, in producing the kind of order I witnessed at Polinter and Franz de Castro.

Third, this book contributes to a recent emergence of monographs, edited volumes and special journal editions published in English on ethnographic prisons research conducted outside Western Europe and Northern America, principal among which Bandyopadhyay (2010), Cheliotis (2014), Darke and Garces (2017b), Garces et al. (2019), Hathazy and Müller (2016), Jefferson and Gaborit (2015), Jefferson and Martin (2014), Jefferson et al. (2014), and Piacentini (2004). More specifically, this is the first social science book originally published in English to focus exclusively on prisons in a Latin American country. In writing the book I am critically aware of the irony that this feat should be accomplished by a researcher from the North. Nelken (2012) distinguishes between three types of comparative research: research undertaken by scholars working from the distance of their home institutions and who are no more than virtually there; research undertaken by scholars that do fieldwork there; and research undertaken by scholars that are fully immersed in the culture of the country they study in respect of the fact that they live there. I fall somewhere between the latter two categories, and for two reasons. For a start, I have lived in Brazil for just one year, from 1993 to 1994, but have spent an average of a month in the country each year since, usually to spend time with friends and family, and in recent years increasingly for teaching and research. Further, my research is participatory and ethnographic. I have accompanied public defenders, human rights advocates and senior government officials to prison, slept in prison, taught in prison, run a focus group in prison, participated in therapeutic activities in prison, had my hair cut and beard trimmed in prison, sat on cell bunks talking about philosophy and religion in prison, and more generally spent many hours hanging out with prison inmates, guards, governors and administrators. I have eaten some of the best but more often the worst meals of my life in prison, picking out the meat while explaining my vegetarianism. One time I skyped home on my mobile in prison. Inmates spoke with my family to assure them I was being well looked after. Another time the same group of inmates stopped me from taking my mobile out of the prison with me for fear I might be mugged while out for a jog. I have found myself being drawn into participating in everyday prison routines. On one occasion, I was momentarily left solely in charge of the entrance to a prison. I have been mistaken as a trusty prisoner more than once. To the extent Brazilian prison cultures are distinct from the outside, I find myself in a stronger position than many Brazilian researchers.

Fourth, and following on from some of these illustrations from my fieldwork, this book is in part based on a short period of ethnographic research conducted while staying (as a guest) at a prison (at Franz de Castro). To my knowledge, Piacentini's (2004) Surviving Russian Prisons is the only other book published in English that is based on ethnographic research conducted during such a sustained (24 hour) period of fieldwork conducted in-situ. Although I will hopefully never truly appreciate what it means to be incarcerated, I do have some understanding of what it means to live in a prison space. The only remotely comparable research I am aware of in Brazil is Debora Diniz's (2015a, b) study of a youth prison, during which she shadowed a team of prison guards.

Finally, this book makes use of inside as well as ethnographic accounts of prison life, including autobiographies, interviews and the academic, auto-ethnographic work of current and former inmates and staff. I chose to do so for two reasons. First, it helped to make up for the shortage in existing academic research on the subject matter, already noted. More important, it corresponded to my wider interest in developing models of co-produced research activism that bridge the gap between the "inside experience" and the "expert knower" through privileging the understanding and standpoints of former and current prison inmates and prison staff (see, inter alia, Aresti and Darke 2016; Aresti and Darke 2018; Aresti et al. 2016; Ross et al. 2014).

Notes

1. Note that, except where otherwise indicated, the individual prisons I refer to in this book are all men's prisons.
2. As in the UK, buildings in Brazil usually have a ground and then first floor. Prisons are an exception in both countries.
3. In this book I do not translate Portuguese words that have a specific meaning in the Brazilian prison context and do not have a precise equivalent in the English language, at least in my native British English. In a country as geographically large and culturally diverse as Brazil, prison slang varies enormously from place to place, although often more in form than substance. I do my best to use more local terms where my knowledge allows. One such word is *faxina*. Words

like *pavilhão* and *galeria*, on the other hand, translate better; perhaps because they describe prison architecture, which we will see is more comparable to its counterpart in the English speaking world than is prison culture.

4. The words *xadrez* and *cela* (cell) are used interchangeably in Brazilian prisons to describe the majority of larger cells in the country, which we will see in Chapter 2 are typically shared by three or more people. Sometimes the words *dormitório* (dormitory) or simply *alojamento* (accommodation) are used. To avoid confusion, I will stick to the word cell throughout this book, but refer to "single" cells when describing cells that comply with the international norm of approximately six square metres.

5. 111 is the number officially recorded as having been killed. It is likely that at least twice this number died. Survivors of the massacre claim the official body count was made only after truck loads of corpses had left the prison (Biondi 2010) and did not include over 100 wounded prisoners that later died in hospital (Varella 1999). Milton Marques Viana, for example, claimed that while he was recovering in the hospital wing of the prison a few days after the killings, other hospitalised survivors spoke of more than 150 dead and 400 wounded (Ramos 2003).

6. A shorter review of Varella's (2008) description of life at Carandiru prison and of the 1992 massacre was previously published as Darke (2012).

7. Note my use of the word prison governor rather prison director. While the latter is more commonly used internationally, only the former is used in the UK.

8. Varella (2004: 32) writes, "how so few could control such a mass of criminals was, for me, the deepest mystery".

9. Carandiru's main blocks each had five floors. The first floors were used for communal activities and included exercise yards or *pátios* (patios), as they are commonly referred to across the Brazilian prison system. The majority of the *faxina* were housed on the second floor. The remaining *faxina* occupied the first cells after the entrances to the three floors above.

10. Unless indicated otherwise in this book, when I describe a place in Brazil I am referring to one of the country's 27 states. So, in this case I am referring to the state rather than the city of Rio de Janeiro.

11. The name Polinter is a pseudonym. It was the term used for the police *carceragem* system in Rio de Janeiro: *o sistema Polinter* ("the Polinter system"). An individual *carceragem* would be referred, for instance, as Polinter de Rio das Ostras or Polinter de Arraial do Cabo (also pseudonyms). One *carceragem* I do refer to by name in Chapter 5 is Polinter de Nova Iguaçu. Although the *carceragem* described in this book has been closed for several years and is easily identifiable from my descriptions to anyone that frequented it, I see no reason to refer to it by its real name, if nothing else but to put off the type of sensationalist, lazy journalism that, for example, followed Human Rights Watch's (2015b) report on prisons in Pernambuco (e.g. Akbar 2015). However, I have every effort to disguise the identity of those that worked or were incarcerated at the lock-up.
12. As at other *carceragens* in Brazil, most had at least been charged with committing a crime. In this book I therefore refer to the people held at police *carceragens* as prisoners or inmates rather than detainees, and use prison as a generic word to describe all types of penal institution. Where it is necessary, I use the term penitentiary to distinguish the common prison system from police custody.
13. A shorter account of this visit was previously published in Darke (2014a).
14. Throughout the remainder of this book, I utilise the terms "Northern", "Global North" or simply "the North" not so much as physical geographical concepts, but in reference to the advanced capitalist economies of the world, most but not all of which are in the Northern Hemisphere. In contrast, I use the terms "Southern", "Global South" or "the South" in reference to less economically developed countries or regions of the world, including Brazil and Latin America.
15. Like Polinter, Franz de Castro is a pseudonym. Franz de Castro was a lawyer who volunteered his services at the first Brazilian prison wing to be managed by the voluntary sector, in São Paulo, in the 1970s. In 1981, he was shot and killed by police while negotiating with inmates that had staged a rebellion at another prison. Today, Franz de Castro is revered within the APAC prison system as a martyr. He is in the process of being canonised.
16. A shorter account of this incident was previously published in Darke (2014b). The following analysis of APAC prisons is also adapted from Darke (2014b).

References

Aas, K. F. (2012). The earth is one but the world is not: Criminological theory and its geopolitical divisions. *Theoretical Criminology, 16*(1), 5–20.

Akbar, J. (2015, October 27). Inside Brazil's toughest jails where inmates rule. *Mail Online*. http://www.dailymail.co.uk/news/article-3289843/Inside-Brazil-s-toughest-jails-inmates-rule-Prisons-dog-chaveiros-sell-crack-cocaine-charge-taxes-gang-rape-murder-rivals-keys.html#ixzz3qRd9moDE. Last accessed 3 November 2015.

Aresti, A., & Darke, S. (2016). Practicing convict criminology: Lessons learned from British academic activism. *Critical Criminology, 24*(4), 533–547.

Aresti, A., & Darke, S. (Eds.). (2018). Twenty years of convict criminology. Under contract with *Journal of Prisoners on Prison, 27*(2).

Aresti, A., Darke, S., & Manlow, D. (2016). Bridging the gap: Giving public voice to prisoners and former prisoners through research activism. *Prison Service Journal, 224*, 3–13.

Arruda, R. F. (2015). *Geografia do cárcere: Territorialidades na vida cotidiana carcerária no sistena prisional de Pernambuco*. Ph.D. thesis, University of São Paulo. http://www.teses.usp.br/teses/disponiveis/8/8136/tde-16062015-125328/pt-br.php. Last accessed 3 February 2017.

Babenco, H., & Kramer, O. (2003). *Carandiru*. Film. Brazil: Globo Filmes.

Babenco, H., Carvalho, W., Gervitz, R., & Faria, M. (2005). *Carandiru: Outros Historias*. Television series. Brazil: Rede Globo.

Bandyopadhyay, M. (2010). *Everyday life in a prison: Confinement, surveillance, resistance*. New Delhi: Orient BlackSwan.

Bassani, F. (2016). *Visita íntima: Sexo, crime e negócios nas prisões*. Porto Alegre: Bestiário.

Biondi, K. (2010). *Junto e misturado: Uma etnografia do PCC*. São Paulo: Teirciero Nome. English version: Biondi, K. (2016). *Sharing this walk: An ethnography of prison life and the PCC in Brazil* (J. F. Collins, Trans.). Chapel Hill: University of North Carolina.

Biondi, K. (2014). *Etnografia no movimento: Território, hierarquia e lei no PCC*. Ph.D. thesis, Federal University of São Carlos. https://www.repositorio.ufscar.br/bitstream/handle/ufscar/246/6378pdf?sequence=1&isAllowed=y. Last accessed 7 April 2017.

Biondi, K. (2016). Author's afterword to the English language edition. In K. Biondi (Ed.), *Sharing this walk: An ethnography of prison life and the PCC in Brazil* (J. F. Collins, Trans.) (pp. 145–176). Chapel Hill: University of North Carolina.

Blaustein, J. (2016). Exporting criminological innovation abroad: Discursive representation, 'evidence-based crime prevention' and the post-neoliberal development agenda in Latin America. *Theoretical Criminology, 20*(2), 165–184.

Blaustein, J. (2017). Ethical criminologists fly economy: Process-orientated criminological engagement abroad. In S. Armstrong, et al. (Eds.), *Reflexivity and criminal justice: Intersections of policy, practice and research* (pp. 357–379). London: Palgrave Macmillan.

Bortoluci, J. H., & Jansen, R. S. (2013). Toward a postcolonial sociology: The view from Latin America. *Postcolonial Sociology, Political Power and Social Theory, 24,* 199–229.

Brant, V. C. (1986). *O trabalhador preso no estado de São Paulo: Passado, presente e expectativas.* São Paulo: Cebrap.

Cain, M. (2000). Orientalism, occidentalism and the sociology of crime. *British Journal of Criminology, 40,* 239–260.

Caldeira, T. (2000). *City of walls: Crime, segregation and citizenship in São Paulo.* Berkeley: University of California.

Câmara dos Deputados. (2008). *CPI do sistema carcerário.* Resource document. http://bd.camara.leg.br/bd/bitstream/handle/bdcamara/2701/cpi_sistema_carcerario.pdf?sequence=5. Last accessed 10 August 2014.

Castro, L. A. (1987). *Criminologia de la liberacion.* Maracalbo: Universidad del Zulia. Portuguese edition: Castro, L. A. (2005). *Criminologia da libertação* (S. Moretzsohn, Trans.). Rio de Janeiro: Revan.

Castro, L. A. (2000). O trinfo de Lewis Carroll: A nova criminologia latino-americana. *Discursos Sediciosos, 5*(9&10), 129–148.

Cheliotis, L. K. (Ed.) (2014). Prison realities: Views from around the World. *South Atlantic Quarterly, 113*(3), 475–502.

Codino, R. (2014). Para uma outra criminologia do terceiro mundo: Perspectivas da criminologia critica no sul (S. Carvalho, Trans.). *Revista Liberdades, 20,* 22–34.

Cohen, S. (1988). *Against criminology.* New Brunswick: Transaction.

Comaroff, J., & Comaroff, J. (Eds.). (2006). *Law and disorder in the postcolony.* Chicago: University of Chicago.

Comaroff, J., & Comaroff, J. (2012). *Theories from the south: Or how Euro-America is evolving towards Africa.* London: Paradigm.

Connell, R. (2006). Northern theory: The political geography of general social theory. *Theoretical Sociology, 35*(2), 237–264.

Connell, R. (2007). *Southern theory: The global dynamics of knowledge in social sciences*. Cambridge: Polity.

Coronil, F. (2000). Towards a critique of globalcentrism: Speculations on capitalism's nature. *Public Culture, 12*(2), 351–374.

Coronil, F. (2004). Latin American postcolonial studies and global decolonization. In N. Lazarus (Ed.), *The Cambridge companion to postcolonial literary studies* (pp. 221–240). New York: Cambride University.

Darke, S. (2012). Estação Carandiru. *Prison Service Journal, 199*, 26–28.

Darke, S. (2013). Inmate governance in Brazilian prisons. *Howard Journal of Criminal Justice, 52*(3), 272–284.

Darke, S. (2014a). Managing without guards in a Brazilian police lockup. *Focaal, 68*, 55–67.

Darke, S. (2014b). Recoverers helping recoverers: Discipline and peer-facilitated reform in Brazilian faith-based prisons. In V. Miller & J. Campbell (Eds.), *Transnational penal cultures: New perspectives on discipline, punishment and desistance* (pp. 217–229). London: Routledge.

Darke, S., & Garces, C. (2017a). Surviving in the new mass carceral zone. *Prison Service Journal, 229*, 2–9.

Darke, S., & Garces, C. (Eds.). (2017b). Informal dynamics of survival in Latin American prisons. *Prison Service Journal, 229*, 1–62.

Darke, S., & Karam, M. L. (2016). Latin American prisons. In Y. Jewkes, et al. (Eds.), *Handbook on prisons* (2nd ed., pp. 460–474). Abington: Routledge. Portuguese version: Karam, M. L., & Darke, S. (2016). Prisões latino americanas (M. L. Karam, Trans.). http://emporiododireito.com.br/leitura/prisoes-latino-americanas-1508702837. Last accessed 17 February 2018. Spanish version: Darke, S., & Karam, M. L. (2017). Las prisiones de América Latina. *Ecuador Debate, 101*, 53–71.

Dias, C. N. (2013). *PCC: Hegemonia nas prisões e monopólio da violência*. São Paulo: Saraiva.

Diniz, D. (2015a). Cadeia de papel: Nome de horror. *Revista Liberdades, 20*, 234–244.

Diniz, D. (2015b). Pesquisas em cadeia. *Revista Direito GV, 11*(2), 573–586. São Paulo.

Dwyer, T. (2012). On the internationalization of Brazilian academic sociology. In A. L. Bialakowsky, et al. (Eds.), *Latin American critical thought: Theory and practice* (pp. 84–104). Buenos Aires: CLASCO.

Feltran, G. S. (2010). The management of violence on the São Paulo periphery: The repertoire of normative apparatus in the PCC era. *Vibrant, 7*(2), 109–134.

Ferreira, V. A. (2016). *Juntando cacos, resgatando vidas: Valorização humana – base do método APAC e a viagem ao mundo interior do prisioneiro – psicologia do preso*. Belo Horizonte: Gráfica o Lutador.

Fonseca, D. S. (2018). Reimagining the sociology of punishment through the global-south: Postcolonial social control and modernization discontents. *Punishment & Society, 20*(1), 8–33.

Foucault, M. (1977). *Discipline and punish*. London: Allen Lane.

França, L. A., Neto, A. S., & Artuso, A. R. (2016). *As marcas do cárcere*. Curitiba: IEA.

Fraternidade Brasileira de Assistência aos Condenados. (2014). *Regulamento Disciplinar APAC*. Resource document. http://www.criminal.mppr.mp.br/arquivos/File/ExecucaoPenal/Mateiral_de_Apoio/APAC/Regulamento_Disciplinar_APACs.pdf. Last accessed 30 December 2017.

Fundação AVSI. (2012). *Um novo olhar além dos muros: O potencial gestão no fortalecimento das APACs de Minas Gerais*. Belo Horizonte: Fundação AVSI.

Garces, C., Martin, T., & Darke, S. (2013). Informal prison dynamics in Africa and Latin America. *Criminal Justice Matters, 91*(1), 26–27.

Garces, C., Darke, S., Duno-Gottberg, L., & Antillano, A. (Eds.). (2019). *Carceral communities: Troubling 21st century prison regimes in Latin America*. Under contract with University of Pennsylvania.

Godoi, R. (2016). Intimacy and power: Body searches and intimate visits in the prison system of São Paulo. *Chámp Penal, XIII.* https://doi.org/10.4000/champpenal.9386.

Goffman, E. (1968). *Asylums: Essays on the situation of mental patients and other inmates*. London: Penguin. Originally published in 1961.

Goifman, K. (2002). Killing time in the Brazilian slammer. *Ethnography, 3*(4), 435–441.

Hathazy, P., & Müller, M. M. (Eds.). (2016). The rebirth of the prison in Latin America: Variations, changes and continuities. *Crime, Law and Social Change, 65*(3), 114–285.

Human Rights Watch. (2015). *The state let evil take over: The prison crisis in the Brazilian state of Pernambuco*. New York: Human Rights Watch.

Inter-American Commission on Human Rights. (2011). *Report on the human rights of persons deprived of liberty in the Americas*. Resource document. http://www.oas.org/en/iachr/pdl/docs/pdf/PPL2011eng.pdf. Last accessed 10 August 2014.

Jefferson, A. M., & Gaborit, L. S. (2015). *Human rights in prisons: Comparing institutional encounters in Kosovo, Sierra Leone and the Philippines*. London: Palgrave Macmillan.

Jefferson, A. M., & Jensen, S. (Eds.). (2009). *State violence and human rights: State officials in the South*. Abingdon: Routledge-Cavendish.

Jefferson, A. M., & Martin, T. M. (Eds.). (2014). Everyday prison governance in Africa. *Prison Service Journal, 202*, 1–51.

Jefferson, A. M., Garces, C., & Martin, T. M. (Eds.). (2014). Sensing prison climates: Governance, survival and transition. *Focaal, 68*, 55–67.

Justiça Global. (2001). *Massacre at Carandiru*. Resource document. http://www.observatoriodeseguranca.org/files/Carandiru%20Prison%20Massacre.PDF. Last accessed 27 October 2015.

Karam, M. L., & Saraiva, H. R. (2017). Ouvindo as vozes de carcereiros brasileiros. Unpublished. English version: Hearing the voices of Brazilian correction officers (M. L. Karam, Trans.). *Prison Service Journal, 229*, 48–50.

Karstedt, S. (2001). Comparing cultures, comparing crime: Challenges, prospects and problems for a global criminology. *Crime, Law and Social Change, 36*(3), 285–308.

Lee, M., & Laidler, K. J. (2013). Doing criminology from the periphery: Crime and punishment in Asia. *Theoretical Criminology, 17*(2), 141–157.

Macaulay, F. (2013). Modes of prison administration, control and governmentality in Latin America: Adoption, adaptation and hybridity. *Conflict, Security and Development, 13*(4), 361–392.

Macaulay, F. (2014). Whose prisoners are these anyway? Church, state and society partnerships and co-production of offender resocialization. In V. Miller & J. Campbell (Eds.), *Transnational penal cultures: New perspectives on discipline, punishment and desistance* (pp. 202–216). London: Routledge.

Macaulay, F. (2015, July 28). Os centros de ressocialização no estado de São Paulo. *JOTA*. https://www.jota.info/especiais/os-centros-de-ressocializacao-no-estado-de-sao-paulo-28072015. Last accessed 28 February 2018.

Madeira, L. M. (2008). *Trajetórias de homens infames: Políticas públicas penais e programas de apoio a egressos do sistema penitenciário no brasil*. Ph.D. thesis, Federal University of Rio Grande do Sul. http://www.lume.ufrgs.br/handle/10183/15656. Last accessed 11 February 2018.

Madeiro, C. (2017, January 22). Em Alcaçuz, presos controlam chave de pavilhões e até entrada de comida. *Amigos de Plantão*. http://marechalonline.net/noticia/em-alcacuz-presos-controlam-chave-de-pavilhoes-e-ate-entrada-de-comida/11317. Last accessed 23 January 2017.

Marques, A. (2010). "Liderança", "proceder" e "igualdade": Uma etnografia das relações políticas no Primeiro Comando da Capital. *Etnográfica, 14*(2), 311–335.

Marques, A. (2014). *Crime e proceder: Um experimento antropológico*. São Paulo: Alameda.
Mascareño, A., & Chernilo, D. (2009). Obstacles and perspectives of Latin American sociology: Normative universalism and functional differentiation. *Soziale Systeme, 15*(1), 72–96.
Mendes, L. A. (2005). *Às cegas*. São Paulo: Companhia das Letras.
Mendes, L. A. (2009). *Memórias de um sobrevivente*. São Paulo: Companhia de Bolso.
Mendes, L. A. (2012). *Cela forte*. São Paulo: Global.
Mendes, L. A. (2015). *Confissões de um homen livre*. São Paulo: Companhia das Letras.
Muñoz, C. (2015, October 20). A privatização perversa das prisões. *Folha de São Paulo*. http://www1.folha.uol.com.br/opiniao/2015/10/1695836-a-privatizacao-perversa-das-prisoes.shtml. Last accessed 3 February 2017.
Nelken, D. (2010). *Comparative criminal justice: Making sense of difference*. London: Sage.
Nelken, D. (2012). Comparing criminal justice. In M. Maguire, et al. (Eds.), *The Oxford handbook of criminology* (6th edn.) (pp. 138–157). Oxford: Oxford University.
Olmo, R. (1981). *America latina y su criminologia*. Delegación Coyoacán: Siglo Ventiuno.
Olmo, R. (1999). The development of criminology in Latin America. *Social Justice, 26*(2), 19–45.
Ottoboni, M. (2006). *Vamos matar o criminoso? Método APAC*. São Paulo: Paulinas.
Pereira, J. (2015). Narrativas silenciadas: Memórias que a morte não apaga. In M. R. Machado & M. R. A. Machado (Eds.), *Carandiru não é coisa do passado* (pp. 159–178). FGV Direito SP.
Piacentini, L. (2004). *Surviving Russian prisons: Punishment, economy and politics in transition*. Cullompton: Willan.
Ramos, H. (2003). *Pavilhão 9: Paixão e morte no Carandiru* (4th ed.). Paris: Gallimard.
Rap, A., & Zeni, B. (2002). *Sobrevivente André du Rap (do Massacre do Carandiru)*. São Paulo: Labortexto.
Rosa, M. C. (2014). Theories of the South: Limits and perspectives of an emergent movement in social sciences. *Current Sociology, 62*(6), 851–867.
Ross, J. I., Darke, S., Aresti, A., Newbold, G., & Earle, R. (2014). Developing convict criminology beyond North America. *International Criminal Justice Review, 24*(2), 121–133.

Sager, T., & Beto, R. (2016). *Central.* Documentary film. Brazil: Panda.
Said, E. (1978). *Orientalism.* New York: Pantheon.
Salla, F. (2006). As rebeliões nas prisões: Novos significados a partir da experiência Brasileira. *Sociologias, 8*(16), 274–307.
Salla, F. (2017). Vigiar e punir e os estudos prisionais no Brasil. *DILEMAS*, special edition no. 2, 29–43.
Salvatore, R. D., & Aguirre, C. (Eds.) (1996). The birth of the penitentiary in Latin America: Towards an interpretive social history of prisons. In R. D. Salvatore & C. Aguirre (Eds.), *The birth of the penitentiary in Latin America* (pp. 1–43). Austin: University of Texas.
Santos, B. S. (2002). *Towards a new legal common sense: Law, globalization and emancipation* (2nd ed.). London: Lexis Nexis Butterworths.
Santos, J. V. T. (2010). The dialogue between criminology and the south's sociology of violence: The policing crisis and alternatives. In M. Burawoy, et al. (Eds.), *Facing an unequal world: Challenges for a global sociology* (pp. 105–125). Taiwan: Institute of Sociology, Academia Sinica.
Santos, J. V. T. (2012). Contemporary Latin American sociology and the challenges for an international dialogue. In A. L. Bialakowsky, et al. (Eds.), *Latin American critical thought: Theory and practice* (pp. 237–271). Buenos Aires: CLASCO.
Santos, B. S., Nunes, J. A., & Meneses, M. P. (2007). Opening up the canon of knowledge and recognition of difference. In B. S. Santos (Ed.), *Another knowledge is possible: Beyond northern epistemologies* (pp. ix–lxii). London: Verso.
Skarbek, D. (2014). *The social order of the underworld: How prison gangs govern the American penal system.* New York: Oxford University.
Sozzo, M. (2006). 'Traduttore traditore': Tradución, importación cultural e historia del presente de la criminología en América Latina. *Cuadernos de Doctrinay Jusrisprudencia Penal, 7,* 354–430.
Sozzo, M. (Ed.). (2017). *Pós-neoliberalismo e penalidade na américa do sul.* São Paulo: Fundação Perseu Abramo.
Steinberg, J. (2016). How well does theory travel? David Garland in the global south. *Howard Journal of Criminal Justice, 55*(4), 514–531.
Steinberg, G., & Sacramento, P. (2004). *O prisioneiro da grade de ferro.* Documentary film. Brazil: California Filmes.
Supervielle, M. (2012). Revitalizing the sociological view in Latin America. In M. Burawoy, et al. (Eds.), *Facing an unequal world: Challenges for a global sociology* (pp. 63–84). Taiwan: Institute of Sociology, Academia Sinica.

Sykes, G. M. (1958). *The society of captives*. Princeton: Princeton University.
Tuhiwai Smith, L. (2012). *Decolonizing methodologies: Research and indigenous People* (2nd ed.). London: Zed.
Varella, D. (2004). Carandiru. *Lancet, 364,* 32–33.
Varella, D. (2008). *Estação Carandiru*. São Paulo: Companhia das Letras. English edition: Varella, D. (2012). *Lockdown: Inside Brazil's most violent prison* (A. Entrekin, Trans.). London: Simon & Schuster.
Varella, D. (2012). *Carcereiros*. São Paulo: Companhia das Letras.
Willys, J. (2015). Os corpos do delito e os delitos do corpo. In M. R. Machado & M. R. A. Machado (Eds.), *Carandiru não é coisa do passado* (pp. 115–133). FGV Direito SP.
Wolfmann, L. C. (2000). *Portal do inferno: Mas há esperança*. São Paulo: WVC Gestão Inteligente Com. Ltda.
Zaffaroni, E. R. (1989). *En busca de las penas perdidas*. Buenos Aires: Editar Sociedad Anónima. Portuguese version: Zaffaroni, E. R. (1991). *Em busca das penas perdidas* (V. R. Pedrosa & A. L. Conceição, Trans.). Rio de Janeiro: Revan.

2

Law and Repression

Of all the inhumanity I have encountered in my prisons research in Brazil, little compares with what I witnessed when I was taken by a criminal lawyer to visit three *carceragens* (lock-ups; units of holding cells) in the state of Paraná. All three were severely overcrowded, and none had any natural light. In one of the *carceragens*, designated for female detainees, the 64 inmates currently held there at least had access to the cell block wing, and a small *pátio* (exercise yard) if they were fortunate enough to receive visits. As the other 12,000 prisoners in the state's *carceragem* system at the time, none were allowed any visits in the first 30 days of their arrest. The women had plenty of complaints to report to the lawyer, but were clearly pleased to talk with us. Many posed for group photographs, afterwards taking the camera to scroll back through the pictures and laugh at their appearances. Like my initial visit to Polinter described in Chapter 1, I left with a deep sense of confusion: anxiety felt by the sheer number of inmates I had seen crowded into such a small space, yet at the same time taken aback by the camaraderie that at that brief moment appeared to exist between them. Most stayed there for up to three months, but some (again like Polinter) had chosen to stay there rather than move into the less crowded penitentiary system, even after trial and sentence. Conditions at the other two *carceragens* were worse still. Few of the male detainees held in these police stations stirred from the bunks or spaces on the floor they lay half-sleeping. The first of the *carceragens* was holding around 140 prisoners, divided up to 20 per four-bunk, six to eight metre square cell. Visitors were required to stand behind a line drawn a metre in front of the metal-grill cell gates. The officer in charge informed me it had previously held as many as 240 inmates. Prisoners showed us swellings and signs of skin diseases on their arms and legs. The atmosphere briefly lifted when the lawyer asked them to pose for pictures. When I look at these photographs today, I am still taken back by the contrast between the inhumanity of the setting in which they were taken and the smiles momentarily captured on the faces of the prisoners.

Conditions at the third *carceragem* were not conducive to even a Brazilian's capacity to make light of a serious situation, however fleetingly. Here, 68 men were held underground in a cellar. Water stains covered the walls, and puddles had formed on the floors. Electric lights hung loosely from the ceilings. Only one prisoner spoke with us or mustered a smile, a young man nicknamed *Homen Aranha* (Spiderman) for his feats climbing residential buildings to burgle upper storey apartments. In prison he was now famous for escaping from a number of institutions, including this *carceragem*, where he had dug a hole through the ceiling. While we were talking, an officer proceeded to pass the prisoners their evening meals through the cell-gate service hatches with one hand while pointing a rifle at them with the other. When the lawyer passed his camera to one of the detainees to take pictures inside one cell, a second officer stroked his hair with his pistol and joked with us that we would have no problem getting the camera back. As we were leaving, this officer took us to the backyard of the *carceragem* where prisoners used to be taken to be beaten. With more than a hint of self-amusement, he claimed the practice only ended after a neighbour complained she could not sleep with the noise of screaming.

According to the most recent official prison statistics (Ministério da Justiça e Segurança Pública 2017: 712, 726)[1] people were imprisoned across Brazil in June 2016, in 1461 prisons. 36,765 of these prisoners were recorded[2] as being held irregularly[3] in police custody, often after conviction, sometimes in separate buildings, but usually in annexes or the basement of police stations, as at Polinter and the three *carceragens* in Paraná described above. 689,510 prisoners were detained in state penitentiaries, and 437 in one of the country's four federal prisons. 40% of prisoners were on remand. 78% of all prisoners were being held in closed units, 15% in semi-open units and five per cent in open conditions (served at a hostel, or more usually at home). 6.5% of Brazilian prisoners are women (Fórum Brasileiro de Segurança Pública 2016).

Brazilian prisons are heavily criticised both at home and abroad, and in governmental as well as academic literature. The United Nations, for example, has described inhumane conditions as endemic to the Brazilian prison system (e.g. United Nations 2008). The most comprehensive Brazilian parliamentary inquiry of recent years (Câmara dos Deputados 2008) was equally damning, concluding that prisoners are treated as human rubbish. In 2015, the Brazilian Minister of Justice, José Eduardo Cardozo condemned his country's prisons as medieval dungeons (Acebes 2017).

In a particularly notable academic intervention, Wacquant (2003: 200) refers to Brazilian prisons as "more akin to concentration camps for the dispossessed, or public enterprises for the industrial storage of social refuse, than to judicial institutions serving any identifiable penological function - be it deterrence, neutralization or rehabilitation". Not only, he explains, are the country's prisons disproportionately populated by the poor and uneducated, but they are also overcrowded and in physical disrepair, lack basic health care and legal assistance, and are characterised by high levels of violence, under-staffing and gang control. Most Brazilian prison ethnographers and scholars that work within a critical criminological framework broadly concur with this opinion.

In this chapter, I provide an overview of the state of Brazilian prisons. We will see Brazilian prisons certainly have few staff, and many are in a state of disrepair. It is also true the daily lives of many Brazilian prisoners are largely shaped by limited access to legal and health services. At the same time, however, the experience of being locked up in Brazil is only part captured by human rights critiques of the failure of authorities to adequately invest in its prison system. This is an obvious yet important point to keep in mind when we shift attention from prison conditions to prison life, as I do from Chapter 3 onwards. For a start, although most Brazilian prisons are unquestionably overcrowded—inmates held in closed units are typically accommodated two to four per single cell, but six per cell is not unusual; it is quite normal to keep inmates held in police custody in conditions of under one square metre per prisoner—at the same time the average Brazilian prisoner spends less time locked up in their cell than his or her counterpart in Western Europe and Northern America. Furthermore, the majority of sentenced prisoners spend at least part of their day in work-related activities, in workshops, informal economies or in-house work. Most of the relatively high number of prisoners (in comparison with the USA or UK, for example) held in open or semi-open units work full-time. At least one day a week, prison gates across the country are opened to visits from inmates' families, lasting up to four hours. Equally significant, although Brazilian prisons may be violent in comparison with Western European or Northern American prisons (though, we will see, not as violent as our Northern theories of prison life might predict) and are often dominated by gangs, they are also characterised by relatively high levels of solidarity among inmates. Finally, in spite of the overcrowding and daytime activity, in my experience Brazilian prisons can be quite orderly places.

Fortunately, then, not all Brazilian prisons are as bad as the *carceragens* of Paraná. Moreover, the *carceragem* system is slowly being dismantled. 39% of all prisoners were held in *carceragens* as recently as 1995 (Human Rights Watch 1998).[4] However, the inescapable truth is Brazilian prison practices that at first sight might be considered relatively good usually arise in response to poor living conditions. For example, prisoners typically rely on their families to make up for the failure of prison authorities to provide them with even the most basic of material goods, including clothes and bedding, while prison authorities often rely on prisoner labour to make up for shortages in officers and support staff. This must be the starting point of any analysis of Brazilian prison life, including (my focus in this book) how and why inmates and staff negotiate and co-produce order. In Chapter 4, I demonstrate that with the exception of a small number of single-cell high security units, all Brazilian prison types are characterised by varying degrees of self-governance, and in ways that provide limited room for comparison with prisons in the Global North. There is an inverse relation between good conditions of work and incarceration and the extent to which Brazilian prisons self-govern. Under-resourced prisons, in other words, depend on staff-inmate collaborations more than better resourced ones.

To repeat the essential point made in Chapter 1, while deprivations tell us much of what it is like to work or be incarcerated in Brazilian prisons, the picture is complete only when we take into consideration their informal dynamics. Over the following chapters, I explore six features that in my view broadly define the Brazilian prison system and what it is like inside the average Brazilian prison, including my focus on the implications of prison staff relying on prisoners to collaborate in running the institutions in which they are held. Four of these (staff shortage, conviviality, co-governance and prison gangs) are directly related to everyday prison life and the production of order. I deal with these matters in Chapters 4 and 6. The other two (Brazil's rapidly expanding prison population and chronic levels of prison overcrowding) form an essential background to all aspects of the experience of prison in Brazil. It is necessary to deal with these first. In exploring the extraordinarily high levels of imprisonment and overcrowding in this chapter, I draw particular attention to a paradigm of globalised crime control that has particular resonance in Brazil: that of criminal justice militarisation. We will see that in this regard, Brazil is ahead of the game in global trends in punishment. In Chapters 3 and 4, I briefly explore a second paradigm of globalised crime control in which Brazil is taking the lead: securitisation of the prison environment. This sets the background to the main focus of the book and of my ethnographic research, on the means by which prison order is maintained through everyday interactions between and among prison inmates and prison staff. Throughout the book, I utilise comparative methodology to explore ways by which, on the one hand, the Brazilian case varies from global averages. In Chapter 7, I give examples of commonalities Brazil retains with other parts of Latin America and the wider Global South.

The Great Incarceration

Scholars of prisons and punishment view the past four decades as a time of global hyperincarceration. 50 nations saw their prison population rise more than half between 1992 and 2004 (Stern 2006). Two thirds of countries saw their prison population increase between 1997 and 2007 (Walmsley 2010). In the late 1990s, around 8 million people were held in prison worldwide (Walmsley 1999). By October 2015, over 10 million people were in prison (Walmsley 2015), nearly half of who in three countries, China, the USA and Russia. Increasing levels of global incarceration are only part explained by increases in the world population or changing demographics, for instance that half of people in the world now live in urban areas (Davis 2007) or that half of the world's population is now under 25 years of age (Jones and Rodgers 2009). Indeed, over the past few decades global levels of police recorded serious crime (i.e. crimes such as burglary, robbery, serious assault, rape and homicide that attract higher levels of imprisonment and longer prison sentences) have increased at a lower rate than prison populations (Heiskanen 2010; Malby 2010).

The USA is often regarded as the main driving force of global punitiveness (Dreisinger 2016). Its prison population increased from around half a million at the beginning of the 1980s to over two million by the end of the century. Since the beginning of the new Millennium, however, the number of American prisoners has risen less sharply, peaking at around two and a quarter million in 2013 (Walmsley 2015). In the same period, Brazil has gone from being one of the lowest (Human Rights Watch 1998) to highest incarcerators in the Americas, and this in addition to the fact prison populations have risen in South and Central America more than any other region on the planet (Coyle et al. 2016; Postema et al. 2017). Most of this increase has occurred in Spanish and Portuguese rather than English-speaking parts of the continent. In Brazil, there are significant differences in the use of prison state to state. For example, while the state of São Paulo had an official prison population rate of 536 per 100,000 national population in June 2016, Bahia had an official prison population rate of 100 per 100,000 national population (Ministério da Justiça e Segurança Pública 2017). Nevertheless, the movement towards mass incarceration is apparent across most of the country. Nor does it show signs of abating. All but three Brazilian states (Bahia; Maranhão; Piauí) have prison population rates that exceed the world average. Moreover, these three states account for less than 5% of all prisoners in the country. While still relatively low, Bahia's prison population increased fourfold from 2000 to a peak of 120 per 100,000 general population in 2010 (Lourenço and Almeida 2013). In terms of absolute numbers of prisoners, Brazil now leads the way in Latin America, lies in third position globally and is quickly catching up with its competitors, China and the USA. At 726,712 adult prisoners in June 2016 (Ministério da Justiça e Segurança Pública 2017), Brazil's official prison population had increased by a quite remarkable 1960 percent from December 1984, when 37,071 adults were in prison (Pavarini and Giamberardino 2011). The previous 20 years[5] before that had seen a far more modest 59% rise, from 23,385 prisoners in December 1964 (ibid.). To put these figures into international context, Brazil imprisoned less people in 1964 and 1984 than England and Wales, despite having a general population two to three times larger. Today Brazil's general population is four times larger than that of England and Wales, but its prison population is seven times larger. Since the start of the Millennium Brazil's official prison population rate has risen from 137[6] per 100,000 national population in December 2000 to 353 per 100,000 in June 2016 (Ministério da Justiça e Segurança Pública 2017). In contrast, the prison population of England and Wales rose by less than 20%, from 124 to 146 per 100,000 national population in 2016 (International Centre for Prison Studies 2017). In October 2013, the world average was 144 per 100,000 national population, just 6% higher than 15 years earlier (Walmsley 2015). International Centre for Prison Studies (2017) estimates the prison population rate in China rose by approximately 10% to 119 per 100,000 national population between 2000 and 2014.[7] In the USA, the rate of imprisonment has barely risen in the twenty-first century at all, from 683 per 100,000 national population in 2000 to 693 in 2014. The Russian prison population plummeted from a rate of

729 per 100,000 national population in 2000 to 448 in 2016. If Brazil's prison population were to triple again over the next 15 years, which it is predicted to do (Leeds 2016), it might find itself to be the highest incarcerator in the world. Brazil, V. M. Batista (2016: 3) writes, is passing through a time in its penal history that may one day be referred to as "the great incarceration".

A breakdown of the prison population provides further detail on the ways in which Brazil is becoming a world leader in incarceration. Four indicators of punitivism are particularly worth noting. First, as previously mentioned, 40% of Brazilian prisoners were officially recorded as being held on remand in June 2016 (Ministério da Justiça e Segurança Pública 2017), significantly higher than the world average of 27%, although lower than the South American average of 50% (Coyle et al. 2016). In total, there were 292,450 remand prisoners, more than any other country besides the USA and a sevenfold increase since 1995, when its remand population was 42,248 (International Bar Association 2010). In São Paulo, 69.4% of all people entering prison in 2015 were remand prisoners (Instituto Sou da Paz 2016). Most criminal suspects are remanded in custody, including nearly all of those arrested for selling drugs (Carlos 2015; Lemgruber et al. 2013). Before certain reforms were made in 2008 and 2015, people typically spent three to five months waiting for their first custody hearing (Conectas 2017), and in some cases more than five years waiting for judicial proceedings to be concluded (International Bar Association 2010).[8] 47% of pretrial detainees were recorded as imprisoned for longer than the international norm of 90 days maximum in June 2016 (Ministério da Justiça e Segurança Pública 2017). A study of the state of Rio de Janeiro, where close to half of prisoners are on remand, found only a third of pretrial detainees eventually received custodial sentences (Lemgruber and Fernandez 2011).

Second is the length of time convicted prisoners spend in custody. 94% of Brazilian prisoners were recorded as serving prison terms of two years or more in May 2014 (Ministério da Justiça 2015); a staggering 47% were serving over eight years, half of who more than 15 years imprisonment. Under the Heinous Crimes Act 1990, the majority of prisoners are required to wait two thirds rather than the "usual" one third of their sentence to be considered for parole. Moreover, thousands of prisoners are held months, sometimes years beyond their official date of release.[9]

Third is the type of crime for which people are remanded in custody or receive prison sentences. Most significant are robbery and the sale of illicit drugs, the latter of which is now legally defined as a heinous crime. 21% of Brazilian prisoners were being held for robbery in June 2016 (Ministério da Justiça e Segurança Pública 2017). Robbery attracts a minimum sentence of 4 years. 30% of prisoners (including 62% of women prisoners) are in for supplying drugs (ibid.), compared to just nine per cent of prisoners in 2005, the year that records began (Karam 2015). The total number of prisoners held in prison for drug supply rose from approximately 47,000 to 126,000 between 2006 and 2011 (Salla et al. 2006). In São Paulo, 39% of prisoners held in June 2015 had been arrested for selling drugs and 35% for robbery (Secretaria de Administração Penitenciária do Estado de São Paulo 2015). Among child prisoners held in administrative detention these figures rise to 41 and 40%, respectively (Dantas et al. 2016). 61% of male and 89% of female prisoners were arrested for selling drugs in Rio Grande do Sul (Hadler et al. 2017). In Rio de Janeiro, the majority of people remanded or sentenced to prison were likewise arrested for selling drugs (Zaccone 2007). Nine out of ten people charged with supplying drugs in Rio de Janeiro are found guilty, three out of four wholly on police testimony (Lins e Silva and Rodas 2017). In addition to restrictions on early release, since the Lei de Drogas (Drugs Law) 2006 a repeat or organised crime related conviction for supplying drugs has carried a minimum sentence of 5 years imprisonment, whatever the quantity, including cannabis as well as cocaine. Many judges give minimum sentences of five years for first time offenders too. Yet selling drugs is by definition a non-violent crime (Valois 2016). Nor do the majority of people carry guns when making drug deals (Zaccone 2007). The Primeiro Comando do Capital (PCC) prohibits guns altogether from *biqueiras* (literally, smoke mouths: places consumers go to buy illicit drugs) in the urban areas under its command in São Paulo (Biondi 2014). Moreover, the legislation makes no distinction between selling drugs and being involved in the sale of drugs (Carvalho and Rodas 2017), both of which fall under the umbrella category of *traficando* (trafficking). Drug possession, on the other hand, was made a non-imprisonable offence under the Drugs Law 2006. When deciding whether to sentence someone for trafficking or possession, judges are required to take account of not only the quantity of drugs found, but also the personal circumstances of the offender and the location of the arrest.

Finally, the Brazilian prison population is young and poor. According to Ministério da Justiça e Segurança Pública (2017), 55% of all Brazilian prisoners are aged between 18 and 29, compared to 18% of the general population of the country. 75% of prisoners left school at or before the statutory minimal age of 14 (ibid.). Ministério da Justiça (2015) estimated the vast majority (68%) of prisoners did not actually complete school. Three in four prisoners were not in formal employment at the time of their arrest (Ministério da Justiça e Segurança Pública 2017). 65% of prisoners are black, indigenous or mixed race, compared to 54% of the general population (ibid.).

Class disparity is built into political, law enforcement and judicial institutional cultures. This is particularly evident in the approach taken to the drug trade. As anywhere else in the world, there is no evidence the Brazilian rich consume illicit drugs any less than the poor. However, the very different approach taken to possessing and selling drugs unashamedly distinguishes between the two. On the streets of Brazil's urban areas, where four in five drug arrests occur (Salla et al. 2006; Valois 2016), there is no shortage of young people willing to act as go-betweens, commonly referred to as *aviões* (airplanes), to take relatively small quantities of drugs from merchants to their customers for very little personal gain. Many do so simply as a means of funding their own consumption (Shimizu and Cacicedo 2016). Yet there exists a de facto assumption among police forces, prosecutors and judges that poor people caught with any quantity of drugs should be charged and sentenced as traffickers (ibid.); the very opposite is the case with the middle classes (Batista 2003a; Zaccone 2007). A study of drug supply prosecutions in the states of São Paulo, Rio de Janeiro, Porto Alegre and Minas Gerais (Valois 2016) found one in four of those arrested had been caught in possession of cannabis only. A similar study of police records in the city of São Paulo (Salla et al. 2012) found 40% of those remanded in custody for selling cannabis had been caught with less than 100 grammes. More than half of people caught with drugs in Rio de Janeiro in 2015 were arrested for supply rather than consumption, yet over a third were in possession of fewer than 15 grammes of cannabis (Instituto de Segurança Pública 2016). Finally, most convicted traffickers are first time offenders (Misse and Vargas 2010).

To a certain extent, explanations for late twentieth-century and early twenty-first-century Brazilian mass incarceration reflect those associated with the global appropriation of American penal policies. These include: cultural punitivism (e.g. Caldeira 1996, 2000); privatisation (e.g. Macaulay 2013); control of the lower classes (e.g. N. Batista 1996; V. M. Batista 2016); and the emergence of a new paradigm of crime control—a "new penology" (Feeley and Simon 1992)—in which offenders are treated as responsible for their actions and criminal justice authorities put less emphasis on dealing with the underlying causes of crime, and instead are increasingly concerned with managing crime rather than rehabilitating offenders (e.g. Dieter 2013; Salla et al. 2006, 2009): as Cohen (1985) described in the context of parallel changes in the regimes of community sentences in the UK, on keeping offenders under preventative surveillance, or teaching them to control their (anti-social) behaviour, rather than the more difficult task of trying to change them as people. At the same time, however, Brazil is far more than an exemplary case of contemporary global punitivism. To regard it as a leader in the global spread of American penality misses much of the richness of Brazilian criminology, including the work of the authors cited above. We will see Brazilian punitivism is qualitatively different to American punitivism, both in its underlying causes and in its expression. Brazil is also increasingly both an exporter and importer of international penal policy norms and might now be regarded as the leading figure in what Garces and I have described as "the new [Latin American] mass carceral zone" (Darke and Garces 2017a: 2).[10,11]

If this claim appears theoretically implausible, it is only so from a Northern perspective. Brazilians are fond of saying theirs is the country of the future, albeit more often in sarcasm. Still, as Hess (1995) noted a quarter of a century ago, there is good reason to believe the post-industrial Global North has always been more likely to be "Brazilianised" than vice versa. Hess puts this down to Brazil's history of racial, religious and cultural intermingling:

> On the one hand, the upper classes are mostly descendants of Europeans, and the language, high culture, and formal institutions are all Western. Brazil is also a Portuguese-speaking Catholic country with a democratic constitution and a capitalist economy. On the other hand, Brazil is something else, something different from the United States, Canada, and the societies of Western Europe. It is a country where Western culture has mixed and mingled with non-Western cultures for centuries… The more one lives in Brazil, the more the Western features of the country appear as a kind of veneer. (Hess 1995: 2)

Hess (1995: 2) concludes that Brazil "may provide the North Americans and Europeans with a glimpse of their own future" (cited in Wacquant 2008: 70). Sadly, this future now appears more likely to be one of economic instability, social exclusion and "punitive containment" (Wacquant 2008: 58). I return to both of these points—plurality and punitivism—in the next section.

It is also important to recognise Brazilian punitivism has historical as well as contemporary roots and is apparent in other areas of criminal justice policy and practice besides sentencing. We will see these include public and private forms of policing. They also include prison overcrowding. It is useful to turn to this second feature of Brazilian prisons identified in the introduction to the chapter before we explore Brazilian criminology in more detail.

Overcrowding

In April 2015 Human Rights Watch visited a number of prisons in Pernambuco. The report that followed (Human Rights Watch 2015b) is a damning indictment of some of the poorest of Brazilian prisons. One of the prisons visited, Penitenciária Agro-Industrial São João, a semi-open prison on Ilha de Itamaracá (Itamaracá Island), had a maximum capacity of 630 but was holding 2300 prisoners. Inmates had to collect water for the cell blocks from taps in the yard that were turned on for just half an hour, three times a day. The second prison, Presídio Agente de Segurança Penitenciária Marcelo Francisco de Araújo, one of three units in the Curado prison complex, Pernambuco (introduced in Chapter 1) had an official capacity of 465 but was holding 1902 prisoners, around 350 on a *seguro* (insurance or vulnerable persons unit) that contained a total of six cells and 36 bunks. Inmates on this wing were locked up 24 hours a day, with just one or two hours unlock at the weekend. At a third prison, Presídio Juiz Antônio Luiz L. de Barros, also in the Curado complex, the Human Rights Watch investigators came across 37 inmates in a windowless, unfurnished cell who had been waiting up to two months for transfer to another prison. As indicated in Chapter 1, Curado has a long history of overcrowding. It also appears to be getting progressively more overcrowded. In the late 2000s, a federal parliamentary investigation found the complex to be operating at nearly 300% capacity, with an inmate population of around 4200 (Câmara dos Deputados 2008). Four years later, it was reported in a federal government report to be holding closer to 5000 inmates (Conselho Nacional de Justiça 2012). By September 2013, a year and a half before Human Rights Watch visited, its inmate population had risen to 6456 (Inter-American Court of Human Rights 2014). Arruda (2015) found there to be insufficient space for everyone to sleep in the cells. Worse still, there was not enough floor space in the corridors for everyone to lie down at the same time.

According to the official prison statistics for June 2016 (Ministério da Justiça e Segurança Pública 2017), two thirds of the country's prisons hold more inmates than they designated. In total, there is a shortfall of 359,048 spaces, leaving the prison system almost 97% overcrowded.[12] The average Brazilian prison remains less crowded than it was two decades ago, when the system was officially operating at around 230% capacity and most remand prisoners were kept in police custody (Human Rights Watch 1998). Still, Brazilian prisons are comparatively far more crowded than their Northern counterparts, at least prisons in

Western Europe. By all accounts, they are also more crowded than they were during much of the second half of the twentieth century, including the country's last period of military dictatorship, 1964–1985.[13] The number of inmates crammed into the remaining *carceragens* such as the ones I visited in Paraná is particularly alarming. Tribuna Popular (2015) lists a number of other *carceragens* in Paraná that are officially more than 10 times over capacity. Among numerous examples of chronic levels of overcrowding in *carceragens* reported by government, human rights and penal reform groups in recent times, public defenders from the Mutirão Carcerário initiative[14] visited a *carceragem* in Pará where 17 prisoners were being held in a four metre long corridor, and a *carceragem* in Paraná where one of the four-bunk cells was found to be holding 30 prisoners (Conselho Nacional de Justiça 2012).[15] However, as Human Rights Watch (2015b) demonstrates, severe levels of overcrowding are encountered in the common prison system as well. 6 in 10 Brazilian inmates were being held in prisons more than double official capacity in June 2014, and almost 1 in 10 in prisons more than 200% overcrowded (Ministério da Justiça 2015). Pernambuco was found to have the worst record in the country. Its prison system was officially operating 265% above capacity; 96% (30,139) of the state's 31,423 inmates were living in overcrowded prisons (ibid.). Other reports of extreme levels of overcrowding in the common Brazilian penal system include:

> The now demolished the Casa de Detenção de São Paulo (Carandiru prison), introduced in chapter one, where 500 vulnerable prisoners were confined to single cells 24 hours a day, six or seven, sometimes up to 10 inmates a time (Human Rights Watch 1998; Varella 2008). In the rest of the prison, at least, cell space per inmate was normally sufficient to allow everyone to sleep on a bunk. At the time of the 1992 police massacre at the prison (also described in Chapter one), the cell block in which the killings occurred had 2069 prisoners and 550 cells. One of the survivors of the massacre describes his cell as measuring 12 square metres and having six bunks. (Ramos 2003)

> A semi-open prison in Ceará whose inmate population peaked at 1688 in 2009, 14 times its official capacity. Legal proceedings led to the immediate release, under evening and weekend house arrest, of 1052 inmates

who worked externally and were previously allowed to sleep at home on weekdays. Prison authorities were given two years to deactivate the prison. (Ministério Público do Ceará 2009)

A closed prison in Goiás with a population of 1435 where on the day public defenders from the Mutirão Carcerário initiative[16] visited a two-person cell was found to be occupied by 35 inmates. (Conselho Nacional de Justiça 2012)

A closed prison in Pernambuco (not one of those covered in Human Rights Watch 2015b) with an official capacity of 426, but found by the Mutirão Carcerário initiative to be holding 2326 inmates. (ibid.)

A high security prison, Penitenciária Jair Ferreira de Carvalho, Mato Grosso do Sul, where the Mutirão Carcerário team found up to 16 inmates sharing each four person cell (ibid.). When I visited the prison in 2017, some of these cells were holding 20 prisoners. Cell block *faxinas* (cleaners or housekeepers) I spoke with on one wing told me their cells, occupied by 10 to 12 prisoners, measured four by two metres. They were given access to the exercise yard for only three hours a day.

In 2008 I made my first visits to active prisons in Brazil (following my visit to the deactivated Carandiru prison three years earlier). At the first prison, a remand unit in São Paulo, Centro de Detenção Provisória da Capital Chácara Belém II, more than 30 inmates were temporarily being held in each 12-bunk cell after one wing had been closed following the discovery of a tunnel (Darke 2013). The cells measured a maximum of eight by three metres. In January 2016 the prison was officially operating at three times capacity, with 844 spaces and 2504 inmates (Secretaria de Administração Penitenciária do Estado de São Paulo, n.d.). Most remand prisons in the state were built to a similar design; all are holding in excess of 2000 prisoners. The most overcrowded wings in São Paulo's remand system now hold between 50 and 60 inmates per cell (Pastoral Carcerária 2016).

In 2010 I visited Penitenciária Alfredo Trajan, one of the largest units in the Gericinó prison complex (commonly referred to as Bangu), Rio de Janeiro. At the time it was not particularly overcrowded, with a population of approximately 700 prisoners. In September 2017, however, the prison was reported to be holding 3087 inmates, three and a half times its current official capacity of 881 (Oliveira 2017).

One of my more recent prison visits was to the largest single prison unit in the country, Cadeia Pública de Porto Alegre (Porto Alegre Public Prison: Central Prison), Rio Grande do Sul, also first mentioned in chapter one. When the prison's inmate population reached 5000 in 2008, more than 150% over official capacity, it was dubbed by Chamber of Deputies (2008) and by the media (Bassani 2016) as the worst prison in the country. In 2017 it was recorded as holding 4670 inmates (Hadler et al. 2017), despite its capacity having been reduced to 1824 after the demolition of one of its crumbling cell blocks in 2014. None of the cell blocks have been renovated since the prison was inaugurated in 1959 (França et al. 2016). Reflecting the situation at the Curado prison complex, Pernambuco, several years ago staff stopped locking prisoners up on many of its current 27 wings for lack of cell space. Cell doors have since been removed. Today the main blocks house in excess of 40 prisoners per eight-bunk cell; at night time hundreds of prisoners sleep side by side across the corridors.[17] In January 2017 the prison was one of 23 in the state temporarily banned by judicial authorities from receiving new prisoners.

Many cells also remain unlocked at the semi-open prison, Penitenciária Feminina do Butantã (Butantã Women's Penitentiary), São Paulo. I visited Butantã for the first time in 2014, and twice again in 2016 with University of São Paulo law students to teach a criminology course to a group of 20 prisoners. In 2016 the prison was holding over 1300 inmates. Like other semi-open units in the country, around half were working full-time, mostly outside the prison. These prisoners were held on the first two floors of the blocks, four to a cell. Each had their own bed. They had access to the whole prison complex 9 am to 5 pm. The prisoners I met were mostly not working and were held on the upper two floors, up to 12 per four-bed cell. These landings were not as crowded as the majority of the wings in Rio Grande do Sul's Central Prison or in Pernambuco's Curado prison complex. However, apart from mealtimes the inmates held there were not allowed outside. They were usually allowed to sleep on mattresses in the corridors, but sometimes their cells would be locked at night.

In 2016 I also visited three units in the Aparecida de Goiânia prison complex, Goiás. One of the units, inaugurated as recently as December 2014, served as the complex's *triagem* (screening; here indicating its holding cells). Pretrial prisoners were held for a month or more after their arrest while it was decided which wings they could be safely allocated in the larger remand prison unit. At the time of my visit the *triagem* was more than three times over official capacity. There were 700 prisoners but only one *pátio*. As at many other prison units in the country, sex offenders, homosexuals and those accused of domestic violence were not accepted by other prisoners. It was also deemed necessary to keep these three prisoner types apart. As a result, unlock was restricted to the legal minimum of two hours a day. One small group of prisoners, young women who had been arrested for infanticide, were locked up 24 hours a day in the unit's *isolamento* (isolation or segregation unit) in cells that, from what I could tell, had no natural light. A few deadly pale faces appeared from tiny glassless windows above head height to bid me good afternoon as I passed through the wing.

Further, official capacity rates are easily manipulated. Brazilian law stipulates prisoners must be held in single cells measuring a minimum of six square metres.[18] Outside the remand system, most of the country's prison cells were built to these international standards (Rolim 2007). However, single occupancy is rare (cf. Human Rights Watch 1998). Brazil does not set minimum conditions for the size of prison cells, although in 2005 the federal government introduced recommendations for the construction and refurbishing of prisons (Ministério da Justiça 2005) that set further standards of seven square metres where a cell is shared by two prison inmates, eight square metres in the case of a four-person cell, and 10 square metres in the case of a six-person cell. These standards fall short of internationally accepted human rights norms, for instance the minimum of four square metres per prisoner held in a multi-occupancy cell set by the Council of Europe Committee for the Prevention of Torture (Coyle et al. 2016). As such, they might be regarded as serving to legitimise, even mystify existing practice, especially in the country's oldest prison establishments, many of which, like their Northern American and Western European counterparts, were originally designed as institutions of silence and solitary confinement (Salvatore 1996). Moreover, even these most minimalistic of standards are a poor reflection of prison practice. Capacity rates are typically calculated on the basis of the number of beds rather than the size of cells. Levels of official overcrowding, in other words, depend on how many beds individual prison governors decide to squeeze or stack in a cell. To give just a few examples of this disjuncture between official occupancy levels and the reality on the ground:

> Câmara dos Deputados (2008) reported visiting a closed prison in Bahia that was officially no more than 50% overcrowded, with 1776 inmates occupying 1200 spaces, yet was holding its inmates six per six metre square cell. In other words, the prison would have been operating within capacity had four prisoners been sharing each single cell. A second (women's) prison in Bahia that was officially operating at 107% capacity required inmates to double up in cells measuring less than three square metres.

Also in the late 2000s, investigators from the United Nations Committee against Torture reported visiting a *carceragem* in Rio de Janeiro that was holding 90 inmates per 30 metre square cell, yet was officially operating at no more than 200% capacity (United Nations 2008). The *carceragem* would therefore have been operating within capacity had it held 30 inmates per 30 metre square cell.

Following my visit to Belém II in 2008, I went on to Penitenciária de Feminina Sant'Ana (Sant'Ana Women's Penitentiary). I visited the prison for a second time in 2017. Sant'Ana is one of Brazil's oldest penal establishments. It was inaugurated in 1920 with a majority of single cells. Originally a men's prison, it is now the largest women's prison in Latin America. From the 1960s to the 1990s it was part of a larger prison complex which also contained Carandiru. In the 1980s most of its cells were still single occupancy (Mendes 2005), but by the 1990s each held two or three inmates (Wolfmann 2000). This continued after it became a women's prison. In January 2008 Sant'Ana had an official capacity of 2400 and a recorded inmate population of 2650 sentenced or remand prisoners, making it officially no more than 10% overcrowded (Darke 2013). By January 2016 it was no longer officially serving as a remand prison. Its recorded inmate population had fallen to 2127, but its capacity had risen to 2696 (Secretaria de Administração Penitenciária do Estado de São Paulo, n.d.). This meant Sant'Ana was officially operating significantly under its certified maximum number of prisoners.

Despite their reputation for being Brazil's most humane prisons (Câmara dos Deputados 2008), cell space is likewise at a premium in the APAC prisons in Minas Gerais, also introduced in chapter one. All APAC prisons operate a strictly observed waiting list to keep them within official capacity, in other words no one sleeps on the floor or on occasional beds. Yet, like those incarcerated in the common prison system, APAC inmates enjoy little space or privacy in their cells. On the closed unit of Franz de Castro prison (a pseudonym), four prisoners shared each eight to 10 square metre cell when I conducted fieldwork there in 2012. The semi-open unit accommodated eight prisoners in each approximately 18 square metre cell. Franz de Castro is the APAC system's flagship prison. Among the other six APAC prisons I visited between 2010 and 2012, at least four units were more crowded than Franz de Castro. Two prisons had literally filled the cells in their semi-open units with as many triple bunk beds that would fit but still allow just enough leg room for inmates to squeeze their way between them. At one of these two prisons inmates on the closed unit similarly slept on triple bunks, in marginally better conditions, but still six per cell measuring no more than eight square metres. The fourth facility, a women's closed unit, housed its inmates six per at most four by two and a half metre cell.[19]

A prison, then, might reduce or even get rid of a problem of overcrowding by simply adding more beds. My attention was drawn to this practice a few years ago at Penitenciária Estadual de Piraquara II (State Penitentiary of Piraquara II), a high security prison in Paraná that I visited in 2012. At the time of my visit the prison had an official capacity of 693 and was holding 687 prisoners. An earlier problem of overcrowding had been solved when an extra layer of bunks was added to the majority of cells, turning them from six to nine bed cells. Each of the cells measured 12.5 square metres. Conselho Nacional de Justiça (2012) similarly report on the temporary use of camp beds in a women's prison it visited in Bahia.

Finally, it should be noted that prisoners working as trusty *faxina* are not usually held in overcrowded cells. Besides getting off the wing during daylight hours, one of the main advantages of taking up a trusty position is that you will most likely get your own bed. Some prisons include wings, often run in partnership with religious voluntary sector organisations, where inmates experience better conditions in exchange for engaging in regimes of full-time work or therapy. I have encountered such wings operating in Central Prison, Rio Grande do Sul, and in the remand unit in the Aparecida de Goiânia prison complex, Goiás. The position for cell block *faxina* is more variable. The *faxina* cell on the wing I visited in Central Prison was occupied by just a few inmates. On the other hand, all gang-affiliated, that is the vast majority of inmates, are expected to live in the same conditions in PCC prisons in São Paulo and Comando Vermelho (CV) prisons in Rio de Janeiro. In later chapters, we will see this includes the majority of trusty *faxina*, who in these two states are mostly selected from gang wings. Working with statistics on average levels of prison overcrowding, in other words, distorts a reality in which some cell blocks, wings and individual cells may be far more overcrowded than others.

Prison overcrowding is a major concern from both human rights and governance perspectives. The severe levels of prison overcrowding in Brazil have negative connotations for relations between and among prison inmates and staff, and for physical and mental health (see, inter alia, Human Rights Watch 1998; Câmara dos Deputados 2008; Inter-American Commission on Human Rights 2011; United Nations 2012). Rates of tuberculosis among prisoners are estimated to be 28 times that of the general Brazilian population; rates of HIV Aids are estimated to be three times higher (Ministério da Justiça 2016b). Of 250 prisoners tested for HIV Aids at Carandiru prison in 1998, seven per cent were positive; in a larger study of 2492 prisoners eight years earlier before crack cocaine had taken over as the hard drug of choice from injectable cocaine, 17% tested positive (Varella 2008). Evidence on deaths in Brazilian prisons is more equivocal. Approximately 1700 people are recorded as dying in Brazilian prisons in 2014, most of natural causes but possibly as many as 500 as the result of criminal violence and up to 100 self-harm and suicide.[20] In comparison, 346 prisoners died in England and Wales in 2016, 174 of natural causes, three as victims of homicide and 120 as the result of self-harm and suicide (INQUEST 2018). At the time of writing (March 2018) 47 cases were still awaiting classification. Considering Brazil has at least seven times more prisoners than England and Wales, these official statistics indicate a prisoner is equally likely to die in either country. A Brazilian prisoner is more likely to suffer from HIV or preventable diseases like tuberculosis, but overall no more likely to die of natural causes. And while they are more likely to be murdered—although we will see in later chapters, less so in states whose prisons are under the control of major gangs—they are less likely to take their own life. A study of state justice ministry archives on prison suicides in Rio Grande do Sul (Negrelli 2006) uncovered 80 suicides over 11 years, equivalent to a rate of 31 per 100,000 prisoners, three times higher than among the state's general population. In 2007, the prison suicide rate in England and Wales was 114 per 100,000 prisoners, over 12 times the rate outside (Department of Health 2009). England and Wales is not exceptional among Western European nations in this regard. Norway (Mathiesen 2012) and France (Fassin 2017) have similar, if not higher levels of self-inflicted death among their prison populations than does England and Wales.

The figures on natural deaths are not quite as surprising as they first appear. The average Brazilian prison is unquestionably less healthy than the average English prison, but at the same time the Brazilian prison population is significantly younger. Almost two thirds of prisoners in England and Wales are over 30 years old, and one in ten prisoners is over 60 (Ministry of Justice 2017c). Less than half of Brazilian prisoners are over 30 and less than one per cent are over 70 (Ministério da Justiça 2016b). The differences in the figures on self-inflicted death are more difficult to explain. According to the World Health Organisation, suicide rates are only slightly (25%) higher in England and Wales than in Brazil outside of prison (World Health Organisation database 2017). More broadly, incidences of non-lethal self-harm also appear to be lower among Brazilian than English prisoners. These divergences cannot be explained by age. In England and Wales, young prisoners are known to be equally vulnerable as older prisoners (Prison Reform Trust and INQUEST 2012). There is no reason to doubt this should be the case in Brazil as well. Nor can these figures be explained by gender. The prison population of both countries is approximately 95% male. That said, in contrast to England and Wales, it is not so clearly the case that women are more vulnerable to self-harm and suicide in prison than men. There have perhaps been 10 self-inflicted deaths in the past decade at Sant'Ana prison.[21] Over the same period, 2007–2016, 37 inmates took their own lives in English women's prisons,[22] which between them hold no more than 50% more than Sant'Ana. Incidences of non-lethal self-harm are registered at Sant'Ana on average once every two weeks. 7657 incidences of self-harm were recorded across the women's prison estate in England and Wales in 2016, involving over a quarter (1152) of prisoners (Ministry of Justice 2017c). The apparent lower level of self-inflicted harm among Brazilian compared to English women prisoners was confirmed to me in visits to Butantã semi-open prison in 2014 and 2016. During the first of these visits, an officer recalled having dealt with a prolific self-harming prisoner only once in her 20 year service. She may well have exaggerated this point. As in England and Wales and anywhere else, prisoners do sometimes turn to self-harm as a means of psychological survival. This Antunes (2017) demonstrates in a recent ethnographic study on the *regime de observação* (observation regime) at Sant'Ana, a wing used to house women sentenced to psychiatric treatment as well as prisoners that have recently arrived or are being punished for breaching prison rules. Still, the point remains that self-harm appears to be comparatively low in Brazilian prisons, and among female as well as male prisoners, in spite of the inhumane conditions within which most prisoners are held. I had the opportunity to explore issues of self-harm and suicide with inmates at one of two lessons I delivered at Butantã prison in 2016. The consensus of opinion among the participants was they were shielded from their otherwise painful experiences of prison by their interpersonal relations with other women prisoners.

The results of research on the mental health of Brazilian prisoners are also counterintuitive. Of 1809 prisoners interviewed in a study by the Department of Psychiatry, University of São Paulo, in the mid-2000s, nearly 40% of women and 20% of men reported symptoms of psychiatric disorder in the past year, two times higher than similar studies conducted among the general population of the state of São Paulo (Andreoli et al. 2014), but lower than comparable studies conducted in the UK, which have shown mental health to be many more times serious an issue inside than outside prison (e.g. Singleton et al. 1998, 2000). Poor mental health is also the single most contributing factor to self-harm and suicide among prisoners in the UK (Scott and Codd 2010; Singleton et al. 1998).

I explore possible explanations for the relatively lower levels of poor mental health, self-harm and suicide among Brazilian prisoners in more detail in Chapter 4. What is important for the purposes of this chapter is that most Brazilian prisons are wholly ill-equipped to deal with inmates' health needs, either physical or psychological. To the extent prisoners survive their experience, the focus of Chapter 4, they usually do so with little direct support from prison staff. A majority of prisons do not even have health centres (Câmara dos Deputados 2008) or any medical cover at all in the evenings and weekends (United Nations 2012). Just 3159 fully qualified medical practitioners (including 567 general practitioners, 1098 nurses and 1265 psychologists) were employed across the entire prison system in June 2016 (Ministério da Justiça e Segurança Pública 2017). Half of prisons do not even have a doctor's surgery (ibid.). In 2015, the prison service of Pernambuco employed a total of 161 health practitioners, 40 health practitioners per shift, to look after the state's 31,000 prisoners (Human Rights Watch 2015b). None of the prisons I have visited in the country were attended by a doctor more than one day a week. São Paulo prison authorities do not supply any doctors at all to a quarter (34) of its 164 prisons (Pastoral Carcerária 2016). Sant'Ana is relatively well staffed in this regard. Although it relies on a voluntary doctor, there were four employed nurses on duty when I last visited in 2017. A remand prison I visited in the interior of São Paulo a few days earlier had also relied on voluntary doctors to take care of its approximately 2100 inmates throughout its 15-year existence. Besides this doctor, who visited on Fridays, just two qualified nurses were usually on duty. A second remand prison I have already mentioned visiting in 2016 in Goiás had recently built a new medical centre but still had only one full-time qualified nurse among its medical staff. At the time the prison was operating with around 2300 inmates, more than three times over capacity.

***

Brazil is a nation of contradictions. Where else would it be perfectly acceptable to hang a Christian cross around the neck of a statue of the Buddha and a spiritist prayer book on his lap? Or for a domestic servant to cry over the death of a sportsman from an elite, land and factory owning family in front of her employer, not having once complained that he paid her the absolute minimum she was legally entitled, equivalent to just £2 for a day's work. Where else would a governor order his staff not to lay hands on people held in his prison, while defending the right for the police to shoot people that resist arrest outside? Or for one closed prison to become internationally recognised as having some of the most humane regimes in the world, while at a closed prison just a few miles away guards have been known to discharge their weapons into cells?

Readers from Southern countries will most likely find these personal experiences less surprising or "exotic" than readers from the North. I have already referred to the Hess' (1995) analysis of the plurality of Brazilian cultures. Of more general application, in an insightful overview of theories of legitimate governance in Africa, Jefferson (2013) stresses the need for Northern scholars to resist thinking in terms of binary oppositions and to recognise that African politics will invariably be unstable and subject to continuous change. Jefferson explores the implications of this observation in the context of prison reform in Sierra Leone and demonstrates how successful local initiatives depend on collaborations between the governors and the governed, in this case state prison authorities and civil society prison reform groups.

Jefferson (2013) suggests instability and change are characteristic of institutions in other parts of the Global South besides Africa. His analysis of the fluidity of African boundaries between the governors and the governed goes to the core of my own observations regarding the informal, interpersonal, clientelistic nature of Brazilian staff-inmate relations and the co-production of prison order that I explore in Chapter 4. More generally, Jefferson's critique of Western binary thinking hints at deeper limitations in the extent to which Northern theories can be used to understand the South. Nuanced accounts are needed that not only take Brazilian and wider Latin American history and social and institutional cultures, but also informality and instability—variation and exception, contradiction and unintended consequences—into account. Reflecting on his historical study of prison life in Lima, Peru, Aguirre writes:

> The role of prisons within the overall structure of the modern state… is contingent upon the nature of that state (liberal, autocratic, oligarchic, military) and the concrete manner in which specific mechanisms and actors operate… a gulf sometimes separates the declared goals of state institutions from their practical implementation… the ultimate form punishment takes will always depend, at its core, on the influence of socially constructed sensibilities. (Aguirre 2005: 11–12)

Of course, prisons should be studied as "cultural artifacts" (Garland 1990: 193, cited in Aguirre 2005: 11) anywhere in the world. The major point here is sensibilities vary from one social context to another in Brazil more than they do in a more culturally homogenous and bureaucratic nation like the UK.

The primary task for any endeavour to synthesise and develop nation or regional-specific theories is to explore how global ideas are, "… appropriated and transformed by very distinct local styles of expression dependent on the political, economic, social and cultural variables of particular institutions and social groups" (Dikötter 2007: 6, cited in Darke and Karam 2016: 461). I present the results of my ethnographic research and my analysis of the plurality of Brazilian prison cultures in the remaining chapters of this book. Over the final pages of this chapter, I briefly introduce some of the most important scholarship I have come to understand as constituting a critical Brazilian penology. In the absence of fieldwork, my overview of sentencing and prison conditions is unavoidably generalised and makes little account for varieties of culture among the elite groups that ultimately determine them, for instance the prosecutors and judges that send people to prison and the government officials that fund prison spaces and material provisions. Political scientists have noted that Brazilian institutions enjoy high levels of bureaucratic autonomy, which on the one hand leads to major variation between decisions made at federal and state level and how they are implemented further down the line (e.g. Macaulay 2007), and on the other hand facilitates major shifts in policies and practices at all levels of government (e.g. Nunes 2015). As far as I am aware, no detailed fieldwork has been conducted in Brazil on the institutional cultures of penal policy makers or actors.

Violent Iberian Realities

The point of departure for any critical analysis of contemporary criminal justice in a Latin American country is to understand law as an illegitimate tool of repression (Castro 1987; Zaffaroni 1989). Notwithstanding the existence of variation and exception previously noted, Brazilian justice continues to be characterised by exclusion, authoritarianism and violence two centuries after the end of Portuguese colonial rule, and decades after the end of the latest period of military rule (see, inter alia, Adorno 2013; V. M. Batista 2003b; N. Batista 1997; Carvalho 1996; Casara 2014; Karam 1996; Neder 1996; Pavarini and Giamberardino 2011). Moreover, like other parts of the Latin American region (Zaffaroni 1989), Brazil continues to be self-consciously and openly exclusionary, authoritarian and violent (Codino 2014). Many Brazilians, especially poor Brazilians in major cities like São Paulo (Caldeira 2000) and Rio de Janeiro (Goldstein 2003), have little faith in either the effectiveness or equity of law. There is no permanent police presence in a quarter of the country's urban areas (Koonings and Kruijt 2009). Rio de Janeiro's *favelas* are on average served by one police officer per 2000 residents (Huggins 2000). Furthermore, Northern liberal democratic theories on separation of state powers, due process and equal application of law could not be further dislocated from the average *favela* resident's lived experience. For vast sections of the Brazilian population the rule of law signifies little more than the rule of the police (Zaffaroni et al. 2003). The life of the poor Brazilian is barely governed by law, let alone governed by laws that can only be enforced according to certain procedures.

Instead, a poor Brazilian's experience of law is typically one of unsolved crime (Caldeira 2002) and arbitrary police violence (Caldeira 2000). In metropolitan Rio de Janeiro, a city of 11 million inhabitants, the police made just 50,000 arrests in 2008, while killing over 1100 (Human Rights Watch 2009).[23] Extra-judicial executions are commonplace (ibid.; Huggins 2000; Human Rights Watch 2016; Zaccone 2015). Many detainees report being beaten in police custody (see Conectas 2017; Foley 2013; Instituto de Defesa do Direito de Defesa 2018; Pastoral Carcerária 2016).

One consequence is that even more serious crimes go largely unreported (Caldeira 2000). In contrast to a country like the UK, where nine in ten crimes the police deal with are brought to their attention by the public, Brazilian police forces encounter a wall of silence across many communities when it comes to investigating crime, again especially in the major Southern cities of Rio de Janeiro (Goldstein 2003; Penglase 2009) and São Paulo (Feltran 2011; Willis 2015). Most people remanded in prison were caught *em flagrante* (in the act) (Carlos 2015). The depth of public distrust of law is reflected in commonly heard expressions like "*direitos humanos é coisa de bandido*" ("human rights are for bandits" or "outlaws") and "*aos meus amigos, tudo; aos meus inimigos, a lei*" ("for my friends, everything; for my enemies, the law"). Regarding the former, in Brazil even the judiciary opposes the internationally recognised notion that human rights are universal and inalienable (Semer 2014). The latter expression was popularised by the country's longest serving president, Getúlio Vargas, in the mid-twentieth cetury (O'Donnell 1998). Despite ruling through martial law for much of his first period in office, 1930–1945, Vargas won democratic elections in 1951. The autocratic sentiments Vargas' words reflected are shared in other parts of Latin America (ibid.). Across the region law is considered a source of injustice more than it is of fairness (Aguirre and Salvatore 2001). "To voluntarily follow the law", O'Donnell (1998: 9) warns, "is [seen as] something that only idiots do… to be subject to the law is not to be the carrier of enforceable rights but rather a sure thing of social weakness".

In terms of sentencing, we have seen Brazil is threatening to move off the scale when it comes to global trends in the use of prison. Certainly in terms of absolute numbers of prisoners, and increasingly in terms of rates of imprisonment, Brazil is leading the way in the emergence of a new, Latin American, mass carceral zone. This does not indicate Brazilian punitivism is just a contemporary matter of concern, however. If we are witnessing anything new at all, it is change in the forms of Brazilian punitivism, not its substance. Prison, in its modern meaning as a place of penal detention, is just the latest in a long series of repressive institutions in the post-colonial era that have openly targeted sections of the population deemed criminally dangerous, threats to state sovereignty, or simply poor, idle or dispensable. These include local authority jails, military dungeons and hulks, industrial schools and workhouses, religious institutions, asylums and charity vice centres, all but the first of which pre-existed the modern prison system by decades, and continued to be used as places of criminal, civil and extra-legal detention years long after the first penitentiaries were built in the mid-nineteenth century (Araújo 2009; Bassani 2016; Koerner 2006). As in other parts of Latin America, due process remained a chimera (Aguirre 2007). In 1830, at least 30 such institutions of detention were in use in the capital city of Rio de Janeiro alone, the largest of which, a military hulk, held 458 sentenced prisoners and escaped slaves (Koerner 2006). The local government ran three civil prisons, the largest of which held 200 people (Araújo 2009). Nor did the modern penitentiary system immediately replace coercive conscription into the army (Salvatore and Aguirre 1996), convict labour (Beattie 2015) or debt servitude, the latter of which was used by the Brazilian government to force people onto plantations up to the mid-twentieth century (Garfield 2010). Further, with the end of slavery towards the end of the nineteenth century many thousands of poor people were confined to agricultural plantations and penal colonies under public order and vagrancy laws (Huggins 1985). Finally, it should also be noted that prison did not replace the Latin American traditions of extra-legal police violence (Costa 2011), "bottom-up legality" (Willis 2016: 37) or private justice (Salvatore and Aguirre 1996), which in their more sinister incarnations continue today in the form of street gangs working in tandem with local police officers (Leeds 1996) or in the form of private militia, *justiceiros* (hit men) and death squads, each made up largely of retired and off-duty police officers—what Leeds (1996) describes as parallel power, and Arias and Goldstein (2010) as violent pluralism (cited in Cavalcanti 2016b; see also, inter alia, Alves 2013; Arias and Barnes 2016; Feltran 2011; Huggins 2000; Huggins and Mesquita 1995, Misse 2007; Penglase 2009; Perlman 2010; Willis 2015).

As for conditions of incarceration, we have seen many prisoners are subjected to severe levels of overcrowding. Few prisoners are held in spaces that comply with the international human rights standards required, for example, by the Council of Europe Committee for the Prevention of Torture. Health care is appalling. Again, it is important to emphasise these are historical as well as modern matters. As previously mentioned, Brazilian prisons were even more overcrowded twenty or more years ago. They were also more deadly. Indeed, Brazilian prisons have been characterised by inhumane living conditions since their inception: in spite of the liberal intentions of the nineteenth-century penal reformers who imported the Northern ideal of the reforming, panoptical prison (Chazkel 2009; Pavarini and Giamberardino 2011); in spite of the early twentieth century and post-war Northern ideal of the rehabilitating prison (Carvalho 2013; Iturralde 2012); and far in excess of the post-industrial, late twentieth century Northern ideal of the warehousing prison (Wacquant 2008). As in other parts of Latin America, Brazil's prisons are historically overcrowded and unhealthy to the point they are more appropriately described as institutions of internment (Birkbeck 2011) than institutions of penal punishment. Most prisoners are fully aware they cannot count on their keepers to sustain them, and that they have been abandoned to their own fate and left to their own devises. The Brazilian penal state makes little effort to hide the fact its prisons are severely under-resourced. The judiciary, on the other hand, continue to hide behind the façade of the rule of law to deny responsibility for the fate of the people they imprison (Caetano 2015; Casara 2016, 2017).

Importantly, unlike their Northern America and Western European counterparts, Latin American prison systems did not emerge during a period of modernisation (Aguirre and Salvatore 2001; Dikötter 2007; Salvatore and Aguirre 1996). In the early nineteenth century, the Brazilian state did not face the threat of either a potentially revolutionary rural peasantry (Prado Júnior 1961) or urban proletariat (Batista 2003a). The Brazilian economy remained agricultural and its work force made up mostly of imported African slaves. Its elites were naturally more concerned with maintaining its slave mode of production than with creating a disciplined, industrial working class; the "useful" slave was simply one that did not rebel (Batista 1996; cf. Huggins 1985). When Latin America's first recognised modern penitentiary, the Casa de Correção da Corte, opened in Rio de Janeiro in 1850 with a regime of daytime work and night-time isolation in spaces of 4.3 square metres, Brazil was very much on the peripheries of global capitalism. It was a major exporter of cotton, tobacco and sugar, the world's leading exporter of coffee, and after three centuries still the world's leading importer of African slaves (Alencastro 2007). However, its economy stagnated throughout much of the nineteenth century and it showed no signs of industrialising. For a country with such a large landmass, Brazil's national population was remarkably small. Its population also included an extraordinarily high proportion of slaves. An estimated 50% of the country's four million inhabitants were held in slavery in 1818 (Beattie 2015). When the transatlantic slave trade finally ended in the mid-nineteenth century, a third of the country's approximately seven million inhabitants were still enslaved (ibid.). In 1849, the province of Rio de Janeiro's recorded population of 557,030 inhabitants included 293,554 slaves. Slavery itself was legal in Brazil until 1888. The nation's economy remained agricultural and its population rural for another hundred years; Brazil did not have a working class to speak of before the second half of the twentieth century (Menegat 2012).

Under these socio-economic circumstances, the reformist vision of the disciplinary prison made little sense to the country's political elites (Dikötter 2007) or prison workers (Bretas 1996). Nineteenth-century penitentiary regulations required inmates to be held in single cells and those sentenced to prison labour subjected to full-time regimes of work and education (Roig 2005). Two years after its inauguration the Casa de Correção still contained just one of an originally planned four wings of 200 individual cells (Pessoa 2014a). A second wing completed in 1856 was instead used to house remand prisoners. The new Casa de Detenção da Corte was designed to hold 160 remand and short-term prisoners serving ordinary rather than prison labour sentences. It was built with 40 individual cells of 14.6 square metres and 20 six-person cells measuring 30 square metres. The Casa de Detenção did not have workshops, but unlike the local authority jails it replaced, different categories of prisoners were meant to be kept apart in an effort to prevent them from contaminating one another with new criminalities (Chazkel 2009; Pessoa 2014b). However, any pretence the Casa de Detenção was designed to reform offenders was soon set aside as it began to be filled with slaves held under civil laws, beggars and children for who the police and local authorities could not find other accommodation, and people sentenced to prison labour and waiting for spaces into become available in the Casa de Correção (Chazkel 2009). As a result, the Casa de Detenção quickly became just as overcrowded and extra-legal as the military and local authority jails it was meant to have replaced. Finally, the prison complex as a whole was poorly ventilated and did not have running water. The Casa de Correção soon yet another "house of disease and death" (Salvatore and Aguirre 1996: 9). 245 prisoners died there by the end of 1869, including 36% of those who had been given two year plus sentences (Bretas 1996). In other words, prisoners died there at a rate of one in six per year. The few judicial detention centres or penitentiaries inaugurated in other parts of Brazil and Latin America in the nineteenth century fared little better (Aguirre 2007).

Like other parts of the Global South, the birth of the prison in Latin America therefore proved to be anything but a belated replication of Western European and Northern American innovations (Dikötter 2007; Salvatore and Aguirre 1996). Instead, the starting point of an analysis of Brazilian justice, including is prisons, should be the country's "violent social reality" of slavery (Batista 2003a: 38). To the extent the concept of prison gained favour in nineteenth-century Brazil, it did so as a result of developments in Northern science rather than liberal ideals, in particular biological theories on the links between crime and evolution, which in Latin America and Brazil in particular were swiftly taken up to legitimise the continued subordination of local indigenous populations and African descendants. Western European and Northern American political ideals of liberty, equality and freedom from degrading treatment were enshrined in Brazil's constitution and penal code in the immediate years after the country gained independence from Portugal in 1822, but these had no impact on the slave economy (Pavarini and Giamberardino 2011) and in practice are yet to be realised for the majority of the population. Prison was constructed as a space of no rights (ibid.). Similar to the attitude taken by colonial rulers in Asia (Dikötter 2007) and other parts of Central and South America (Aguirre 2007), in the post-colonial era Brazil's

European-descendent elites continued to regard Brazil's "native" populations as intrinsically dangerous and beyond reform. Today, Brazil remains the most unequal country in Latin America, and the closest to its slavery past (Barrata 2003).

Finally, no critical analysis of the country's penal system is complete without reference to the specificities of Portuguese colonisation, and in particular the Iberian monarchical and Jesuit traditions of militarism, absolutist hierarchy, law as moral interventionism, corporal punishment and religious crusade. Cut off from continental Europe by the Pyrenees mountain range, N. Batista (2000) explains the Iberian Peninsula developed its socio-economic identity in the sixteenth to eighteenth centuries in relative isolation to the other major colonial powers. The political and legal customs that emerged during this early modern period were notably draconian. The legacies of these "Iberian matrixes" (Batista 2000) are key to understanding the extraordinary depth of violence associated with Brazilian slavery. (The sheer extent of the Brazilian slave trade can be largely explained by the peninsula's geography: Portugal started trading in African slaves as early as 1550.) Iberian matrixes also help to explain Brazil's history of informality and clientelism (Batista 2016). Of particular importance for this chapter, the early modern Iberian traditions of slavery, militarism and crusade help to explain the discriminatory and absolutist nature of Brazilian justice today: the fact, for instance, that deterministic theories of human behaviour and social defence theories of law continued to dominate legislation and legal training (Batista 2000; Neder 1996; Zaffaroni et al. 2003) as well as administrative criminology (Batista 2009, 2011) throughout both the nineteenth and twentieth centuries.[24]

It is therefore of little surprise that the global new penology of the late twentieth century and early twenty-first century has found such a receptive audience in Brazil. So too the neo-liberal economic and political ideals of deregulation, privatisation and responsibilisation, and the related criminological theories of rational choice and underclass. Brazilian liberalism has always been fundamentally elitist (Pereira 1997, cited in Goldstein 2003). Unlike post-war Western Europe and Northern America, Brazil did not have a welfare state to leave behind (Cavalcanti 2016b; Macaulay 2007; Perlman 2010).

More generally, across Latin America there is little if any correlation between those countries that have most adopted neo-liberal economic agendas and those that have seen the steepest rise in prison population (Darke and Graces 2017b; Sozzo 2017). In a review of the application of Garland's (2002) work on the move beyond penal welfarism in the USA and UK, Salla et al. (2006) explain Brazil already had a well-established criminology of the other. N. Batista (2000) starts his historical study of the legacies of early modern Iberian justice with a simple yet pertinent example: in Brazil persistent petty shoplifting will nearly always be considered a crime when it is done by a poor child, but as a family issue if it is done by a middle-class child. A second example I have highlighted in this chapter is the wholly differential treatment by prosecutors and judges of poor and rich teenagers and young adults involved in the sale or consumption of drugs. A third example is the differential treatment of "VIP" remand prisoners, for example politicians, church ministers, army officers, lawyers, judges, professional journalists and people with degrees from top universities, who have the legal right under the 1941 Penal Code and subsequent revisions to await trial in a separate prison or cell to "common prisoners" or under home detention where these are not available (Zapater 2017). A middle class or "respectable poor" offender convicted of a less serious crime also has a reasonable chance to serve their whole sentence in open or semi-open conditions. The "good delinquent", N. Batista (1997: 145–147) explains, may sometimes be made an example of to divert attention from the otherwise blatant selectivity of Brazilian justice, but he or she will still be deemed worthy of "resocialisation". In contrast, the habitual, "dangerous offender" will always be deemed in need of repression. He or she will be treated as fully responsible for what they have done. As V. M. Batista (2003a: 38) puts it, "in Brazil, authoritarianism and liberalism [have always been] two sides of the same coin".

None of this is to say Brazil does not have a major problem of serious, violent crime. 61,283 violent criminal deaths were registered in 2016, including 2666 committed during robbery (Fórum Brasileiro de Segurança Pública 2017). The majority of violent deaths involve the use of firearms. On average, 38,000 people die from gunshot wounds annually (Cavalcanti 2016a). In São Paulo recorded violent criminal deaths peaked at 1000 a month in 1992. In the 25 years since I first visited São Paulo, many of my friends and family have been victims of gun-related crime. Close acquaintances have been burgled at gunpoint, robbed at gunpoint, shot while resisting kidnapping, even tortured at gunpoint.

Nevertheless, punitive public attitudes go well beyond personal experiences of crime. 87% of Brazilians were found to support legislative proposals to reduce the age of adult criminal responsibility to 16 (Phillips 2015), even though youths can already be imprisoned for up to three years,[25] and irrespective of the fact youth prisons are not that much more humane than adult prisons (Griffin 2017). Opinion polls have also consistently found more than half of Brazilians to agree with the expression "*bandido bom é bandido morto*" ("a good outlaw is a dead one") (Caldeira 2000; Fórum Brasileiro de Segurança Pública 2016). In a public opinion survey in 10 capital cities (Cardia 2012), half of the participants agreed the police would be justified to act violently towards an incarcerated person who had tried to escape (cited in Cavalcanti 2016b). Rio de Janeiro's *favela* residents accept police killings as an inevitable part of young men's involvement in the drug trade (Zaluar 1994, cited in Penglase 2010). At least a third of Paulistanos (residents of the city of São Paulo) expressed support for the police slaughter of 111 or more inmates at Carandiru prison in 1992 (Caldeira 2000). When the internationally acclaimed Tropa de Elite (Elite Force) (Padilha and Prado 2007) was played in cinemas, some audiences missed the film's central message on police violence and corruption and cheered on police killings of teenage drug dealers in scenes reminiscent of American audiences' reactions to watching Rocky Balboa beat the Soviet Union boxer Ivan Drago in Sylvester Stallone's jubilant film Rocky IV (Chartoff et al. 1985). Except Rocky IV was a tale of patriotism, external enemies and just revenge rather than the elimination of enemies within. More on the matter of enemies in a moment. In Brazil, I have spent hours with people whose opinions I otherwise have the upmost respect for questioning the view that the police should get away with shooting armed robbers and drug dealers in the back while they are making their escape. On numerous occasions, I have also found myself having to explain sentences are actually shorter in the UK, that people caught with small quantities of drugs are rarely given custodial sentences, and that life without parole, perpetual prison as Brazilians refer to it, is far from the norm anywhere in the Northern world, even for intentional murder, and even in the USA. In my experience, both these assumptions—that the police should sometimes kill; that Brazil is soft on crime—are based less on ignorance as on popular notions of justice.

Still, it is all too easy to dismiss Brazilian punitivism as pre-modern and barbaric. To conclude and summarise this chapter, Brazilian punitivism is intricately bound up with political and social conceptions of the rule of law, which as O'Donnell (1998) observes has very different meaning in Latin American than Northern American or Western European vocabulary. Or at least it did until recently. Politically, Brazil is arguably a world leader in global trends towards austere prison conditions as well as mass incarceration. Or to put it another way, prisons in the Northern world are now catching up with how prisons have always been in Brazil. Like other parts of the Global South, Brazil did not have much of an old penology to move on from, just as it has never had an inclusive, liberal state. To utilise Foucault's (1977) classic account of the birth of the penitentiary in Western Europe, Brazilian prisons were never complete institutions that aimed to transform inmates through segregation, continuous observation, discipline and training (Koerner 2006; Teixeira et al. 2016). Callously legitimised by a criminology of apartheid (Zaffaroni 2006, cited in Batista 2009) and politics of ever-continuing fear (Batista 2003b, 2018) and exception (Carvalho 1996), Brazilian justice has always been militarised; and prisoners have always been treated as public enemies, as threats to be neutralised due to the social group they come from, rather than as people in need of individual, personalised support. And to borrow from Gledhill's (2015) analysis of class conflict over Latin American land rights, Brazilian elites have been at "war with the poor" since the land was discovered by Europeans in the 1500s. It is only in its latest version that this conflict is constructed as a crusade against drugs (Batista 2016; Carvalho 1996; Karam 2009).

As for public punitivism, distrust of the rule of law betrays deeper, rational discontent with democracy. For the poor, democracy is historically regarded less as a tool for political participation as a tool for legitimising state over informal community controls (Holston 2008). As in other parts of Latin America, Brazil's post-dictatorship democratic settlement has been characterised by a "cool authoritarianism" (Zaffaroni 2006, cited in Darke and Karam 2016) that maintains the formal structures of democracy while continuing to rule through violence and oppression. Few poor residents in Rio de Janeiro would have failed to see the symbolic significance when on 4 April 2014 armed military police entered its largest *favela* area, Complexo de Maré, accompanied by 2000 soldiers and marines to re-establish a permanent police presence almost fifty years to the day after the military coup of 1964. The operation was hailed as one of the most major successes in the state's Unidade de Polícia Pacificadora (Police Pacification Unit: UPP) programme, started in 2008. Complexo de Maré has an estimated population of around 140,000 residents. Yet the average Brazilian national is less concerned with the failures of the country's democracy as are critical academics, liberal and left wing lawyers. Police killings have doubled in Rio de Janeiro over the past five years, reversing an initial halving of police killings when the UPP programme began. 1035 people were killed by Rio de Janeiro police between January and November 2016 (Human Rights Watch 2018). Similarly, levels of non-state violence have levelled off since 2012 following a decade of decline. UPPs now operate in 38 of the state's *favelas*, the residents of which are increasingly critical of the state's failure to supplement police presence with promised investment in infrastructure, health and education. The police have also come under attack for failing to control local drug markets, and for an increasing number of shoot outs with drug gangs in occupied *favelas* in which residents have been caught in the crossfire. In a major survey of Complexo de Maré residents (Silva 2017), just 31% of 1000 interviewees agreed the UPP programme made them safer. 21% of respondents felt less safe than they had done previously. Still, as recently as August 2017 an opinion poll found two thirds of residents in UPP *favelas* continued to support the initiative overall (Economist, 5 October 2017). The irony is that the first years of the 1964–1985 dictatorship coincided with a period of economic prosperity and lower levels of urban violence (Perlman

2010). In Chapter 6, we will see class consciousness was awoken among prisoners during the dictatorship period, as attention switched from internal to external enemies and poor criminals found themselves sharing prison spaces with middle-class revolutionaries. For the emerging working class more generally, it was a period of relative stability. In 2008, a cross-national public survey found 53% of Brazilians would support a return to military dictatorship if it were to the advantage of the economy (Salla and Ballesteros 2008). Similar results were observed across Latin America (Perlman 2010).

Notes

1. The true figure is higher than this. For example, these official statistics do not include 24,628 children held in administrative detention at the end of 2014 (Fórum Brasileiro de Segurança Pública 2017). The age of criminal responsibility is 18. However, a child of 12 or over that has committed a criminal "infraction" may be detained under the Estatuto da Criança e do Adolescent (Children and Adolescents Act) 1990 for up to three years for "social and education measures" (Bochenek and Delgado 2006), even if they turn 18 during this period. Nor do the official statistics include 147,937 individuals recorded as subject to 24 hour home detention in May 2014, while on remand or in place of open prison (Conselho Nacional de Justiça 2014).
2. Official statistics on police detention are particularly questionable. 37,444 people were recorded as being in police custody in May 2014 (Ministério da Justiça 2016b), close to 10,000 more than 27,950 recorded just half a year earlier (Ministério da Justiça 2015). These latter figures did not include data from 13 states (Fórum Brasileiro de Segurança Pública 2015). The May 2014 figures still excluded data from two states. The figures from seven other states were recorded five months earlier, in December 2013. Similarly, the June 2016 figures (Ministério da Justiça e Segurança Pública 2017) did not include data from six states. The figures provided for four states were recorded in December 2015.
3. According to the Lei de Execução Penal 1984 (Penal Enforcement Act 1984), all pretrial detainees must be held in a *cadeia pública* (public

prison), run by prison authorities, once their arrest has been processed. In some states the police are still left to hold on to detainees for several months until places become available.
4. In the mid-1990s, 32,000 prisoners were held in police custody just in São Paulo (Human Rights Watch 1998), across 174 *carceragens* (Biondi 2000). The *carceragem* system was gradually dismantled in the state in the 2000s. However, an estimated two per cent, approximately 1000, of the state's prisoners are still held in police stations today (Filho 2017). Rio de Janeiro's 16 police *carceragens*, the subject matter of Chapter 5, were deactivated in the early 2010s. Paraná's *carceragens* are slowly closing down. In 2011, they peaked at 15,000 prisoners. In June 2016, they still held a registered 9826 prisoners (Ministério da Justiça e Segurança Pública 2017).
5. Brazil was ruled through military dictatorship in this period. I also return to the significance of this later.
6. Brazil's child prison population has likewise risen sharply, from 4245 in 1996 (Carvalho 2013).
7. These figures do not include an estimated 650,000 people held in administrative detention, including pretrial prisoners. If they were included, International Criminal Policy Institute (2015) explains China would have a prison population rate of 165. The world average would rise to 155.
8. A federal government initiative set up in August 2008, the Mutirão Carcerário (Joint Custodial Effort), led to the release by November 2009 of 16,466 prisoners held in pretrial custody for legal irregularities, for example being held beyond the length of time they were likely to be sentenced, 1 in 5 cases examined (International Bar Association 2010). By January 2012, this figure had risen to 36,673 prisoners (Foley 2012). Following a pilot programme in Maranhão (Human Rights Watch 2015a), a second federal state initiative to guarantee custody hearings within 24 hours of arrest, Audiência de Custódia (Custody Hearing), was piloted in São Paulo from February 2015 and subsequently introduced across the country between July and October 2015. Of approximately 75,000 cases examined by April 2016, 47% (35,000) led to the detainee being released on bail (Ministério da Justiça 2016a). More specific figures are provided state by state. In São Paulo, 9722 prisoners (47% of the 20,721 cases examined) had been released under the

initiative by 13 October 2015 (ibid.). According to the latest available official figures, 186,455 cases had been examined nationwide by January 2017, of which 54% led to the prisoner's release (Pastoral Carcerária 2017a). At the time of writing, however, the initiative has still spread little beyond state capitals and is operating in only a third of judicial districts overall (Instituto de Defesa do Direito de Defesa 2018).
9. In 2010, the Mutirão Carcerário initiative moved onto the wider prison system. 310,079 cases were examined, of which 9% (24,884) resulted in prisoners being released for having already served their sentence (Conselho Nacional de Justiça 2012).
10. I am again indebted to Chris Garces for coining this phrase. Over the past few years, Garces and I have worked on a number of collaborative writing and research projects aimed at developing comparative theoretical and empirical insights into prisons and prison life in the Latin American region.
11. A second aspect of the Latin American mass carceral zone I do not deal with in this book is a similarly extraordinary rise in community sentences, from 80,364 in 1995, the year they were introduced (Carvalho 2013) to 671,078 in 2009, the latest year figures were published (Darke and Karam 2016). A third aspect, dealt with in Chapter 3, is the effect of mass incarceration on poor, urban communities.
12. Note that the deficit was significantly smaller in December 2014, when there were a similar number (250,318) of spaces; the prison system was officially 67% overcrowded (Ministério da Justiça 2016b). Neither Ministério da Justiça (2016b) nor Ministério da Justiça e Segurança Pública (2017) included spaces in police *carceragens* in their calculations of prison capacity. If they had likewise excluded prisoners held in police detention in their calculations of inmate numbers, they would have recorded official rates of overcrowding approximately five per cent points lower. The official rates of overcrowding would have reduced further still had they taken account of the fact the majority of prisoners held in open conditions end up serving their time in their own homes.
13. Two reliable accounts of prison conditions in the dictatorship period are Coelho's (2005) study of prisons in Rio de Janeiro and Mendes' (2009) memoirs of being imprisoned in Carandiru, both of which I explore in detail in Chapter 4. The prisons described by these authors were often violent and, like the majority of Brazilian prisons today,

poorly resourced. However, neither author mentions the prisons being particularly overcrowded. Coelho provided detail of the sizes of the cells and number of occupants in each of the cell blocks of seven prisons, including three remand and two high security units. By far the worst among these were the cells in one block at Presídio Ary Franco, where the equivalent space was 1.5 square metres per prisoner. Ary Franco is known as the *porta de entrada* (entrance door) to Rio de Janeiro's prison system. It is also informally referred to as the state's *prisão do castigo* (punishment prison), the place to send the most unruly guards and inmates.
14. See n. 8.
15. These are reminiscent of previous reports on the former police *carceragens* of São Paulo and Rio de Janeiro. Human Rights Watch (1998), for example, cited a newspaper report of a *carceragem* in São Paulo city where two prisoners were held per square metre. Lemgruber (2005) described a *carceragem* in Rio de Janeiro where 65 prisoners were being held in a cell measuring 12 square metres.
16. See n. 8.
17. For visual images of overcrowding at Central Prison, see the Facebook page of Judge Sidinei Brzuska: https://www.facebook.com/sidinei.brzuska?fref=ts (last accessed 18 January 2018). Brzuska is an executive judge responsible for overseeing the prison.
18. Lei de Execução Penal 7210/84, art. 88(b).
19. This is where the comparisons with the common prison system end. APAC prisoners are only locked up between 10 p.m. and 7 a.m. At Franz de Castro inmates on the semi-open wing are allowed to stay up later when there were football matches on television, which in Brazil start at 9 p.m. Nevertheless, the fact even the APAC prison system does not respect inmates' need for personal space and privacy is indicative of the inhumanities of the Brazilian prison system as a whole. In the common prison system the utilitarian view that conditions in prisons need to be poorer than outside plays an important part as it does in many other countries around the world, including the UK. The APAC methodology is premised in the view that conditions inside prison should replicate conditions outside.
20. 1151 prisoners are recorded as dying in 2014 (Fórum Brasileiro de Segurança Pública 2016). Of these 570 are recorded as dying of natural causes, 312 as meeting violent deaths, 106 as taking their own lives and 55 as dying as the result of accidents; 108 deaths were not

classified (ibid.). These figures do not include the states of São Paulo or Rio de Janeiro, which hold close to 50% of the country's prisoners between them. Ministério da Justiça (2016b) recorded figures for the second half of 2014 for these two states of 278 prison deaths in São Paulo and 86 prison deaths in Rio de Janeiro. Of these 354 deaths, 287 were recorded as having natural causes, 10 were recorded as murders, 24 as suicides and eight as accidental. 35 deaths were not classified. According to a freedom of information request a further 250 prisoners died in São Paulo in the first half of 2014 (Arcoverde 2016). São Paulo prison authorities later confirmed that a total of 482 prisoners had died that year, 450 of natural causes (Adorno 2017). My suggestion that homicides may have in reality accounted for up to a third, 500, of all registered deaths among Brazilian prisoners in 2014 is based on anecdotal evidence that many deaths with no recorded cause are likely to have been murders. It also takes account of further anecdotal evidence that some recorded suicides and accidental deaths are in fact murders dressed up as drug overdoses (Dias and Salla 2013; Human Rights Watch 1998; Sager and Beto 2016). My estimate is also informed by research conducted for Câmara dos Deputados (2008). Of 105 prison deaths across the country analysed in that parliamentary investigation, 29 (28%) were found to be violent. 63 (60%) were found to have natural causes, and nine (nine percent) to be suicides. Four (four percent) of the deaths were found to be accidental.

21. I have spoken about the issue of self-inflicted death with a number of people who have worked or been imprisoned at Sant'Ana. None have recalled more than one or two suicides occurring in any one year. Most speak of suicide occurring in occasional years. In September 2017 news emerged of an apparent wave of suicides at the prison in recent months. Pastoral Carcerária (2017b) reported that four prisoners took their lives at the prison between the beginning of July and the middle of August 2017. Prison authorities later confirmed three suicides in 2017; one suicide was recorded at the prison in 2016 (Reis 2017).
22. See https://www.inquest.org.uk/deaths-in-womens-prisons.
23. Official statistics on police killings in the state São Paulo peaked at 1428 in 1992 (Caldeira 2002), and at 1195 in Rio de Janeiro in 2003 (Gay 2009). In 2015 São Paulo police officially killed 856 citizens (Fórum Brasileiro de Segurança Pública 2017). Rio de Janeiro police killed 925 civilians (ibid.).

24. Critical scholars also stress that racism remains endemic to Brazilian society. In my personal experience, it is tied up with attitudes towards poverty and class. One of my first experiences of this was a fictional drama on the 1990 s national television programme Você Decide (You Decide). In the first episode I watched the audience had to vote on whether the show should end with the removal of a kidney from an unconscious poor, black teenager to save the life of a middle-class white woman who had been involved in a serious car accident. The teenager had been shot in the back by a police officer after stealing a loaf of bread. What struck me most was not that the audience voted to save the woman's life—in a real life situation I might have done the same—but the clear prejudices on which the writers of the programme were playing.
25. See n. 1.

References

Acebes, M. C. (2017, January 18). Brazil's correctional houses of horror. *Foreign Affairs*. https://www.foreignaffairs.com/articles/brazil/2017-01-18/brazil-s-correctional-houses-horror. Last accessed 9 March 2017.

Adorno, S. (2013). Democracy in progress in contemporary Brazil: Corruption, organized crime, violence and new paths to the rule of law. *International Journal of Criminology and Sociology, 2*, 409–425.

Adorno, L. (2017, September 1). Com salário de R$7.400, faltam médicos nos presídios de SP; prisões têm 41 mortes por mês. *UOL*. https://noticias.uol.com.br/cotidiano/ultimas-noticias/2017/09/01/em-media-41-presos-morrem-sob-a-custodia-do-estado-de-sp.htm. Last accessed 5 September 2017.

Aguirre, C. (2005). *The criminals of Lima and their worlds: The prison experience, 1850–1935*. Durham, NC: Duke University.

Aguirre, C. (2007). Prisons and prisoners in modernising Latin America. In F. Dikötter & I. Brown (Eds.), *Cultures of confinement: A history of the prison in Africa, Asia, and Latin America*. Ithaca, NY: Cornell University.

Aguirre, C., & Salvatore, R. D. (2001). Writing the history of law, crime, and punishment in Latin America. In R. D. Salvatore, et al. (Eds.), *Crime and punishment in Latin America*. Durham, NC: Duke University.

Alencastro, L. F. (2007). Brazil in the south Atlantic: 1150–1850 (E. Suari, Trans.). *Mediations, 23*(1), 125–174.

Alves, J. A. (2013). From necropolis to blackpolis: Necropolitical governance and black spatial praxis in São Paulo, Brazil. *Antipode, 46*(2), 323–339.

Andreoli, S. B., Santos, M. M., Quintana, M. I., Ribeiro, W. S., Blay, S. L., Geraldo, J. V. T., & Mari, J. J. (2014). Prevalence of mental disorders among prisoners in the state of São Paulo, Brazil. *PLoS ONE, 9*(2). https://doi.org/10.1371/journal.pone.0088836.

Antunes, S. A. (2017). Para habitar entre grades: Táticas de [sobre]vida na prisão. *ARACÊ, 4*(4), 116–135.

Araújo, C. E. M. (2009). *Cárcares imperiais: Correção do Rio de Janeiro. Seus detentos e o sistema império, 1830–1861*. Ph.D. thesis, State University of Campinas. http://repositorio.unicamp.br/handle/REPOSIP/280976. Last accessed 15 June 2017.

Arcoverde. (2016, January 7). A cada mês, 40 detentos morrem nos presídios paulistas. *Fiquem Sabendo*. http://www.fiquemsabendo.com.br/2016/01/a-cada-mes-40-detentos-morrem-nos-presidios-paulistas-2. Last accessed 24 February 2017.

Arias, E. D., & Goldstein, D. M. (2010). Violent pluralism: Understanding the new democracies of Latin America. In E. D. Arias & D. M. Goldstein (Eds.), *Violent democracies in Latin America* (pp. 1–34). Durham, NC: Duke University.

Arias, E. D., & Barnes, N. (2016). Crime and plural orders in Rio de Janeiro, Brazil. *Current Sociology, 65*(3), 448–465.

Arruda, R. F. (2015). *Geografia do cárcere: Territorialidades na vida cotidiana carcerária no sistena prisional de Pernambuco*. Ph.D. thesis, University of São Paulo. http://www.teses.usp.br/teses/disponiveis/8/8136/tde-16062015-125328/pt-br.php. Last accessed 3 February 2017.

Barrata, A. (2003). Prefácio. In V. M. Batista (Ed.), *Difíceis ganhos fáceis: Drogas e juventude pobre no Rio de Janeiro* (2nd ed., pp. 15–34). Rio de Janeiro: Revan.

Bassani, F. (2016). *Visita íntima: Sexo, crime e negócios nas prisões*. Porto Alegre: Bestiário.

Batista, N. (1996). Fragmentos de uma discurso sedicioso. *Discursos Sediciosos, 1*(1), 69–77.

Batista, N. (1997). A violência do estado e os aparelhos policiais. *Discursos Sediciosos, 2*(4), 145–154.

Batista, N. (2000). *Matrizes ibericas do sistema penal brasileiro*. Rio de Janeiro: Freiras Bastos.

Batista, V. M. (2003a). *Difíceis ganhos fáceis: Drogas e juventude pobre no Rio de Janeiro* (2nd ed.). Rio de janeiro: Revan.

Batista, V. M. (2003b). *O medo na cidade do Rio de Janeiro*. Rio de Janeiro: Revan.
Batista, V. M. (2009). Novas funções do cárcere no Brasil contemporâneo. In R. T. Oliveira & V. Mattos (Eds.), *Estudos de execução criminal: Direito e psicologia* (pp. 17–27). Belo Horizonte: Tribunal de Justiça de Minas Gerais.
Batista, V. M. (2011). *Introdução crítica à criminologia brasileira*. Rio de Janeiro: Revan.
Batista, V. M. (2016). *A questão criminal no brasil contemporâneo*. São Paulo: Fundação Bienal de São Paulo.
Batista, V. M. (2018, February 21). O falacioso discurso de segurança pública. *Nova Democracia*. http://anovademocracia.com.br/noticias/8272-exclusivo-professora-vera-malaguti-comenta-a-intervencao-militar-no-rio. Last accessed 28 February 2018.
Beattie, P. M. (2015). *Punishment in paradise: Race, slavery, human rights, and a nineteenth-century Brazilian penal colony*. Durham: Duke University.
Biondi, K. (2014). *Etnografia no movimento: Território, hierarquia e lei no PCC*. Ph.D. thesis, Federal University of São Carlos. https://www.repositorio.ufscar.br/bitstream/handle/ufscar/246/6378.pdf?sequence=1&isAllowed=y. Last accessed 7 April 2017.
Birkbeck, C. (2011). Imprisonment and internment: Comparing penal institutions North and South. *Punishment and Society, 13*(3), 307–332.
Bochenek, M., & Delgado, F. (2006). Children in custody in Brazil. *Lancet, 367*, 696.
Bretas, M. L. (1996). What the eyes can't see: Stories from Rio de Janeiro's prisons. In R. D. Salvatore & C. Aguirre (Eds.), *The birth of the penitentiary in Latin America* (pp. 101–122). Austin: University of Texas.
Caetano, H. (2015, July 20). O juiz e a banalidade do mal. *Justificando*. http://justificando.cartacapital.com.br/2015/07/20/o-juiz-e-a-banalidade-do-mal. Last accessed 3 February 2017.
Caldeira, T. (1996). Fortified enclaves: The new urban segregation. *Public Culture, 8*, 303–328.
Caldeira, T. (2000). *City of walls: Crime, segregation and citizenship in São Paulo*. Berkeley: University of California.
Caldeira, T. (2002). The paradox of police violence in democratic Brazil. *Ethnography, 3*, 235–263.
Câmara dos Deputados. (2008). *CPI do sistema carcerário*. Resource document. http://bd.camara.leg.br/bd/bitstream/handle/bdcamara/2701/cpi_sistema_carcerario.pdf?sequence=5. Last accessed 10 August 2014.
Cardia, N. (2012). Os direitos humanos segundo a pesquisa 'Atitudes, normas culturais e valores em relação a violação de direitos humanos e violência'. In

Núcleo de Estudos da Violência (Ed.), *5º relatório nacional sobre os direitos humanos no Brasil* (pp. 39–49). Resource document. São Paulo: NEV-USP. http://www.nevusp.org/downloads/down265.pdf. Last accessed 17 April 2017.

Carlos, J. O. (2015). *Drug policy and incarceration in São Paulo, Brazil*. London: International Drug Policy Consortium.

Carvalho, S. (1996). *A política criminal de drogas no Brasil*. Rio de Janeiro: LUAM.

Carvalho, S. (2013). Theories of punishment in the age of mass incarceration: A closer look at the empirical problem silenced by justificationism (the Brazilian case). *Open Journal of Social Sciences, 1*(4), 1–12.

Carvalho, S., & Rodas, S. (2017, February 20). É absolutamente ilegítimo que o Estado limite o uso de qualquer droga. *Consultor Jurídico*. http://www.conjur.com.br/2017-fev-20/entrevista-salo-carvalho-professor-direito-penal-ufrj. Last accessed 21 February 2017.

Casara, R. (2014). Segurança pública: Facismo e polícia. In R. C. Junior (Ed.), *Criminologia do cotidiano* (pp. 263–280). Rio de Janeiro: Lumens Juris.

Casara, R. (2016, July 9). Na pós-democracia, os direitos e garantias fundamentais também são vistoscomo mercadorias. *Justificando*. http://justificando.cartacapital.com.br/2016/07/09/na-pos-democracia-os-direitos-e-garantias-fundamentais-tambem-sao-vistos-como-mercadorias. Last accessed 21 February 2017.

Casara, R. (2017). *Estado pós-democrático: Neo-obscurantismo e gestão dos indesejáveis*. Rio de Janeiro: Civilização Brasileira.

Castro, L. A. (1987). *Criminologia de la liberacion*. Maracalbo: Universidad del Zulia. Portuguese edition: Castro, L. A. (2005). *Criminologia da libertação* (S. Moretzsohn, Trans.). Rio de Janeiro: Revan.

Cavalcanti, R. P. (2016a). Armed violence and the politics of gun control in Brazil: An analysis of the 2005 referendum. *Bulletin of Latin American Research*. https://doi.org/10.1111/blar.12476.

Cavalcanti, R. P. (2016b). *Over, under and through the walls: The dynamics of public security, police-community relations and the limits of managerialism in crime control in Recife, Brazil*. Ph.D. thesis, University of London. http://westminsterresearch.wmin.ac.uk/18353. Last accessed 7 April 2017.

Chartoff, R., Winkler, I., & Stallone, S. (1985). *Rocky IV*. Film. United States: United Artists.

Chazkel, A. (2009). Social life and civic education in the Rio de Janeiro city jail. *Journal of Social History, 42*(3), 697–731.

Codino, R. (2014). Para uma outra criminologia do terceiro mundo: Perspectivas da criminologia critica no sul (S. Carvalho,Trans.). *Revista Liberdades, 20*, 22–34.

Coelho, E. C. (2005). *A oficina do diablo. E outros estudos sobre criminalidade*. Rio de Janeiro: Record

Cohen, S. (1985). *Visions of social control*. Cambridge: Polity Press.

Conectas. (2017). *Tortura Blindada: Como as instituições do sistema de justiça perpetuam a violência nas audiências de custódia*. Resource document. http://www.conectas.org/arquivos/editor/files/Relato%CC%81rio%20completo_Tortura%20blindada_Conectas%20Direitos%20Humanos(1).pdf. Last accessed 7 March 2017.

Conselho Nacional de Justiça. (2012). *Raio-x do sistema penitenciário brasileiro*. Resource document. http://www.cnj.jus.br/images/pesquisas-judiciarias/Publicacoes/mutirao_carcerario.pdf. Last accessed 4 January 2016.

Conselho Nacional de Justiça. (2014). *Novo Diagnóstico de Pessoas Presas no Brasil*. Resource document. http://www.cnj.jus.br/images/imprensa/Pessoas_presas_no_Brasil_1.pdf. Last accessed 10 August 2014.

Costa, A. T. M. (2011). Police brutality in Brazil: Authoritarian legacy or institutional weakness? (T. Thompson, Trans.). *Latin American Perspectives, 38*(5), 19–32.

Coyle, A., Fair, H., Jacobson, J., & Walmsley, R. (2016). *Imprisonment worldwide: The current situation and an alternative future*. Bristol: Policy.

Dantas, H. S., Silveira, C. M., & Rovaron, M. (2016). Adolescências inscritas na ilegalidade. A Lei 11.343/2006 e os adolescentes em cumprimento de medida socioeducativa. *Boletim IBCCRIM, 24*, 15–17.

Darke, S. (2013). Inmate governance in Brazilian prisons. *Howard Journal of Criminal Justice, 52*(3), 272–284.

Darke, S., & Garces, C. (2017a). Surviving in the new mass carceral zone. *Prison Service Journal, 229*, 2–9.

Darke, S., & Garces, C. (Eds.). (2017b). Informal dynamics of survival in Latin American prisons. *Prison Service Journal, 229*, 1–62.

Darke, S., & Karam, M. L. (2016). Latin American prisons. In Y. Jewkes et al. (Eds.), *Handbook on prisons* (2nd ed., pp. 460–474). Abington: Routledge. Portuguese version: Karam, M. L., & Darke, S. (2016). Prisões latino americanas (M. L. Karam, Trans.). http://emporiododireito.com.br/leitura/prisoes-latino-americanas-1508702837. Last accessed 17 February 2018. Spanish version: Darke, S., & Karam, M. L. (2017). Las prisiones de América Latina. *Ecuador Debate, 101*, 53–71.

Davis, M. (2007). *Planet of slums*. London: Verso.

Department of Health. (2009). *The Bradley report*. Resource document. http://www.rcpsych.ac.uk/pdf/Bradley%20Report11.pdf. Last accessed 27 June 2017.

Dias, C. N., & Salla, F. (2013). Organized crime in Brazilian prisons: The example of the PCC. *International Journal of Criminology and Sociology, 2*, 397–408.

Dieter, M. S. (2013). *Política criminal actuarial: A criminologia do fim da história*. Rio de Janeiro: Revan.

Dikötter, F. (2007). The prison in the world. In F. Dikötter & I. Brown (Eds.), *Cultures of confinement: A history of the prison in Africa, Asia, and Latin America* (pp. 1–14). Ithaca, NY: Cornell University.

Dreisinger, B. (2016). *Incarceration nations: A journey to justice in prisons around the world*. New York, NY: Other.

Fassin, D. (2017). *Prison worlds: An ethnography of the carceral condition*. Cambridge: Polity.

Feeley, M., & Simon, J. (1992). The new penology: Notes on the emerging strategy of corrections and its implications. *Criminology, 30*, 449–474.

Feltran, G. S. (2011). *Fronteiras de tensão: Política e violência nas periferias de São Paulo*. São Paulo: Unesp.

Filho, J. J. (2017). *Administração Penitenciária: O controle da população carcerária a partir da gestão partilhada entre diretores, judiciário e facções*. Ph.D. thesis, Fundação Getulio Vargas. http://bibliotecadigital.fgv.br/dspace/handle/10438/18432. Last accessed 10 July 2017.

Foley, C. (2012). The Mutirão Carcerário. In C. Foley (Ed.), *Another system is possible: Reforming Brazilian justice* (pp. 13–29). London: International Bar Association.

Foley, C. (2013). *Protecting Brazilians from torture: A manual for judges, prosecutors, public defenders and lawyers* (2nd ed.). Resource document. International Bar Association. http://www.conectas.org/arquivos/editor/files/Relato%CC%81rio%20completo_Tortura%20blindada_Conectas%20Direitos%20Humanos(1).pdf. Last accessed 6 July 2017.

Fórum Brasileiro de Segurança Pública. (2015). *Anuário brasileiro de segurança pública*. São Paulo: Fórum Brasileiro de Segurança Pública.

Fórum Brasileiro de Segurança Pública. (2016). *Anuário brasileiro de segurança pública*. São Paulo: Fórum Brasileiro de Segurança Pública.

Fórum Brasileiro de Segurança Pública. (2017). *Anuário brasileiro de segurança pública*. São Paulo: Fórum Brasileiro de Segurança Pública.

Foucault, M. (1977). *Discipline and punish*. London: Allen Lane.

França, L. A., Neto, A. S., & Artuso, A. R. (2016). *As marcas do cárcere*. Curitiba: IEA.

Garfield, S. (2010). The environment of wartime migration: Labor transfers from the Brazilian Northeast to the Amazon during World War II. *Journal of Social History, 42*(3), 989–1019.

Garland, D. (1990). *Punishment and modern society: A study in social theory.* Oxford: Clarendon.

Garland, D. (2002). *The culture of control: Crime and social order in contemporary society.* Oxford: Oxford University.

Gay, R. (2009). From popular movements to drugs gangs to militaries: An anatomy of violence in Rio de Janeiro. In K. Koonings & D. Kruijt (Eds.), *MegaCities: The politics of urban exclusion and violence in the global south* (pp. 29–51). London: Zed.

Gledhill, J. (2015). *The new war on the poor.* London: Zed.

Goldstein, D. M. (2003). *Laughter out of place: Race, class, violence, and sexuality in a Rio shantytown.* Berkeley: University of California.

Griffin, J. (2017, March 3). Is brutal treatment of young offenders fuelling crime rates in Brazil? *The Guardian.* https://www.theguardian.com/global-development/2017/mar/03/brazil-crime-rates-brutal-treatment-young-offenders. Last accessed 8 March 2017.

Hadler, O. H., Guareschi, N. M. F., & Scisleski, A. C. C. (2017). Observances: Psychology, public security policies and incarcerated youth. *Pesquisas e Práticas Pscicossociais, 12*(4), e2271.

Heiskanen, S. (2010). Trends in police-recorded crime. In S. Harrendorf, et al. (Eds.), *International statistics on crime and justice* (pp. 21–48). Helsinki: European Institute for Crime Prevention and Control.

Hess, D. J. (1995). Introduction. In D. J. Hess & R. Matta (Eds.), *The Brazilian puzzle: Culture in the borderlands of the western world* (pp. 1–30). New York: Columbia University.

Holston, J. (2008). *Insurgent citizenship: Disjunctions of democracy and modernity in Brazil.* Princeton: Princeton University.

Huggins, M. K. (1985). *From slavery to vagrancy in Brazil.* New York, NY: Rutgers University.

Huggins, M. K. (2000). Urban violence and police privatization in Brazil: Blended invisibility. *Social Justice, 27*(2), 113–134.

Huggins, M. K., & Mesquita, M. (1995). Scapegoating outsiders: The murders of street youth in modern Brazil. *Policing and Society, 5,* 265–280.

Human Rights Watch. (1998). *Behind bars in Brazil.* New York: Human Rights Watch.

Human Rights Watch. (2009). *Lethal force: Police violence and public security in Rio de Janeiro and São Paulo.* New York, NY: Human Rights Watch.

2 Law and Repression 93

Human Rights Watch. (2015a). *The state let evil take over: The prison crisis in the Brazilian state of Pernambuco*. New York, NY: Human Rights Watch.
Human Rights Watch. (2015b). *Brazil: Prison crisis spurs rights reform*. São Paulo: Human Rights Watch.
Human Rights Watch. (2016). *Good cops are afraid: The toll of unchecked police violence in Rio de Janeiro*. New York, NY: Human Rights Watch.
Human Rights Watch. (2018). *World Report 2018*. New York, NY: Human Rights Watch.
INQUEST. (2018). *Deaths in prison*. http://www.inquest.org.uk/statistics/deaths-in-prison. Last accessed 19 January 2018.
Instituto de Defesa do Direito de Defesa. (2018). *Audiências de custódia: Panorama nacional*. Resource document. http://www.iddd.org.br/wp-content/uploads/2017/12/Audiencias-de-Custodia_Panorama-Nacional_Relatorio.pdf. Last accessed 12 January 2018.
Instituto de Segurança Pública. (2016). *Panorama das apreensões de drogas no Rio de Janeiro 2010–2016*. Resource document. http://arquivos.proderj.rj.gov.br/isp_imagens/uploads/RelatorioDrogas2016.pdf. Last accessed 16 February 2017.
Instituto Sou da Paz. (2016). *Panorama dos dados divulgados pela Secretaria da Segurança Pública de São Paulo*. Resource document. http://www.soudapaz.org/noticia/sou-da-paz-lanca-panorama-2015-dos-dados-divulgados-pela-secretaria-da-seguranca-publica-de-sao-paulo. Last accessed 18 May 2016.
Inter-American Commission on Human Rights. (2011). *Report on the human rights of persons deprived of liberty in the Americas*. Resource document. http://www.oas.org/en/iachr/pdl/docs/pdf/PPL2011eng.pdf. Last accessed 10 August 2014.
Inter-American Court of Human Rights. (2014, May 22). *Order of the Inter-American Court of Human Rights*. Provisional measures regarding Brazil. Matter of the penitentiary complex of Curado. Resource document. http://www.corteidh.or.cr/docs/medidas/curado_se_01_ing.pdf. Last accessed 6 May 2016.
International Bar Association. (2010). *1 in 5: The crisis in Brazil's prisons and criminal justice system*. Resource document. http://www.ibanet.org/Article/Detail.aspx?ArticleUid=9a841b12-4a44-41db-a4bd-4433e694e2ba. Last accessed 10 August 2014.
International Centre for Prison Studies. (2017). *World prison brief*. http://www.prisonstudies.org/world-prison-brief. Last accessed 21 December 2017.
Iturralde, M. (2012). O governo neoliberal de ainsegurança social na América Latina: Semelhanças e diferenças com o Norte Global. In V. M. Batista (Ed.), *Loïc Wacquant e a questão penal no capitalism neoliberal* (pp. 169–191). Rio de Janeiro: Revan.

Jefferson, A. M. (2013). The situated production of legitimacy: Perspectives from the global south. In J. Tankebe & A. Liebling (Eds.), *Legitimacy and criminal justice: An international exploration* (pp. 248–266). Oxford: Oxford University.

Jones, G., & Rodgers, D. (Eds.). (2009). *Youth violence in Latin America: Gangs and juvenile justice in perspective.* New York, NY: Palgrave Macmillan.

Karam, M. L. (1996). A esquerda punitiva. *Discursos Sediciosos, 1*(1), 79–92.

Karam, M. L. (2009). Estado penal, novo inimigo interno e totalitarismo. In R. T. Oliveira & V. Mattos (Eds.), *Estudos de execução criminal: Direito e psicologia* (pp. 127–133). Belo Horizonte: Tribunal de Justiça de Minas Gerais.

Karam, M. L. (2015, December 24). Mulheres presas. *Empório do Direito.* http://emporiododireito.com.br/mulheres-presas-por-maria-lucia-karam. Last accessed 24 June 2017.

Koerner, A. (2006). Punição, disciplina e pensamento penal no brasil do século xix. *Lua Nova, 68,* 205–242.

Koonings, K., & Kruijt, D. (Eds.). (2009). *MegaCities: The politics of urban exclusion and violence in the global south.* London: Zed.

Leeds, E. (1996). Cocaine and parallel politics in the Brazilian urban periphery. *Latin American Research Review, 31,* 47–85.

Leeds, E. (2016). *The Brazilian prison system: Challenges and prospects for reform.* WOLA: Advocacy for Human Rights in the Americas. Resource document. http://www.psych.org/edu/other_res/lib_archives/archives/200604.pdf. Last accessed 18 January 2017.

Lemgruber, J. (2005). *The Brazilian prison system: A brief diagnosis.* Eugene, OR: University of Oregon.

Lemgruber, J., & Fernandez, M. (2011). *Impacto da assistência jurídica a presos provisóriso: Um experiment na cidade de Rio de Janeiro.* Rio de Janeiro: Associação pela Reforma Prisional and Centro de Estudos de Segurança e Cidadania. English version: Lemgruber, J., & Fernandez, M. (2012). Legal aid and pre-trial prisoners: An experiment in the city of Rio de Janeiro. In C. Foley (Ed.), *Another system is possible: Reforming Brazilian justice* (pp. 31–53). London: International Bar Association.

Lemgruber, J., Fernandes, M., Cano, I., & Musumeci, L. (2013). *Usos e Abusos da Prisão Provisória no Rio de Janeiro.* Rio de Janeiro: Associação pela Reforma Prisional and Centro de Estudos de Segurança e Cidadania.

Lins e Silva, T., & Rodas, S. (2017, February 21). Mesmo sem provas, acusado de tráfico e furto começa o processo condenado. *Consultor Jurídico.* http://www.conjur.com.br/2017-fev-20/entrevista-salo-carvalho-professor-direito-penal-ufrj. Last accessed 22 February 2017.

Lourenço, L. C., & Almeida, O. L. (2013). "Quem mantém a ordem, quem cria desordem": Gangues prisionais na Bahia. *Tempo Social, 25*(1), 37–59.

Macaulay, F. (2007). Knowledge production, framing and criminal justice reform in Latin America. *Journal of Latin American Studies, 39*, 627–651.

Macaulay, F. (2013). Modes of prison administration, control and governmentality in Latin America: Adoption, adaptation and hybridity. *Conflict, Security and Development, 13*(4), 361–392.

Malby, S. (2010). Homicide. In S. Harrendorf, et al. (Eds.), *International statistics on crime and justice* (pp. 7–20). Helsinki: European Institute for Crime Prevention and Control.

Mendes, L. A. (2005). *Às cegas*. São Paulo: Companhia das Letras.

Menegat, M. (2012). *Estudos sobre ruínas*. Rio de Janeiro: Instituto Carioca de Criminologia.

Mathiesen, T. (2012). Scandinavian exceptionalism in penal matters: Reality or wishful thinking? In T. Ugelvik & J. Dullum (Eds.), *Penal exceptionalism? Nordic prison policy and practice* (pp. 13–37). London: Routledge.

Ministério da Justiça. (2005). *Diretrizes básicas para construção, ampliação e reforma de estabelecimentos penais*. Resource document. http://www.justica.gov.br/seus-direitos/politica-penal/transparencia-institucional/biblioteca-on-line-2/biblioteca-on-line-manuais/manual-diretrizes-basicas-construcao-2005.pdf. Last accessed 15 December 2015.

Ministério da Justiça. (2015). *Levantamento nacional de informações penitenciárias infopen, junho de 2014*. Resource document. http://www.justica.gov.br/seus-direitos/politica-penal/relatorio-depen-versao-web.pdf. Last accessed 15 December 2015.

Ministério da Justiça. (2016a). *Implementação das audiências de custódia no brasil: análise de experiências e recomendações de aprimoramento*. Resource document. http://www.justica.gov.br/seus-direitos/politica-penal/politicas-2/alternativas-penais-1/arquivos/implementacao-das-audiencias-de-custodia-no-brasil-analise-de-experiencias-e-recomendacoes-de-aprimoramento-1.pdf. Last accessed 11 October 2016.

Ministério da Justiça. (2016b). *Levantamento nacional de informações penitenciárias infopen, dezembro de 2014*. Resource document. http://www.justica.gov.br/seus-direitos/politica-penal/infopen_dez14.pdf. Last accessed 24 October 2016.

Ministério da Justiça e Segurança Pública. (2017). *Levantamento nacional de informações penitenciárias: Atualização - Junho de 2016*. Resource http://www.justica.gov.br/news/ha-726-712-pessoas-presas-no-brasil/relatorio_2016_junho.pdfdocument. Last accessed 21 December 2017.

Ministry of Justice (2017). *Safety in custody quarterly bulletin*, December 2016. Resource document. https://www.gov.uk/government/statistics/safety-in-custody-quarterly-update-to-december-2016–2. Last accessed 4 June 2017.

Ministério Público do Ceará. (2009). *Justiça interdita Colônia Agropastoril do Amanari*. http://www.mpce.mp.br/servicos/asscom/releases.asp?icodigo=893. Last accessed 7 January 2016.

Misse, M. (2007). Illegal markets, protection rackets and organized crime in Rio de Janeiro. *Estudos Avançados, 61*, 139–157.

Misse, M., & Vargas, J. D. (2010). Drug use and trafficking in Rio de Janeiro. *Vibrant, 7*(2), 88–108.

Neder, G. (1996). Absolutismo e punição. *Discursos Sediciosos, 1*(1), 191–206.

Negrelli, A. M. (2006). *Suicídio no sistema carcerário: Análise a partir do perfil biopsicossocial nas instituições prisionais no Rio Grande do Sul*. Master's degree dissertation, Pontifical Catholic University, Rio Grande do Sul. http://tede.pucrs.br/tde_busca/arquivo.php?codArquivo=510. Last accessed 27 June 2017.

Nunes, R. M. (2015). The politics of sentencing reform in Brazil: Autonomous bureaucrats, constrained politicians and gradual policy change. *Journal of Latin American Studies, 47*(1), 121–148.

O'Donnell, G. (1998). *Polyarchies and the (un)rule of law in Latin America*. Resource document. Kellogg Institute. http://kellogg.nd.edu/publications/workingpapers/WPS/254.pdf. Last accessed 20 April 2017.

Oliveira, H. (2017, 5 September). Rafael Braga com tuberculose: A contradição da lei antidrogas que zela pela saúde pública. *Justificando*. https://portal-justificando.jusbrasil.com.br/noticias/495868237/rafael-braga-com-tuberculose-a-contradicao-da-lei-antidrogas-que-zela-pela-saude-publica. Last accessed 7 September 2017.

Padilha, J., & Prado, M. (2007). *Tropa de elite*. Film. Brazil: Zazen.

Pastoral Carcerária. (2016). *Tortura em tempos de encarceramento em massa*. Resource document. http://carceraria.org.br/wp-content/uploads/2016/10/tortura_web.pdf. Last accessed 22 November 2016.

Pastoral Carcerária. (2017a, December 21). *Como uma nomeação pode colocar as audiências de custódia em xeque*. http://carceraria.org.br/como-uma-nomeacao-pode-colocar-as-audiencias-de-custodia-em-xeque.html. Last accessed 18 January 2018.

Pastoral Carcerária (2017b, August 17). *Pastoral Carcerária pede MP apure suicídios em presídio feminino em SP*. http://carceraria.org.br/pastoral-carceraria-pede-que-mp-apure-suicidios-em-presidio-feminino.html. Last accessed 5 September 2017.

Pavarini, M., & Giamberardino, A. (2011). *Teoria da pena e execução penal: Uma introdução crítica*. Rio de Janeiro: Lumen Juris.

Penglase, B. (2009). States of insecurity: Everyday emergencies, public secrets, and drug trafficker power in a Brazilian favela. *PoLAR. Political and Legal Anthropology Review, 32*, 47–63.

Penglase, B. (2010). The owner of the hill: Masculinity and drug-trafficking in Rio de Janeiro, Brazil. *Journal of Latin American and Caribbean Anthropology, 15*(2), 317–337.

Pereira, A. (1997). *Elitist liberalism: Citizenship, state violence, and the rule of law in Brazil*. Paper presented at the XX International Congress of the Latin American Studies Association, April, Guadalajara, Mexico.

Perlman, J. E. (2010). *Favela: Four decades of living on the edge in Rio de Janeiro*. New York: Oxford University.

Pessoa, G. T. A. (2014a, August 18). *Casa de Correção*. http://linux.an.gov.br/mapa/?p=6333. Last accessed 9 March 2017.

Pessoa, G. T. A. (2014b, December 15). *Casa de Detenção*. http://linux.an.gov.br/mapa/?p=7400. Last accessed 9 March 2017.

Phillips, D. (2015, June 16). Brazil divided over how to deal with its teenage criminals. *The Guardian*. https://www.theguardian.com/world/2015/jun/16/brazil-teenage-criminals-juvenile-rehabilitation. Last accessed 8 March 2017.

Postema, M., Cavallaro, J., & Nagra, R. (2017). Advancing security and human rights by the controlled organisation of inmates. *Prison Service Journal, 229*, 57–62.

Prado Júnior, C. (1961). *Formação do brasil contemporâneo (colônia)* (6th ed.). São Paulo: Editôra Brasiliense.

Prison Reform Trust, & INQUEST. (2012). *Fatally flawed: Has the state learned lessons from the deaths of children and young people in prison?* Resource document. http://inquest.org.uk/pdf/reports/Fatally_Flawed.pdf. Last accessed 17 August 2017.

Ramos, H. (2003). *Pavilhão 9: Paixão e morte no Carandiru* (4th ed.). Paris: Gallimard.

Reis, V. (2017, August 30). MP analisa denúncia de 'suicídios em série' em penitenciária feminina de SP. *O Globo*. http://g1.globo.com/sao-paulo/noticia/mp-analisa-denuncia-de-suicidios-em-serie-em-penitenciaria-feminina-de-sp.ghtml. Last accessed 5 September 2017.

Roig, R. D. E. (2005). *Direito e prática histórica da execução penal no brasil*. Rio de Janeiro: Revan.

Rolim, M. (2007). Prisão e ideologia: Limites e possibilidades para a reforma prisional no brasil. In S. Carvalho (Ed.), *Crítica à execução penal* (2nd ed., pp. 77–115). Rio de Janeiro: Lumen Juris.

Sager, T., & Beto, R. (2016). *Central*. Documentary film. Brazil: Panda.
Salla, F., & Ballesteros, P. (2008). *Democracy, human rights and prison conditions in South America*. Paper prepared for the Research Project of Geneva Academy of International Humanitarian Law and Human Rights. Resource document. University of São Paulo. http://www.nevusp.org/downloads/down227.pdf. Last accessed 16 February 2017.
Salla, F., Gauto, M., & Alvarez, M. C. (2006). A contribuição de David Garland: A sociologia da punição. *Tempo Social, 15*(1), 329–350.
Salla, F., Ballesteros, P., Mavila, O., Mercado, F., Litvachky, P., & Museri, A. (2009). *Democracy, human rights and prison conditions in South America*. São Paulo: University of São Paulo.
Salla, F., Jesus, M. G. M., & Rocha, T. T. (2012, October). Relato de uma pesquisa sobre a Lei 11.343/2006. *Boletim IBCCRIM, 20,* 10–11.
Salvatore, R. D. (1996). Penitentiaries, visions of class, and export economies: Brazil and Argentina compared. In R. D. Salvatore & C. Aguirre (Eds.), *The birth of the penitentiary in Latin America*. (pp. 194–223). Austin: University of Texas.
Salvatore, R. D., & Aguirre, C. (Eds.). (1996). The birth of the penitentiary in Latin America: Towards an interpretive social history of prisons. In R. D. Salvatore & C. Aguirre (Eds.), *The birth of the penitentiary in Latin America* (pp. 1–43). Austin: University of Texas.
Scott, D., & Codd, H. (2010). *Controversial issues in prison*. Maidenhead: Open University.
Secretaria de Administração Penitenciária do Estado de São Paulo. (n.d.). *168 unidades prisionais*. http://www.sap.sp.gov.br/uni-prisionais/cdp.html. Last accessed 12 January 2016.
Secretaria de Administração Penitenciária do Estado de São Paulo. (2015). *Levantamento presos X delitos*. Resource document. http://www.sap.sp.gov.br/download_files/pdf_files/levantamento_presosxdelitos.pdf. Last accessed 19 November 2015.
Semer, M. (2014). A serpente que só pica os pés descalços: Desigualdade e direito penal. In R. C. Junior (Ed.), *Criminologia do cotidiano* (pp. 185–199). Rio de Janeiro: Lumens Juris.
Shimizu, B., & Cacicedo, P. (2016). Crítica à estipulação de critérios quantitativos objetivos para diferenciação entre traficantes e usuários de drogas: Reflexões a partir da perversidade do sistema penal em uma realidade margina. *Boletim IBCCRIM, 24,* 8–9.

Silva, E. S. (2017). *A ocupação da Maré pelo exército brasileiro: Percepção de moradores sobre a ocupação das forças armadas na Maré*. Rio de Janeiro: Redes da Maré.

Singleton, N., Meltzer, H., & Gatward, R. (1998). *Psychiatric morbidity among prisoners in England and Wales*. London: Office for National Statistics.

Singleton, N., Bumpstead, R., O'Brien, M., Lee, A., & Meltzer, H. (2000). *Psychiatric morbidity among adults living in private households, 2000*. London: Office for National Statistics.

Sozzo, M. (Ed.). (2017). *Pós-neoliberalismo e penalidade na américa do sul*. São Paulo: Fundação Perseu Abramo.

Stern, V. (2006). *Creating criminals: Prisons and people in a market society*. London: Zed Books.

Teixeira, A., Salla, F. A., & Marinho, M. G. S. M. C. (2016). Vadiagem e prisões correcionais em São Paulo: Mecanismos de controle no firmamento da República. *Estudos Históricos, 29*(58), 381–400.

United Nations. (2008). *Report on Brazil* CAT/C/39/2. Resource document. http://www2.ohchrorg/english/bodies/cat/docs/AdvanceVersions/cat.c.39.2.doc. Last accessed 27 February 2018.

United Nations. (2012). *Report on the visit of the subcommittee on prevention of torture and other cruel, inhuman or degrading treatment or punishment to Brazil*. CAT/OP/BRA/1. Resource document. http://www2.ohchr.org/english/bodies/cat/opcat/docs/CAT-OP-BRA-1_en.pdf. Last accessed 27 February 2018.

Valois, L. C. (2016). *O direito penal da guerra às drogas*. Belo Horizonte: D'Plácido.

Varella, D. (2008). *Estação Carandiru*. São Paulo: Companhia das Letras. English edition: Varella, D. (2012). *Lockdown: Inside Brazil's most violent prison* (A. Entrekin, Trans.). London: Simon and Schuster.

Wacquant, L. (2003). Towards a dictatorship over the poor: Notes on the penalization of poverty in Brazil. *Punishment and Society, 5*(2), 197–205.

Wacquant, L. (2008). The militarization of urban marginality: Lessons from the Brazilian metropolis. *International Political Sociology, 2*, 56–74.

Walmsley, R. (1999). *World prison population list*. London: Home Office.

Walmsley, R. (2010). Trends in world prison population. In S. Harrendorf, et al. (Eds.), *International statistics on crime and justice* (pp. 153–166). Helsinki: European Institute for Crime Prevention and Control.

Walmsley, R. (2015). *World prison population list* (11th ed.). London: International Centre for Prison Studies.

Willis, G. D. (2015). *The killing consensus: Police, organized crime, and the regulation of life and death in urban Brazil*. Oakland: University of California.

Willis, G. D. (2016). Before the body count: Homicide statistics and everyday security in Latin America. *Journal of Latin American Studies, 49*, 29–54.

Wolfmann, L. C. (2000). *Portal do inferno: Mas há esperança*. São Paulo: WVC Gestão Inteligente Com. Ltda.

World Health Organisation. (2017). *Suicide rates, age standardized*. http://www.who.int/gho/mental_health/suicide_rates/en/. Last accessed 12 June 2017.

Zaccone, O. (2007). *Acionistas do Nada: Quem são os traficantes de drogas*. Rio de Janeiro: Revan.

Zaccone, O. (2015). *Indignos de vida. A forma juridical da política de extermínio de inimigos na cidade de Rio de Janeiro*. Rio de Janeiro: Revan.

Zaffaroni, E. R. (1989). *En busca de las penas perdidas*. Buenos Aires: Editar Sociedad Anónima. Portuguese version: Zaffaroni, E. R. (1991). *Em busca das penas perdidas* (V. R. Pedrosa & A. L. Conceição, Trans.). Rio de Janeiro: Revan.

Zaffaroni, E. R. (2006). *El enemigo en el derecho penal*. Madrid: Dykinson.

Zaffaroni, E. R., Batista, N., Alagia, A., & Slokar, A. (2003). *Direito Pena Brasileiro – Primeiro volume*. Rio de Janeiro: Revan.

Zaluar, A. (1994). *Condomínio do diablo*. Rio de Janeiro: Revan.

Zapater, M. (2017, February 3). Prisão com ala VIP: Qual a necessidade de cela especial? *Justificando*. http://justificando.cartacapital.com.br/2017/02/03/prisao-com-ala-vip-qual-necessidade-de-cela-especial. Last accessed 24 February 2017.

3

The Northern Massacres

In January 2017, the legitimacy of the Brazilian prison system came under deep scrutiny following a series of violent encounters between rival gangs in the North of the country. Three incidences were particularly deadly. In the late afternoon of 1 January, prisoners affiliated to the Família do Norte (Northern Family: the FDN) gang took control of the closed unit of the Anísio Jobim complex in Manaus, the capital of the state of Amazonas. By the time prisoners handed the unit back to authorities the following morning, 56 prisoners were reported to have been killed, mostly on the *seguro* (insurance or vulnerable persons unit), which among its other inmates held 26 men affiliated to Brazil's largest gang, São Paulo's Primeiro Comando da Capital (PCC). The estimated death toll later increased to 66 (Filho 2017). Some of the victims' bodies were mutilated. Severed heads were put on display to lay the FDN's mark on the PCC territory. Mutilated bodies were thrown over the wall for media consumption. Reports from survivors suggested the killings spiralled out of control. In their frenzy, the killers also turned on sex offenders and police informants, most of who were also being held, as is normal practice, on the *seguro*, but some of who had chosen to stay on wings controlled by the FDN rather than risk being associated with the

PCC. State authorities subsequently transferred the survivors out of the complex to a recently deactivated prison unit in another part of the city. A request was made for leaders of the FDN at the prison to be transferred to high-security federal prisons. During its investigations into the incident, the civil police found evidence guards had allowed the FDN to smuggle arms into the prison in the days before they carried out the atrocity (Souza 2017).

In the first of two major responses to the Anísio Jobim massacre, on 6 January, PCC affiliates killed a reported 33 non-gang-affiliated prisoners on the *seguro* of the semi-open unit Monte Cristo in the neighbouring Amazonian city of Boa Vista, in the state of Roraima. Three months earlier, on 16 October 2016, the PCC had killed 10 other inmates at the prison, including Waldiney de Alencar Sousa, one of the most senior figures in the PCC, who had been sent to the Amazonian region to lead efforts to take control of its prisons, only to defect to Rio de Janeiro's Comando Vermelho (CV) (Ribeiro et al. 2016). The *seguro* mixed inmates that had been expelled or had chosen not to recognise the gang's right to rule with other vulnerable prisoners such as sex offenders and child killers, as is prison practice across the country. Trophy videos of *seguro* prisoners being decapitated, quartered and disembowelled were circulated on social media. In one particularly disturbing video distributed through WhatsApp, prisoners used the blood from their victim to write *aqui é o PCC* (here is the PCC) on the floor (Estadão, 7 January 2017). This time state authorities chose not to move either the perpetrators or survivors of the massacre to other prisons. However, the state Secretary of Justice followed the example set by authorities in Amazonas and put in a request for gang leaders to be transferred into the federal prison system.

The spate of violence culminated with the reported murder by the PCC of yet another 26 prisoners on 14 January at the Alcaçuz prison complex close to the city of Natal, 1700 miles east of Manaus in the state of Rio Grande do Norte. Again, the death toll was probably higher. A number of unidentified, charred bodies were not included in the count (Biondi 2017b). Two months later, 71 prisoners remained unaccounted for (Melo and Rodrigues 2017). This time the PCC's victims were affiliated to a second of its rivals, the Sindicato do Crime do Rio Grande do Norte (Rio Grande do Norte Crime Union: the SRN). Again the victors marked the territory with the mutilated bodies of their victims, which were laid out on the ground to form the letters PCC. Alcaçuz stayed at the centre of mainstream and social media attention for another week as PCC and SRN prisoners were photographed and filmed by journalists and other prisoners hanging out and squaring up to one another in the grounds of the complex and on the roofs of cell blocks brandishing knives and waving banners. The prison complex had been damaged beyond repair in March 2015 during previous statewide prison riots and was to be deactivated in 2017 when new prisons were due to be inaugurated. National and world media outlets reported the complex was now under the control of prisoners. On 20 January, a particularly headline-grabbing report (Zauli 2017) emerged from Brazil's largest media network O Globo claiming FDN prisoners had paused their rebellion to hold an evangelical service. Like most other media outlets, O Globo failed to grasp or at least explain to its audience that although prisoners were still refusing to stay inside the cell blocks, the emergency had in effect ended by the morning of 15 January. Prison authorities had immediately responded to the killings by sending in construction workers to mend the damage to a poorly constructed wall that had separated the PCC and SRN units, and then within a few days to replace it with a stack of shipping containers. No reports emerged of either of the two warring factions obstructing these workers or challenging the special forces that accompanied them. On 18 January, 220 FDN prisoners were transferred from the prison and 230 prisoners with no gang allegiance brought in to take their place, again with no reported resistance. State authorities finally decided to force the issue on 27 January. Gang banners were removed and Rio Grande do Norte and Brazilian national flags planted in their place. Again a request was made for the gang leaders that had orchestrated the killings to be moved into federal custody.

One media report (Madeiro 2017) that did not catch so much public attention helps explain the apparent delayed response to the Alcaçuz tragedy. For some time, the prison complex had been staffed by trusty inmates recruited from the *seguro*. These inmates were in charge of daily routines inside the prison, including escorting prisoners and visitors to and from the cell blocks, the entrances to which they carried keys. The cell blocks themselves were under the control of the PCC and SRN. One guard explained to the journalist there were just six officers on each shift, despite the complex holding over 1000 prisoners. "The prisoners are free", he continued; "we don't have access to [the complex]… our access ends at the gates". But for the armed stand-off between the PCC and the SRN while the physical barrier between them was being reinforced, to all intents and purposes life at the prison had returned to normal within hours of the killings. If it hadn't been for the continuing media attention, there would have been little reason for state authorities to send in the troops.

***

Brazil's president, Michel Temer, came under heavy criticism from Brazil's liberal left for not commenting in public for several days after the Anísio Jobim tragedy, and for continuing to downplay the significance of the massacres altogether. Critics claimed these were not exceptional events, as Temer was accused of suggesting, but symptoms of a system in crisis. In place of announcing new measures, on 6 January 2017, President Temer's administration chose to bring forward the publishing of a national public security action plan (Ministério da Justiça e Cidadania 2017) it had been working on since late 2016, most of which merely listed actions that were already in place and/or included in the action plans published under the previous three administrations headed by former presidents Dilma Rousseff, Luiz Inácio Lula da Silva and Henrique Cardoso. A small number of additional measures were added in later announcements during or shortly after the massacres. Even if they were fully implemented, Temer's critics claimed, none of the pre-existing or new measures relating to prisons would do much to solve the immediate problem at hand—gang-orchestrated violence—let alone deal with its underlying causes. Criticism of the government's reaction to the northern massacres can be broken down into four broad areas, none of which is fully satisfactory.

The first area of critique focuses on the seeming phenomenon[1] of the "inside-outside" (Dudley and Bargent 2017; Lessing 2016) gang and its involvement in drug markets. It concerns a refusal to acknowledge major gangs like the PCC and CV are symptoms rather than causes of the increasingly punitive stance taken towards the production and sale of drugs. On 17 January, judicial authorities conducted an audit of criminal court records to establish the current size of the prison population. The report that followed (Conselho Nacional de Justiça 2017) found 29% of prisoners were inside for selling drugs. It is argued gangs would be weaker, perhaps not exist at all if drugs were legal, especially in prison (on the outside, they might continue to compete with legal entrepreneurs). By controlling prisons, gangs indirectly control drug markets outside prison. They do not typically sell drugs themselves, but instead through a system of franchising. When someone purchases drugs from a gang on licence and does not repay their debts, there will be nowhere to hide besides the *seguro* or the *isolamento* (segregation unit) the day they end up in prison themselves.

According to this analysis, drug prohibition policies are largely to blame for the proliferation of gangs like the PCC and CV, not vice versa. This alternative explanation for the Brazilian gang phenomenon has its merits, but is incomplete. Drug legalisation or reduced criminalisation may be valid demands in their own right, but they would not make a great deal of difference to prison gangs. In Chapter 6, we will see all major Brazilian prison gangs emerged from the ground and continue to act as institutions of (alternative) governance as well as drug-trafficking organisations. The majority of prisoners involved in gang activities today are likewise not involved in the drug trade. For a start, few international traffickers end up in prison. Also, as we saw in Chapter 2, the vast majority of people imprisoned in the Brazilian war on drugs were arrested for their involvement in local drug markets and were at the very bottom of the chain, most often caught in possession of just a few grammes of cocaine or cannabis. For the ordinary PCC, FDN or SRN affiliated prisoner incarcerated in Anísio Jobim, Monte Cristo and Alcaçuz, whose involvement in the drug trade has never been more than to make ends meet, we will see the massacres—or at least the premeditated aspects of the massacres—most likely had more to do with their concern for personal safety and well-being than their concern to make a living in prison. Most prisoners that benefited from the massacres would have had a stake in the mutual aid and protection provided by the PCC, CV and its allies, not their drugs.

Nor are Brazilian prison gangs always as authoritarian as is often assumed, at least for the ordinary prisoner who is accepted into the inmate body—the *coletivo* (collective)—and abides by its rules. In Chapter 6, we will see this is particularly the case for larger gangs like the PCC and CV. Punishment beatings are by no means uncommon,[2] but Brazil's prison gang phenomenon has reduced, not increased inmates' vulnerability to predatory, expressive and arbitrary violence. It is equally misguided to treat these gangs first and foremost as rent-seeking organisations. Today, the CV and PCC profit little from prisoners. The PCC does not charge or have any kind of system for collecting fees from inmates or their families. Quite the opposite, we will the PCC's success is largely grounded in its opposition to the exploitation of prisoners. Anyhow, as I will explain in a moment, even to the extent Brazil's criminal organisations do profit from their control over prison spaces and do govern through violence, many prisoners are still better off with than without them.

Finally, at least one major Brazilian prison gang—the Povo de Israel—does not operate outside as well as inside prison and is not involved in the drug trade besides regulating the supply and use of illicit substances by inmates on its wings. Its members do not consider themselves career criminals. For this reason, I will avoid using the terms criminal or inside-outside gang. Instead, I will refer more specifically to drug-trafficking and prison gangs. The Povo de Israel is Rio de Janeiro's largest prison gang. I introduced this gang in Chapter 1, and deal with it in some detail in Chapter 5.

The next two areas of critique focus more attention on the state of the Brazilian prison system. The first of these extends from the government's failure to fully acknowledge the contribution of prison conditions to the massacres. Principally, the January 2017 action plan was criticised for failing to add to previous announcements the government would provide R$800 million (£200 million) of federal funds to state prison authorities for 20,000 to 25,000 more prison spaces in addition to the approximately 20,000 new prison spaces already planned for 2017 by state prison authorities. The action plan set a target of a 15% reduction in overcrowding by the end of 2017. Alcaçuz is reported to have been operating more than 50% over capacity at the time of the massacres, with approximately 1150 prisoners and 620 spaces (Globo, 14 February 2017), Monte Cristo twice over capacity, with 1475 prisoners and 750 spaces (Folha de São Paulo, 30 January 2017), and Anísio Jobim close to three times capacity, with a reported population of 1224 crammed into just 454 spaces (BBC, 2 January 2017). 45,000 new prison spaces may not be sufficient to meet the targeted reduction in overcrowding considering the sheer size and year on year increase in the prison population in recent decades. Conselho Nacional de Justiça (2017) recorded a total of 654,372 prisoners in January 2017, five percent more than the 622,731 prisoners recorded two years earlier in Ministry of Justice official statistics for December 2014 (Ministério da Justiça 2016). This figure, based on court records, turned out to be an underestimation. In Chapter 2, we saw official statistics released later in the year (Ministério da Justiça e Segurança Pública 2017) indicated the prison population had already reached 726,712 by June 2016, fully 15% higher than in December 2014. We also saw there had been a small decrease in the number of prison spaces during this 18 month period, and that the official prison occupancy rate had risen from 167 to 197%. Even if it had been achieved (there is no evidence that it was), a 15% reduction in overcrowding would have marked no more than a return to the December 2014 situation, and there is nothing to indicate that such a high level of prison building continued into 2018. Under Rousseff's presidency, the federal government cut central funding to state prison authorities from R$111 million (£28 million) in 2014 to R$12 million (£3 million) in 2015 and R$17 million (£4 million) in 2016 (Amora and Cancian 2017). A year after the massacres, a media report (Maisonave 2018) painted a bleak picture of conditions at Anísio Jobim, Monte Cristo and Alcaçuz. All three prisons/prison complexes were reported to still be operating at between one and a half and double official capacity. No additional work, education or other purposeful activity programmes had been introduced. At Anísio Jobim, prisoners were instead spending more time locked up in their cells. Prisoners held at Monte Cristo had recently rioted after not receiving meals.

In Chapter 2, we saw prison overcrowding is indeed a cause for major concern in Brazil. However, demands for prison building—or its corollary, decarceration—as a means of tackling the kind of gang-orchestrated violence witnessed in January 2017 are again largely amiss. Poor prison conditions may help to explain the excesses of violence witnessed in the massacres, especially at Anísio Jobim, if not the initial calculated decisions to kill. Inhumanity is a cause of anger, anxiety and desensitisation, all of which are known to make individuals more prone to violence. Yet, as I also emphasised in that chapter, Brazilian prisons have never been humane. We saw overcrowding has been a continuing aspect of imprisonment in the country for most of its penal history, as have material deprivations and wholly inadequate health and social services. Anyhow, there are far worse prisons in the country than Monte Cristo or in the Anísio Jobim or Alcaçuz complexes that have not seen rebellions or serious incidences of violence for many years. When I ask Brazilian prisoners and prison workers why this might be the case, they usually come up with the same answer. Prisons *não explodem* (do not explode) because their inmates do not want them to.

This takes us on to the third area of liberal critique, which focuses on staffing shortages. In this case, President Temer's critics are rightly concerned that prison governors have increasingly abdicated responsibility for the day-to-day running their institutions to inmates as the numbers of officers and support staff at their disposal has failed to keep up with rising prisoner numbers. Well-staffed prisons are preferable to inmate-run prisons. A substantial reduction in overcrowding might reduce the ordinary prisoner's reliance on gangs for his or her welfare, so long as it were accompanied by other improvements in living conditions, but unless there were also a radical investment in staffing levels inmates would still be vulnerable to abusive or unpredictable individuals. Nor would they have many other options but violence when, for instance, they needed to collect unpaid debt. In Chapter 4, we will see that across Brazil prison authorities today employ too few guards to maintain a presence on the majority of cell block wings. In some prisons, like those in the Alcaçuz complex, officers do not even maintain a presence in the space between the entrances to cell blocks and the individual wings within them: the *miolo* (core), as it is sometimes referred to in Rio de Janeiro (Karam and

Saraiva 2017). In these circumstances, it is only natural that prisoners should rely on alternative forms of governance.

What liberal commentators often fail to point out, however, is that like poor prison conditions, staff shortage is a normal feature of the Brazilian penal system, and that the average Brazilian prison has always been administered with the cooperation and inclusion of its inmates. This we will see in Chapter 4. On 18 January, Temer announced plans for a new federal level rapid reaction force to deal with prison rebellions. An existing military elite force, originally set up to support the police, would also be made available to prison authorities for searching prison wings. These reactionary measures may help to reduce the excesses of violence associated with prison rebellions, but they will not have any effect on ordinary staffing levels or the ordinary state of (co-produced) prison governance.

A fourth and final area of critique concerns the attention the current administration, like its predecessors, has instead put on tackling gangs through securitising prisons. Here, I am again only in part agreement with the government's liberal opponents. The action plan provided R$200 million (£50 million) to build five new 220 cell single-cell federal prisons. The first four federal prisons were inaugurated between 2006 and 2009, each with 208 single cells. A fifth prison is five years behind schedule. A number of state prisons are also designated as high security. Some of these prisons have whole wings of single cells available for inmates that have committed serious disciplinary offences and who may be held in isolation for up to 30 days; note that prisoners can also be held in isolation indefinitely for their own protection. But even here it is not uncommon for prisoners to be held two or more per cell. Prison authorities do not keep statistics on how many prisoners are held in isolation under these measures. We do know, however, that in December 2014 Brazil's state-level high-security estate included 299 spaces designated specifically for prisoners subject to what is known as the Regime Disciplinar Diferenciado (Differentiated Disciplinary Regime: RDD) (Ministério da Justiça 2016). Federal prisons also include cells reserved for RDD. RDD was introduced as state-level administrative measures after major prison riots in São Paulo in 2001 and Rio de Janeiro in 2002. It was given statutory footing under federal law in 2003. It can be imposed for up to 360 days at a time. Federal and RDD prisoners are supposed to be restricted to their legal right to two hours a day unlock and two hours a week family visits, the latter of which conducted from behind a glass screen. If the new proposed federal prisons are eventually built, Brazil will still have no more than 2500 federal prison or state prison RDD spaces, enough to hold little more than a quarter of a percent of the country's projected 2020 prison population.

Besides this reality of insufficient capacity, Temer's focus on securitisation is also misguided. Federal prisons and the RDD disciplinary system were both introduced to deal with prison gangs; they aim to break gangs through isolating their leaders (Dias and Salla 2017; Filho 2013). However, this approach is premised in the view that the most successful gangs develop into structured, hierarchical organisations. The mafia paradigm of organised crime on which it is based is increasingly discredited in research on drug markets (Woodiwiss and Hobbs 2009), as are the decapitating strategies that accompany it. Mexican president Calderón's 2006–2012 *mano duro* (hard hand or zero tolerance) strategy of imprisoning or killing gang leaders, for instance, increased rather than decreased gang-related violence as drug-trafficking organisations splintered rather than disbanded (Boullosa and Wallace 2015; Gledhill 2015). The mafia or cartel myth is used to legitimise exceptionally punitive responses to organised crime in Southern as well as Northern America (Zaffaroni 1996).

In Chapter 6, we will see Brazil's so-called criminal gangs are even less structured than their counterparts in Mexico or other countries on the cocaine trail from Southern to Northern America. This point is not acknowledged by many of Temer's critics. Some of the country's more radical prison researchers go so far as to say that, whatever their origins, today the PCC and CV cannot really be described as hierarchical organisations. Biondi (2010, 2014) describes the PCC, for instance, as an organisation of criminals rather than as a criminal organisation, without origin or endpoint, that is not defined by its members, and is interpreted differently in every prison and *quebrada* (literally, broken; here meaning ghetto).[3] Similarly, Barbosa (2006: 126) describes the CV as a network without a centre, as a "conjunct of alliances" between the leadership of numerous *favelas* that might not meet or coordinate their actions at all if it were not for spending time together in prison. According to these authors, neither gang has a clearly defined, vertical, centralised command structure. Brazilian gangs are also less profitable than many of their Southern and Central American competitors, and arguably more under the pay of corrupt politicians and police officers than vice versa. According to Brazilian police estimates, the PCC makes R$200 million ($60 million) a year from its illicit activities, 80% of which from drugs (Karam 2018). By comparison, drug trafficking was estimated to account for seven percent of gross domestic product in the cocaine-producing Andean countries of Colombia, Peru and Bolivia in the 1990s (Green and Ward 2004). Drug-trafficking gangs claimed to have paid fees to as many as a third of Colombia's parliamentarians (ibid.). Today, traffickers working on the northern cocaine trail from the Andes mountains to consumers in the USA make as much as $40 billion a year profit in Mexico (Count the Costs, n.d.). A few years ago Mexico's largest gang, the Sinaloa, was estimated to make $3 billion a year (Keefe 2012). The main beneficiaries of the eastern cocaine trail through Brazil to Africa and Europe are international trafficking organisations like the Italian Ndrangheta mafia (Saviano 2015), which allegedly utilises the PCC to shift cocaine from Paraguay to Brazil's largest port, Santos, from where it is exported across the Atlantic (Attanasio 2017). The Ndrangheta was estimated to have made over €25 billion from drugs in 2008, and to control 40% of the international trade in cocaine (ibid.). Also important are individual drug entrepreneurs like Luiz Carlos da Rocha (Ramsay 2014), who is said to have supplied up to five tonnes of cocaine produced in Peru and Bolivia directly to Brazil's criminal networks in São Paulo and Rio de Janeiro every month for 30 years until his arrest close to the border with Paraguay (BBC, 2 July 2017).

Is it not so clearly the case that Brazilian gangs are the main benefactors of the local drug markets either. Rio de Janeiro's police, for instance, were deeply involved in organised crime long before the city became a centre for the international drug trade (Arias and Barnes 2016; Misse 2007). In 2017, a group of corrupt military police officers was claimed to have made $5 million a year from drugs in just one of the state capital's municipalities (Clavel 2017). Today, a significant minority of Rio de Janeiro's *favelas* are governed by militia groups rather than drug-trafficking gangs. In chapter 2, I noted militia groups are made up mostly of retired police officers or police officers working off duty. They make most of their money through extortion, but are increasingly accused of being drawn into the very drug markets they claim to have taken over *favelas* to put to an end (ibid.). The point is that Rio de Janeiro's gangs are not sufficiently organised or resourced to compete with the police. As Zaccone (2007) puts it, citing Christie's (2000) abolitionist critique of the war on drugs in the USA, the many hundreds of thousands of people imprisoned under the Brazilian drug war are *acionistas do nada* (shareholders in nothing). Zaccone is a senior civil police officer in Rio de Janeiro who is now educated to PhD level and regular speaks at universities and academic conferences. I introduced him in Chapter 1. Zaccone (2007) was published from his master's degree thesis. His conclusions on the lack of organisational structure among Rio de Janeiro's major gangs are worth citing in length:

> Members of supposed "organisations" like the CV, CVJ (Youth Red Command), Terceiro Comando (Third Command) and ADA (Friends of Friends) are not so connected as to be able to carry out joint operations… In the best (or worst) case scenario, each of these groups is able [only] to provide men and armaments during disputes over sale territories; they organise themselves only for the acquisition of prohibited substances […] [According to research recently cited in the media] 25 percent of teenage *favelados* (*favela* residents) in the city work in organised crime. Seeing that there are one million *favelados* in Rio, they concluded, an army of *marginais* (marginal people) is in formation… The idea there is an army of *marginais* being formed through the market in illicit drugs is as much a fantasy as the existence of chemical weapons in Iraq. (Zaccone 2007: 109, 120)

In São Paulo, the situation is little different. Salla et al. (2012) analysed police records on 667 people remanded in custody in the city between December 2010 and January 2011 for selling drugs. Just 12 of these records made any reference to organised crime. This does not indicate that most illicit drug deals on the streets of the city have nothing to do with the PCC. The illicit economy is governed by PCC rules of engagement—or at least localised interpretations of PCC rules of engagement—across much of the state. However, like Rio de Janeiro and most major cities across the country, São Paulo's prison gangs operate as much as ideals as physical realities.

In addition to increased spaces in federal prisons, Temer's action plan provided state prison authorities a further R$400 million (£100 million) of central funds to spend on security. This money was specifically divided between R$150 million (£38 million) for mobile signal blocking equipment, R$80 (£20 million) for body scanners, R$72 (£18 million) for electronic tags and R$98 million (£25 million) for weapons. Of these measures, only body scanners will have improved the situation of prisoners, whose visitors are still subjected to degrading strip and cavity searches in much of the country. Under Rousseff's presidency, in 2014, the government initiated a policy to end such practices once metal detectors or similar equipment were available, but some states and many individual prisons have yet to comply. Mobile signal blocking will make it more difficult for gang members to manage illicit activities on the outside but will not necessarily reduce their power within the prison system. Brazilian prison gangs have other ways of communicating between one prison and another. The PCC's *salves* (broadcasts or communiqués) are also delivered word of mouth through prisoners' families and lawyers.

More generally, the federal government's emphasis on high-security prisons, mobile phone blocking and so on in the aftermath of the northern prison massacres is more rhetoric than reality. Two points can be made here. First, even the limited federal government agenda has not been matched at state level. Existing efforts to securitise the country's prison systems have been largely corrupted by the same gangs for which they were targeted (Macaulay 2007). There are significantly less RDD prisoners today than there were a decade ago, when the first federal prison was inaugurated. In São Paulo, the official RDD population has fallen from 515 in August 2003 (Carvalho and Freire 2007) to 109 in December 2014 (Ministério da Justiça 2016). By 2016, this figure had dropped further, to approximately 85 prisoners, not all of who were being held under these conditions for gang-related activity (Filho 2017). There is little or no provision for RDD in Rio de Janeiro or in Paraná, whose prison systems are dominated by the CV and PCC. Instead, prison authorities continue to make use of ordinary disciplinary proceedings, which I have already noted allow for up to 30 days single-cell confinement. In São Paulo, senior members of the PCC have not been sent to federal supermax prisons, and have only occasionally been put on RDD (Dias and Salla 2017). In December 2016, the PCC's long-standing leader, Marcos Willians Herbas Camacho (also known as Marcola[4]), was returned to RDD for only the third time in the past 10 years.

Second, the country's high-security estate is not actually that secure, at least by the prison standards established in Northern countries that officially prioritise public protection over rehabilitation, as is the case in the USA and UK. Prisoners in the USA's far larger supermax prisons and other single-cell high-security units often spend days at a time locked up and generally do not have contact with other prisoners when they are given time—rarely more than an hour—out of their cells (Ross 2013). Most of Brazil's RDD and federal prisoners spend their two hours unlock in association, not that I am suggesting this is anything to be proud of.[5] This includes Marcola, who at the time of writing (January 2018) had just been returned to Penitenciária Presidente Maurício Henrique Guimarães Pereira (better known as Venceslau II) after completing a maximum 12 month period of (quasi) isolation at São Paulo's only purpose-built RDD facility, Centro de Reabilitação de Penitenciária Presidente Bernardes (Bernardes Penitentiary Rehabilitation Centre). It also includes Márcio dos Santos Nepomuceno (also known as Marcinho VP), perhaps the second best-known CV leader, who has been held in federal custody for the past 10 years. The head of the CV, Luiz Fernando da Costa (known as Fernandinho Beira-Mar), on the other hand, has spent long periods in the federal prison system in total isolation, where he has now been imprisoned for twelve years.[6] In Rio de Janeiro, the headquarters of the CV is currently Penitenciária Dr. Serrano Neves, one of 25 units within the 28,000 inmate-strong Gericinó prison complex introduced in Chapter 2. The complex is more commonly referred to by the area in which it is situated, Bangu; this particular unit is commonly known as Bangu IIIa. While officially designated high security, Bangu IIIa is made up of multi-occupancy cells, which like most other prison cells in the country are open to exercise yards for much of the daytime. A few senior CV figures lower down the leadership hierarchy are held close-by in a 48 single-cell unit, Penitenciária Laércio da Costa Pellegrino, Bangu I, along with prisoners affiliated to other prison gangs. According to the latest federal government inspectorate report on the prison (Conselho Nacional de Política Publica e Penitenciária 2014), just 14 of these cells were occupied at the unit at the beginning of 2014. Bangu I is officially Rio de Janeiro's top security prison. Opened in the late 1980s to hold gang leaders (Gay 2015), it was also the first modern single-cell prison to be inaugurated in the country. It is perhaps Brazil's highest security prison as well. By all accounts, prisoners are usually[7] confined to these cells for 22 hours a day, as RDD and most federal supermax prisoners. Like the majority of federal prisoners, they spend unlock in association. In a recent media interview (Costa and Andrade, n.d.), an animated Marcinho VP told journalists the Bangu I regime was tougher than federal prison regimes. Prisoners did not have access to an exercise yard and were only allowed televisions, radios or even ventilation on good behaviour. There was no natural light. Visits were restricted to the legal minimum of two hours a week, and intimate visits not allowed altogether. Televisions, radios, extended and intimate visits, in other words, were the norm in federal prisons. Marcinho VP served time at Bangu I alongside Fernandinho Beira-Mar in 2002.

Besides the relatively small number held under special legal procedures (in federal prisons, under RDD, or serving disciplinary punishments), inmates held in Brazil's wider high-security estate experience few more restrictions than they would in ordinary prisons. First and foremost, they are typically held in shared cells. It is also unusual for these inmates to be confined to their cells for more than 20 hours a day—again, anything but humane, but at the same time, falling far short of international standards associated with the supermax prison model. The PCC leadership is held alongside Marcola at Venceslau II, 400 hundred miles from the capital. A 2014 television exposé (Globo 2014) of the wing occupied by Marcola and the PCC's other main leaders showed most of its cells were shared by two or more prisoners (although Marcola himself appeared to have his own cell). Yet the prison was operating a third under official capacity. Unlock was restricted to three hours a day, but during this period, Marcola was seen to be freely mixing (and it was alleged, organising and commanding) with dozens of other PCC prisoners.

I have visited three state-level high security prisons: Penitenciária Jair Ferreira de Carvalho, Mato Grosso do Sul, Penitenciária Estadual de Piraquara II, Paraná, and the Unidade Especial Disciplinar (Special Disciplinary Unit) in the Complexo Penitenciária de Mata Escura (Mata Escura prison complex), Bahia. I introduced the first two of these prisons in Chapter 2. Jair Ferreira de Carvalho receives PCC prisoners from across the country. Like most other closed prisons in Brazil, inmates are held there in multi-occupancy cells. There is no single-cell wing used to separate gang leaders or troublesome inmates from other prisoners. Piraquara II is also designated for PCC prisoners. It includes four small, single-storey wings containing a total of 32 single cells. However, as in Rio de Janeiro, inmates on these wings are not held under RDD, but are instead separated from other inmates under ordinary disciplinary procedures. The prison was officially operating within capacity when I visited, and had solved a previous problem of overcrowding by simply adding an extra layer of bunks to its previous six-bed cells (see Chapter 2). Most inmates were held on these (now) nine-bed-cell wings. Like other penal institutions in the country, guards did not maintain a presence on the wings during unlock at either of the three prisons, and were required to communicate with the inmate body only through their representatives.[8] In this sense, these inmates' experiences of security likewise ended at the entrance to the prison wings. In the aftermath of the northern prison massacres, state prison authorities decided to search Jair Ferreira de Carvalho for drugs and weapons, but were only able to do so with the aid of 500 federal troops (Globo, 15 February 2017). Within a week of my visiting the prison, one inmate was reported to have been murdered (Ribeiro 2017) and three inmates to have escaped (Mendonça 2017). In December 2016, a group of prisoners were reported to have broken onto the *isolamento* during the night to execute another prisoner (César 2016). In September 2017, another prisoner was reported to have been executed on the *isolamento*, although this time by his own cellmates (Holsback 2017). The relative insecurity of Brazil's high-security estate was further exposed in 2014 when Piraquara II experienced a major rooftop protest. Two guards and seven inmates from the *isolamento* were held hostage for 24 hours before authorities agreed to transfer 43 PCC prisoners to lower security and semi-open units.

The UK confines relatively few prisoners to solitary confinement either, and a quarter of prisoners share cells originally built for single occupancy. However, lock-up is increasingly the norm. A third of remand and short-term prisoners (who serve their time in local prisons such as Pentonville and Wormwood Scrubs in London) spend 22 hours or more a day under lock-up (HM Inspectorate of Prisons 2017), albeit usually in shared cells—many of which built to nineteenth-century standards of as little as 5.5 square metres (ibid.)—and, in further contrast to Brazilian RDD, if not federal supermax prisoners, with in cell televisions and radios if they are well behaved. In a recent visit to Pentonville prison, Council of Europe (2017) found that on an average day only around half of the prisoners were unlocked for more than two and a half hours a day. The maximum time any prisoner spent outside his cell was five hours and 30 minutes a day. Most prisoners do not get out of their cells at all over the weekend except to collect their food. Unlock is also regularly cancelled during the week due to staff sickness. Further, most British prisoners have the right to a two-hour visit just every other week, although they are at least allowed to meet up with their family around a table and to have a certain amount of physical contact, again in contrast to Brazilian RDD prisoners.

In Chapters 4–6, we will see the ordinary Brazilian prison environment is securitised in the sense it usually operates under tacit agreements between staff and inmate collectives: that the latter will maintain discipline on the cell block wings and cooperate with prison administrators, guards and other inmates working alongside them. Such co-governance works for the majority of prisoners, but the imbalance between everyday staff and inmate authority means it is fragile and, as we saw in the case of the 2017 northern massacres, occasionally breaks down altogether. We will also see that over the past half-century prisoners have become more organised and more politicised as Brazil first became a military dictatorship and later one of the most punitive and exclusive democratic societies in the world. This trajectory—from loose, localised systems of situated inmate and staff-inmate interdependencies and negotiations, to a more politicised, collectively negotiated system has given Brazilian prison order a little more certainty. By default, it also makes Brazil a world leader in a second aspect of the global trend towards securitisation: securitising of the prison environment. This phenomenon has naturally played out differently from state to state in a country as large as Brazil, as well as from prison to prison. Still, we will see it is possible to make a number of generalisations. One norm common to most prisons is that if and when prisoners do decide to rebel, no harm should come of prison staff or their trusty *faxinas* (cleaners or housekeepers). We saw this in Varella's (2008) account of late twentieth century rebellion at the Casa de Detenção de São Paulo (Carandiru prison) in Chapter 1, as well as during the northern prison rebellions.

***

The analysis above is a longer version of two scholarly articles I published in the immediate aftermath of the massacres (Darke 2017; Darke and Garces 2017b). To summarise: we have seen liberal commentary on the 2017 northern massacres and the Brazilian government's reaction to them focused on four major issues: the self-defeating, counterproductive war on drugs; the poor state of the prison system; the absence of guards on prison wings; and the failure of the country's non-existent or corrupted securitisation agenda over the past decade to manage prison gangs, let alone deal with the fallout from the more recent breakdown in relations between the PCC and CV over the trade in cocaine. Each of these areas of critique is found wanting. Brazilian prison gangs are involved in a lot more than illicit drug markets and neither the country's impoverished prisoners nor overstretched prison managers could get by without them. The staff-inmate power dynamics that emerge in these abandoned spaces are complex and in constant flux. Disruptions or shifts in power may be accompanied by violence, some of which may not be intended or foreseen by its organisers. Finally, with no clear gang leadership to target, the government's purported decapitating strategy would make little difference even if it were to exist.

In the remainder of this chapter, I aim to demonstrate that the massacres, or at least the prison gang orchestrated aspects of the massacres, were the result of a short rather than long-term crisis, and moreover a crisis in prison governance as opposed to drug prohibition policies or prison conditions. Most people imprisoned for trafficking, to repeat, are only involved at the edges of the drug trade and are more concerned with surviving than profiting from their incarceration.

The provider of prison governance at the centre of attention, the PCC, was formed 1700 miles away from Manaus and 1300 miles from Recife, following the equally horrific prison massacre 25 years ago when elite police forces killed 111 mostly first-time offenders at Carandiru, mostly with machine guns or pistols fired at point-blank range (see Chapter 1). Today, the PCC governs the lives of 250,000 or more prisoners in São Paulo, and perhaps a million residents in its *quebradas*. In Chapter 6, we will see that through its regulation of illicit markets, banning of weapons, crack cocaine and sexual violence, dealings with police and prison officers, oversight of *normas* (norms) or *regras do convívio* (rules of communal living) (Marques 2010), or *regras de proceder* (rules of procedure) (Marques 2014; Ramalho 2002) and quasi-legal systems of dispute resolution, the PCC has been instrumental in radically reducing levels of violence on both sides of the prison wall.

Much of the analysis of the prison tragedies, both in support and critique of the Brazilian government's position, centres on the fact the PCC is now disputing prison and urban spaces on the opposite side of the country, moreover with Brazil's second largest gang—the CV— that until recently also confined its operations to the South. The most immediate cause of the massacres appears to be a breakdown in relations between the PCC and the CV, although the precise details or extent of the rift have yet to be clarified. The Brazilian media have published a number of documents from late 2016 claiming to be PCC *salves*, but these are littered with contradictions. In Chapter 4, we will see it has become increasingly difficult to trace the origins of individual *salves* as the PCC has evolved into a more horizontal organisation. Moreover, that PCC *salves* are increasingly treated as suggestions of good practice rather than as instructions or indicators of general policy. The lack of clarity over the origins and authority of the late 2016 and early 2017 *salves* was to be expected. A series of contradicting *salves* also emerged the last time the PCC was involved in serious conflict, when in 2012, dozens of young PCC affiliates and police officers died in series of tit-for-tat assassinations on the streets of São Paulo (Biondi 2014).

What is broadly agreed is that, having always managed to avoid conflict previously, tensions grew between prisoners affiliated to the two gangs in late 2016 after the CV was seen to have formed alliances with the PCC's northern rivals, including the FDN and SRN. Certainly, the Anísio Jobim, Monte Cristo and Alcaçuz massacres were the most serious of a number of violent conflicts between PCC affiliates and other gangs in the Amazonian region since October 2016, when another 21 prisoners died, including the 10 at Monte Cristo mentioned earlier. It is also generally accepted that the two gangs specifically fell out over control of the eastern cocaine trail, which increasingly flows through the Amazon basin and Northern Brazil as well as the established route through Paraguay and the Brazilian states of Mato Grosso do Sul and São Paulo. Yet no major PCC-CV conflicts have been reported since the massacres.[9] However, no one has yet issued a *salve* announcing the truce between the PCC and CV has been restored.

Still, the risk of further conflicts will continue until prisoners in the north of Brazil either defeat or more likely accept the PCC as their authority. Today, the PCC is present in prisons across each of the 26 Brazilian states (Manso and Dias 2017). Temer might hope that the PCC one day controls every cell block in the country. There has not been a major prison rebellion in São Paulo since the PCC consolidated control over 90% of its prisons in the mid-2000s (Adorno and Dias 2016; Biondi 2017a). In the meantime, there is little Brazilian authorities will likely do but sit back and observe the disruption in prison governance run its course. This may be a controversial and negative conclusion, but it is the right one to make. It comes from three interpretations of the relationship between the Brazilian state and its prisons. For one, it might be argued the Brazilian state does not have any other choice. In Chapters 4 and 6, we will see it has ceded control of the day-to-day administration of its prisons. As Guaracy Mingardi, former national public security sub-secretary, turned academic, put it in a media interview in the aftermath of the massacres, "the Brazilian state is waiting to see, because it has no idea what to do to intervene" (EXAME, 23 January 2017). Second, any suggestion the state were to make to humanise its prisons and to invest in prison staffing would fall largely on deaf ears. Few expressed any sympathy for the victims of the massacres. There was barely a public outcry. A number of politicians, including national and local government officials, went so far as to applaud the massacres (Acebes 2017). Finally, from a more critical perspective, it is important to emphasise that the Brazilian state benefits from the distorted reality of organised crime the massacres are commonly believed to represent (Shimizu 2011). The attention on organised crime diverts attention away from its own failings, not only to invest in prisons but also to deal with violent crime, outside as well as inside.

A major purpose of this book, then, is to complement top-down macro-perspectives on the Brazilian prison gang phenomenon with an additional area of analysis that focuses on the everyday realities of prison culture, inmate and staff-inmate relations. The prison massacres, I have indicated, represented a disruption or progression in a system of co-produced governance that for decades has kept the average Brazilian prison in better order, and enabled the average Brazilian inmate to better endure their prison experience. From the perspective presented here, the ebbs and flows of prison gangs relate to changes in prison governance as well as prison conditions and drug markets. Accordingly, important questions that neither Temer's administration nor its critics have adequately answered are: firstly, whether inmate collectives might eventually arise in the North that are sufficiently organised to provide the depth of hegemonic governance that the PCC provides in São Paulo, with or without the assistance of prison staff; and secondly, whether there will be further moments of crisis as power differentials between groups of prisoners is disputed along the way. For inmates at the top of prison hierarchies, there is money to be made from drugs. But the common prisoner is more concerned with matters of everyday governance. As any other community, prison communities need governance institutions to protect them, make their lives more predictable (Skarbek 2014), and in prisons as impoverished as they are in Brazil, to provide for their everyday needs. In January 2017, prisoners rioted and killed in the north of Brazil for control over territories of mutual aid and protection as well as territories of commerce. Moreover, their dispute was with other prisoner collectives, not with prison authorities, even less so their official keepers working on the ground, who we will see in Chapter 4, they do not necessarily blame for the excesses of the Brazilian penal state. It is no coincidence there were no reports of any serious harm coming to prison staff. The breakdown in order was the cause of a rift in gang relations, not prisoner-staff relations.

Central to my interpretation, then, is that Brazilian prisons have always been impoverished. This much I established in Chapter 2. We saw prison governors have never had sufficient material or human resources to run their establishments without the full cooperation of the people held there. In the following chapters, I focus as much on twentieth as twenty-first-century literature in order to demonstrate that prison governance was co-produced long before the existence of statewide or nationwide prison gangs. From the perspective of those incarcerated and working in prison, who have a shared interest in their institutions being orderly, the prison gang phenomenon is best understood as a development of an existing tradition of co-produced prison governance, symbolised by the position of the *faxina*. Indeed, it might be said there is not actually that much extraordinary about the contemporary Brazilian prison gang. *Faxinas* were described in detail, for instance, in the classic autobiographic account by the writer Graciliano Ramos (Ramos 2015, originally published in 1953) of his time served as a political prisoner in the Casa de Detenção (House of Detention), Instituto Penal Cândido Mendes (Cândido Mendes Penal Institution), and Casa de Correção (House of Correction), Rio de Janeiro in the 1930s, Edmundo Campo Coelho's (2005) and William da Silva Lima's (1991) accounts of researching and being imprisoned in Rio de Janeiro in the 1980s, and in José Ricardo Ramalho's (2002), Luiz Alberto Mendes' (2005, 2009, 2015), and Drauzio Varella's (2008, 2012) accounts of researching, being incarcerated and working voluntarily in São Paulo prisons from the late 1960s.

The term inmate *faxina* dates back to at least the 1920s (Süssekind 2014). Interestingly, Brazil's largest neighbour, Argentina, also makes use of the word cleaner as a more general term for trusty prisoner (Salla et al. 2009). However, I have yet to come across the term being used to describe inmate leaders or teams of prisoners working in the cell blocks under the instruction of inmate leaders other than in Brazil. Unfortunately, the historical and geographical origins of these two categories of prison worker, and the words used to describe them are beyond the scope of this book.

Still, over the following chapters, I occasionally draw upon historical and contemporary examples from other countries to provide some international context to the Brazilian tradition of co-produced prison governance. Most important, these include colonial and modern-day inmate governance systems from the Global South. They also include the largely antiquated, trusty prisoner and inmate leadership systems identified in Northern American prisons literature in the mid-twentieth century (see, inter alia, Cloward 1960; Crouch and Marquart 1989; Marquart and Roebeck 1985; McWhorter 1981; Sykes 1956, 1958), as well as the *pridúrki* system utilised in the gulags of the Soviet period (see, inter alia, Applebaum 2003; Gregory 2008; Solzhenitsyn 1963, 1975) and the *kapo* system utilised in the Nazi concentration camps of the Second World War (see, inter alia, Frankl 2004; Levi 1987, 1989). I have not conducted fieldwork or archival research on prison life outside of Brazil, and so I can only make the broadest of comparisons. However, it is useful to do so, if only to identify areas of potentially productive future research, and to counter the overly negative conclusion some might reach that a country like Brazil is beyond international understanding and reform (see Chapter 1).

Brazilian prisoners have always assumed responsibilities for domestic and administrative tasks. The extent they do so depends in a large part on the availability of guards and other prison workers. We will see this is also generally the case in other parts of the world too, North and South. In contrast to many countries, however, certainly those in the Global North, today Brazilian prison staff continue to not only formally delegate responsible for daily domestic and administrative routines such as cleaning, distributing meals and clerical work, but also to informally delegate responsibility for security and inmate discipline, alongside or in the place of prison guards. In some prisons, inmates are entrusted with keys to individual cells to lock up and unlock their companions. In others, certain prisoners may be entrusted with keys to the cell blocks and wings themselves. I introduced all of this in Chapter 1. In the Brazilian context, I distinguish between two ideal types of inmate working in prison management, one officially on behalf of the prison administration, and the other officially on behalf of the *coletivo*. I describe these as trusty and cell block *faxinas*. Despite these official differences, both work with the implicit, sometimes explicit support of the prison administration. We will see the relationship between Brazilian prison staff and prison inmates is often very much reciprocal and negotiated. On many prison wings, at least one cell, typically the one closest to the entrance, is dedicated to cell block *faxinas*. These prisoners are often the only ones that talk with prison guards. They form one side of the *ligação* (link) between the prison administration and the inmate body. Sometimes, trusty *faxinas* take the place of guards on the other side of the *ligação*. At Porto Alegre Public Prison (Central Prison) in Rio Grande do Sul, described in Chapter 2, the *ligação* is made up of the *prefeitura* (prefects, Rio Grande do Sul's equivalent to cell block *faxinas*) stationed on one side of a wing entrance, and *plantões de chave* (key shifts, in Rio Grande do Sul prison slang: the state's equivalent to Pernambuco's *chaveiros*—key holders—described in Chapter 1) working on the other. In São Paulo, less than one percent of inmates in many PCC prisons are official gang members (*irmãos* or *irmãs:* brothers or sisters), but every PCC wing has its cell block *faxina*. These prisoners are not necessarily gang members, although some—especially those working on the *ligação*—will often have been selected as potential gang members. Some prisons run according to PCC rules with no oversight from "baptised" gang members at all (Biondi 2010).

Yet my purpose in writing this book is not only to explore similarities to the past. We will see co-governance is also a specifically contemporary phenomenon. In the modern-day era, staff have come to rely even further on inmates to collaborate and self-govern. Like other parts of Latin America (Darke and Garces 2017a; Darke and Karam 2016), Brazilian prisoners have also become increasingly organised.

Before we continue, it is also useful to remind the reader that Brazilian prisons, like Brazilian society more generally, are as notable for their peculiarities as commonalities, from one time to another, and within as well as between different states, even between different cell blocks and wings (Biondi 2010). I emphasised this point in Chapter 2. Comparative criminology emerged as a sub-discipline in the late twentieth century in the context of increasing similarities and cooperation between criminal justice institutions both nationally and globally. More generally, Pakes (2015) reminds us, much social science is concerned with making comparisons, within as well as between one country and another. This is especially the case in a country as large and culturally varied as Brazil. The point I am making here is that irrespective of the internationalising (and within Brazil, nationalising) of prison gangs, institutional cultures continue to vary significantly from one Brazilian prison to another. We will see my distinction between trusty and cell block *faxina* serves as a useful ideal type, but that the differences between the two are not always clear cut and are particularly blurred with regard to those that work in the *miolo*. At the Curado prison complex in Pernambuco, for example (described in Chapter 1), the official title for the trusty position of *chaveiro* has in recent years been changed to *representante* (representative). In the following chapters, we will see the term *representante* has historically been associated with inmate leaders. At Curado, *representantes* are selected by prison staff but only with the consent of other prisoners (see, inter alia, Arruda 2015; Câmara dos Deputados 2008a; Human Rights Watch 2015; Mecanismo Nacional de Prevenção e Combate à Tortura 2017; Muñoz 2015). This ambiguity is demonstrated in an interview with a prisoner held there in the early 2010s:

> [You need to] learn how live within the norms created by prisoners… These norms are based in respecting one another and also visitors… The *chaveiro* passes these norms on… There is a lot of violence between prisoners; we need to organise and help one another. There are cell blocks where there are many fights, where they stab each other, where it's each to their own. There are cell blocks where the *chaveiro* interferes and where you are not allowed to fight. (Arruda 2015: 126)

This shared recognition of the need for prison order and blur between inmate and staff powers and responsibilities goes to core of what I mean by prison governance being co-produced. Moreover, the fact that Brazilian prison order is locally negotiated means the selection and responsibilities of participating prisoners vary from one prison to another.

Still, in Chapter 6, we will see the presence of major prison gangs has led to a certain level of consistency, especially when it comes to more serious matters of potential conflict. For example, one highly disputed space in prison is the kitchen, where workers not only gain access to the food eaten by their enemies, but also access to knives. Even where meals are delivered by external companies, as is increasingly the case, disputes arise over who will transport them within the cell block and deliver them to the wings. In some of the prisons I have visited outside of Rio de Janeiro and São Paulo, kitchens were staffed by prisoners from the *seguro*. In others, kitchen workers were held on a separate wing altogether. In both cases, inmates typically cooked for other inmates working in trusty positions, and sometimes also for prison staff. In a few prisons, the kitchen served the *coletivo* as well. In São Paulo's prisons, PCC affiliated prisoners prepare and transport all food served to the *coletivo* (Marques 2014). At Penitenciária Feminina de Sant'Ana (Sant'Ana Women's Penitentiary, introduced in Chapter 2), these PCC selected prisoners carry the title of *boieiras* (loosely translatable as servers of lunch boxes). Cell block *faxinas* also managed the prison kitchen at Carandiru before it was closed in 1995 (Varella 2008). The same occurs at CV prisons in Rio de Janeiro (Karam and Saraiva 2017).

More generally, in some of the prisons I describe visiting in this book, I found all inmates formally working (and remunerated) as trusty *faxina* were selected only from the *seguro*, and only by prison staff, while in other prisons I met inmates working in trusty *faxina* positions who had been selected by gang leaders. The latter is increasingly the case in the CV and PCC controlled prisons of Rio de Janeiro and São Paulo, where there are a decreasing number of *seguro* prisoners from which to choose them, in part due to prison authorities choosing to dedicate whole prison units to a particular gang, and in São Paulo increasingly due to prisoners that do not consider themselves to be career criminals—older prisoners, evangelical prisoners, those working in the formal economy—being accepted onto PCC controlled wings. In Rio de Janeiro, some prison units are fully reserved as *seguros*.

To complicate matters further, we will see there are significant differences between prisons under the control of different gangs. The varieties of prison co-governance in Brazil are illustrated in a fascinating interview held in Rio de Janeiro in 2015 with two university students who also worked as prison officers (ibid.). One of the guards, who worked at a CV prison in the Bangu complex, described how gang-affiliated prisoners filled all but the most skilled trusty positions (for which inmates were brought in from the complex's *seguro*). The second guard, who worked at a Third Command (Terceiro Comando: TC) prison, described a very different set-up in which trusty *faxina* were selected from both gang and *seguro* wings (ibid.). As for power relations between and among prison inmates and prison staff, the first guard emphasised the CV gained its legitimacy by not diverging from established inmate codes, while the second guard emphasised that the TC understood the prison governor ultimately set the rules. Yet both stressed the importance of prison staff negotiating with the gang *conselhos* (councils), whether guards or governors of individual prisons or, in the case of the *conselho* of CV leaders held at Bangu IIIa, the governor of the entire prison complex. Moreover, both interviewees stressed that the balance of power regularly changed, depending on who was currently in charge. The first guard had seen the leadership of the CV at the prison change five times in the year he had been working there. Some rules came from those at the top of the CV hierarchy in Bangu IIIa and had not changed, for example the rule that prisoners did not turn their backs on officers while being strip-searched after family visits. Local rules, on the other hand, had changed with each prisoner administration. For instance, guards were currently kept under prisoner observation in the exercise yard during visiting hours, while a short time ago, they had not been.

A few months later, I was able to follow up on some of these issues in a conversation with the second of the two guards. When I asked what roles trusty *faxinas* played in his TC prison, he explained it varied shift to shift, that is depending on which team of guards was on duty. Some of the trusty *faxina* were entrusted with keys to the cell block, but not by his team. Gang leaders currently appointed prisoners to work on the TC side of a cell block *ligação*, but this simply reflected the view taken by the most recent prison governor. In the past, trusty *faxina* had worked both inside and outside of the cell blocks. *Não tem padrão* (there is no pattern), he added.[10] As noted in Chapter 1, every prison under the command of the most organised of gangs, the PCC, has its own peculiar *ritmo* (rhythm) (Biondi 2010; Marques 2014). In at least two PCC prisons I have visited, the power to select cell block *ligação* was as much in the hands of staff as prisoners. Although the PCC made the initial selections, prison staff were able to veto or later insist on the removal of particular inmates with whom they decided they were unable to work.

Notes

1. In this book, I utilise the term phenomenon in its popular as well its scientific usage; that is in the context of things that are considered unusual or of special significance.
2. For testimonies of prison violence, see Foley (2013) and Pastoral Carcerária (2016).
3. *Quebrada* is a relatively new term. It might be regarded as São Paulo's equivalent to the term *favela*, which is used across the country to describe illegal and quasi-legal, poor residential areas. However, it is a broader term used to distinguish poor from middle-class or upper-working class, urban areas. It is akin to the term ghetto in the USA.
4. Marcola explains the origins of his nickname in a fascinating four-hour interrogation in a 2006 congressional inquiry (Câmara dos Deputados 2008b). He explains he was homeless from the age of nine. Like many other children living on the streets of São Paulo in the 1970s and 1980s, he slept in a large square in the centre of the city, Praça da Sé. Today, the square is largely populated by immigrants from West Africa and Haiti. As other homeless children, Marcola turned to sniffing *cola* (glue). I cover Marcola's interrogating in detail in Chapter 6.
5. Note too that many federal prisoners are also regularly allowed time out of their cells for work and education. This has been noted by a number of news channels and documentary makers who have been allowed to film inside the prisons and interview inmates. Dreisinger (2016) also spoke with inmates in education when she visited Catanduvas federal prison, Paraná, in 2014.

6. Note that in Mexico, the heads of criminal organisations have also been held in supermax facilities since the 2000s, but after a series of early protests were allowed 12 hours a day in association as well as extended family visits (O'Day and O'Connor 2013).
7. In 2016, it was reported that a group of seven senior CV prisoners briefly held at Bangu I had been allocated their own wing and allowed out of their cells during much of the daytime. They had been removed from Bangu IIIa and were waiting transfer into the federal prison system. The state prisons minister who had taken the decision was temporarily suspended by judicial authorities (Globo, 28 June 2016).
8. Although prison staff did not talk directly with them. One prisoner, who took the role of *o orelho* (the ear), would communicate messages from prison staff. A second prisoner, *o voz* (the voice), would return with the reply.
9. This does not mean that there have not been serious incidences of violence related to disputes between groups of prisoners, some of which might identify as gangs. One of the more deadly episodes of prison violence in the 12 months after the northern massacres occurred on 1 January 2018, when nine prisoners were reported to have been killed in the semi-open unit of the Aparecida de Goiânia prison complex, Goiás (introduced in Chapter 2). Media claims that different cell blocks have fallen under the control of the PCC and CV have not been verified. Nor has evidence arisen of any of the offenders or victims being involved in major gangs. The prison gang phenomenon has not reached either the prison complex or the city of Goiânia, as I discovered when I visited in 2016.
10. Personal communication, prison officer, Rio de Janeiro, 6 April 2016.

References

Acebes, M. C. (2017, January 18). Brazil's correctional houses of horror. *Foreign Affairs.* https://www.foreignaffairs.com/articles/brazil/2017-01-18/brazil-s-correctional-houses-horror. Last accessed 9 March 2017.

Adorno, S., & Dias, C. N. (2016). Cronologia doa "ataques de 2006" e a nova configuração de poder nas prisões na última decada. *Revista Brasileira de Segurança Pública, 10*(2), 118–132.

Amora, D., & Cancian, N. (2017, January 4). Em meio a superlotações, governo federal seca repasses para presídios. http://www1.folha.uol.

com.br/cotidiano/2017/01/1846864-em-meio-a-superlotacoes-governo-federal-seca-repasses-para-presidios.shtml. Last accessed 15 March 2017.
Applebaum, A. (2003). *Gulag: A history of the soviet camps*. London: Allen Lane.
Arias, E. D., & Barnes, N. (2016). Crime and plural orders in Rio de Janeiro Brazil. *Current Sociology, 65*(3), 448–465.
Arruda, R. F. (2015). *Geografia do cárcere: Territorialidades na vida cotidiana carcerária no sistena prisional de Pernambuco*. Ph.D. thesis, University of São Paulo. http://www.teses.usp.br/teses/disponiveis/8/8136/tde-16062015-125328/pt-br.php. Last accessed 3 February 2017.
Attanasio, A. (2017, September 9). 'Narcosur': As conexões da máfia italiana com o PCC e os cartéis latino-americanos. *BBC*. http://www.bbc.com/portuguese/internacional-41196027. Last accessed 11 September 2017.
Barbosa, A. R. (2006). O baile e a prisão: Onde se juntam as pontas dos segmentos locais que respondem pela dinâmica do tráfico de drogas no Rio de Janeiro. *Cadernos de Ciências Humanas, 9*(15), 119–135.
Biondi, K. (2010). *Junto e misturado: Uma etnografia do PCC*. São Paulo: Teirciero Nome. English version: Biondi, K. (2016). *Sharing this walk: An ethnography of prison life and the PCC in Brazil* (J. F. Collins, Trans.). Chapel Hill: University of North Carolina.
Biondi, K. (2014). *Etnografia no movimento: Território, hierarquia e lei no PCC*. Ph.D. thesis, Federal University of São Carlos. https://www.repositorio.ufscar.br/bitstream/handle/ufscar/246/6378.pdf?sequence=1&isAllowed=y. Last accessed 7 April 2017.
Biondi, K. (2017a, January 23). The extinction of sexual violence in the prisons of São Paulo, Brazil. http://uncpressblog.com/2017/01/23/karina-biondi-the-extinction-of-sexual-violence-in-the-prisons-of-sao-paulo-brazil. Last accessed 7 March 2017.
Biondi, K. (2017b). Prison violence, prison justice: The rise of Brazil's PCC. *NACLA Report on the Americas, 49*(3), 341–346.
Boullosa, C., & Wallace, M. (2015). *Narco history: How the United States and Mexico jointly created the Mexican drug war*. New York: Or Books.
Câmara dos Deputados. (2008a). *CPI do sistema carcerário*. Resource document. http://bd.camara.leg.br/bd/bitstream/handle/bdcamara/2701/cpi_sistema_carcerario.pdf?sequence=5. Last accessed 10 August 2014.
Câmara dos Deputados. (2008b). No title. Resource document. http://www1.folha.uol.com.br/folha/cotidiano/20060708-marcos_camacho.pdf. Last accessed 17 July 2017.

Carvalho, S., & Freire, C. R. (2007). O regime disciplinar diferenciado: Notas críticas à reforma do sistema punitivo brasileiro. In S. Carvalho (Ed.), *Crítica à execução penal* (2nd ed., pp. 269–281). Rio de janeiro: Lumen Juris.

César, R. (2016, December 5). Nove presos teriam executado detento em área de isolamento, denuncia Sinsap. *Correio do Estado*. http://www.correiodoestado.com.br/cidades/campo-grande/nove-presos-teriam-executado-detento-em-area-de-isolamento-denuncia/292800. Last accessed 4 October 2017.

Christie, N. (2000). *Crime control as industry: Towards gulags, western style?* London: Routledge.

Clavel, T. (2017, June 29).'Largest ever' police corruption case unfolds in Brazil's Rio de Janeiro. *InSight Crime*. http://www.insightcrime.org/news-briefs/brazil-largest-ever-police-corruption-case-unfolds-rio-de-janeiro-state. Last accessed 14 July 2017.

Cloward, R. A. (1960). Social control in the prison. In R. Cloward, et al. (Eds.), *Theoretical studies in social organization of the prison* (pp. 20–48). New York: Social Science Research Council.

Coelho, E. C. (2005). *A oficina do diablo. E outros estudos sobre criminalidade.* Rio de Janeiro: Record.

Conselho Nacional de Justiça. (2017). *Reunião especial de jurisdição.* Resource document. http://www.cnj.jus.br/files/conteudo/arquivo/2017/02/b5718a7e7d6f2edee274f93861747304.pdf. Last accessed 3 March 2017.

Conselho Nacional de Política Publica e Penitenciária. (2014). *Relatório de inspeção extraordinária em estabelecimentos penais no estado do Rio de Janeiro.* Resource document. https://www.justica.gov.br/seus-direitos/politica-penal/cnpcp-1/relatorios-de-inspecao-1/relatorios-de-inspecao-2014-1/relatorio-de-inspecao-extraordinaria-rj-jan-21-2014.pdf. Last accessed 25 June 2017.

Costa, F., & Andrade, V. (n.d.). O poder do crime. *UOL*. https://www.uol/noticias/especiais/marcinho-vp.htm#tematico-1. Last accessed 21 October 2017.

Council of Europe. (2017). *Report to the government of the United Kingdom on the visit to the United Kingdom carried out by the European Committee for the prevention of torture and inhuman or degrading treatment or punishment (CPT) from 30 March to 12 April 2016.* CPT/Inf (2017). Resource document. https://rm.coe.int/CoERMPublicCommonSearchServices/DisplayDCTMContent?documentId=090000168070a773. Last accessed 18 April 2017.

Count the Costs. (n.d.). *The war on drugs: Wasting billions and undermining economies*. Resource document. http://www.countthecosts.org/sites/default/files/Economics-briefing.pdf. Last accessed 17 August 2017.

Crouch, B., & Marquart, J. (1989). *An appeal to justice: Litigation reform of Texas prisons*. Austin, TX: University of Texas.

Darke, S. (2017, January 26). Who is really in control of Brazil's prisons? *The conversation*. https://theconversation.com/who-is-really-in-control-of-brazils-prisons-71391. Last accessed 23 June 2017.

Darke, S., & Garces, C. (2017a). Surviving in the new mass carceral zone. *Prison Service Journal, 229*, 2–9.

Darke, S., & Garces, C. (2017b, January 9). What's causing Brazil's prison massacres? *Centre for Crime and Justice Studies*. https://www.crimeandjustice.org.uk/resources/whats-causing-brazils-prison-massacres. Last accessed 23 June 2017.

Darke, S., & Karam, M. L. (2016). Latin American prisons. In Y. Jewkes et al. (Eds.), *Handbook on prisons* (2nd ed., pp. 460–474). Abington: Routledge. Portuguese version: Karam, M. L., & Darke, S. (2016). Prisões latino americanas (Karam, M. L., Trans.). http://emporiododireito.com.br/leitura/prisoes-latino-americanas-1508702837. Last accessed 17 February 2018. Spanish version: Darke, S., & Karam, M. L. (2017). Las prisiones de América Latina. *Ecuador Debate, 101*, 53–71.

Dias, C. N., & Salla, F. (2017). Formal and informal controls and punishment: The production of order in the prisons of São Paulo. *Prison Service Journal, 229*, 19–22.

Dreisinger, B. (2016). *Incarceration nations: A journey to justice in prisons around the world*. New York: Other.

Dudley, S., & Bargent, J. (2017, January 19). The prison dilemma: Latin America's incubators of organized crime. *InSight Crime*. http://www.insightcrime.org/investigations/prison-dilemma-latin-america-incubators-organized-crime. Last accessed 15 June 2017.

Filho, J. J. (2013). The rise of the supermax in Brazil. In J. I. Ross (Ed.), *The globalization of supermax prisons* (pp. 129–144). New Brunswick, NJ: Rutgers University.

Filho, J. J. (2017). *Administração Penitenciária: O controle da população carcerária a partir da gestão partilhada entre diretores, judiciário e facções*. Ph.D. thesis, Fundação Getulio Vargas. http://bibliotecadigital.fgv.br/dspace/handle/10438/18432. Last accessed 10 July 2017.

Foley, C. (2013). *Protecting Brazilians from torture: A manual for judges, prosecutors, public defenders and lawyers* (2nd ed.). Resource document. International Bar Association. http://www.conectas.org/arquivos/

editor/files/Relato%CC%81rio%20completo_Tortura%20blindada_ Conectas%20Direitos%20Humanos(1).pdf. Last accessed 6 July 2017.

Frankl, V. E. (2004). *Man's search for meaning*. London: Rider. Originally published in 1947.

Gay, R. (2015). *Bruno: Conversations with a Brazilian drug dealer*. Durham, NC: Duke University.

Gledhill, J. (2015). *The new war on the poor*. London: Zed.

Globo. (2014). *Domingo Espetacular revela rotina de um presídio de segurança maxima*. Television documentary. https://www.youtube.com/watch?v=XAziwMDOCnE. Last accessed 19 January 2018.

Green, P., & Ward, T. (2004). *State crime: Governments, violence and corruption*. London: Sage.

Gregory, P. R. (2008). *Lenin's brain and other tales from the secret Soviet archives*. Stanford: Hoover International.

HM Inspectorate of Prisons. (2017). *Life in prison: Living conditions*. Resource document. http://www.justiceinspectorates.gov.uk/hmiprisons/wp-content/uploads/sites/4/2017/10/Findings-paper-Living-conditions-FINAL-.pdf. Last accessed 11 October 2017.

Holsback, L. (2017, 22 September). Preso é assassinado em pavilhão de isolamento da Máxima. *Capital News*. http://www.capitalnews.com.br/policia/preso-e-assassinado-em-pavilhao-de-isolamento-da-maxima/309277. Last accessed 4 October 2017.

Human Rights Watch. (2015). *The state let evil take over: The prison crisis in the Brazilian state of Pernambuco*. New York: Human Rights Watch.

Karam, M. L. (2018, 22 February). O uso indevido das forças armadas em atividades de segurança pública. *Cunsultor Jurídico*. https://www.conjur.com.br/2018-fev-22/maria-lucia-karam-uso-indevido-militares-seguranca-publica. Last accessed 28 February 2018.

Karam, M. L., & Saraiva, H. R. (2017). Ouvindo as vozes de carcereiros brasileiros. Unpublished. English version: Hearing the voices of Brazilian correction officers (M. L. Karam, Trans.). *Prison Service Journal, 229*, 48–50.

Keefe, P. R. (2012, June 15). Cocaine incorporated. *The New York Times Magazine*. http://www.nytimes.com/2012/06/17/magazine/how-a-mexican-drug-cartel-makes-its-billions.html. Last accessed 5 July 2017.

Lessing, B. (2016). *Inside out: The challenge of prison-based criminal organizations*. Resource document. The Brookings Institution. https://www.brookings.edu/wp-content/uploads/2016/09/fp_20160927_prison_based_organizations.pdf. Last accessed 19 April 2017.

Levi, P. (1987). *If this is a man*. London: Abacus. Originally published in 1947.

Levi, P. (1989). *The drowned and the saved*. London: Abacus. Originally published in 1986.

Lima, W. S. (1991). *Quatrocentos contra um: Uma história do Comando Vermelho*. Rio de Janeiro: ISER.

Macaulay, F. (2007). Knowledge production, framing and criminal justice reform in Latin America. *Journal of Latin American Studies, 39,* 627–651.

Madeiro, C. (2017, January 22). Em Alcaçuz, presos controlam chave de pavilhões e até entrada de comida. *Amigos de Plantão*. http://marechalonline.net/noticia/em-alcacuz-presos-controlam-chave-de-pavilhoes-e-ate-entrada-de-comida/11317. Last accessed 23 January 2017.

Maisonave, F. (2018, January 11). Até mutirão de Cármen Lúcia empaca, e prisões seguem superlotadas no país. *Folha de São Paulo*. http://www1.folha.uol.com.br/cotidiano/2018/01/1949577-ate-mutirao-de-carmen-lucia-empaca-e-prisoes-seguem-superlotadas-no-pais.shtml. Last accessed 18 January 2018.

Manso, B. P., & Dias, C. N. (2017). PCC, sistema prisional e gestão do novo mundo do crime no Brasil. *Revista Brasileira de Segurança Pública, 11*(2), 10–29.

Marquart, J., & Roebeck, J. (1985). Prison guards and "snitches". *British Journal of Criminology, 25*(3), 217–233.

Marques, A. (2010). "Liderança", "proceder" e "igualdade": Uma etnografia das relações políticas no Primeiro Comando da Capital. *Etnográfica, 14*(2), 311–335.

Marques, A. (2014). *Crime e proceder: Um experimento antropológico*. São Paulo: Alameda.

McWhorter, W. (1981). *Inmate society: Legs, half-pants and gunmen: A study of inmate guards*. Saratoga, CA: Century Twenty One.

Mecanismo Nacional de Prevenção e Combate à Tortura. (2017). *Relatório anual 2016–2017*. Resource document. http://www.sdh.gov.br/noticias/pdf/mecanismo-nacional-de-prevencao-e-combate-a-tortura-lanca-relatorio-anual-2016-2017-2. Last accessed 28 June 2017.

Melo, J. G., & Rodrigues, R. (2017). Notícias de uma massacre anunciado e em andamento: O poder de matar e deixar morrer à luz do massacre no presidio de Alcaçus, RN. *Revista Brasileira de Segurança Pública, 11*(2), 48–62.

Mendes, L. A. (2005). *Às cegas*. São Paulo: Companhia das Letras.

Mendes, L. A. (2009). *Memórias de um sobrevivente*. São Paulo: Companhia de Bolso.

Mendes, L. A. (2015). *Confissões de um homen livre*. São Paulo: Companhia das Letras.

Mendonça, M. (2017, May 22). Três fogem do Presídio de Segurança Máxima da Capital. *Correio do Estado*. http://www.correiodoestado.com.br/cidades/campo-grande/tres-fogem-do-presidio-de-seguranca-da-maxima-da-capital/304389. Last accessed 21 June 2017.

Ministério da Justiça. (2016). *Levantamento nacional de informações penitenciárias infopen, dezembro de 2014*. Resource document. http://www.justica.gov.br/seus-direitos/politica-penal/infopen_dez14.pdf. Last accessed 24 October 2016.

Ministério da Justiça e Cidadania. (2017). *Plano nacional de segurança pública*. Resource document. http://www.justica.gov.br/noticias/plano-nacional-de-seguranca-preve-integracao-entre-poder-publico-e-sociedade/pnsp-06jan17.pdf. Last accessed 5 March 2017.

Ministério da Justiça e Segurança Pública. (2017). *Levantamento nacional de informações penitenciárias: Atualização - Junho de 2016*. Resource document. http://www.justica.gov.br/news/ha-726-712-pessoas-presas-no-brasil/relatorio_2016_junho.pdf. Last accessed 21 December 2017.

Misse, M. (2007). Illegal markets, protection rackets and organized crime in Rio de Janeiro. *Estudos Avançados, 61,* 139–157.

Muñoz, C. (2015, October 20). A privatização perversa das prisões. *Folha de São Paulo*. http://www1.folha.uol.com.br/opiniao/2015/10/1695836-a-privatizacao-perversa-das-prisoes.shtml. Last accessed 3 February 2017.

O'Day, P., & O'Connor, T. (2013). Supermaxes south of the border. In J. I. Ross (Ed.), *The globalization of supermax prisons* (pp. 35–48). New Brunswick, NJ: Rutgers University.

Pakes, F. (2015). *Comparative criminal justice*. Cullompton: Willan.

Pastoral Carcerária. (2016). *Tortura em tempos de encarceramento em massa*. Resource document. http://carceraria.org.br/wp-content/uploads/2016/10/tortura_web.pdf. Last accessed 22 November 2016.

Ramalho, J. R. (2002). *Mundo do crime: A ordem pelo avesso* (3rd ed.). Rio de Janeiro: Graal.

Ramos, G. (2015). *Memórias do Cárcere* (49th ed.). Rio de Janeiro: Record.

Ramsay, G. (2014, June 27). A closer look at Brazil-bound drug networks. *Insight Crime*. http://www.insightcrime.org/news-analysis/a-closer-look-at-brazil-bound-drug-networks. Last accessed 6 July 2017.

Ribeiro, L. (2017, 17 May). Agente penitenciário encontra detento morto em presídio de segurança maxima. *Capital News*. http://www.capitalnews.com.br/policia/agente-penitenciario-encontra-detento-morto-em-presidio-de-seguranca-maxima/304806. Last accessed 21 June 2017.

Ribeiro, A., Corrêa, H., & Fonseca, H. (2016, October 25). As rebeliões em presídios são um aviso: A selvageria está à solta. *ÉPOCA*. http://epoca.globo.com/tempo/noticia/2016/10/o-crime-esta-em-guerra-maiores-faccoes-brasileiras-romperam.html. Last accessed 28 February 2017.

Ross, J. I. (2013). Invention of the American supermax prison. In J. I. Ross (Ed.), *The globalization of supermax prisons* (pp. 10–24). New Brunswick, NJ: Rutgers University.

Salla, F., Ballesteros, P., Mavila, O., Mercado, F., Litvachky, P., & Museri, A. (2009). *Democracy, human rights and prison conditions in South America*. São Paulo: University of São Paulo.

Salla, F., Jesus, M. G. M., & Rocha, T. T. (2012, October). Relato de uma pesquisa sobre a Lei 11.343/2006. *Boletim IBCCRIM, 20*, 10–11.

Saviano, R. (2015). *Zero, zero, zero*. London: Allen Lane.

Shimizu, B. (2011). *Solidariedade e grefarismo nas facções criminosas: Um estudo criminológico à luz da psicologia das massas*. São Paulo: Instituto Brasileiro de Ciências Criminais.

Skarbek, D. (2014). *The social order of the underworld: How prison gangs govern the American penal system*. New York: Oxford University.

Solzhenitsyn, A. (1963). *One day in the life of Ivan Denisovich*. London: Penguin.

Solzhenitsyn, A. (1975). *The gulag archipelago: Volume 2*. New York: Harper and Row.

Souza, F. (2017, September 1). Polícia diz que agentes facilitaram massacre de presos em Manaus e indicia 210 detentos. *BBC*. http://www.bbc.com/portuguese/brasil-41118908. Last accessed 6 September 2017.

Süssekind, E. (2014). *Estratégias de sobrevivência e de convivência nas prisões do Rio de Janeiro*. Ph.D. thesis, Fundação Getulio Vargas. http://bibliotecadigital.fgv.br/dspace/handle/10438/13390. Last accessed 15 June 2017.

Sykes, G. M. (1956). The corruption of authority and rehabilitation. *Social Forces, 34*(3), 257–262.

Sykes, G. M. (1958). *The society of captives*. Princeton, NY: Princeton University.

Varella, D. (2008). *Estação Carandiru*. São Paulo: Companhia das Letras. English edition: Varella, D. (2012). *Lockdown: Inside Brazil's most violent prison* (A. Entrekin, Trans.). London: Simon and Schuster.

Varella, D. (2012). *Carcereiros*. São Paulo: Companhia das Letras.

Woodiwiss, M., & Hobbs, D. (2009). Organized evil and the Atlantic alliance: Moral panics and the rhetoric of organized crime policing in America and Britain. *British Journal of Criminology, 49*(1), 106–112.

Zaccone, O. (2007). *Acionistas do Nada: Quem são os traficantes de drogas*. Rio de Janeiro: Revan.

Zaffaroni, E. R. (1996). "Crime Organizado": Uma categoricação frustrada. *Discursos Sediciosos, 1*(1), 45–67.

Zauli, F. (2017, January 20). Presos interrompem rebelião em presídio do RN para culto evangélico. *O Globo*. http://g1.globo.com/rn/rio-grande-do-norte/noticia/2017/01/presos-interrompem-rebeliao-em-presidio-do-rn-para-culto-evangelico.html. Last accessed 28 February 2017.

4

Surviving through the *Convívio*

Brazil, then, has a long history of inmate self-governance and staff-inmate collaboration that ordinarily maintains order and ordinarily facilitates prisoner survival. This (trusty and cell block) *faxina* (cleaner or housekeeper) system must first and foremost be understood in the context of acute under-resourcing and abdication by state authorities of responsibility for maintaining their prisons and the welfare of those incarcerated or working in them. While the Brazilian prison *faxina* system varies from one place and time to another, the poorer the prison the more likely its inmates will have developed reciprocal systems of mutual aid and protection. The poorer the prison, the more prison staff also rely on the inmates under their care to maintain discipline and prison security and to manage prison routines. Prisoner collectives—gangs for want of a more appropriate word—naturally compete over the benefits of the *faxina* system, as do individual prisoners. In Brazil, there exists a relatively strong cultural identity among prisoners, who often refer to themselves in the singular, as being one inmate body, as one *coletivo* (collective). Collective inmate identity mitigates against the potential dominance of predatory individuals and gangs. In the past few decades, larger gangs have emerged that operate in more than one cell block and in more than one prison. Most, but not all, of these gangs also operate in the urban community from which their affiliates come and their families usually still reside. The Primeiro Comando da Capital (PCC) is the most advanced and successful of these self-proclaimed criminal organisations.

This statement breaks down equates with the four essential features of Brazilian prison life identified in Chapter 2, the first three of which I focus on in this chapter: the insufficient levels of staffing required to maintain security and discipline, let alone manage everyday routines; the informal, convivial nature of prisoner and, to a lesser but still important extent, staff-prisoner relations; staff dependency on prisoners and their families as well as inmate dependency on prison staff; and the increasing significance to prison governance of gangs that often cross the boundaries between one prison to another, and between prisons and urban communities, and in most cases are considered and consider themselves to be criminal. Like the high levels of prison overcrowding and subsequent deprivations explored in that chapter, staff shortage, conviviality, co-governance and gangs make the experience of imprisonment very much different in Brazil than in Northern America and Western Europe. Conviviality—the art of living communally, however begrudgingly—has been at the centre of the Brazilian prison experience since the country opened its first penal penitentiary in 1850. Prison inmates have always depended as much on each other as on prison staff for their most basic of needs. Prison staff have always depended on prison inmates to individually and collectively run prison regimes. Major prison gangs are a more recent manifestation.

Staff Shortage

Across the Brazilian prison system 78,163 people were employed as guards and 8900 as administrators in June 2016 (Ministério da Justiça e Segurança Pública 2017). A further 3294 police officers worked full time in prison.[1] These figures equate to an inmate–officer ratio of eight to one.[2] To put these figures into North-South comparative context, the best resourced and most human rights respecting prison systems in the world, such as those to be found in the Nordic countries of Denmark,

Sweden, Finland, Norway and Iceland, employ one member of staff for every prisoner (Ugelvik 2016). England and Wales saw a 26% reduction in prison staff in its public prisons between 2010 and 2016 (Prison Reform Trust, n.d.). It now employs 33,327 staff, including 22,679 guards (Ministry of Justice 2017). These figures indicate that in England and Wales there is approximately one prison officer per three prisoners held in public prisons. In some prisons, the effective inmate-officer ratio is reported to have fallen as low as 50 to one, taking into account work shift patterns and staff sickness (Council of Europe 2017). Pentonville prison employs a total of 196 guards, less than 50 a shift, to watch over more than 1300 inmates (ibid.). Under these circumstances, prisoners are increasingly kept to their cells for their safety and the safety of officers. Activities are increasingly cancelled. At a prison I visited in 2015 officers had resorted to leaving one staff member in charge of each wing while the remaining officers moved wing to wing to allow prisoners at least one hour a day in association. At another prison I visited in 2017 some prisoners had had their time out of cell restricted to as little as 30 minutes a day. Council of Europe (2017) also encountered a number of prisoners that spent more than 23 hours a day locked up in their cells in the segregation unit of a prison holding youths aged 18–21. In 2017, legal proceedings were brought over the case of a 16 year old who was locked up for 23 hours and 30 minutes a day for two months at Feltham Young Offenders Institute in London (Bowcott 2017). This treatment was held to breach the child's right to education under the European Convention of Human Rights, but not to constitute degrading inhumane or degrading treatment (Travis 2017).

That Brazilian prisons should continue to function with more than twice the number of inmates per guard than the prison system of England and Wales defies (Northern) common sense. Staff shortages are felt hardest at the front line. The first positions that need to be filled are at the entrances to the prison and its cell blocks. Guards are also regularly withdrawn from cell blocks to escort prisoners to and from court, and to make up for shortages in office clerks. Prison guards are also regularly absent on sick leave. In a survey of 100 officers in a women's prison in Minas Gerais (Mattos 2010), a third of respondents stated they had taken extended periods of time off work for health reasons.

I have already mentioned that prison guards do not maintain a presence in the majority of Brazilian prison wings today. This fact alone makes it difficult to draw meaningful comparisons between prison life in Brazil, Northern America and certainly Western Europe. The average Brazilian prisoner has little daily contact with prison guards once they have been registered and delivered to the leaders of their wing or cell block. This is most notably the case with police *carceragens* (lock-ups; units of holding cells), which are often managed with barely any staff at all. When Human Rights Watch visited a *carceragem* in Rio Grande do Norte in the late 1990s, it found three police officers responsible for 646 prisoners (Human Rights Watch 1998). A decade later UN Committee against Torture (2009) reported visiting a *carceragem* in Rio de Janeiro where 1405 prisoners were being guarded by six officers. The three *carceragens* I visited in Paraná (see Chapter 2) were much smaller and each had at least two officers on duty. However, it is quite possible there was only one officer on duty at night time, as we will see in the next chapter I discovered to have been common practice at the, since deactivated, *carceragem* in Rio de Janeiro (Polinter) I researched in 2010.

However, staffing shortages are clearly endemic to the prison system as a whole. When I visited Central Prison, Rio Grande do Sul in 2016 it was operating with on average one staff member on duty per 68 prisoners. Inter-American Court of Human Rights (2013) found the prison employed a total of 370 police officers—the prison was taken over by the military police following a major rebellion in the mid-1990s—meaning there might have been one officer on duty per 40 prisoners. Two years later, staffing levels were found to have decreased to 340 officers (Mecanismo Nacional de Prevenção e Combate à Tortura 2015). By 2017, the prison was operating with no more than 295 officers (Hadler et al. 2017). In Chapter 3, we saw there were six officers per shift in the Alcaçuz prison complex at the time of the northern massacres. Anísio Jobim was reported to employ a total of 153 staff (Mecanismo Nacional de Prevenção e Combate à Tortura 2016), among which as few as four guards may have been on duty when the rebellion began (Cowie 2017). The most extreme example cited in governmental reports on prison conditions I am aware of is the Curado complex in Pernambuco. In Chapter 1, I cited a parliamentary investigation (Câmara dos

Deputados 2008) that found five officers in charge of the 4200 prisoners held there. More recent reports indicate the complex is still operating with as few as one officer per 400–500 inmates (Pastoral Carcerária/PE et al. 2014; Mecanismo Nacional de Prevenção e Combate à Tortura 2017). Among the prisons I have visited, Penitenciária Alfredo Trajan left a particularly deep impression. As noted in Chapter 2, this prison is situated in the vast Bangu prison complex. Bangu is made up of 25 units and holds approximately 28,000 prisoners. In 2010, I spent an afternoon at Alfredo Trajan, Bangu II, with a public defender and a group of law students providing legal advice to prisoners. As we drove through the prison complex, we passed dozens of special prison force officers going through military drills. Several ordinary prison officers searched us at the entrance to the unit. Passing through security into the main cell block was like entering into a different world. Over the next few hours attending prisoners in a *pátio* (exercise yard), only one prison guard was ever present. He was one of eight officers on his shift, including the officers stationed at the entrance to the prison. At the time the prison held around 700 inmates. I later discovered this to be quite usual across the whole of the prison complex. A few years earlier Penitenciária Dr. Serrano Neves (Bangu IIIa), a maximum security prison in the complex holding Comando Vermelho (CV) leaders, was reported to have ten guards on duty at a time its 780 inmates were on hunger strike (Caldeira 2003). Another prison unit, holding 1200 CV inmates, was recently reported to have a maximum of nine officers on duty, just five of which stationed inside the cell block. These *guardas de miolo* (core guards) were the only prison staff in everyday contact with inmates (Karam and Saraiva 2017).

At first sight, it might seem the Brazilian prison system is going through a temporary staffing crisis as authorities have simply not been able to keep abreast of the rapidly increasing numbers of prisoners. It is true staffing levels were higher in the recent past. In 1994, São Paulo prison authorities had 14,702 employed staff and a prison population of 31,842 (Adorno and Salla 2007). By 2006, São Paulo's prison population had quadrupled to 125,523 inmates, but prison staff numbers had not even doubled, to 25,172 (ibid.). Over the next eight years its prison population climbed dramatically to 220,030, while prison staff rose by barely a third, to 32,679 (Ministério da Justiça 2016). In June 2016, São Paulo's prison population had reached 240,061 inmates (Ministério da Justiça e Segurança Pública 2017).

But twenty years acute understaffing equates to more than a crisis. Anyhow, São Paulo's inmate–staff ratio was no better in 1994 than England and Wales' inmate–staff ratio is today. Human Rights Watch (1998) reported finding one officer on duty per 100 or more inmates in numerous prisons across the country, including the Casa de Detenção de São Paulo (Carandiru prison, introduced in Chapter 1), which at the time held a fifth of São Paulo's sentenced prisoners. Although Carandiru employed close to 1000 people in the 1990s (Varella 2012), a maximum of 90 guards were ever on duty (Mendes 2015). The period following the country's 1964–1985 military dictatorship was also an exceptionally good time for prison staffing in São Paulo. Later in the chapter we will see the state's first post-dictatorship government was unusually concerned with prison reform. In the 1970s, Carandiru prison employed around 200 staff, equivalent to little more than 50 staff per shift, to take care of more than 5500 prisoners (Ramalho 2002). Wolfmann (2000) refers to having just two guards on duty in cell blocks eight or nine when he was governor of Carandiru in the early 1980s. Outside of São Paulo, the only other account of Brazilian prisons of the dictatorship era I am aware of that provides detail on staffing levels is Coelho's (2005) study of seven prisons in Rio de Janeiro in the early 1980s, first published in 1987. Inmate–guard ratios, barring sickness, withdrawal to perform administrative duties, escort prisoners to and from court and so on, ranged from 12:1 (670 inmates; 55 guards) at a maximum security prison to 50:1 (1253 inmates; 25 guards) at a remand prison. As continues to be the norm in Brazilian prisons today, guards were divided into four teams, each working 24 hours on, 72 hours off.

Whatever the era and whatever the prison type, historical, ethnographic and autobiographical accounts of Brazilian prison life invariably refer to prison governors relying on prisoners to collaborate and self-govern. Brazil's first two penitentiaries, the *casas de correção* (houses of correction) of Rio de Janeiro and São Paulo, likewise operated with minimal staffing levels throughout the second half of the nineteenth century and first half of the twentieth century (Koerner 2006; Salla 2015).

Brazil's first remand prison, Rio de Janeiro's Casa de Detenção (House of Detention), employed 34 staff to oversee as many as 400 inmates in 1928 (Chazkel 2009). One prisoner was appointed to maintain order in each cell (ibid.). João do Rio (1905), a regular visitor to the Casa de Detenção, also wrote of prisoners earning the right to wear prison guard uniforms and working as *serventes* (servants). Similarly, Bretas (1996) cites an autobiography of a political prisoner from 1926 that described food being served by a "convict servant". Bretas also cites 1895 and 1922 journalistic accounts of a long-term prisoner who, when he eventually moved on to Cândido Mendes prison (described in detail in Chapter 6), worked as the "supervisor of the prisoners' uniforms" (Bretas 1996: 115). At both the Casa de Detenção and Casa de Correção, most domestic and maintenance work was conducted by slaves and free slaves right up to abolition (Araújo 2009; Chazkel 2009; Koerner 2006). As late as 1879, slaves made up 28% of the 7225 prisoners that spent time in the Casa de Detenção (Chazkel 2009). One year before abolition in 1888 it only held 19 slaves; however, 385 of its prisoners were free slaves (ibid.). In Chapter 6, we will see Ramos (2015) described virtually every aspect of prison work being delegated to inmates when he was incarcerated for a short period in Rio de Janeiro's prison system in the mid-1930s. If there was ever a golden age for Brazilian prisons, it might have been in Rio de Janeiro during the country's first period of full democracy, 1945–1964. Barbosa (2005) reports that older guards in the state reminisce of this period as a time when increased federal investment allowed state prison authorities to provide more social assistance and specialised prison work, as well as sufficient material provisions for prison administrators not to rely on inmates' families. During this period, staff–inmate relations were also relatively good, allowing guards to maintain more control over prison discipline (Coelho 2005).[3] Nevertheless, any improvements in prison conditions in the post-Second World War period were not matched by improvements in prison staffing. Prisons continued to rely on inmates to self-govern and to work alongside staff in administrative, supervisory and disciplinary capacities.[4]

Today's prison governors are certainly accustomed to managing without guards. Inmate self-governance is ingrained into everyday prison routines across the country. It is also supported by all but the earliest prison architecture. Of the prisons I have visited in the country, only São Paulo's Penitenciária Feminina de Sant'Ana (introduced in Chapter 2) was built along the classic Northern American or Western European model of individual cells separated by long, narrow landings. We have seen Sant'Ana was inaugurated in the early twentieth century. The archetypical modern Brazilian prison is instead divided into self-contained blocks of cells facing onto—and in some cases, like Carandiru, surrounding—a *pátio* (see Fig. 4.1). This is the case, for instance, at each of the three prisons/complexes (Anísio Jobim, Monte Cristo and Alcaçuz) at the centre of the 2017 massacres in the Northern states of Amazonas, Boa Vista and Rio Grande do Norte. As we saw in Chapter 3, guards do not have a daytime presence in the cell blocks at these or indeed most other Brazilian prisons.

Since São Paulo closed its system of police *carceragens* in the 2000s, it has built dozens of remand prisons under a similar design. Each unit

Fig. 4.1 A cell block *pátio* at the deactivated Carandiru prison, São Paulo, Brazil. Photograph taken by the author, 8 April 2005

4 Surviving through the *Convívio*

has a capacity of approximately 700 prisoners and contains eight wings for gang-affiliated prisoners, four each side of a wide corridor, as well as a *seguro* (insurance or vulnerable persons unit) and *isolamento* (segregation unit) (see Fig. 4.2). The gang wings each contain a *pátio* and four 12-bunk cells to one side (see Fig. 4.3), although each holds three to four times the number of prisoners than available spaces. The gates to the cells are generally left open between seven and eight in the morning and four and five in the afternoon. Prison staff ordinarily have no need to enter the wings and are stationed either at the entrance to the prison or in the corridor running between them. Besides the barred gate entrances to the wings, there is limited visibility. From the corridor, there is no way for a guard to see what is going on in the cells.

Fig. 4.2 A wooden model of a modern remand prison in São Paulo, showing the main cell block with the roof removed from the central corridor and cells on four of the prison's ten wings. The first two wings, to the forefront of the picture, contain the *seguro* to the viewer's left and the *isolamento* to the viewer's right. The other wings all house gang-affiliated prisoners

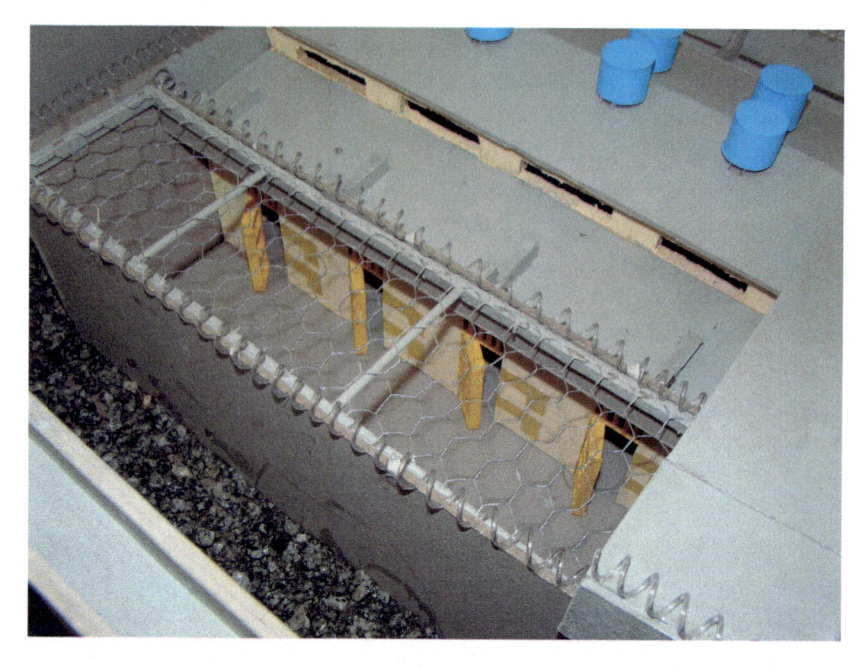

Fig. 4.3 A wooden model of a modern remand prison in São Paulo, showing the entrances to the four cells on one of the gang wings, and the *pátio* that prisoners have access to during the day

I have visited two remand prisons in São Paulo. As mentioned in Chapter 2, the first visit, to Belém II in 2008, was my first experience of entering a functioning Brazilian prison. I was escorted through the prison by the governor and head of security and otherwise encountered no more than half a dozen other prison guards besides those stationed at the outer prison wall. Prisoners were not under observation in the *pátios*, but at the entrance to one of the wings I noted two guards in conversation with inmate leaders. I discovered later that its sister prison, Belém I, had been found to be operating with a total of 15 officers despite having 2000 prisoners (Miraglia and Salla 2008). Several years later I visited an almost identical remand prison an hour drive from São Paulo city. The prison was operating with approximately 2100 prisoners and 110 staff, of which a maximum of 12 officers were on duty each shift. To make matters worse, one officer per shift had been withdrawn from guarding duties to make up for shortages in administration. Officers were not required to enter the wings to lock up prisoners. At the end of the day, inmate leaders would send prisoners back to their cells before the entrances to the cells were closed electronically.

How Brazilian prisons manage with 100–200 prisoners for each officer on duty, and up to 400 prisoners per officer stationed in the cell blocks, is the major subject of this book. I turn to the ways and means by which inmates explicitly and implicitly negotiate prison order with each other and with prison staff later. First it is necessary to explore the cultural conditions that make such collaborative governance possible.

Conviviality

Before I started researching in Brazil, I had never found much use for the words *éticas* (ethics), *convivência* (conviviality), *coletivo* or *convívio* (both here meaning collective, *coletivo* as a concrete noun as well as an adjective; *convívio* as an abstract noun) in the context of prisons. Over the past eight years of fieldwork, I have increasingly come to realise the way these words are used by Brazilian inmates is crucial to understanding how prisoners relate to one another, and how the institutions in which they are incarcerated operate. Quite different to my experiences of visiting and teaching[5] in English prisons, my interviews and informal conversations in Brazilian prisons about everyday prison governance inevitably end up being drawn towards issues relating to how inmates have to negotiate prison life among themselves and with prison staff to the tiniest detail so as to get by with limited resources: what we might call a prison's informal dynamics of survival.[6] To a greater or lesser extent, I have also found direct or indirect references to these two themes—coexistence and co-survival—alongside the wider issue of prisoner participation in each of the ethnographic, historical and firsthand accounts of Brazilian prison life I review in this book, most but not all of which written about Rio de Janeiro or São Paulo: principally, Arruda (2015), Bassani (2016), Beattie (2015), Biondi (2010), Chazkel (2009),

Coelho (2005), Dias (2013), Karam and Saraiva (2017), Lima (1991), Lourenço and Almeida (2013), Marques (2014), Mendes (2009, 2015), Ramalho (2002), Ramos (2015), Rap and Zeni (2002), Silva (2011), and Varella (2008, 2012).

As I have come to understand it, to be part of the *coletivo*,[7] and subject to its *éticas/regras do convívio*,[8] is to come under the mutual protection and aid of the inmate body: to be recognised and recognise your fellow prisoners as victims of a historical system of injustice that starts with precarious conditions of living in poor, urban areas—in Rio de Janeiro referred to in general as the *comunidade* (community); in São Paulo as the *periferia* (periphery) or *quebrada* (broken)—and ends in an overcrowded and unhealthy prison. To be ejected or not to be accepted into the *coletivo* (as a sex offender, contract killer, police informant, drug addict or affiliate of a different gang, for example) means to join the ranks of the police and prison guards, in the street and prison slang of São Paulo to become a *coisa* (thing) (Biondi 2014) or in Rio de Janeiro an *alemão* (German) (Barbosa 2005; Goldstein 2003). Those with no place among the *coletivo* have no choice but to get out, to move onto the *seguro* or, if they cannot live by the rules of communal living there either, to move onto the *isolamento*. Yet to be outside the *coletivo*—in São Paulo not to be identified as a *ladrão* (thief), *homen sujeito* (fellow man) or *cara de proceder* (procedure man) (Marques 2014)—does not always mean to be an enemy. This also applies to "good cops" and "good officers". The real enemy of the *coletivo* is the punitive state. To repeat a key point from Chapter 3, it is the institution of the state, not its servants, against which the *coletivo* is ultimately opposed, as the following officers' accounts of working at CV and Third Command (TC) prisons in Rio de Janeiro make clear:

> In CV units everything has to be negotiated. They have an inmate council with legitimacy to create consensus in order to avoid disagreements. […] My objective is to always maintain the respect that exists between the prisoner and the guard… This respect is not constructed by force but by the righteousness of my conduct inside. Nobody disturbs me, because they can see that I'm doing my job in the right way. (Karam and Saraiva 2017: 1, 5)

The TC's discipline is not the same as the CV's. The CV's conception of *coletivo* is much stronger. [...] The prisoners say "this guard is a fellow man"... If you work within their legality, their ethics, you will not suffer any form of retaliation. The prisoners know when an inmate is wrong: even when you reprimand this inmate, the other prisoners do not go against you... you also cannot become known as a quitter. (Karam and Saraiva 2017: 2, 5)

Besides Biondi (2013, 2014), I have not come across the words *éticas*, *convivência*, *convívio* or *coletivo* in any anthropological studies of crime and justice in Brazil's poor, urban areas, although Feltran (2011, 2012) and Hirata (2010) refer to their participants entering the *convívio* rather than the *seguro* when discussing experiences of going to PCC controlled prisons. I return to the work of Biondi and Feltran in a moment.

However, collective identity and consciousness of repression are enduring themes in nearly all research in Brazil's *favelas/quebradas*. As I emphasised in Chapter 2, young Brazilian men from the urban ghettos are used to being regarded, and often regard themselves, as career criminals, as *bandidos* (outlaws) or *ladrões* (thieves) just for the fact that they are poor and do not work in the formal, licit economy. It is often noted that Brazil's twentieth-century dictatorships met minimal public resistance in part due to a lack of class consciousness amongst its population. This has not been my experience since I first visited the country in 1993. Among prisoners in particular, there is little pretence that things could be otherwise. They quite openly describe themselves as in conflict with the law. The shared sense of community that arises from such recognition of mutual suffering inevitably plays a part in encouraging cultures and institutions of mutual aid and protection.

In her account of the everyday struggles of women in a *favela* in Rio de Janeiro, Donna Goldstein (2003) describes the use of black humour as a tool of defiance to the structural inequalities of class, race and gender. Although Goldstein does not focus specifically on young people or collective responses to suffering, she writes extensively on both of these issues in the context of young men's involvement in gangs. Goldstein emphasises *favela* community cohesion is built upon opposition to the police, and that gangs would continue to be a major part of community life even without the drug trade. Gangs, she explains, provide communities with means of dispute resolution and young men with a means of identity that they are unable to obtain in the formal economy. In the absence of a legitimate police and judicial system, the community she studied tolerated gang violence and even police violence so long as it was seen to be fairly applied and its victims deserving. The major concern was that their community increasingly went through "cycles of calm and violence" (Goldstein 2003: 176) as wiser heads—both gang leaders and local police officers—were sometimes deposed by younger, more volatile men or by "bad police" interested in extorting rather than working with the community.

In contrast to the women at the centre of the study, however, Goldstein (2003) describes young men's oppositional culture as ultimately destructive and apolitical. In my view, this is not the only conclusion Goldstein might have drawn from her data presented. Goldstein is keen not to describe the gang lifestyle in which many poor, young men get involved as wholly irrational and emerging from false consciousness. Citing the classic works on British and American subaltern street culture of Stuart Hall (1991) and Philippe Bourgois (1995), she utilises cultural production theory to explain how young men growing up in poverty are conscious of who they are and remain agents of their own futures, but are limited in the choices they can make, especially how to succeed in the legal economy. Nevertheless, she could have gone one step further. "They, like most people in the United States", Bourgois (1995: 54) writes in regard to his Latin American-descendent New York City crack-dealing participants, "firmly believe in individual responsibility. For the most part, they attribute their marginal living conditions to their own psychological or moral failings [….] Like most people in the United States, drug dealers and street criminals are scrambling to obtain their piece of the pie as fast as possible" (ibid.: 326). Bourgeois' participants, in other words, considered conventional success to be a possibility, and something for which they should really strive. In contrast, the young Brazilian men with whom Goldstein engaged had "very few success stories other than soccer players and musicians" (Goldstein 2003: 99) to provide counter-narratives.[9] They were aware they could never earn enough money legally to achieve what was socially expected of them as husbands and fathers, and while they might be scornful to others that worked for slave wages, they did not lack so much solidarity with their wider community. Similarly, Goldstein's participants had quite different life chances to the young black American men at the centre of Elijah Anderson's (1999) ethnography of 1980s poverty in the city of Philadelphia. Anderson's participants had a black middle class to which to aspire. Their neighbourhoods were divided between those that turned to the oppositional culture and violence of the streets and those that remained determined to get by through legitimate means, and despite understanding there were structural barriers to success in poor, black communities, blamed others for not doing the same. The informal networks of community support and protection Goldstein describes as emerging from gang culture in the *favela* were driven by more than the young men's investment in masculine, patriarchal culture and the lure of drugs money. Their oppositional culture was less destructive. It was also shaped, or at least tempered in good measure by their community's need for some form of governance institution in place of the police.

More specifically relevant to my focus on community self-governance are Boaventura Santos' (2002) analysis of the use of quasi-legal forms of dispute prevention and settlement by a residents association in a *favela* in Rio de Janeiro, Benjamin Penglase's (2009, 2010) analysis of the relationships between the CV, local communities and the police, also in a *favela* in Rio de Janeiro, and Gabriel Feltran's (2010, 2011, 2012) analysis of PCC governance and community politics in the periphery of the city of São Paulo. Santos refers to the *favela* he studied as Pasargada. He originally conducted his research in 1970, several years prior to the birth of the CV and PCC and Brazil's emergence as a player in the international trade in cocaine, but at a time when *favelas/quebradas* had already emerged as loci for the sale of cocaine and cannabis to local drug consumers. While the civil disputes the residents association dealt with were mostly over property, they often also involved matters of nuisance and minor criminal activity. However, the residents association avoided getting involved in accusations of crime, in part due to fear of drug dealers and other career criminals, but mostly due to the community's negative relationship with the police. The residents association knew it would lose the faith of the community if it were to report crime to such an ostracised institution as the police. If, on the other hand, it were to deal with criminal matters itself, it could "expose itself to the arbitrary actions of an authoritarian state, and might be outlawed" (Santos 2002: 115).

Santos (2002) does not discuss the position of young people in the *favela*. Of importance for the present study, like Goldstein (2003) he is unequivocal about the Pasargada community's understanding of their socio-economic standing in Brazilian society. Santos concludes:

> Pasargada law is an example of an informal and unofficial legal system developed by urban oppressed classes... to achieve the survival of the community... In this instance, class conflict is characterized by mutual avoidance... and adaptation... Pasargada law achieves its informality and flexibility through selective borrowing from the official legal system... the Brazilian state has tolerated a settlement it defines as illegal... it has allowed the settlement to acquire a status we may call alegal or extralegal. (Santos 2002: 155)

By the early twenty-first century, Rio de Janeiro's residents associations had been forced to cede much of their power to drug gangs, who ended the practice of locally electing resident association leaders and killed or evicted those that were opposed to gang rule (Gay 2009; Perlman 2009). At the same time, gangs like the CV have become more splintered and volatile as the lure of drugs money has gradually taken precedence over community protection in the eyes of young people, and the CV's original members have been replaced by younger men (Penglase 2009). Penglase's (2009, 2010) ethnography paints a less solidaristic picture of community-gang-local cop relations than that of Goldstein (2003) conducted just a decade earlier. Penglase (2009) describes the security provided by gangs as illegitimate and police dealings with gangs as corrupt (cf. Zaluar 1994). Violent police intrusions into the *favela*, he claims, are used by the CV as an excuse to justify their protection rackets and the continuing of a wholly asymmetric system of power. Still, the participants he quotes in his study spoke as favourably of the role gangs played in regulating violence in the community as the participants quoted by Goldstein, which they likewise contrasted heavily to the arbitrary violence of the institution of the police. Like Goldstein, Penglase finds the gang in the *favela* he studied to be currently headed by a popular *dono do morro* (owner of the hillside), in contrast his participants told him to other parts of the city. What concerned residents was what might happen when this CV leader was eventually deposed, killed or arrested. Penglase might also have interpreted his findings differently. While his research participants he quotes spoke in terms of reciprocity, Penglase concludes that, "far from being founded on consensus, drug trafficking power in [the *favela*] was founded upon a highly unequal and uneven exchange, built out of fear and the threat of violence *as much as* upon social ties" (Penglase 2009: 55—emphasis added).

In an ethnographic study of PCC dominated *quebradas* in the peripheries of São Paulo, Feltran (2010, 2011, 2012) is less reluctant to describe local gang-community-police relations as relatively stable and legitimate. While Penglase warns against taking the stance of those involved in drug trafficking and gang activity, Feltran does not distinguish between the reliability of the views expressed by his research participants and pays specific attention to the voices of young adults. Like Santos (2002) and Goldstein (2003), Feltran also puts class politics at the centre of his analysis. Any study of the relationship between ghettos and the public sphere in a country as asymmetric and hierarchical as Brazil, Feltran (2011) emphasises, must take three polar opposites between political philosophical theories and social realities as its starting point: the distance between, egalitarianism and social inequality, the rule of law and police repression, and pluralism and access to power. These three themes resonate with my own take on the openly repressive nature of law and criminal justice in the country outlined in Chapter 2. Feltran (2011) goes on to demonstrate ways in which families and grass roots social movements in the *periferia* draw on their understanding of the collective suffering of their geographical communities in their responses to the gradual drift of young men from the world of work to the world of crime.

As for the prison gang phenomenon, at the time of Feltran's research (the mid- to late 1990s) the PCC was little more than a decade old, yet had already established control over most of São Paulo's prison system and much of São Paulo city's *periferia*. In contrast to Penglase's (2009) analysis of CV-community relations, Feltran (2011) demonstrates the PCC was rapidly attaining hegemony among the people it governed in place of the police. Furthermore, the PCC regulated street crime with the implicit agreement of local police (Feltran 2010, 2012). As Willis (2015, 2016) illustrates through ethnographic research conducted on homicide detectives in the city, such "bottom up legality" (Willis 2016: 37), parallel power (Leeds 1996), violent pluralism (Arias and Goldstein 2010) or my preferred term co-governance played a part in a two-thirds drop in homicide in São Paulo in the first decade of the twenty-first century alongside socio-demographic changes such as a falling youth population and economic prosperity (Peres et al. 2011; cf. Feltran 2012; Manso 2012, 2016; Willis 2009). The total number of homicides fell from 12,818 recorded cases in 1999 to 4320 in 2010 (Folha de São Paulo, 1 February 2011). By the mid-2000s, the PCC had not only begun to regulate drug markets, but had also institutionalised a pre-existing system of community dispute resolution, *debates* (debates), to deal with accusations of violence and theft committed by *bandidos* or *homens de crime* (men of crime) against their own communities, and governed by the *lei de crime* (law of crime) (Feltran 2010) rather than the law of the land. This quasi-legal system would run alongside resident association-run systems of civil dispute resolution, and also the official criminal justice system, which was reserved for the crimes of other citizens: *trabalhadores* (workers). Feltran found local police officers and PCC leaders not only knew each other, but actively negotiated in the exchange of offenders and bribes.

A second ethnographic study of ghetto life that draws specifically upon the voices of young people, albeit not young men involved in street gangs or in the drug trade, is Roxana Cavalcanti's (2016b, 2017) study of police-youth relations in Recife, Pernambuco. Cavalcanti does not focus on issues of self-governance or coexistence. However, her study is particularly relevant here for its depth of empirical detail on political consciousness among ghetto residents. Moreover, it is possibly the only detailed ethnographic study to give voice to young men's experiences of repressive crime control practices in the north of Brazil. Like the participants in Goldstein's (2003) and Feltran's (2010, 2011) research, what is striking about the young people Cavalcanti interviewed and observed is their depth of understanding of the structural conditions under which their peers turned to gangs and became victims of police violence. In contrast to these and other ethnographic studies of *favelas* and *quebradas* in Rio de Janeiro and São Paulo, however, Cavalcanti finds her participants to be less critical of the police than of drug gangs, who she emphasises are not so organised in the north of the country as they are in the south. Cavalcanti also finds her participants to have well-developed notions of what an accountable and ethical police force might look like. One of her 17-year-old respondents explains:

> We need the demilitarisation of the police. The way it is now, they don't make us feel safer, they don't protect the community, their impact is negative. They don't respect residents – and if you're poor, you're treated like a bandit. (Fieldwork interview, Cavalcanti 2016b: 211)

My final example of conviviality and co-governance in Brazilian ghettos comes from the work of Karina Biondi in São Paulo. I have already referred to Biondi's work numerous times in this book. Alongside Camila Dias, whose work I cover in some detail in Chapter 6, Biondi is Brazil's leading academic expert on the PCC. She is also unique in being the only ethnographer of crime to have conducted in-depth studies inside as well as outside prison, the former of which conducted while visiting her partner, who was serving time in a PCC prison. Some of her work has been translated or more recently first published in English (Biondi 2010, 2017b, c, d, 2019). As I have already noted, a central concern of all of Biondi's research is the organisational structure—or rather the absence of structure—of the PCC, whose presence, I also indicated in Chapter 3, is claimed by inmates in prisons that have very few, if any official "baptised" gang members (*irmãos* or *irmãs*: brothers or sisters) at all (Biondi 2010). Most relevant here is Biondi's doctoral research conducted in a provisional town outside the capital city (Biondi 2014), part of which was published as Biondi (2013). The main findings of the study are summarised in the afterword to the English version of Biondi (2010).

Biondi (2014) is ultimately a postmodern anthropological study that gives weight to the standpoints and knowledge of her participants and aims to deconstruct existing political and social scientific theories on governance, in particular the notions of territory, hierarchy and law. Building upon her previous master's degree prisons research (published as Biondi 2010), which found the PCC to be a loose, heterogeneous organisation, Biondi (2014) describes the PCC not as a whole but as a coming together of numerous and constantly shifting "movements" without territorial or temporal limits. As a result, the leadership of the PCC is neither fixed, organised or all powerful. Nor, as we saw in Chapter 3, is its ideology or its *salves*, which Biondi (2013) suggests are better understood as recommendations than as codes or commands. In contrast to the formal legal system, even its system of dispute resolution, its *debates*, are largely indeterminate. PCC *debates* are based on legal notions of procedural propriety—requiring witness testimony, pleas for mitigation and majority guilt finding—but they do not adhere to notions of legal precedence or judicial seniority (cf. Feltran 2011). Their factual outcomes (guilt or innocence) depend on the consensus of opinion among those who happen to be there (Biondi 2014; cf. Marques 2010a, 2014).

I return to Biondi's work in more detail in Chapter 6, in the context of prison gangs. Just two points need introducing to wrap up here. First, Biondi's aim is not to depoliticise ghetto self-governance or to downplay the significance or legitimacy of the PCC. Quite the opposite, she applies her ontological framework to the PCC's most enduring, guiding principles, principally those of *paz* (peace), *justiça* (justice), *luta* (fight), *liberdade* (liberty), *união* (union), *ética* (ethics) and *igualdade* (equality). Distinguishing her work from that of her colleague and fellow PCC researcher Adalton Marques (2010a, b, 2014), Biondi explains her focus to be the internal dynamics of the PCC: to describe variation in meaning and understanding "inside of the PCC" (Biondi 2014: 34), not to question the work of those that focus their efforts on exploring the origins and consequences of the PCC's ideologies.

Second and more generally is Biondi's emphasis on the informality of the PCC's justice. Returning to the points I developed from the work of Hess (1995) and Jefferson (2013) in Chapter 2, and my introduction to the term *jeito* (way) in Chapter 1, it might be said that Brazil has always been postmodern in the sense that irrespective of the country's visible and undeniable social inequalities and injustices, everyday human relations are shaped just as much by everyday social interactions as they are by socio-economic circumstances, and are characterised by flexibility and negotiation. This might be more obvious to a foreign observer whose first points of reference are the bureaucracies of the Global North. In a recent reflection on her research, Biondi arrives at a point that to me is not at all surprising now I have grown accustomed to the chaos of a country in the Global South:

> This phantom-like presence of the PCC even compelled me to abandon the ethnographic pursuit of multi-locality – according to which the PCC would be simultaneously active in several places – on behalf of an ethnographic approach that attempted to explore how everyday mundane micro-political practices could generate something like "the PCC". (Biondi 2019: n.p.)

Co-governance

It is hardly surprising that the Brazilian poor should be somewhat unified in opposition to class adversity at this historical juncture. Brazil is a nation in conflict. The post-dictatorship, neoliberal economic reforms of the late twentieth century left the country extremely divided. Democratisation reinforced to the poor that they were not biologically or socially inferior and did not need to defer to unjust authority. Moreover, today Brazilian society is as much socially as economically divided (Caldeira 1996, 2000). Poor people are systematically and blatantly excluded from middle-class residential areas and shopping malls, increasingly even from their beaches.

In Chapter 2, we saw that since the days of African and indigenous slavery, Brazilian elites have consistently used the rule of law as a tool of repression. Marxist conflict theories have been utilised by social and political scientists and historians to correlate violent and manifest oppression with intra-class division and violence. Catholicism and more recently evangelicalism act as particularly powerful conservative counter forces to working class solidarity. So too terrestrial television, whose live peak time news regularly includes journalists visiting crime scenes and police stations to interview victims, witnesses and perpetrators.[10] Paternalistic attitudes towards the poor also help maintain a sense of class inferiority (Goldstein 2003; Santos 2002). As for crime, desire to possess the latest material goods undoubtedly pushes some people into predatory behaviour and normalised violence, as it does anywhere else. Masculinity is also a particular concern. Machismo has been identified as one of the main drivers of both domestic and street violence across Latin America (Karstedt 2001). With limited career prospects in the licit economy young men turn to violence as a means of performing masculinity. For some, serious violence comes to be regarded a rite of passage to mark their transition from boys to men (Drybread 2014). Young men involved in gangs may resort to serious violence as an expressive means of reaffirming their power (Penglase 2010).

Yet oppression also produces resistance. Brazilian socio-economic inequalities are too extreme, too open and too institutionalised to divide the poor to the same extent that they are in the neoliberal economies of the Global North. Or indeed to produce quite the same degree of mismatch between socio-economic expectations and opportunities that Northern strain theory has identified as underlying much interpersonal violence. There is no real Brazilian dream to speak of. Few pretend someone from the ghetto can make it into the ranks of the middle classes so long as they try hard enough. Extreme inequality is as much a root cause of anger and frustration in Brazil as it would be anywhere else. However, anger and frustration are causes of solidarity as well as violence.

More surprising perhaps is that cultures of mutual protection and survival shape aspects of life in Brazil's impoverished prisons as well as its impoverished ghettos. Studies of prison life in the UK, for example, are unequivocal in linking prison overcrowding and other material deprivations with institutional neurosis, anxiety and depression, and ultimately poor mental health and violence, both self-inflicted and directed towards others (for an overview of the pains of imprisonment in the UK, see Scott and Codd 2010).

In Chapter 2, we also saw Brazilian prison conditions can be extraordinarily inhumane, and that interpersonal violence—but less so self-inflicted violence—is a major concern. At the same time, however, levels of violence vary enormously prison to prison, and from one year to another, and in ways that do not always bear relation to variation in material conditions. For instance, 55 prisoners were murdered in the Curado prison complex in 2008 (Inter-American Court of Human Rights 2014), but a much smaller number, 13 prisoners, between August 2011 and February 2014 (Pastoral Carcerária et al. 2014). A recent spate of violence in the complex resulted in the deaths of 12 prisoners from January to August 2016 (Inter-American Court of Human Rights 2016). There were 280 recorded murders in Central Prison over a four-year period, 2009–2012, but none in 2013 (Inter-American Court of Human Rights 2013). In the past few years, there have been several suspicious deaths at the prison, in which murders are likely to have been disguised as drug overdoses, but there has been a dramatic drop in violent deaths overall (Sager and Beto 2016).[11]

These figures suggest that like its *favelas* and *quebradas*, Brazil's prisons go through cycles of relative calm and violence, depending on who has the right over life and death and how strong is their authority. Gangs regulate violence in prisons across much of the country, but they are often both internally and externally unstable. Their leaders may be challenged by other prisoners lower down the gang hierarchy. They may also be challenged by rival gangs, or they may lose the confidence of their *coletivo*. They tend to work with limited resources and may rely on the collaboration of prison staff as much as other prison inmates. Major incidences of calculated prison violence are often symptoms of temporal restructurings in governance. This may take some time—for instance, the PCC took six years to gain control of the maximum security Jair Ferreira de Carvalho prison, introduced in Chapter 3, after authorities began transferring prisoners there from São Paulo in 2000, during which time rival gang leaders were often murdered and decapitated—or they might be settled by an incidence of extreme violence like that witnessed in the Anísio Jobim prison complex in 2017. At the same time, orchestrated violence may have the undesired effect of temporarily unleashing irrational, expressive violence (Green and Ward 2009). We saw the prisoners involved in the Anísio Jobim massacre were most likely motivated by matters of territory and group identity, but that once the Família do Norte's initial objective to kill PCC affiliates had been achieved, the emotions of the killers took over.

Still, the point remains that Brazilian prison gangs increase levels of mutual aid and protection on the whole. This is the focus of Chapter 6. To give some figures on reductions in violence in the country's most gang-dominated prison systems for now, in São Paulo the number of recorded violent deaths in prison fell from 117 in 1999, when the PCC was still in its infancy, to 14 in 2016, and this despite a 350% rise in the number of prisoners (Biondi 2017a). Rio de Janeiro, whose prison system has been dominated by the CV and other major gangs since the 1980s, recorded 7 violent prison deaths in 2013, 10 violent prison deaths in 2015 and 6 violent prison deaths in the first seven months of 2017 (Costa and Bianchi 2017). We will see Rio de Janeiro's prisons are generally less stable than São Paulo's prisons[12]—note, for example, that 21 violent deaths were recorded in 2016 (ibid.). Nevertheless, with an inmate population of over 40,000, even 21 violent deaths makes Rio de Janeiro's prisons some of the safest in the country.

In Chapter 1, I noted Skarbek's (2014) analysis of the role gangs have played in reducing violence in North American prisons. Skarbek utilises rational choice theory to demonstrate prison violence is largely predictable when inmates lack other means to deal with conflicts in their cooperative pursuits for social order and economic activity, for example over money lent and borrowed. In a more recent paper, Skarbek (2016) explores literature on inmate self-governance with in other parts of the world, including my own work on Brazil, and extends his analysis beyond his initial focus on extra-legal regulation of illicit markets to more basic areas of potential everyday conflicts among prisoners. In Brazil, reported examples of *regras de convívio/proceder* utilised to govern everyday relations between prisoners in different prisons include: not winding up (*xingando*) other inmates (an example given to me by a Rio de Janeiro remand prison officer I spoke with in 2016: see Chapter 3); maintaining hygienic living conditions, whereby all inmates have regular showers and wear flip-flops rather than shoes in their cells (examples cited from former prisoner memoirs in Marques 2014; and by Apple 2017, in an interview with the partner of a man imprisoned in the early 2010s); wearing t-shirts and allowing privacy during family visits, especially when it is someone's turn to have sex with their partner in the cell (ibid.); burning a twisted strip of toilet paper after going to the toilet to help disguise the smell (also cited from prisoner memoirs in Marques 2014); being able to eat in peace, with no one brushing their teeth or going to the toilet before you are finished (Coelho 2005); having a period of quiet to sleep, and the right to progress—typically from the toilet to the *praia* (beach or floor), at first besides the toilet, later towards the back of the cell, and eventually up to one of the *beliches* (bunk beds)— the longer you are have been in the cell (ibid.) or in prison (Biondi 2010, 2013); not wearing dark glasses (an example given by a prisoner interviewed in Arruda 2015); not showering during visiting times (Bassani 2016); and having to share out the food and other basic goods brought in by your family in their weekly *jumbos* (introduced in Chapter 1) with your cellmates in order, for instance, that everyone gets something more than the same old prison food to eat—*marmitas* (meal boxes), typically composed of rice, spaghetti, a few beans, a few bits of vegetable and some lumps of beef, mixed together in an aluminium bowl—to eat (another example given in Apple 2017, and an example I return to in my own fieldwork presented in the following chapter).

Rational choice theory goes a long way towards explaining the need for such informal rules to govern relations between people living in such proximity as prisoners do in Brazil. To repeat a second key point first made in Chapter 1, conflict is only in the interest of the toughest and most predatory of prisoners. Forced to share small spaces and scarce resources, Brazilian prisoners are particularly exposed to situations of potential conflict, and once they are involved have little place to hide. In this sense, collective self-governance emerges out of necessity. With so few human or material resources at their disposal, prison officers likewise have little choice but to cooperate with prison inmates to get their jobs done (Moraes 2005).

What is more difficult to explain through rational choice theory is the origins of prison order, or the ways in which prison order evolves, and in one place compared to another. These questions require a cultural analysis (Kaminski 2004). Nor is rational choice theory well suited to explaining how the human need for governance and protection is achievable in prisons quite as dehumanising as many are in Brazil; and moreover, from a rule utilitarian position, why prisoners form pro-social cultures of mutual aid that are not always in their individual interests and/or go beyond purely rational, economic reasoning and into the realm of moral choices.[13] Neither does rational choice theory fully explain why Brazilian prisoners appear to better survive psychologically and are less likely to resort to harming themselves than their counterparts in the Northern world. Self-interest and limited choices play some part in most decisions to self-harm (Gambetta 2009; Kaminski 2004). Most self-inflicted harms in prison are essentially cries for help and most prison suicides are essentially accidental (Scott and Codd 2010). Maybe some Brazilian prisoners do not ultimately resort to self-harm because they have little to gain from prison authorities and/or little to escape—bullying, extortion and so on—from other prisoners. However, many others will not need to contemplate self-harm or suicide in the first place.

To make further sense of these apparent contradictions, it is useful to expand on two further points initially made in Chapter 1. First of these is the sheer volume of human interaction. Despite their overcrowding, Brazilian prisons continue to be hives of everyday activity, professional, interpersonal and social relations and negotiations, in sharp contrast to the increasingly inactive and isolating prison regimes in many parts of Western Europe and Northern America. We have seen Brazilian prisoners typically sleep in multi-occupancy cells of at least four people, and that these cells are generally unlocked during daylight hours, in some of Brazil's most overcrowded prisons during the night time as well. For many prisoners time out of cell means no more than access to wing corridors and *pátios*. For up to one in ten prisoners it also means time to earn small amounts of money and their legal right to a day's remission in sentence for every three days officially working for the prison administration as trusty *faxina*. A further one in eight prisoners gain remission for their involvement in full-time (four hours a day) education.[14] In addition to remission, close to one in seven inmates gain the opportunity to earn a higher salary in prison workshops and/or for private contractors. Of the prisons I have visited, Sant'Ana was most progressive in this regard. The workshops that were built at the end of each wing corridor in the early twentieth century are still in full use today.[15] Approximately one third (800) of its inmates were in full-time paid work when I was last there in 2017. Another 120 were in full-time education.

Even disciplinary measures do not usually result in isolation. The cells on Sant'Ana's *isolamento* each hold up to seven women (Antunes 2016). But for the relatively small number of those held in single cells in high security prisons (in supermax facilities, under the RDD regime, or up to 30 days for breaching prison rules), Brazilian prisoners therefore serve little of their time alone. In certain regards these conditions of communal, yet overcrowded living are an extreme version of the painful and debilitating conditions described in the classic sociological and social psychological accounts of Sykes (1958) and Goffman (1961) of a high security prison and a secure psychiatric hospital in mid-twentieth-century USA. One of both Sykes' and Goffman's main concerns was the effect on inmates of lack of privacy, in particular (to utilise Goffman's phraseology) the effects of contamination and exposure. It is virtually impossible for Brazilian prisoners to maintain personal space or to keep secrets. Prison authorities have few records on the people under their care, but prisoners get to know a lot about each other. In this sense, Brazilian prisons are qualitatively very different. Prisoners naturally develop interpersonal and pro-social skills as well as skills of reciprocal exchange and conflict negotiation when living so close to others. Or at least the conditions in which they find themselves are less conducive to them losing the skills with which they entered prison. When we discussed explanations for the relatively low number of self-inflicted deaths in Brazilian prisons during one of the classes at Penitenciária Feminina do Butantã, São Paulo (see Chapter 2), inside students emphasised the importance of interpersonal, affective relationships. They added that most women experienced same-sex relationships in prison. A number of women referred to their partner inside prison as their husband or wife. Antunes (2016) also notes the importance of romantic and sexual relationships among prisoners in her ethnographic research at Sant'Ana prison, where most of the women I taught had started their sentence; as does Varella (2017) in his reflections on working voluntarily at Sant'Ana since 2006.

Following from this are everyday dealings between cell block *faxina*, trusty and prison staff, in particular the few staff that continue to work in the cell blocks, in the *miolo* (core). When I started researching Brazilian prisons in the late 1990s, I did not anticipate the extent I would find inmate self-governance to be accepted by guards, and conversely the extent to which the functions performed by prison guards, including trusty *faxinas* working alongside guards, to be accepted by prisoners. Again, these relationships are usually, but not always restricted to reciprocal or economic exchanges. We have seen prisoners distinguish between "bad guards" that rely on arbitrary violence and "good guards" that respect their *éticas*. For their part, prison guards find themselves being drawn into inmate cultures (see, inter alia, Coelho 2005; Mendes 2015; Moraes 2005; Varella 2008).

Second is the contact Brazilian prisons, or at least Brazilian men's prisons, retain with their local community. Brazilian prisons and communities are materially as well as symbolically connected (Moore 2017). I have noted prison authorities rely on inmates' families to make up for shortages in basic provisions much as they rely on the inmates themselves to collaborate and self-govern. More than 400,000 people are registered to visit prisoners in São Paulo (Godoi 2016). In 2012, prison authorities in Rio Grande do Sul recorded over one million visits to its 30,000 prisoners (Bassani 2016). This included 260,000 visits to Central Prison, up to 1700 each Saturday and Sunday (ibid.). In São Paulo, there were more than two million registered prison visits in the first half of 2013 (Godoi 2015). Family visits naturally keep prisoners in closer contact with the outside world than would be the case otherwise. Provisions are delivered by inmates' families both outside and during visiting times. During visiting and other *jumbo* delivery times, impromptu street markets arise around prisons as merchants sell their wares to better off families to save them from having to purchase and travel with everything in advance (The best off can order deliveries online; one delivery company has developed a *jumbo* Android Application). Most male prisoners receive weekly visits for up to four hours unsupervised in the *pátios*, where they will eat together and, if space allows, might go for a walk together. Many of these prisoners will also receive intimate visits, usually during ordinary visiting hours in the vacated cells. Rotas for intimate visits are normally left to the *coletivo* (Bassani 2016; Godoi 2016). In England and Wales, by contrast, most prisoners are allowed two visits a month, lasting up to two hours. Prisoners usually receive their visitors in a hall where they are monitored by guards and CCTV cameras (Hutton 2016). A Brazilian prisoner's right to two-hour weekly visits is among the few laws that is respected and often exceeded by prison authorities. Popular criticism of intimate visits focuses not on the rights it gives to prisoners, but on stories, not too far from reality, of visitors forming sexual relations with prisoners they had never met on the outside. When I explained to a group of inmates at Central Prison that British prisoners were prevented from having sex with their heterosexual partners, I left them in fits of laughter.

The connections between prisons and communities are by no means restricted to contact between prisoners and their families. I doubt any Northern prisons researcher would not be taken aback the first time they witnessed a long queue of families outside a male prison on a Saturday or Sunday morning patiently waiting with their *jumbos*. Less visible but also significant are the volunteers that provide vital services to prisoners. These include professionally qualified medical staff, as previously mentioned, lawyers and educationalists, prison reform and prisoner support groups, and above all churches. They also include university students like the ones I accompanied to Bangu II in 2010 and Butantã in 2016. My 2016 visit to Central Prison also included a rehabilitation project run by a lawyer with the support of dozens of volunteers, including university students. More recently I visited the Xuri Prison Complex, Espírito Santo, with a group of law students working voluntarily for the complex's executive judge.

Moreover, Brazilian prisons and communities are interconnected through gangs. In Chapter 3, we saw that much governmental and media analysis of Brazilian prison gangs focuses attention on the role they play in servicing the illicit drug trade on the outside. This interpretation of Brazilian prison gangs tells an important part of the story. However, the picture is more complex and nuanced than this, as I demonstrated in the case of the 2017 northern prison massacres and in my brief overview in this chapter of informal governance in Brazil's urban *favelas* and *quebradas*. The prison gangs-as-protection-racket approach starts from the view gangs are inherently predatory and exclusionary, and that any egalitarian vision groups like the CV and PCC in Brazil might once have honestly claimed to have was eventually corrupted by the lure of the money that could be made from their "captured" markets. It is equally plausible to argue the reality is quite the opposite in Brazil: that prison gangs are shaped more by everyday social interactions and matters of survival; and that the blatant injustices of the war on drugs, of which almost half of prisoners are victims, has further entrenched prisoners' common cause. From this perspective, the term criminal gang is largely misleading. We have seen the poor young men that make up more than half of Brazil's prison population are quite used to being treated as career criminals however much they are actually involved in crime. Being a *bandido* is an identity that is shared with all of their peers that make their living from the illicit economy.

***

In the overcrowded and under-resourced prisons of Brazil, codes of prison conduct have evolved from decades of social interactions that govern almost every aspect of an inmate's relations to others, including prison staff. These are all comparable, but more intense versions of the inmate codes in Northern prisons originally explored in the classic American sociology of prison life literature of the mid-twentieth century (e.g. Clemmer 1940; Irwin 1970; Sykes 1958) and later adapted to the realities of prison life in post-industrial Northern societies today (e.g. in English, Cohen and Taylor 1972; Crewe 2009; Mathiesen 1965; Skarbek 2014). These *regras de convívio/proceder* are, I contend, more strongly tied to inmates' images of themselves as a homogenous group, bound together through poverty and resistance to a punitive state, yet at the same time less concerned with opposing the authority of prison staff. Indeed, many *regras*, especially but not restricted to those designed to govern staff-inmate relations, are negotiated and agreed with guards and prison managers.

In an extensive ethnographic study of prisoner relations and organisation originally conducted at Carandiru prison in the mid-1970s, Ramalho (2002) identified five categories of *regra de proceder* or *lei da massa* (law of the masses). These covered in cell behaviour, commerce, morality, solidarity and dealings with guards. Prisoners Ramalho interviewed at Carandiru referred to themselves as *malandros* (scoundrels or tricksters; people who get round the rules) more than they did *bandidos* or *ladrões*, as was more common in the "pre-PCC" (Dias 2013) era. The term *massa* referred to the *malandro*'s or *bandido*'s collective outlaw identity in prison, although one prisoner explained the *massa* did not discriminate against *trabalhadores*, for example those that had been arrested for drug use or white collar crime, as inside prison everyone suffered the same. Ramalho's interviewees used the term *coletivo* only when referring more specifically to their cellmates.

I introduced examples of common modern-day codes of in cell behaviour earlier in the chapter. At Carandiru in the 1970s, these likewise covered some of the most basic of human needs. Ramalho (2002) gave the following two examples: not touching anything that was not yours, and being quiet and not smoking while others were sleeping. As with the other *leis da massa*, the first layer of responsibility for managing in cell behaviour fell to *juizes da xadrez* (cell judges), usually the longest in the cell, who also represented his cellmates in their dealings with prison guards. Prisoners Ramalho interviewed explained that even food could be the cause of fatal conflict, as some prisoners would save a little of each meal to share with their family during their weekend. Sleep needed to be respected by everyone: "Just because [a *malandro*] is locked up or delinquent, it doesn't mean he should necessarily *não tem educação* (not be educated, in Brazil used in the sense that someone has not been socialised)" (prisoner interviewed in Ramalho 2002: 39). In 2002, the PCC-affiliated prisoner responsible for the fifth floor of cell block nine repeated a similar message on camera in the documentary film O Prisioneiro da Grade de Ferro (The Prisoner of the Iron Bars) (Steinberg and Sacramento 2004). After telling the interviewers—themselves also prisoners held in the same cell block—how important it was to brief new prisoners on the *dia a dia* (day to day) of the prison, he explained, "he needs to learn. He is in prison. Prison is his school".

Codes relating to commerce put equal emphasis on collecting as paying debts. Those that were owed money were equally likely to resort to stealing as those that were in debt to them. At the time, drug debts were not the most serious concern at the prison, as the market in drugs was regulated by (trusty) *faxinas*: "After the sun goes down... everyone is locked up", a prisoner explained, "Not them. Those that work in the *faxina* are free until 9pm. They do not snitch... they carry grass" (Ramalho 2002: 40). With the crack-cocaine epidemic of the 1990s, however, drug debts became a greater concern (Steinberg and Sacramento 2004; Varella 2008). Debts were usually settled on a Monday, sometimes violently for addicts whose families had not brought in money over the weekend (Human Rights Watch 1998; Steinberg and Sacramento 2004). An inmate nurse interviewed for Human Rights Watch (1998) told the researchers 10 prisoners died violently at the prison every year. In Chapter 3, I explained that in the mid- to late 2000s the PCC managed to reduce levels of violence in São Paulo's prisons in large part through banning the sale and consumption of crack. I return to this matter in Chapter 6.

Codes of solidarity were not concerned with maintaining opposition to prison staff but with mutual aid and protection amongst prison inmates, including those that worked for the prison administration. The rule was simple: treat your companions well, most importantly treat the *faxina* well. Regarding the former, one prisoner explained:

> The good *malandro* is one who dispenses his humanity to his companion. He sees his companion cleaning every day and goes up and gives him some support. Even in the other cell I used to live in, when it was my turn to clean, I always had two or three of my companions to help me... But the one that stays in bed, intimidating others to do it, that's the bad *malandro*. He has nothing to do with *malandragem* (trickery), he is ignorant, lacks principles... (Ramalho 2002: 161)

As for the latter, the *massa* depended on *faxinas* not only for the circulation of drugs, but also meals and other material goods. The prison administration also depended on *faxinas*. The prison simply could not operate without them. The same prisoner, who worked as a *faxina* in cell block nine, explained:

> It's the prisoner that does everything. Here a prisoner makes food, a prisoner pays for food, a prisoner does the cleaning. An employee does nothing. An employee only manages, administrates. Watches over you, punishes you if you make a mistake… If the inmates do nothing here, nothing works in the prison. Have a look, you only see inmates working. You just see the employee himself signing paper. (Ramalho 2002: 151)

Other *faxinas* worked and were accommodated in the administration block (cell block two), where they had access to prison administrators and visiting lawyers, both of whom prisoners depended on for their legal rights to early release, family visits, etc. These *faxinas* also had to be relied upon not to inform. Those that did were ostracised by the *massa*. Indeed, only those seen to treat all prisoners equally and to *adiantar o lado do outro* (advance their side) were considered part of the *massa*. A prisoner who worked as an office clerk *faxina*, helping prisoners get the documentation they needed for their families to visit, explained, "they say, that one's a good *malandro*… a decent person" (ibid.: 40). In the following two chapters, we will see prisoners working as trusty *faxina* today continue to tread a fine line between being seen to work for prison authorities—*fechando com a polícia* (closing with the police)—and working with prison authorities on behalf of the *coletivo*. This is a particular concern when prisoners work alongside or in place of guards, especially when they are entrusted with keys.

Codes of morality dealt specifically with sexual relations between prisoners. Homosexual relations were strictly forbidden. Ramalho described this as one of two fundamental rules. A prisoner could not approach another prisoner for sex, and someone offered sex had to enact revenge. However, there were nuances in the meaning of the word homosexual. Two exceptions to the ban on sex between prisoners were allowed. Transvestites, who were regarded as playing the role of women, remained part of the *massa*, as did those with whom they formed relationships or were paid or given favours for casual sex. Older prisoners were also allowed to abuse young prisoners, who were blamed for not being able to defend themselves or being well connected enough to be protected. A prisoner unable to resist abuse was then expected either to work as a prostitute or to form a relationship with one of their abusers, again taking the female role. Today, homosexuality is accepted in some but not all of São Paulo's men's prisons (Salvadori and Dias 2016). We have seen it is regarded as ordinary for women to form sexual relations in at least two major São Paulo prisons. Fortunately, we will see all forms of sexual violence largely disappeared from São Paulo's prisons over the next few decades, as prisoners at first banned sex between older and younger prisoners (Mendes 2015), and cell block *faxina* (Varella 2008) and later the PCC (Biondi 2017a) banned the use of rape and all other forms of violence.

The second fundamental rule, and Ramalho's final category of inmate code, was that prisoners did not inform on each other. While codes against homosexuality were based on maintaining the *massa*'s image of itself as a group of men, codes against informing helped maintain its image as a group of career criminals, and so the division between, "the prisoner and the police, the laws of the *massa* and the rules of the prison" (ibid.: 47). Yet cooperating with prison staff, like sex, was considered an essential part of prison life. Ramalho identified two nuances in the meaning of the word inform as used at the prison.

The first of these nuances follows the previous point regarding the position of the trusty *faxina* working in administration. Some were selected as soon as they arrived at the prison, but most had started in the other cell blocks and were now close to release. They worked alongside or in the place of prison staff in every kind of auxiliary position, as porters, cleaners, office clerks, handymen, cooks, educationalists, nurses, even hairdressers. Ramalho explained that while these prisoners were referred to as informants, other prisoners accepted it was inevitable they would work closely with prison staff, and as I have already emphasised, realised the prison was ungovernable without them. A *faxina* compared his situation to the story of the three little monkeys that do not see, hear or speak. These "three succinct rules"—to see, but to notice nothing, to hear but to remain deaf, and to keep your mouth firmly shut—made up the wider "law of silence" at the prison (Marques 2014: 54). Prison staff understood *faxinas* should never be asked to talk about other inmates outside the immediate context they were dealing with them.

The second exception related to *juizes da xadrez*, who Ramalho described as the point of contact between the two systems of (inmate and prison) rules. A prisoner explained the role of a *juiz da xadrez* as the following:

> The *juiz da xadrez* is the person designated by the chief of discipline, for example, the person who is the oldest in the cell. He has to watch over the cell, to keep order and respect so there is not too much mess... he the second responsible, after the head of discipline. To avoid all those annoyances, conversations, those little things that [prisoners] would usually take to the head of discipline – a complaint that [a cellmate] does not let him sleep, that he messes with him... the head of discipline is obliged, in fact the *juiz da xadrez* is obliged to look at everything to see if the person can remain in the cell or not. If not, then he communicates this to the chief of discipline. (Ramalho 2002: 61).

In other words, order was produced by the *juiz da xadrez* with the support of prison officers working in the cell blocks. The two systems of rules they represented were ultimately compatible. Underlying both was the common desire to prevent conflict. Just as there were good and bad *malandros*, there were good and bad officers. Good officers were those that had most contact and a positive attitude towards the *massa*. It was their job to watch over prisoners to prevent escapes, but also as another inmate put it, "to make sure we don't go without food... and to make sure we don't stab anyone" (ibid.: 64). Like the good *malandro*, the good officer was likely to be experienced, a third inmate explained, one that had become "half a prisoner" (ibid.: 66) due to having worked at the prison twelve hours a day for many years. The governor of the prison at the time was well respected by inmates. New officers, on the other hand, had to be taught the ways of the prison. In Chapter 3, we saw prison managers in São Paulo continue to work closely with prisoner representatives, and still have a say in which prisoners they work with.

As the *faxina*, the *juiz da xadrez* was therefore effectively both prisoner and guard. He occupied an uncertain, often unstable and precarious position somewhere in between. Prison staff had their liberty intact, but as I have already noted in this chapter, they still had to think and act like an inmate to get their jobs done. In the next chapter, we will see the staff-inmate relations Ramalho discovered in São Paulo in the 1970s differed little to those I found in my own study of a *carceragem* in Rio de Janeiro more than forty years later.

Ramalho (2002) stands out as one of just two detailed ethnographic studies of a Brazilian prison completed before the turn of the century. The other, Coelho (2005), introduced earlier in this chapter, described a similar system of co-produced governance in 1980s Rio de Janeiro in which prison routines were mostly administered by (again trusty) *faxinas*—in Rio de Janeiro also referred to as *colaboradores* (collaborators) or more recently in CV prisons *zeladores* (caretakers) (Karam and Saraiva 2017)—while inmate discipline was maintained with the support of *xerifes* (sheriffs; Rio de Janeiro's equivalent at the time to São Paulo's *juizes da xadrez*). Like the *juiz da xadrez*, Rio de Janeiro's *xerife* acted as the *ligação* (link: see Chapter 3) between inmates and the prison administration, representing the former and accounting to the latter. He needed to maintain the confidence and respect of both his cellmates and prison staff. The default position was that the *xerife* should be the person longest in the cell. Coelho also described a figure not mentioned by Ramalho, cell *faxinas*, usually prisoners that did not have family visits, who the *xerife* would select to keep the cell clean in return for their share of some of the goods brought in by other prisoners' families. We will see this tradition continues in Rio de Janeiro in the CV era.

Coelho likewise regarded inmate organisation and staff-inmate cooperation as inevitable aspects of everyday prison governance:

> The discipline, security and relative tranquillity in [our] prisons fundamentally depends on the willingness of the mass incarcerated to spontaneously submit and cooperate… there is no cooperation without

negotiation; and negotiation does not happen without leadership. (Coelho 2005: 36)

Besides instructing their cellmates and reporting and negotiating with officers, however, the *xerife*'s role was largely limited to maintaining in cell hygiene and alimentation. There existed among Rio de Janeiro's prisoners a fundamental rule that *criminoso não manda em criminoso* (a criminal does not tell another criminal what to do). As a result, *xerifes* did not adjudicate or administer penalties for prisoner indiscipline. This remained the responsibility of prison staff.

***

With the emerging of the cell block *faxina* system from the 1980s, today the position of the *juiz da xadrez* has all but disappeared from São Paulo's prison system. Rio de Janeiro's *xerifes*, on the other hand, continue to operate within a two-tiered system that includes cell as well as cell block representation. The prisons I have visited or read about in other Brazilian states are evenly split between these two broad ideal types of staff-inmate co-governance. I explore similarities and differences in today's prison environments between São Paulo, Rio de Janeiro and other Brazilian states in Chapter 6. For now I will focus on commonalities, and on the pre-gang era. I have already noted that the convivial nature of everyday inmate and staff-inmate relations Ramalho (2002) found at Carandiru and Coelho (2005) found in Rio de Janeiro are reflected in the autobiographical accounts of prisoners and prison workers in the two states. Before their prisons came to be dominated by major gangs around the turn of the century, confrontation and violence remained integral parts of the prison experience in these states, but daily interactions between and among prison inmates and prison staff were still governed by professional, interpersonal and social relations, customs and informal regulations that, while undoubtedly fragile, served to mitigate against the strains towards disorder and conflict the under-resourced and under-staffed prison environments otherwise produced.

Two series of first-hand accounts of life at Carandiru and other prisons in the São Paulo serve to illustrate these points. The first is Mendes'

(2005, 2009, 2012, 2015) autobiographical texts on his experiences of serving more than thirty years in custody from the early 1970s, the first of which written and published while he was at Carandiru. Today Mendes works as a writer and as a volunteer on an anti-violence project that he co-designed and delivers at a community prison, Centro de Ressocialização Social de Limeira (Limeira Resocialisation Centre), described in Chapter 7. As a young prisoner, Mendes experienced periods of isolation and beatings, having been arrested for the murder of a security guard, and killing another prisoner soon after arriving at Carandiru prison. Prior to arriving at the prison in 1972, he experienced three months of what he described as intensive torture while held as a 19 year old in police custody. After approximately a year he was transferred to the adjacent Penitenciária do Estado de São Paulo (São Paulo State Penitentiary; today Sant'Ana). Mendes returned to Carandiru 23 years later, having served time in several other prisons. Not surprisingly, he was transferred yet again when his first autobiography was about to be published. He briefly returned to Carandiru for a final time in 2001. His first autobiography, Mendes (2009), focuses on his experiences of police *carceragens* and prison from the first time he was arrested and tortured as a fifteen year old until his first experience of being incarcerated as an adult at Carandiru and then at the Penitenciária do Estado. The book was originally published in 2001. Mendes (2005) picks up the story at the Penitenciária do Estado from the early 1980s, after he had passed through what he calls his "personal revolution" (Mendes 2009: 400) and made the decision to stop fighting the world, start reading and studying, and eventually teach literature classes. He almost completed a law degree at the Pontifical Catholic University of São Paulo, but one day absconded, was later rearrested for robbery, and eventually returned to the prison. Mendes (2012) is a collection of short reflections that he wrote during and after prison. Mendes (2015) focuses on the period after his return to Carandiru in 1995 as a middle-aged man, having returned to robbery once more while on home leave from a semi-open prison unit. Mendes is unique among prisoner/former prisoner autobiographers to have witnessed the rise of the PCC first hand.

Mendes (2009) paints a far more disorderly picture of Carandiru in the 1970s than Ramalho (2002). In a large part, this might be explained by the two authors' very different experiences: one an angry young man who had suffered at the hands of the police and prison officers since he was 14 or 15 years old and had now been sentenced to over 100 years, of which he knew he would serve at least 30; the other an outsider, a middle-class researcher who it should be added was not able to spend much time or conduct many interviews with prisoners besides the trusty *faxinas* held in cell block two. Important for current purposes is the emphasis Mendes likewise places on the role played by cell leaders, who he refers to as *condes* (counts) or *barões* (barons) rather than *juizes da xadrez*, as well as the camaraderie he felt towards his cellmates. In contrast to Ramalho, however, Mendes dedicates little attention to trusty *faxinas*. Instead he focuses attention on the position of the *faxinas* housed in one of the main cell blocks. More than Ramalho, Mendes also emphasises the relative strength of inmate as opposed to staff governance at the prison. The main role played by guards, he writes, was to lock and unlock gates and cell doors. The main cell blocks were largely left in the hands of these latter *faxinas*. Towards the end of the book, Mendes recounts a time at the Penitenciária do Estado when, having been held naked in isolation for several days as a 21 year old, the head *faxina* of his cell block angrily castigated the head of security that had put him there. In a more detailed account of the incidence, originally written in 1999, Mendes (2012) goes on to recount that the director of security's immediate response was to give him his clothes back and to persuade the prison governor to end the practice altogether. In Chapter 6, we will see the Penitenciária do Estado was not under the command of the PCC or another prison-wide gang before the turn of the century.

Unlike the prisoners interviewed by Ramalho, Mendes (2009) has little good at all to say about prison guards at either prison. He describes them as relying on informers and arbitrary violence. His position on inmate violence is more nuanced. Troubles that started before prison were regularly settled inside. Occasionally scores between rival gangs would end in killings. However, Mendes makes it clear the prison was going through a particularly violent period at the time he was there. In Mendes (2005), he describes a very different time at the Penitenciária do Estado in the early 1980s when, following a particularly progressive governor allowing in cell televisions, home leave for Christmas, and most important of all inmates to elect a prison-wide *comissão* (commission) of representatives from each cell block to oversee the work of *faxinas* working on their wings, "there had not been a single act of violence for six months" (Mendes 2005: 25). Moreover, Mendes does not mention *faxinas* abusing their power at either prison.

Furthermore, Mendes only once mentions a prison guard being attacked, at Carandiru in 1974, albeit mortally by an inmate who was seriously mentally ill. The officer had unlocked his cell to allow a team of shock troops to administer punishment beatings following an incidence between rival gangs. This, Mendes writes, was the only time he heard of an officer being killed in the thirty years he spent inside: "I always heard it said that instead of killing fellow sufferers, a prisoner should kill the guard that beat him… now it had become a fact" (Mendes 2009: 391).

When Mendes returned to Carandiru in the mid-1990s, the prison was up for closure following the 1992 massacre and was in a poor state of repair. Prison authorities were providing no more than meals and a there were a diminishing number of guards. Mendes (2015) found cell block routines to now be fully in the hands of the prisoners. The *faxina* housed in the cell blocks were selected and commanded by their *coletivos* and headed by what he describes as *notáveis* (observers)—"the smartest and most experienced outlaws" (Mendes 2015: 145). The half dozen or so guards typically on duty in cell block eight, where he was held as a reconvicted prisoner, only entered the wings together and only at unlock and lock-up. Failure to repay drug debts had become a major source of violence, but as previously mentioned, sexual violence had fallen dramatically as the inmate body had banned the abuse of younger prisoners. Mendes does not mention any system of cell leadership still operating at the prison. Instead, inmate codes were judged through *debates* involving groups of prisoners (I return to this important point in a moment). Decisions to kill were made by the *notáveis*. Mendes also describes more cooperation between prisoners and guards in 1990s

Carandiru than he had a quarter of a century earlier, some of which more by default than design—for instance, guards leaving the cell blocks to self-regulate—and some of which more openly negotiated—for instance, decisions over who to place in which cell. During the 1990s, cell block *faxinas* put an end to the practice of taking staff hostage to gain transfer out of the prison. However, Mendes puts this decision down to preventing violent retaliation rather than an improvement in staff-inmate relations. His understandable distrust of prison staff continued—"For me staff were always staff. However friendly they were, you couldn't trust them. At times of rebellion they would turn into demons, with iron bars in their hands to beat us… they preferred to sacrifice us than to lose their jobs" (Mendes 2015: 257).

The second series of first-hand accounts I highlight here are Varella's (2008, 2012) memoirs of working voluntarily as a doctor at the prison in the 1990s. I have already dealt with Varella (2008) in some depth, in Chapter 1. Alongside Mendes' autobiographies, Varella's prison writings confirm the position of the cell leader faded away at Carandiru in the late twentieth century, while the position of the *faxina* working within the main cell blocks evolved much closer to what it is today. Varella only indirectly refers to cell leaders once, when recounting an older prisoner reminiscing of the effectiveness of in cell discipline in previous times when he had needed to ask permission to take off his shoes from the person that "had been longest in the cell" (Varella 2008: 192). As previously noted, Varella likewise places his analysis of everyday order in the cell blocks squarely on the role of the *faxina*. Further, in contrast to the 1970s, the *faxina* described by Varella, like Mendes, was more closely tied to the *coletivo* and its codes of conduct/conflict management—its *regras de procedimento* (rules of procedure) (Varella 2008: 78)—and less to the prison administration. Unlike Ramalho, neither Varella nor Mendes uses the term *faxina* in the context of the trusty prisoners housed in cell block two, although Varella does describe them as prisoners that work with the confidence of the prison administration. Instead they refer to these prisoners in terms of the clerical and domestic tasks they performed. Most likely it was to distinguish the pre-existing trusty prisoner system from the new cell block, inmate-led system that the term was eventually retained only for prisoners working within the latter. In Chapter 3, we saw the PCC continues to describe its workers as *faxinas*. In Rio de Janeiro, on the other hand, the term has been largely reserved for trusty prisoners, although we have seen such prisoners are equally likely to be referred to as *colaboradores* or, more recently, *zeleadores*. In previous chapters, I have noted the use of altogether different terms in other parts of the country, for instance in Rio Grande do Sul and Pernambuco.

In this chapter, we have seen the emergence of a system of (inmate commanded) cell block *faxina* forms a major background to the modern-day criminal prison gang phenomenon in the two Brazilian states in which Brazil's first and largest of these gangs—the PCC and CV—emerged. It is for this reason I questioned the limitations of applying an organised crime perspective to the 2017 northern prison massacres. It appeared to me that those who did so based their reasoning on an outdated, if not wholly incorrect interpretation of the PCC and CV, and on an assumption—not yet established in academic research, nor supported by the events themselves—that Brazil's northern and southern prison gangs are similar, or that the PCC and CV mean the same thing in different parts of the country.

I started this book with Varella's (2008) account of the 1992 Carandiru prison massacre. Although the killings were carried out by police officers rather than prisoners in that incident, it was likewise the result of a momentary break down in governance, and likewise came to symbolise the late twentieth-century/early twenty-first-century prison gang. Before we move onto the subject of prison gangs in detail over the next two chapters, I conclude this chapter by reminding the reader of the key points I have made regarding Brazilian prison life in the book so far, as they related to the pre-CV and PCC era in Rio de Janeiro and São Paulo, where most of the relatively limited amount of historical and criminological research on prison life in the country has been produced. For consistency of illustration, I will focus on Carandiru.

First, regarding inmates' adjustments to prison life, we have seen most prisoners were able to form reciprocal and sometimes affective relations with their companions in spite, if not as a result of, the appalling conditions of overcrowding and material deprivation.

Second, regarding inmate leadership, we have seen Carandiru's cell block *faxina* could only govern with the confidence of the wider body of prisoners and were eventually taken over by it. Like the *juizes de xadrez* or *barões* described by Ramalho (2002) and Mendes (2009), and the *xerifes* described by Coelho (2005) in Rio de Janeiro, those that rose to the top of the cell block hierarchies tended to be those with most experience of prison. These prisoners were not necessarily the ones with the greater criminal reputation outside, although Dias (2013) points out, some crimes will always gain a prisoner greater respect than others, especially crimes associated with social banditry (I would add this is more so in a country like Brazil, where we have seen there exists a strong cultural tradition of positive social images of crime, as represented in the figure of the *malandro* or *bandido*). Dias gives the example of bank robbery, for which most of the original founders of the CV and PCC were imprisoned. Besides time spent in prison, Varella emphasises, the most influential prisoners were also likely to be natural leaders, those with the best sense and most ability to resolve disputes and form alliances. Physical strength or reputation for violence was not important: "the leader is the one that knows how to hear the voice of reason" (Varella 2008: 81).

Third, and again reflecting the position of the former *juiz de xadrez/ xerife*, we have seen that while the prison administration could no longer openly select or deselect cell block *faxinas* by the 1990s, or at least not their leaders, at Carandiru the new cell block-wide inmate hierarchies continued to work with the tacit support of the prison administration. We also saw this in Chapter 1, in Varella's (2012) account of the immediate reaction by prisoners and guards in cell block eight when shock troops entered cell block nine in 1992 to brutally put down a riot. More than Mendes (2015), Varella (2008) emphasises that the secret to order at the prison was dialogue and mutual respect between staff and cell block *faxinas*. This arose naturally, Varella continued, from their interdependency and everyday dealings with each other. Varella gives the example of the head *faxina* of cell block nine handing someone who had asked permission to kill and then backed down over to prison guards to be moved to the *isolamento* in cell block nine. "You're not a criminal", Varella (2008: 79) recounts the head *faxina* telling him, "you're a joke". One of the current prison guards in Rio de Janeiro I have cited several times in this chapter makes an almost identical point about the relationship between officers and inmates at his CV prison (Karam and Saraiva 2017). He describes two kinds of prisoner: the *bandido* and the *comédia* (comedian), the *comédia* being the undisciplined prisoner who does not follow the established, negotiated rules. At Carandiru prison, Varella continues, staff did not have to interfere with the order maintained by the cell block *faxina* until someone was killed. The same point was also made to me by another Rio de Janeiro prison worker I interviewed in 2010 (I return to this in Chapter 5). Even then, Varella concludes, it was no more than a matter of putting the relevant cell block on lockdown and waiting for someone to assume responsibility, usually a drug addict finding an opportunity to clear his debts.

As an extension of this third point, we have seen that while staff-inmate relations were largely defined by reciprocal exchanges, prisoners remained vulnerable to occasional institutional violence. Varella (2008, 2012), in particular, lends support to the conclusion that by the turn of the century guards increasingly managed the prison through negotiation. More specifically, it seems that after the return to democracy in the mid-1980s, São Paulo prison staff stopped using violence as an ordinary tool of discipline (Varella 2012; see also Wolfmann 2000). After the public scandal caused by the 1992 massacre, and the threat posed to staff outside prison with the subsequent emergence of the PCC, Varella (2012) claims officer violence was almost eliminated altogether. However, it appears the case that guards continued to resort to punishment beatings as a reactionary measure, and that this is better understood as a matter of institutional practice than as a case of deviant staff culture or the continued presence of individual, vindictive guards.

These three conclusions—concerning mutual interests, legitimacy and co-governance—are supported by the memoirs of others imprisoned Carandiru in the late twentieth century, for instance José André de Araújo (also known as André du Rap) (Rap and Zeni 2002) and

Hosmany Ramos (2003). Rap, a survivor of the 1992 massacre, spent most of the 1990s in prison, including six years at Carandiru, where he served months of his time locked up 24 hours a day in one of the prison's *isolamentos*. Rap and Zeni (2002) contain a series of letters written by Rap while in prison, and transcripts of four interviews he gave in 2001. Ramos, a middle-class doctor and longer-term prisoner, was also present at the massacre, although not in cell block nine. He had been imprisoned at Carandiru since 1981. Ramos (2003) contains a series of accounts of the experiences of people with whom he lived at the prison, including another survivor of the massacre, Milton Marques Viana.

Rap's reflections are as striking for their positive portrayal of inmate culture at the prison as his account of the massacre and his experience of disciplinary punishments. This he contrasts with the poor treatment he suffered at the hands of prison officers. He tells his interviewer he arrived at the prison fearful for his life, but quickly made friendships and picked up the importance of getting immersed in its *coletividade* (collectivity), which included letting the cell block *faxinas* get on with their jobs. Rap goes on to recount stories of the relations he formed with his cellmates and the support networks he encountered, and continuously returns to themes of solidarity and mutual respect. Even more than Mendes (2005, 2009, 2012, 2015) or Varella (2008, 2012), Rap and Zeni (2002) focuses attention on the depth of social interaction at the prison that inevitably arose from prisoners being continually in one another's company. Among many passages I could have chosen as illustrations of Rap's dealings with his cell block hierarchy (who he refers to individually using grammatically correct Portuguese as *faxineiros* rather than the more commonly used word, *faxinas*):

> In the day to day, you form friendships with your companions. You get used [to prison]. You are there, the *faxineiro* comes, takes the change from your hand, you greet him, "what's up brother, how's it going". He says, "pass by my cell later for a chat. Which *quebrada* are you from?... You need to have social skills. Get used to the *ritmo* (rhythm). At meal times

you can't get in the way of the food trolley. You have to be respectful when the *faxineiro* is doing the mopping. It's your companions' work". (Du Rap and Zeni 2002: 49)

Ramos (2003) writes little about *faxinas* in his accounts of the experiences of his companions at the prison, besides one story that features a *juiz da xadrez* preparing a meal at Christmas, and calming a situation when one of his cellmates tells another prisoner he is not invited to eat. In contrast to Rap and Zeni (2002), Ramos (2003) focuses on tensions as well as camaraderie between Carandiru's inmates. Still, it is the latter that attracts most of his attention. In one notable passage, Ramos describes a quote from a former state justice secretary that had been reproduced and left for many years on the door of a cell. It read:

> Understand that, compared to the *mendigo* (tramp), the *ladrão* is better. The *mendigo*... is a loser who gave up the fight... Not the *ladrão*. [He] reacts and takes on society. Risks his liberty and his life. Continues fighting, doesn't accept his destiny.... (Ramos 2003: 236–237)

In the preface to the book, Ramos reflects:

> My prison experience gave me the opportunity to know from close up the suffering and conflict between men... people who experienced at every moment the limits of violence, of life and death [...] It's a world the reader... will love not only for the extraordinary, but also for the secret connection that exists in all of us... my stories demonstrate that it is possible to rediscover human sensibility and solidarity – indispensable counterpoints to the solitary life and anguish of prison. (Ramos 2003: 11, 12)

The significance of the new cell block *faxina* system is also highlighted in two media depictions of Carandiru prison, both of which fictionalised accounts of real events first described by Varella (2008). Less known outside of Brazil is the television drama series Carandiru: Outras Histórias (Carandiru: Other Stories) (Babenco et al. 2005), of which Varella was the main script writer. The first episode focuses on a *debate* attended by dozens of prisoners who decide in a show of hands that an inmate is not required to kill a second inmate who had started a relationship with his wife in the time between the two being imprisoned. The issue at stake was that wives having affairs while they were imprisoned was a major cause of anxiety to prisoners, and so the second inmate's actions were prejudicial to the prisoner body as a whole and should normally have been dealt with inside rather than after prison. In another *debate* referred to in Varella (2008), attended by more than 40 prisoners, an inmate was sentenced to death having himself murdered a cellmate without permission. His victim had refused to allow him to use their cell to take crack cocaine.

The second is the opening part of the internationally acclaimed film Carandiru (Babenco and Kramer 2003), which I explained in Chapter 1 was based on Varella (2008). In the opening scene the head of a cell block *faxina*, Moacir, is seen on a wing corridor negotiating a dispute between two prisoners, Lula and Peixeira, who are held in separate cells and are now being restrained by their cellmates. Lula had attacked Peixeira after discovering he had killed his father on the outside. The prison governor shortly arrives accompanied by a number of guards and Varella, who is in the prison for the first time. Moacir apologises on behalf of Lula for his inexperience, for seeking to take revenge without permission and moreover, in contrast to the *debate* depicted in Babenco and Kramer (2003), for bringing an issue into the prison that should have been left to the street. Later the governor tells Varella, "they're not prisoners [here], they own this place. The only reason this place does not explode is because they don't want it to". As Varella leaves that evening he is followed to the entrance to the cell block by Moacir and two other *faxinas*, who ask him if he will return to the prison. The following day Varella is seen attending Moacir in the cell block surgery, who tells him how difficult it is to sleep with all of his responsibility. Varella (2008) recounts a similar episode in which the head of the cell block nine *faxina* explains he cannot switch off during the night: "I'm the judge of the cell block. The judge on the street works a few hours and goes home... I work 24/7. He only has to decide if the accused goes to prison... I sign off the death penalty" (Varella 2008: 81).

Notes

1. Special police forces are sometimes employed to patrol prison complexes or respond to prison riots. The Gericinó (Bangu) prison complex in Rio de Janeiro, introduced in Chapter 2, also has its own police station. A few prisons are run by the police rather than penitentiary authorities. This includes one of the country's largest prison units, Porto Alegre Public Prison (Central Prison), Rio Grande do Sul, also introduced in Chapter 2.
2. An additional 20,758 people were recorded as employed in health, education and social services, or as lawyers. I have not included these staff for the moment simply because it is difficult to make meaningful comparison with other countries. In some countries, e.g. Norway, health, education and social welfare are all provided by national services. In other countries, e.g. England and Wales, education and social welfare are often provided as a prison officer specialism.
3. It is not clear these improvements in Rio de Janeiro's prison conditions were matched in São Paulo. Varella (2012) and Wolfmann (2000) describe São Paulo's prisons operating in the 1950s under a progressive system of 90 days single cell confinement followed by a period of confinement in collective cells before moving on to semi-open conditions. Salla (2015), on the other hand, describes the 1950s as a period of deteriorating prison conditions. Following a major prison rebellion in 1952, in which eight soldiers, two police officers and four guards as well 15 inmates were killed, a number of semi-open prisons were inaugurated. However, any immediate gains were short-lived. In Chapter 2, we saw Brazil holds a relatively large number of prisoners in semi-open conditions today, but that these facilities are often just as overcrowded as the rest of the prison system.
4. For analysis of the roles delegated to prisoners at one of Brazil's other major nineteenth-century penal institutions, see Peter Beattie's (2011, 2015) historical research on the country's largest penal colony of the period, the Island of Fernando de Noronha, Pernambuco. At its peak, in the 1870s and 1880s, the island was populated by more than 1500 convicts. Prisoners (usually but not necessarily imprisoned soldiers—"military convicts"—who made up one in five prisoners) occupied most of the guard-like as well as domestic positions. Only a handful of prisoners were locked up at any given time. The

majority lived in huts, often with their families, and were supervised in their daytime work by "convict sergeants" and "convict corporals". Night time curfews were enforced by "convict police".
5. In England I teach a foundation level criminology module at HMP Pentonville and run undergraduate and postgraduate criminology reading groups at HMP Grendon and HMP Coldingley.
6. Here I am again indebted to my colleague Chris Garces, who first used made use of the concept informal prison dynamics in Garces et al. (2013).
7. Or similar terms signifying collective identity such as *massa* (mass), as used by prisoners in Sager and Beto's (2016) documentary on Central Prison, Rio Grande do Sul, and in Ramalho's (2002) and Lima's (1991) accounts of prison life in the 1970s and 1980s covered below.
8. Or similar terms signifying expected ways of conducting yourself. For example, PCC-affiliated prisoners use the terms *ética* and *disciplina* (discipline) interchangeably (Biondi 2014). Arruda (2015) also found the terms *disciplina* and *regras do convívio*, and further *codigos de convivência* (codes of conviviality), in common use at Curado prison in Pernambuco. Bassani (2016) refers to prisoners' *regras de boa convivência* (rules of good conviviality) in Central Prison, Rio Grande do Sul.
9. See also Perlman (2010). Perlman describes a process of post-dictatorship economic decline in which *favela* residents have become increasingly marginalised from the licit economy to the point in which, "even the lucky few who get a job for a minimum salary and work overtime still do not earn enough to support their families" (Perlman 2010: 162).
10. For an analysis of the effect such crime reporting has on public perceptions of crime and justice in a poor community in the north of the country, see Garmany (2009).
11. Some of the drop in recorded prison homicides in São Paulo is also likely explained by an increase in faked suicides (Dias and Salla 2013). However, as noted in Chapter 3, the number of recorded suicides is also low.
12. As my Rio de Janeiro colleague Maria Lúcia Karam once jokingly put it to me, even São Paulo's criminal gangs are more organised.
13. These two points were suggested to me by Gary Taylor, a BA Philosophy student imprisoned at HMP Grendon, during a reading group session that focused on the final draft of Chapter 1.
14. Note that the same day plans for a rapid reaction force were made public in the aftermath of the 2017 northern prison massacres, the

Ministry of Work made a separate and little reported announcement it would set aside R$30 million (£7.5 million) to provide professional work training schemes for up to 15,000 prisoners.
15. Ministério da Justiça (2016) recorded a total of 115,805 working prisoners in December 2014. 37,388 were employed by prison authorities in trusty positions. 49,153 were employed in workshops and/or contracted by private companies. Most, but not all of these were sentenced prisoners. 29,264 prisoners in open and semi-open units were employed externally. 74,436 prisoners were registered as studying. 26% of all working prisoners were recorded as receiving their statutory right to three quarters of the national minimum wage in June 2016 (Ministério da Justiça e Segurança Pública 2017). This included few prisoners held in closed conditions. Women prisoners typically earn R$200 (£50) a month at Sant'Ana, less than a quarter of minimum wage.

References

Adorno, S., & Salla, F. (2007). Criminalidade organizada nas prisões e os ataques do PCC. *Estudos Avançados, 21*(61), 7–29.
Anderson, E. (1999). *Code of the street: Decency, violence and the moral life of the inner city*. New York: W. W. Norton.
Antunes, S. A. (2016). Produção de corpos e categorias de pessoas nos fluxos de uma penitenciária feminina. *Revista Florestan Ferbandes, 3*(1), 63–71.
Apple, C. (2017, May 8). Como o PCC garantiu a segurança do meu marido dentro da prisão. *Vice*. https://www.vice.com/pt_br/article/wnkn7y/pcc-garantiu-seguranca-do-meu-marido-prisao. Last accessed 30 June 2017.
Araújo, C. E. M. (2009). *Cárcares imperiais: Correção do Rio de Janeiro. Seus detentos e o sistema império, 1830–1861*. Ph.D. thesis, State University of Campinas. http://repositorio.unicamp.br/handle/REPOSIP/280976. Last accessed 15 June 2017.
Arias, E. D., & Goldstein, D. M. (2010). Violent pluralism: Understanding the new democracies of Latin America. In E. D. Arias & D. M. Goldstein (Eds.), *Violent democracies in Latin America* (pp. 1–34). Durham, NC: Duke University.
Arruda, R. F. (2015). *Geografia do cárcere: Territorialidades na vida cotidiana carcerária no sistena prisional de Pernambuco*. Ph.D. thesis, University of São

Paulo. http://www.teses.usp.br/teses/disponiveis/8/8136/tde-16062015-125328/pt-br.php. Last accessed 3 February 2017.

Babenco, H., & Kramer, O. (2003). *Carandiru*. Film. Brazil: Globo Filmes.

Babenco, H., Carvalho, W., Gervitz, R., & Faria, M. (2005). *Carandiru: Outros Historias*. Television series. Brazil: Rede Globo.

Barbosa, A. R. (2005). *Prender e dar fuga biopolítica, sistema penitenciários e tráfico de drogas no Rio de Janeiro*. Ph.D. thesis, Federal University of Rio de Janeiro. http://www.uece.br/labvida/dmdocuments/prender_e_dar_fuga_biopolitica_sistema_penitenciario.pdf. Last accessed 1 May 2017.

Bassani, F. (2016). *Visita íntima: Sexo, crime e negócios nas prisões*. Porto Alegre: Bestiário.

Beattie, P. M. (2011). The jealous institution: Male nubility, conjugality, sexuality, and discipline on the social margins of imperial Brazil. *Comparative Studies in Society and History, 53*(1), 180–209.

Beattie, P. M. (2015). *Punishment in paradise: Race, slavery, human rights, and a nineteenth-century Brazilian penal colony*. Durham: Duke University.

Biondi, K. (2010). *Junto e misturado: Uma etnografia do PCC*. São Paulo: Teirciero Nome. English version: Biondi, K. (2016). *Sharing this walk: An ethnography of prison life and the PCC in Brazil* (J. F. Collins, Trans.). Chapel Hill: University of North Carolina.

Biondi, K. (2013). O PCC: Da organização á ética. In A. R. Barbosa, et al. (Eds.), *Etnografias em uma fronteira difusa* (pp. 23–34). Rio de janeiro: Universidade Federal Fluminense.

Biondi, K. (2014). *Etnografia no movimento: Território, hierarquia e lei no PCC*. Ph.D. thesis, Federal University of São Carlos. https://www.repositorio.ufscar.br/bitstream/handle/ufscar/246/6378.pdf?sequence=1&isAllowed=y. Last accessed 7 April 2017.

Biondi, K. (2017a, January 23). *The extinction of sexual violence in the prisons of São Paulo, Brazil*. http://uncpressblog.com/2017/01/23/karina-biondi-the-extinction-of-sexual-violence-in-the-prisons-of-sao-paulo-brazil. Last accessed 7 March 2017.

Biondi, K. (2017b). 'It was already in the ghetto': Rap, religion and crime in the prison. Interview with Djalma Oliveira Rios, aka 'Cascão'. *Prison Service Journal, 229*, 45–47.

Biondi, K. (2017c). Movement between and beyond the walls: Micropolitics of incitements and variations among São Paulo's prisoners' movement the 'PCC' and the prison system. *Prison Service Journal, 229*, 23–25.

Biondi, K. (2017d). Prison violence, prison justice: The rise of Brazil's PCC. *NACLA Report on the Americas, 49*(3), 341–346.

Biondi, K. (forthcoming 2019). Facing up to the PCC: Theoretical and methodological strategies to approaching Brazil's largest "prison gang". In C. Garces, et al. (Eds.), *Carceral communities: Troubling 21st century prison regimes in Latin America*. Under contract with University of Pennsylvania.

Bourgois, P. (1995). *In search of respect: Selling crack in el barrio*. Cambridge: Cambridge University.

Bowcott, O. (2017, April 25). Child locked in cell for more than 23 hours a day at Feltham, high court told. *The Guardian*. https://www.theguardian.com/society/2017/apr/25/single-unlock-prison-regime-breached-youths-rights-court-told?CMP=share_btn_tw. Last accessed 26 April 2017.

Bretas, M. L. (1996). What the eyes can't see: Stories from Rio de Janeiro's prisons. In R. D. Salvatore & C. Aguirre (Eds.), *The birth of the penitentiary in Latin America* (pp. 101–122). Austin: University of Texas.

Caldeira, T. (1996). Fortified enclaves: The new urban segregation. *Public Culture, 8*, 303–328.

Caldeira, T. (2000). *City of walls: Crime, segregation and citizenship in São Paulo*. Berkeley: University of California.

Caldeira, C. (2003). Bangu 3: Desordem e ordem no quartel-general do Comando Vermelho. *Insight Inteligênçia, 22*, 91–115.

Câmara dos Deputados. (2008). *CPI do sistema carcerário*. Resource document. http://bd.camara.leg.br/bd/bitstream/handle/bdcamara/2701/cpi_sistema_carcerario.pdf?sequence=5. Last accessed 10 August 2014.

Cavalcanti, R. P. (2016a). Armed violence and the politics of gun control in Brazil: An analysis of the 2005 referendum. *Bulletin of Latin American Research*. https://doi.org/10.1111/blar.12476.

Cavalcanti, R. P. (2016b). *Over, under and through the walls: The dynamics of public security, police-community relations and the limits of managerialism in crime control in Recife, Brazil*. Ph.D. thesis, University of London. http://westminsterresearch.wmin.ac.uk/18353. Last accessed 7 April 2017.

Cavalcanti, R. P. (2017). Marginalised youth, violence and policing: A qualitative study in Recife, Brazil. *Contemporary Social Science, 12*, 227–241.

Chazkel, A. (2009). Social life and civic education in the Rio de Janeiro city jail. *Journal of Social History, 42*(3), 697–731.

Clemmer, D. (1940). *The prison community*. New York: Holt, Rinehart and Winston.

Coelho, E. C. (2005). *A oficina do diablo. E outros estudos sobre criminalidade*. Rio de Janeiro: Record.

Cohen, S., & Taylor, L. (1972). *Psychological survival: The experience of long term imprisonment*. Harmondsworth: Penguin.

Costa, F., & Bianchi, P. (2017). "Massacre silencioso": Doenças tratáveis matam mais que violência nas prisões brasileira. *UOL*. https://noticias.uol.com.br/cotidiano/ultimas-noticias/2017/08/14/masacre-silencioso-mortes-por-doencas-trataveis-superam-mortes-violentas-nas-prisoes-brasileiras.htm. Last accessed 8 September 2017.

Council of Europe. (2017). *Report to the Government of the United Kingdom on the visit to the United Kingdom carried out by the European Committee for the Prevention of Torture and Inhuman or Degrading Treatment or Punishment (CPT) from 30 March to 12 April 2016*. CPT/Inf (2017). Resource document. https://rm.coe.int/CoERMPublicCommonSearchServices/DisplayDCTMContent?documentId=090000168070a773. Last accessed 18 April 2017.

Cowie, S. (2017, March 27). Brazil's prisons: A battleground in the drug wars. *Al Jazeera*. http://www.aljazeera.com/indepth/features/2017/02/brazil-prisons-battleground-drug-wars-170219053354497.html. Last accessed 5 April 2017.

Crewe, B. (2009). *The prisoner society: Power, adaptation and social life in an English prison*. Oxford: Oxford University.

Dias, C. N. (2013). *PCC: Hegemonia nas prisões e monopólio da violência*. São Paulo: Saraiva.

Dias, C. N., & Salla, F. (2013). Organized crime in Brazilian prisons: The example of the PCC. *International Journal of Criminology and Sociology, 2*, 397–408.

Drybread, K. (2014). Murder and the making of man-subjects in a Brazilian juvenile prison. *American Anthropologist, 116*(4), 752–764.

Feltran, G. S. (2010). The management of violence on the São Paulo periphery: The repertoire of normative apparatus in the PCC era. *Vibrant, 7*(2), 109–134.

Feltran, G. S. (2011). *Fronteiras de tensão: Política e violência nas periferias de São Paulo*. São Paulo: Unesp.

Feltran, G. S. (2012). Governo que produz crime, crime que produz governo: Políticas estatais e políticas criminais na gestão do homicídio em São Paulo. *Revista Brasileira de Segurança Pública, 6*(2), 232–255.

Gambetta, D. (2009). *Codes of the underworld: How criminals communicate*. Princeton, NJ: Princeton University.

Garces, C., Martin, T., & Darke, S. (2013). Informal prison dynamics in Africa and Latin America. *Criminal Justice Matters, 91*(1), 26–27.

Garmany, J. (2009). The embodied state: Governmentality in a Brazilian favela. *Social and Cultural Geography, 10*(7), 721–739.

Gay, R. (2009). From popular movements to drugs gangs to militaries: An anatomy of violence in Rio de Janeiro. In K. Koonings & D. Kruijt (Eds.), *megacities: The politics of urban exclusion and violence in the global south* (pp. 29–51). London: Zed.

Godoi, R. (2015). *Fluxos em cadeias: As prisões em São paulo na virada dos tempos*. Ph.D. thesis, University of São Paulo. http://www.teses.usp.br/teses/disponiveis/8/8132/tde-05082015-161338/pt-br.php. Last accessed 3 July 2017.

Godoi, R. (2016). Intimacy and power: Body searches and intimate visits in the prison system of São Paulo. *Chámp Penal, XIII*. https://doi.org/10.4000/champpenal.9386.

Goffman, E. (1961). On the characteristics of total institutions. In D. Cressey (Ed.), *The prison: Studies in institutional organization and change*. New York: Holt, Rinehart and Winston.

Goldstein, D. M. (2003). *Laughter out of place: Race, class, violence, and sexuality in a Rio shantytown*. Berkeley: University of California.

Green, P., & Ward, T. (2009). Violence and the state. In R. Coleman, et al. (Eds.), *State, power, crime* (pp. 116–128). London: Sage.

Hadler, O. H., Guareschi, N. M. F., & Scisleski, A. C. C. (2017). Observances: Psychology, public security policies and incarcerated youth. *Pesquisas e Práticas Pscicossociais, 12*(4), e2271.

Hall, S. (1991). The local and the global: Globalization and ethnicity. In A. King (Ed.), *Culture, globalization and the world-system* (pp. 19–39). London: Macmillan.

Hess, D. J. (1995). Introduction. In D. J. Hess & R. Matta (Eds.), *The Brazilian puzzle: Culture in the borderlands of the western world* (pp. 1–30). New York: Columbia University.

Hirata, D. V. (2010). *Sobreviver na universidade: Entre o mercado e a vida*. Ph.D. thesis, University of São Paulo. http://www.teses.usp.br/teses/disponiveis/8/8132/tde-03032011-122251/pt-br.php. Last accessed 13 April 2017.

Human Rights Watch. (1998). *Behind bars in Brazil*. New York: Human Rights Watch.

Hutton, M. (2016). Visiting time: A tale of two prisons. *Probation Journal, 63*(3), 347–361.

Inter-American Court of Human Rights. (2013). *Precautionary measure no. 8–13. Matter of persons deprived of liberty at the central penitentiary of Porto Alegre regarding Brazil, 30 December 2013*. Resource document. https://www.oas.org/en/iachr/decisions/pdf/Resolution14-13(MC-8-13).pdf. Last accessed 17 April 2017.

Inter-American Court of Human Rights. (2014, May 22). *Order of the Inter-American Court of Human Rights.* Provisional measures regarding Brazil. Matter of the penitentiary complex of Curado. Resource document. http://www.corteidh.or.cr/docs/medidas/curado_se_01_ing.pdf. Last accessed 6 May 2016.

Inter-American Court of Human Rights. (2016). *Medidas provisórias a respeito do brasil. Assunto do compexo penitenciário de Curado de 23 de Novembro 2016.* Resource document. http://www.corteidh.or.cr/docs/medidas/curado_se_04_por.pdf. Last accessed 17 April 2017.

Irwin, J. (1970). *The felon.* Berkeley: University of California.

Jefferson, A. M. (2013). The situated production of legitimacy: Perspectives from the global south. In J. Tankebe & A. Liebling (Eds.), *Legitimacy and criminal justice: An international exploration* (pp. 248–266). Oxford: Oxford University.

Karam, M. L., & Saraiva, H. R. (2017). Ouvindo as vozes de carcereiros brasileiros. Unpublished. English version: Hearing the voices of Brazilian correction officers (M. L. Karam, Trans.). *Prison Service Journal, 229*, 48–50.

Karstedt, S. (2001). Comparing cultures, comparing crime: Challenges, prospects and problems for a global criminology. *Crime, Law and Social Change, 36*(3), 285–308.

Kaminski, M. M. (2004). *Games prisoners play: The tragic worlds of Polish prisoners.* Princeton: Princeton University.

Koerner, A. (2006). Punição, disciplina e pensamento penal no brasil do século xix. *Lua Nova, 68*, 205–242.

Leeds, E. (1996). Cocaine and parallel politics in the Brazilian urban periphery. *Latin American Research Review, 31*, 47–85.

Lima, W. S. (1991). *Quatrocentos contra um: Uma história do Comando Vermelho.* Rio de Janeiro: ISER.

Lourenço, L. C., & Almeida, O. L. (2013). "Quem mantém a ordem, quem cria desordem": Gangues prisionais na Bahia. *Tempo Social, 25*(1), 37–59.

Manso, B. P. (2012). *Crescimento e queda dos homicídios em SP entre 1960 e 2010: Uma análise dos mechanismos da escolha homicida e das carreiras no crime.* Ph.D. thesis, University of São Paulo. http://www.teses.usp.br/teses/disponiveis/8/8131/tde-12122012-105928/pt-br.php. Last accessed 13 April 2017.

Manso, B. P. (2016). *Homicide in São Paulo: An examination of trends from 1960–2010.* Cham: Springer.

Marques, A. (2010a). *Um "debate" sobre o estado de "isento" no Primeiro Comando da Capital.* Paper presented at the 27th Brazilian Anthropology Reunion, 1–4 August 2010. Unpublished.

Marques, A. (2010b). "Liderança", "proceder" e "igualdade": Uma etnografia das relações políticas no Primeiro Comando da Capital. *Etnográfica, 14*(2), 311–335.

Marques, A. (2014). *Crime e proceder: Um experimento antropológico.* São Paulo: Alameda.

Mathiesen, T. (1965). *The defences of the weak: A study of a Norwegian correctional institution.* London: Tavistock.

Mattos, V. (2010). *De uniforme diferente: O livro das agentes.* Belo Horizonte: Fundação MDC.

Mecanismo Nacional de Prevenção e Combate à Tortura. (2015). *Relatório de visita ao presidio central de Porto Alegre, Rio Grande do Sul.* http://www.sdh.gov.br/sobre/participacao-social/comite-nacional-de-prevencao-e-combate-a-tortura/representantes/presidio-central-de-porto-alegre. Last accessed 5 September 2017.

Mecanismo Nacional de Prevenção e Combate à Tortura. (2016). *Relatório devisita a unidades prisionais de Manaus – Amazonas.* Resource document. http://www.sdh.gov.br/sobre/participacao-social/sistema-nacional-de-prevencao-e-combate-a-tortura-snpct/mecanismo/Unidades_Prisionais_de_Manaus___AM.pdf. Last accessed 5 September 2017.

Mecanismo Nacional de Prevenção e Combate à Tortura. (2017). *Relatório anual 2016–2017.* Resource document. http://www.sdh.gov.br/noticias/pdf/mecanismo-nacional-de-prevencao-e-combate-a-tortura-lanca-relatorio-anual-2016-2017-2. Last accessed 28 June 2017.

Mendes, L. A. (2005). *Às cegas.* São Paulo: Companhia das Letras.

Mendes, L. A. (2009). *Memórias de um sobrevivente.* São Paulo: Companhia de Bolso.

Mendes, L. A. (2012). *Cela forte.* São Paulo: Global.

Mendes, L. A. (2015). *Confissões de um homen livre.* São Paulo: Companhia das Letras.

Ministério da Justiça. (2016). *Levantamento nacional de informações penitenciárias infopen, dezembro de 2014.* Resource document. http://www.justica.gov.br/seus-direitos/politica-penal/infopen_dez14.pdf. Last accessed 24 October 2016.

Ministério da Justiça e Segurança Pública. (2017). *Levantamento nacional de informações penitenciárias: Atualização - Junho de 2016.* Resource document. http://www.justica.gov.br/news/ha-726-712-pessoas-presas-no-brasil/relatorio_2016_junho.pdfdocument. Last accessed 21 December 2017.

Ministry of Justice. (2017). *National Offender Management Service workforce statistics bulletin, 30 September 2016.* Resource document. https://www.gov.uk/

government/uploads/system/uploads/attachment_data/file/567178/noms-workforce-statistics-30-September-2016.pdf. Last accessed 22 March 2017.

Miraglia, P., & Salla, F. (2008). O PCC e a gestão dos presídios em São Paulo: Entrevista com Nagashi Furukawa. *Novos Estudos, 80*, 21–41.

Moore, H. (2017). Imprisonment and (un)relatedness in northeast Brazil. Ph.D.thesis, University of Toronto.

Moraes, P. R. B. (2005). *Punição, encarceramento e construção de identidade professional entre agents penitenciários*. São Paulo: Instituto Brasileiro de Ciências Criminais.

Pastoral Carcerária/PE, Serviço Ecumênico de Militância nas Prisões, Pastoral Carcerária Nacional, Justiça Global and Harvard Law School. (2014). *4⁰ contrainforme dos representantes dos beneficiários, MC 199-11: Pessoas privadas da liberdade no Presídio Professor Aníbal Bruno e outros, estado de Pernambuco, Brasil*. Resource document. http://arquivoanibal.weebly.com/uploads/4/7/4/9/47496497/19_-_2014_02_18_-_4o_contrainforme_dos_representantes_-_mc_199-11_-pub.pdf. Last accessed 16 December 2015.

Penglase, B. (2009). States of insecurity: Everyday emergencies, public secrets, and drug trafficker power in a Brazilian favela. *PoLAR: Political and Legal Anthropology Review, 32*, 47–63.

Penglase, B. (2010). The owner of the hill: Masculinity and drug-trafficking in Rio de Janeiro, Brazil. *Journal of Latin American and Caribbean Anthropology, 15*(2), 317–337.

Peres, M. F. T., Almeida, J. F., Vicentin, D., Cerda, M., Cardia, N., & Adorno, S. (2011). Queda dos homicídios no Município de São Paulo: Uma análise exploratória de possíveis condicionantes. *Revista Brasileira Epidemiol, 14*(4), 709–721.

Perlman, J. E. (2009). Megacity's violence and its consequences in Rio de Janeiro. In K. Koonings & D. Kruijt (Eds.), *Megacities: The politics of urban exclusion and violence in the global south* (pp. 52–68). London: Zed.

Perlman, J. E. (2010). *Favela: Four decades of living on the edge in Rio de Janeiro*. New York: Oxford University.

Prison Reform Trust. (n.d.). *Bromley briefings prison fact file: Autumn 2016*. Resource document. http://www.prisonreformtrust.org.uk/Portals/0/Documents/Bromley%20Briefings/Autumn%202016%20Factfile.pdf. Last accessed 21 March 2017.

Ramalho, J. R. (2002). *Mundo do crime: A ordem pelo avesso* (3rd ed.). Rio de Janeiro: Graal.

Ramos, H. (2003). *Pavilhão 9: Paixão e morte no Carandiru* (4th ed.). Paris: Gallimard.

Ramos, G. (2015). *Memórias do Cárcere* (49th ed.). Rio de Janeiro: Record.
Rap, A., & Zeni, B. (2002). *Sobrevivente André du Rap (do Massacre do Carandiru)*. São Paulo: Labortexto.
Rio, João do. (1905). *O memento literário*. Paris: Garnier.
Sager, T., & Beto, R. (2016). *Central*. Documentary film. Brazil: Panda.
Salla, F. (2015). Rebelião na Ilha Anchieta em 1952 e a primeira grande crise na segurança pública paulista. *DILEMAS, 8*(4), 633–658.
Salvadori, F., & Dias, C. N. (2016, June 3). Quem disse que a bandidagem não tolera estuprador? *Ponte*. https://ponte.org/crime-organizado-estupro. Last accessed 15 June 2017.
Santos, B. S. (2002). *Towards a new legal common sense: Law, globalization and emancipation* (2nd ed.). London: Lexis Nexis Butterworths.
Scott, D., & Codd, H. (2010). *Controversial issues in prison*. Maidenhead: Open University.
Silva, A. M. C. (2011). *Participo que… Desvelando a punição intramuros*. Rio de Janeiro: Publit.
Skarbek, D. (2014). *The social order of the underworld: How prison gangs govern the American penal system*. New York: Oxford University.
Skarbek, D. (2016). Covenants without the Sword? Comparing prison self-governance globally. *American Political Science Review, 110*(4), 845–862.
Steinberg, G., & Sacramento, P. (2004). *O prisioneiro da grade de ferro*. Documentary film. Brazil: California Filmes.
Sykes, G. M. (1958). *The society of captives*. Princeton, NY: Princeton University.
Travis, A. (2017, July 4). Prolonged solitary confinement of boy at Feltham YOI 'breached human rights'. *The Guardian*. https://www.theguardian.com/society/2017/jul/04/feltham-yoi-high-court-human-rights. Last accessed 5 July 2017.
Ugelvik, T. (2016). Prisons as welfare institutions? Punishment and the Nordic model. In Y. Jewkes, et al. (Eds.), *Handbook on prisons* (2nd ed., pp. 388–402). Abington: Routledge.
Varella, D. (2008). *Estação Carandiru*. São Paulo: Companhia das Letras. English edition: Varella, D. (2012). *Lockdown: Inside Brazil's most violent prison* (A. Entrekin, Trans.). London: Simon and Schuster.
Varella, D. (2012). *Carcereiros*. São Paulo: Companhia das Letras.
Varella, D. (2017). *Prisioneiras*. São Paulo: Companhia das Letras.
Willis, G. D. (2009). Deadly symbiosis? The PCC, the state, and the institutionalization of violence in São Paulo, Brazil. In G. Jones & D. Rodgers

(Eds.), *Youth violence in Latin America: Gangs and juvenile justice in perspective* (pp. 167–182). New York: Palgrave Macmillan.

Willis, G. D. (2015). *The killing consensus: Police, organized crime, and the regulation of life and death in urban Brazil*. Oakland: University of California.

Willis, G. D. (2016). Before the body count: Homicide statistics and everyday security in Latin America. *Journal of Latin American Studies, 49*, 29–54.

Wolfmann, L. C. (2000). *Portal do inferno: Mas há esperança*. São Paulo: WVC Gestão Inteligente Com. Ltda.

Zaluar, A. (1994). *Condomínio do diablo*. Rio de Janeiro: Revan.

5

Managing without Guards

In this chapter, I report on a study of the working lives of police officers and prisoners at one of the 16 police *carceragens* (lock-ups; units of holding cells) in the state of Rio de Janeiro where I completed my first Brazilian prison fieldwork study in September 2010. Until its closure in 2013, Rio de Janeiro's *carceragem* system held a significant minority of the state's prisoners awaiting trial, sentence or the outcome of appeals, sometimes in separate buildings but more often in annexes or the basements of police stations. I refer to this particular *carceragem* as Polinter.

In Chapter 1, I offered an extended account of my first visit to Polinter. I described how I was initially inspired to research Brazilian prisons following a visit five years earlier to the recently deactivated Casa de Detenção de São Paulo (Carandiru), and by the accounts I subsequently read of people that had worked, been incarcerated or researched there of the relative everyday orderliness of the prison in spite of its infamy for overcrowding, degrading living conditions and acute shortage of prison guards (explored in detail in Chapter 4). I returned to Brazil in 2008 to visit two active prisons in São Paulo (Centro de Detenção Provisória da Capital Chácara Belém II and Penitenciária Feminina de Sant'Ana, both introduced in Chapter 2), and again in 2010, this time to Rio de Janeiro and Minas Gerais, to select a prison for fieldwork. This latter research trip included visits to Penitenciária Alfredo Trajan (Bangu II), also introduced in Chapter 2, and APAC de Nova Lima, introduced in Chapter 1. However, it was my visit to Polinter that left the greatest impression and set the tone for my next eight years of research and writing.

In Chapter 2, we saw 36,765 people were recorded as being held illegally by the police in June 2016, approximately 13% of the country's pre-trial detainees and 5% of its total prison population. In June 2012, the first year in which official statistics were collated from the majority (all but four) of the 19 states that continued the practice, a full eight percent of Brazilian prisoners were in the custody of the police (41,220 of 508,357 total prison population) (Ministério da Justiça 2012). In June 2010, two months before I conducted the study at Polinter, an estimated 3000 were in police custody in Rio de Janeiro (Folha de São Paulo, 4 April 2010), 2500 of which in the metropolitan city area (Lemgruber and Fernandez 2011). As in the rest of the country, most were held in *carceragens*—in the basement or in annexes to police stations—rather than in ordinary police holding cells.

In Chapter 2, I noted that under Brazilian law a person cannot be held by the police after their arrest has been processed. But as authorities try to keep control over numbers in the official prison system (colloquially known as the *sistema*: system), in many states, the police are left to hold on to detainees for months until places become available. By default, the police are also left to take on the role of guards. We will see the few officers who worked at Polinter received no extra resources to manage the hundreds of detainees left in their charge, let alone to attend to their social, personal or medical needs. There were no administration, health, education or other support staff to provide services to prisoners. *Marmitas* (meal boxes: see Chapter 4) were delivered three times a day. Otherwise, the people that worked at the *carceragem* had to be creative if they were to do anything more than secure the perimeter walls.

In September 2010, I spent an intensive three weeks researching at Polinter. On the first day, I was welcomed by the coordinator of Rio de Janeiro's *carceragem* system, Orlando Zaccone (also introduced in Chapter 1). Zaccone soon left me in the hands of the deputy governor, before he headed off to another appointment (the governor, who had changed since my previous visit, was away that morning). The deputy governor immediately introduced me to Polinter's two most senior trusty prisoners (although at first, I assumed them to also be police officers), before himself heading back to his position in the administration office. Over the next few hours, I moved back and forth between the office and the entrance to the cell block, where these two prisoners remained stationed. The deputy governor explained they were former police officers who had killed *bandidos* (outlaws). I later discovered they answered directly to the governor and did not take orders from this deputy. They spent most of the day outside the cell block, where they could best monitor the work of the other trusty prisoners under their command, and from where they could directly oversee one of the most risky procedures at the *carceragem*, the movement of prisoners to and from the wings. When the governor arrived, the deputy took me on a quick tour of the cell block. That was the only time I saw him even approach the cell block in the three weeks I was there.

From the second day, I arrived between 9 a.m. and 10 a.m. each morning and left at around 7 p.m. I spent most of my hours at the *carceragem* sitting around in the office and courtyard between the front gate and cell block, observing and casually chatting with the people that worked there. By the end of the second week, I was on good speaking terms with the police officers and most of the trusty prisoners that worked outside the cell block: in the office, the courtyard, the visitors' reception, the kitchen and so forth. In the third week, I focused more attention on the work of prisoners in the cell block. I eventually negotiated spaces to conduct more formal interviews with 21 key informants.

After the first day, I only entered the wings themselves for a few brief moments. I had been granted access from Zaccone, but on condition I was accompanied by the deputy governor or the *chefia* (management, as I later realised, indicating the governor and his head trusty prisoners).

Not only would it have been difficult to speak in confidence with prisoners, but we will see the *carceragem* was too thinly staffed to allow the governor or his head trusty prisoners (henceforth referred to collectively as the *chefia*) to take much time out of their ordinary work routines. What I could do was accompany one of them on the rare occasion they entered a wing other than to unlock the cells at the beginning of the day and to lock prisoners up again in the evening. Instead, I spent most of my time in the cell block observing and talking with the trusty prisoners and inmate leaders that manned the entrances to the wings and visiting rooms. The space between the entrance to a cell block and its wings is sometimes referred to as the *miolo* (core) in Rio de Janeiro (see Chapter 3). At Polinter, it was referred to in more abstract terms, as the *ligação* (link), most likely we will see because it measured only a few square metres. I introduced the concept of the *ligação* in Chapter 3 and return to it in more detail here.

At lunchtime, I ate with the *chefia* in a small room by the entrance to the *carceragem*, which doubled as a bedroom for one of the two head trusty prisoners. Wherever something was happening—new prisoners arriving, the families of prisoners arriving for visits with their *jumbos* (bags of food and other basic goods) ready for inspection, prisoners or their families being escorted to and from the visiting rooms, cell block and so on—I would be close by mentally taking note before heading to the office to write down my observations and reflections. It became a running joke among some of my participants that I never sat still, that I was a "ninja" researcher who would appear one moment and disappear the next. I shortly found myself being drawn into the routines of the prison, in particular answering queries from prisoners' families and other visitors (mostly lawyers and church groups), many of who we will see assumed I was working there. I was sometimes asked to accompany the police officer stationed at the front gate (usually this role was fulfilled by a trusty prisoner). Fortunately, this meant no more than greeting and directing visitors, or passing messages to the governor or deputy governor when someone unexpectedly arrived. Once I found myself temporarily in charge of the front gate when the officer stationed there had to be elsewhere. When someone knocked, I asked them to wait until the officer returned. No other police were present at the *carceragem* at the time.

When I arrived at Polinter, there had not been a murder in any of Rio de Janeiro's *carceragens* for two years. Nor had there been an escape from Polinter for more than a year, but over the following 12 months, there were four, one involving an exchange of gunfire. In Chapter 1, I noted Zaccone had previously inaugurated an award-winning civil police initiative, Projeto Carceragem Cidadã (Citizen Police Lock-up Project), in 2008, while governor of a second *carceragem* in the city, Nova Iguaçu. The project resulted in various improvements to the regime at Nova Iguaçu, including medical assistance and a library. At the time of my study, health and education centres were in the process of being built at Polinter. A small *pátio* (exercise yard) had recently opened for prisoners held on one wing. A second *pátio* was being constructed for prisoners on the other. During his tenure, Zaccone actively campaigned for the closure of Rio de Janeiro's *carceragens*. By the time he moved on in February 2011, they were no longer receiving new prisoners.

Besides the obvious difficulties of researching in a second language (and moreover, a second language tainted with local prison slang: my Brazilian colleague who transcribed the interviews complained that at times my participants were barely speaking Portuguese), the most mentally tiring aspect of the research was that I was often given contradicting facts or differing versions of the same events. Occasionally, I suspected that I was being lied to, but most of the time, I had the impression my participants simply wanted to answer my questions, however, much they actually knew. There was also the constant worry of negotiating the boundaries of my research. I quickly discovered my access to potential interviewees also depended on the relationship I was able to form with the head trusty prisoners. By asking the same thing to different people, and finding different ways to ask the same thing of the same people, I gradually found the answers to most of my doubts; and through repeated reminders to the head trusty prisoners I eventually interviewed everyone I wanted.

Most exhausting of all were the (likewise often contradicting) emotions I experienced from one day to the next. I had sensibly chosen to stay in a hotel over an hour away to gain some mental distance from the research, but my good intention to go for a run along the beach in the evenings was soon replaced by the comfort of cigarettes and the hotel bar. I had too much to recover from (and reflect on). For example, while I became aware that some of the trusty prisoners had killed on multiple occasions, and felt uncomfortable (and indeed angered) by the continuous sexist and homophobic banter that many tried to involve me, by the time the research ended I had begun to enjoy their company and feel empathy towards them. The last day of research ended with hugs, photographs, promises to visit me in London, and jokes from the governor that if I got into trouble with the police outside he would always have a job for me (that is as a trusty prisoner), but that they would have to learn to cater better for vegetarians. (After three weeks of rice, beans, poached eggs, lettuce and tomato, I nodded in agreement).

Still, despite my depth of immersion in the routines of Polinter, the three-week time frame restricted the amount of data that I was able to gather, and the trust that I was able to establish with my research participants. As Waldram (2009) reminds us, captured populations such as prisoners are often anxious to tell their stories to outside researchers, but at the same time are likely to be initially wary of someone new. These limitations were further compounded, as previously mentioned, by restrictions to my access to certain parts of the *carceragem*. Principally, the fact I only entered the wings accompanied by the *chefia* most likely created further suspicion among inmate leaders regarding my insider/outsider status. Indeed, in interview, the head prisoner on the *seguro* (insurance or vulnerable persons unit) questioned whether I was an inmate—that is a trusty prisoner—as well as a researcher. It also left me largely dependent on inmate leaders and trusty prisoners for knowledge of life in the cell block and the views of the wider inmate body (the *coletivo*: collective), with whom I had no opportunities to talk without an officer or trusty prisoner by my side. This limitation was most poignant regarding the gang wing. Most trusty prisoners had at least some understanding of the *seguro*, having spent several months there before being entrusted to work. However, I only became aware of two that had started on the gang wing, where in common with other prisons in the state (see Chapter 6), inmates were banned from working as trusty prisoners and would be ejected from the gang for doing so. One had started out on the gang wing at Polinter, then transferred to another *carceragem* in the state, and returned to Polinter to become a trusty prisoner. The other had been transferred to Polinter a year after becoming a trusty prisoner at his first *carceragem*. He emphasised he had never been involved in any form of gang-related activity on the outside. Yet he remained concerned someone might recognise him in the future. His family had moved away from the area in which he had lived. (For analysis of the potentially serious consequences post-prison of being seen to have collaborated, see Silva 2008b.)

Finally, in such a confined, controlling space, most of my conversations and observations were of groups rather than individual officers and prisoners, or else were regularly interrupted. This was a particular concern in the case of the inmate leaders and trusty prisoners, who, as I will explain, spent their working day continuously in the company of others. While I was able to arrange times and places to supplement the observational research with private interviews, in the case of the gang wing (I describe the wings in a moment), the six interviewees arrived together, and only two sat down to talk. Interviews with trusty prisoners were mostly held in the head trusty prisoners' bedroom, which was used by officers and other more senior trusty prisoners at lunchtime to eat and watch television. Interviews with prisoners on the wings were held in the lawyers' visiting room. I approached officers and trusty prisoners personally for interviews. Interviews on the wings were negotiated through the head inmate leaders. With limited understanding of the pressure inmate leaders might put on individuals to participate, this raised potential ethical concerns regarding the informed consent of interviewees (see Waldram 1998). In the event, inmate leaders selected themselves for interview. Considering the role we will see inmate leaders played in speaking on behalf of the *coletivo*, the lack of confidence they may have had in my position vis-à-vis the prison administration, and the broader "law of silence" that Rio de Janeiro's gangs impose among *favela* residents (see Chapter 4), this was always likely to be the case.

Much of this chapter is borrowed from a previous published article I dedicated fully to Polinter (Darke 2014). The analysis I present in the conclusion is mostly borrowed from Darke (2013). This was the first publication in which I made use of the concept of co-governance to describe and analyse Brazilian everyday prison dynamics, although I did not utilise that specific term. Here I have added additional detail from my field notes in places as well as from conversations I have had since with people that worked or visited there, including Zaccone. I also repeat a number of the points about Polinter that I first made in Chapter 1. I gave Darke (2014) the title of Managing without Guards in a Brazilian Police Lockup—part duplicated here—to reflect the fact the *carceragem* was not only administered by the police with the support of its prisoners, but that at the time of the study, the police and prisoners were successfully doing so. At the time, my then 11-year-old daughter suggested an alternative title: No Guards; Prisoners in Charge. Besides sounding a little childish and sensationalist, it did not reflect the complexities of co-governance. Neither, we saw in Chapter 3, does the organised crime perspective favoured by Brazilian authorities and some of the less critical research on the Brazilian prison gang phenomenon. In retrospect, No Guards; Prisoners in Charge might have made a good title, although it would have been necessary to add a question mark. I have used it as the subtitle for the conclusion to this chapter.

***

On the first day of research, Polinter was holding 464 male prisoners,[1] most incarcerated for the first time. The majority had arrived following arrest, but a few had been transferred from other *carceragens* to work as trusty prisoners (I return to this important point later in the chapter). Most preferred to stay there to be close to their families and, we will see, due to the way their families were treated when they came to visit (this is a second major point I return to). Others were waiting to be selected to join the dozen or so prisoners transferred to remand prisons each Friday morning (and could not afford to pay to be put at the front of the waiting list). Most prisoners remained there between six months and a year; some had been there for several years. Some had already been tried and sentenced;

a few had already served the minimum time required to move to a semi-open prison unit. At Polinter, the only free legal advice prisoners received was from a lawyer working pro bono for a voluntary sector non-governmental organisation that visited every other Saturday morning (though, we will see, the police employed a number of more educated prisoners to liaise with the courts over judicial hearings). Prisoners typically waited two months for their case to be reviewed by the state's public defence service and seven months for their first judicial hearing. The consequences of these delays were serious for the majority of prisoners. In Chapter 2, I cited research at the time (Lemgruber and Fernandez 2011) which showed just a third of pre-trial detainees in Rio de Janeiro were eventually sentenced to imprisonment. A later study (Instituto de Defesa do Direito de Defesa 2018) found fewer than one in twenty people arrested *em flagrante* (caught in the act) in Rio de Janeiro were represented by a lawyer while their detention in police custody was processed.

There are four features of life at Polinter common to other Brazilian prisons I should emphasise by way of introduction. First was the number of employed staff. At the time of research, a total of five police officers worked at the *carceragem*. Two *plantonistas* (literally, on duty; here meaning guards) worked 12-hour shifts at the front gate. Two more police officers, the governor and deputy governor, worked during the daytime. The governor usually arrived at lunchtime. The fifth and only woman police officer worked Monday to Friday. Her role was to lightly frisk the majority of (female) visitors. (Unlike many prisons in the country, visitors were not put through the humiliating experience of being strip-searched: see Chapter 2.) A few other officers came and went during the week, transporting prisoners to and from court appearances or, bringing newly arrested detainees from nearby police stations or, as just mentioned, transferring existing inmates to remand prisons. As in other *carceragens* in the state, there were no paid support staff.

Instead, the *carceragem* was mostly run by its prisoners. For the purposes of my research, this was its most relevant feature. Polinter's *chefia* was in charge of approximately 45 trusty prisoners. As for governance on the wings, the first thing a person that arrived at Polinter was asked was, "*tem facção?*" ("are you in a criminal gang?"). What qualified him as being in a gang was not active membership but coming from an area under gang control. If the new prisoner was from an area controlled by a gang other than the one assigned to Polinter, the CV, he was sent to the *triagem* (holding cell) to await transfer to another *carceragem*.[2] If he indicated that he did not want to be associated with gangs (which was often the situation with older prisoners), or it was otherwise decided that he would not be accepted by them (for instance, because of his sexuality, if he had been arrested for a sexual offence, or if he had worked for one of the militia groups that has in recent years taken control of over a third of Rio de Janeiro's *favelas*: see Chapter 2), he went to the *seguro*, where he would find himself subject to the authority of the latest prisoner gang phenomenon to hit Rio de Janeiro, the Povo de Israel (People of Israel). Formed in the mid-2000s at a prison designated for prisoners not affiliated with existing gangs (Caldeira 2007; Silva 2011), the Povo de Israel is unique among major Brazilian prisoner organisations in that it has no links to gang hierarchies on the outside. Membership begins and ends at the prison gate. Prisoners on the *seguro* at Polinter did not consider the Povo de Israel to be a criminal gang.[3] The head of the Povo de Israel was from a well educated background. His sister, who introduced herself to me during a visit, was fluent in English and spoke with an American accent.

The third key feature of life at Polinter was the physical space. The *carceragem* occupied just 1200 square metres. It had been converted from police stables. At the start of the study, 74 prisoners were accommodated in single rooms or dormitories above the cell block (the previous stables) and office, or in communal areas off the wings; from what I could tell, every indoor area besides the office and toilets was utilised. This number included the prisoners that worked as *colaboradores* (collaborators, one of Rio de Janeiro's terms for trusty prisoners; the one preferred by those working as trusty prisoners at Polinter and which I will use from now on).[4] The remainder were officially kept off the wings for their safety, for instance, as sons of politicians or judges, former militia or police (though, as I have already suggested, ex-police were particularly likely to be offered *colaborador* positions, as they also were at the state's other *carceragens* at the time: see, e.g., Soares 2012).[5] Some had paid a *propina* (fee or bribe) to avoid the wings. This practice has been noted in other prisons in Rio de Janeiro (see, e.g., Silva 2011). The cell block measured perhaps 400 square metres. Here, 390 prisoners were divided between the two (CV and *seguro*) wings, in a total of nine cells (five of which were on the *seguro*), each measuring approximately 25 square metres and containing 12 bunks. Each cell was represented by one prisoner (the *representante de cela*: cell representative), and each wing had one *representante geral* (general representative). When I first visited, the cell block held nearer to 550 prisoners. A year before that, some cells had contained over 90 prisoners. One research participant claimed his cell had held 103 prisoners.

Finally, in spite of the crowding, Polinter was a hive of organised activity between 8 a.m. and 7 p.m., mostly surrounding the distribution of food and collection of rubbish, visits from families of prisoners, of which there were more than 1000 each week, and mid-morning and mid-afternoon Mass, led by local church groups. At noon and again at 6 p.m., prisoners on the CV wing held further prayers, followed by a chant of allegiance. When someone was released, which occurred around 7 p.m. some evenings when court officials arrived with the results of the day's proceedings, the CV wing again broke into chant.

In the following two sections, I document the formal and informal roles played by prisoners in running Polinter, and the benefits they gained. In doing so, I have two purposes. The first is to elaborate on the institutional character of inmate collaboration and self-ordering at the *carceragem*: to demonstrate that it would not have been possible for Polinter to operate in the way that it did without the full participation of its inmates. My second purpose is to explore what it meant for prisoners to run the *carceragem*, in terms of the order they produced. I conclude with a discussion of the implications of the *ritmo da cadeia* (prison rhythm, as Rio de Janeiro and São Paulo inmates often refer to an established prison order: see, *inter alia*, Barbosa 2005; Marques 2014, whose work I cover in the next chapter) at the *carceragem* for our understanding of everyday governance in penal institutions, like Polinter, that manage with limited space and few resources. We will see staff dependence on inmates presents a series of questions concerning not only order, but also authority and legitimacy, concepts that are at the centre of criminological prison studies.

The *Colaboradores*

The work of the *colaboradores* could be categorised into 14 areas of activity. Nine of these involved janitorial or clerical duties that would not be considered particularly unusual even in the relatively well-resourced prisons of the Global North. Important for current purposes, however, is that they were performed almost exclusively by prisoners, and largely without officer supervision. Three of these positions (which I call "the handyman", "the chef" and "the nurse") were performed by individual prisoners. Most of the handyman's time was taken up fixing fans, making furniture and repairing cars. Alongside the *propina* charged for sleeping in beds outside of the wings, his workshop was one of many additional sources of income we will see the police utilised to sustain the regime. He made repairs for the *carceragem*, individual police officers and other private clients.[6] The chef cooked for the police and *colaboradores*. The nurse was solely responsible for the medical care of all 464 prisoners; nine in ten of who he claimed were on some form of medication. As for the other *colaboradores*, working in the place of prison staff brought a number of advantages, including better food, quicker access to medical attention and judicial assistance, greater contact with their families (who were allowed to visit all day Saturday and Sunday and to pass by at the end of each working day) and the right to wear jeans and trainers and personal effects like watches and jewellery. Furthermore, in common with inmates working as trusty prisoners in other Brazilian prisons, they also gained the statutory right to one day remission in sentence for every three days worked, but not their legal entitlement to 75% of the minimum salary.

Most important to the *colaboradores* I interviewed, working also meant not being held on the wings, where there was little to keep prisoners occupied, little natural light and little space to move around or sleep comfortably. The handyman, nurse and chef slept on mattresses where they worked; in the case of the nurse, this was on the examination couch in between attending inmates that had fallen ill during the night or new prisoners that had arrived with injuries or withdrawing from crack or alcohol.[7] Like the majority of *colaboradores*, they had been in the *carceragem* system for at least a year (one *colaborador* had been at Polinter for 32 months), and had spent several months on the wings before being offered the chance to work. *Colaboradores* were chosen according to their willingness to work and the skills and other resources they could offer (for instance, some in the office worked with their own computers; the nurse gained his position after his nephew, a paramedic working for the fire service, approached the police with an offer to redirect medicines donated to the fire service on to the *carceragem*), but primarily for their perceived trustworthiness. Most important, the police had to be confident they would not try to escape. In practice, this meant having a good disciplinary record, and a stable family that regularly visited. Most had also been imprisoned for violent rather than drug offences, which in the eyes of the police made them less likely to be deceitful (*malandros*: see Chapter 4) and less likely to consider themselves *bandidos*. Six years later, I learnt from an officer working in a TC (Terceiro Commando) remand prison (see Chapter 3) that this was the norm in other prisons in Rio de Janeiro as well. Besides those that had paid to get onto the *colaborador* wing (in Chapter 2, we saw trusty prisoners usually live in less crowded conditions), most of the *colaboradores* in his prison had been arrested for homicide.

The remaining prisoners responsible for janitorial or clerical tasks were divided into teams, led by inmates the police considered most trustworthy. The governor described how he had brought most of these *colaboradores* from his previous *carceragem*. The governor he replaced had likewise taken "his *colaboradores*" away to his new *carceragem*. At least five of these *colaboradores*, including the two head *colaboradores* already mentioned (and to whose roles I return in a moment), were former police officers, all, it seemed, likewise convicted of homicide. These more senior *colaboradores* had few restrictions on their movements and were at liberty to frequent the courtyard at lunchtime or in the evening before retiring to single rooms. From time to time, they would leave Polinter to purchase supplies outside, again reflecting practice in Rio de Janeiro's other *carceragens* of the period (again, see, as example, Soares 2012).[8] However, those working under them had to return to their quarters outside working hours. The largest team ("the porters") was comprised of nine prisoners incarcerated for fixed terms of 30, 60 or 90 days for not paying child maintenance. They spent much of the day shifting rubbish bins and boxes of food to and from the wings. Other responsibilities included sweeping the courtyard, cleaning the bathrooms, opening and closing internal gates for police vans and making coffee. Due to their relatively minor offences and short sentences, they were not considered escape risks and were not closely monitored. Their final duty of the day was to clean the visiting rooms, where they subsequently slept.

The remainder of the *colaboradores* slept in their own beds, though in dormitories rather than single rooms. Two other teams of perhaps six prisoners were involved in janitorial work: checking, registering and delivering the *jumbos* brought in by families during visiting hours (9–11 a.m., 11:30 a.m.–1:30 p.m., 2–4 p.m. and 4:30–6:30 p.m., Monday to Friday)[9] ("the registers"); and selling additional goods to prisoners on the wings (the *cantineiros* or "canteen workers"). The goods brought in by their families were particularly valued by prisoners. In addition to food, families were allowed to bring in cleaning products, clothes, medicines and cigarettes. The internal goods market (the *cantina*: canteen) was a particularly important source of finance for the *carceragem*, as it is in many other Brazilian prisons (I explore this tradition in the following chapter). Four prisoners were involved in this work. Chilled two-litre bottles of soft drinks sold in their dozens, perhaps hundreds, each day for R$4 (£1); burger and chips for R$4 (£1) and R$6 (£1.50); and packets of cigarettes for R$5 (£1.25). Most items were sold during visiting hours, for prisoners to share with their families. As there was no paid work at the *carceragem* for prisoners on the wings, these goods were purchased with money brought in by their families. Towards the end of the day, bulk sales were made for distribution to the cells. In both cases, common prisoners[10] initially paid their *representantes*, who made the purchases on their behalf.[11] Some *colaboradores* had been given permission (no doubt, involving some form of commission or *propina*) to supplement their incomes through selling additional items brought in by their own families. One sold origami; another sold beaded flip-flops made to order by his wife; another sold cakes to his fellow *colaboradores*. The cakes were delivered fresh to the *carceragem* at the end of the working day.

Two small teams of prisoners were involved in clerical work. These were the only *colaboradores* at the *carceragem* that were supervised by officers as well as team leaders. Four prisoners ("the receptionists") sat throughout the day alongside the woman police officer by the main entrance, noting down visitors' names, collecting their bags and *jumbos*, identification cards and mobile phones and writing down the cell numbers of those they were visiting on pieces of paper for them to take to the *colaboradores* working in the cell block, at the entrances to the visiting rooms. Another three prisoners ("the clerks") worked alongside the deputy governor in the office. Their main tasks were to maintain records and, as previously explained, correspond with lawyers and judges. New visitors also had to register with them.

More extraordinary were the tasks carried out by inmates involved in guarding prisoners held on the wings. Again, these tasks were performed with minimal police supervision. Prisoners were employed as guards in six principle ways. The first concerned surveillance. More generally, the police relied on *colaboradores* accommodated above the cell block to listen out for attempts to escape. In addition, a number of *colaboradores* ("the watchmen") patrolled the courtyard at night. Some of these prisoners may have been armed.

Next, two *colaboradores* ("the escorts") were responsible for guarding the prisoners held on the wings when they were being registered in the office, and handcuffing and accompanying them to and from the cell block. At least 15 others ("the turnkeys") worked at the entrance to the cell block, in a six-way intersection (the *ligação*) measuring perhaps 10 square metres alongside the *colaboradores* involved in selling confectionaries and fast food. In this space, two barred doors led to the visiting rooms, and two solid doors to rooms used for conjugal visits. Two twin-gate *gaiolas* (cages) led onto the wings. The turnkeys working at the *gaiolas* were the only *colaboradores* required to wear uniforms (blue T-shirts with the word *apoio* [helper] printed on the back). During visiting hours never a minute went by when prisoners, families or fast food did not pass through the area, the latter from the *cantina*, which was located in a smaller, unused cell. Money was continuously exchanged through the *gaiolas* and doors to the visiting rooms between the *cantineiros* and *representantes*. Prison meals also passed through this area. Large rubbish bins full of empties moved in the opposite direction.

At the end of visits, the fourth and perhaps most controversial *colaborador* task was carried out. Families were moved into the courtyard, at which point senior *colaboradores* from across the *carceragem* descended on the visiting rooms to strip-search the *representantes* and common prisoners who had received visits. The period immediately following visits was considered the most dangerous. It is the only part of the daily routine in which common prisoners were congregated and uncuffed outside the wings, and hence the most likely time for rebellion; and the only time of day I sensed tension and anxiety on the part of the *colaboradores*. As a security measure, families were kept on-site until common prisoners had returned to the wings. After the final visit of the day, cell doors were locked for the night, and senior *colaboradores* began their last guard-like duty, the *confere* (check). Cells were emptied one by one and their occupants counted and seated along the length of the wing corridors, with their hands behind their heads. Meanwhile, the cells were searched for tunnels, contraband material and tampering with locks and bars. One evening, I was there a *colaborador* returned from the *confere* with two halves of a broken hacksaw blade. The last task of the *colaboradores* concerned their role supporting *representantes* in maintaining order. Where possible, incidences of disorder were left to *representantes* to deal with. However, if a fight broke out *representantes* were unable to control, *colaboradores* would enter with the police to separate the prisoners involved. *Representantes* reported prisoners considered too difficult to control for transfer. All of my research participants refuted any suggestion *colaboradores* might occasionally resort to violence, though a number, including the governor and the *representante geral* on the CV wing, referred to *colaborador* (and, indeed, police) brutality in the past. The CV leader also claimed violence continued in some of Rio de Janeiro's other *carceragens*. One of Zaccone's first instructions when becoming coordinator of Rio de Janeiro's *carceragens* was to ban the police from "*mexendo com os presos*" ("messing with the prisoners"). This meant an end to the systematic practice of punishment beatings, which continue across much of the state's prison system today (see Chapter 4). Punishment beatings were also the norm in Rio de Janeiro's *carceragem* system before Zaccone was put in charge. In a biographical account of a drug trafficker's journey through Rio de Janeiro's prison system in the mid-2000s that I have already cited twice in this chapter, former National Security Secretary, Luiz Soares (2012: 147), describes the state's *carceragen*s as operating under four Ps: "*pau, porrada e porrete, porra!*" ("stick, beating and clubbing, fuck you!").

We have seen that highest ranking of all *colaboradores* were two prisoners who worked directly for the governor. They were effectively the general managers of Polinter and second in command to the governor, and exercised greater day-to-day authority than the remaining police officers, who rarely left their posts (in the office; at the front gate; in the visitors' reception). While the governor was off duty, they were effectively in charge. While the police referred to the governor and his head *colaboradores* as Polinter's *chefia*, prisoners referred to them as Polinter's *administração* (administration). Both carried mobile phones, which they used to organise deliveries and to communicate with the governor when he was away. In Chapter 1, I noted they also carried keys to the cell block and to the back entrance of the *carceragem*, which they opened for families to leave at the end of visits, as well as to receive supplies. We will see in a moment that at least one of them also had a key to the arms cabinet. The first of these two prisoners oversaw the markets in confectionaries and fast food (the *cantina*) and other items *representantes* asked to purchase from outside. He acted as stock taker, cashier and accountant.[12] I refer to him as Polinter's 'finance manager'. The other head *colaborador* acted as the middleman between the governor, senior *colaboradores* and *representantes*. He was essentially Polinter's 'operating manager'. *Colaboradores* might not have physically abused common prisoners. However, the operating manager appeared to have licence to assault other *colaboradores*. On the last Friday morning of the research, he hit a junior *colaborador* (who had been accused of trying to escape when taking out rubbish bins) open handed in front of the deputy governor, before handcuffing him and putting him into a police van alongside common prisoners about to be transferred. In the confusion, one of the drivers forgot his weapon. As the van was leaving, the finance manager rushed to the arms cabinet, cocked the driver's stored rifle and passed it to him through the van window.

The *Representantes*

Equally important to the management of Polinter were the roles played by the *representantes* in organising life on the wings. We have seen that at Polinter, as at many other prisons in Brazil, the police and their *colaboradores* did not enter the wings between unlock and lockdown so long as the *coletivo* and its *representantes* were able to ensure daily routines ran smoothly and prisoners were disciplined and under control. As expected, nor did the police or their *colaboradores* have any direct involvement in the appointment of *representantes,* their deputies or their work teams, who were instead chosen by their cell and wing mates. (Although, again reflecting practice in other prisons in Rio de Janeiro and other parts of the country, including the equally gang-dominated São Paulo [see Chapter 3], it is likely officers could effectively deselect prisoners appointed to positions lower down the CV hierarchy by simply refusing to work with them.) Some research participants spoke of *representantes* being elected; others spoke in terms of "natural leaders" or the most "experienced" prisoners assuming positions (which we have seen in previous chapters is also ordinary practice in São Paulo and other parts of the country). Significantly, most downplayed the hierarchical nature of the inmate leader system. Indeed, on the *seguro* at least, the only privilege gained by becoming a *representante* was the opportunity to spend the whole of the daytime out of the cells. Moreover, as at other penal institutions across Brazil, it appeared a *representante*'s authority depended as much upon him remaining accountable to and retaining the confidence of the *coletivo* as gang hierarchies (though to a certain degree, this might equate to the same thing: several research participants, including the governor, emphasised *representantes* lived in fear of what might happen to them when they eventually moved on to the *sistema* if they failed to do so). This, we will see in a moment, meant enforcing and themselves following long-established codes of conduct designed to facilitate solidarity among prisoners and to enable them to keep their heads down and serve their time. As Antônio Barbosa (2005, 2007) explains, the CV and other prison gangs in Rio de Janeiro (including, I would add, the Povo de Israel) have brought levels of order that prison administrators have historically been unable to achieve on their own. I return to Barbosa's work in Chapter 6.

As should already be apparent, the first duty of the *representantes* was to deal with the police and *colaboradores* on behalf of the *coletivo*: to work on the other side of the *ligação*. This mostly involved their everyday dealings with the turnkey *colaboradores*, for instance, to call prisoners with visits or appointments in the office or medical room or to purchase from the *cantina*. *Representantes* explained it was not practical to give every common prisoner licence to congregate around the entrances to the wings and visiting rooms, where *colaboradores* were stationed. More interesting in terms of prison governance, *representantes* were consulted by the *chefia* on decisions affecting the *coletivo*, including as I have already noted, decisions to transfer prisoners that threatened the status quo. This I witnessed on two occasions when common prisoners acted aggressively towards the escorts. Following the first, less serious incident, when the governor of the *carceragem* was off duty, one of the head *colaboradores* (the operating manager) approached the CV wing *representantes*, who assured him they would be able to deal with the inmate in question. The other, more serious incident, when an inmate from the *seguro* physically lashed out at his escort, was dealt with by the governor. After the governor had spoken with the Povo de Israel *representantes*, he sent the operating manager to the office to instruct one of the clerks to put the offending prisoner on the list of transferees.

More generally, the governor held meetings with the *representantes*, collectively known as the wings' *comissões* (committees; see Chapter 4), to discuss prison order and inmate needs. "I try to help them with everything they need," the governor elaborated. "In return they give me discipline" (fieldwork interview, 17 September 2010). *Colaboradores* and *representantes* likewise emphasised the usefulness of the police having just a few people to deal with and to be held responsible by the police and the *coletivo* when things went wrong.

Besides negotiating on behalf of their *coletivo* and working on the *ligação*, one of the main roles of the *representantes* was to manage routines on the wings. This could be divided into two areas of activity. The first involved organising teams to distribute meals and bulk purchases from the *cantina*, and to clean the corridors, visiting areas and (on the CV wing) the newly constructed *pátio*. Second, *representantes* organised a number of rotas, for instance, for spending time out of cell, having a haircut, making coffee or preparing food on in cell stoves (each prisoner was, for instance, allowed 500 grammes of coffee powder, one loaf of bread and three packets of instant noodles per week as part of his *jumbo*), receiving conjugal visits or maintaining in cell hygiene such as cleaning, washing clothes or showering. The only major facet of prisoners' day-to-day lives that did not have a rota was sleeping. Those that had been at Polinter the longest had first choice of bunks and (on the CV wing) opportunity to sleep in the relatively cool *pátio*. Poorer prisoners (e.g., those whose families did not visit or bring them money) were often paid to take on their cellmates' chores.

Representantes played a further role in meeting the needs of individual prisoners. Inmates were expected to provide needier prisoners (usually those that did not receive visits) and new prisoners arriving on the weekend (when there were no visits on the wings) with essential goods such as their prison dress (Bermuda shorts, white T-shirt, flip-flops), toiletries, medicines and food to supplement their prison meals. To a large extent, this relied on individual prisoners, who were expected to share out some of the goods brought in by their families with more needy prisoners (on the CV wing this was considered obligatory). In Chapter 4, we saw this is common practice among prisoners across the country. However, much was also organised by the *representantes*, who kept hold of items left behind by former prisoners (in the case of the CV wing) and maintained a *caixinha* (collection box) into which prisoners who received family visits were also expected to contribute (the Povo de Israel also made use of a *caixinha*, but this was managed by the wing *pastores* [church ministers] rather than the *representantes*). The *caixinhas* were used, among other things, to provide a welcome kit for new prisoners and bus fares for freed prisoners, and to buy communal items such as cleaning products, electric ovens, cooking utensils, fans and televisions. One of the most recent items *representantes* on the CV wing had asked permission to buy was paint, which they needed to decorate a shrine in the new *pátio*.

Like the janitorial and clerical tasks played by *colaboradores* outside the wings, none of these inmate roles were particularly out of the ordinary per se, either in a global or historical context, including in the Global North (except that they were again performed with little police interference or supervision). Again, what was most unusual, at least in comparison with prisons in the North, was the institutional character of this prisoner self-ordering. Both on and off the wings, it was not so much useful as necessary for the five officers that worked at Polinter to pass on responsibilities for managing the *carceragem* to prisoners.

Of particular significance for our understanding of governance at the *carceragem*, police reliance on prisoners extended to the role *representantes* played within the *coletivo* in overseeing inmate codes of conduct. As at other prisons in the country (see Chapters 4 and 6), these covered, among other things, dealings with the police (principally, not to impede the work of the police and their *colaboradores* in maintaining prison routines, discipline and security, but otherwise not to inform), in cell behaviour (e.g., not to touch others' belongings and to be quiet at night) and inmate solidarity (e.g., not to be aggressive, to share items brought in by families and to respect other prisoners' visitors). On the CV wing, the requirement to respect the work of *colaboradores* as well as the police stood in contrast to the official position the *coletivo* took on its own affiliates working for the prison administration (although we have already seen in practice this meant little more than no longer having the right to be recognised as a gang associate, and not having an option to return to a CV wing in the future). In Chapter 6, we will see gang-affiliated prisoners across Brazil accept some inmates need to work alongside or in the place of prison staff if, for example, their meals are to be delivered or their families are able to visit. As at any other prison, personal problems were to be sorted out on the street, while disputes with prison management were to be avoided until (in the case of the CV) an order came from higher up the gang hierarchy for state-level rebellion (I also return to this point in Chapter 6 in the context of São Paulo's PCC). Rules regarding inmate solidarity were, if anything, stricter than at the average Brazilian prison. In such appalling living conditions and with so few resources, it was deemed absolutely necessary to avoid any form of aggressive behaviour. Both wings were free of crack cocaine and weapons. In the three weeks I did not hear anyone curse, or even raise their voice. Besides the governor and CV *representante geral*, only one of my participants used a swear word during interview. In the cramped conditions of the *carceragem* it was important that extra care was taken not to upset prisoners' families. I quickly learnt, like the turnkeys, to step out of the way of visitors, hold gates open for them in the cell block and turn away when they reached the visiting rooms.

Of course, as alternative orders in Rio de Janeiro's *favelas* are subject to cycles of violence (Goldstein 2003) and occasional abuse by gang leaders (Penglase 2009) (see Chapter 4), even the most established inmate *coletivos* are likely to occasionally lose authority. One research participant, for example, spoke in depth of a brief period nine months earlier when a group of prisoners calling themselves the Nova Aliança (New Alliance) had temporarily taken over from the Povo de Israel and ruled the *seguro* through extortion and unprovoked beatings. As for the present, I was aware that notwithstanding the option *representantes* had to report more troublesome prisoners to the police for transfer into the *sistema*, the power wielded by *representantes* was likewise based at least in part on the potential of violence. One *colaborador* referred to inmate punishment beatings being directed towards the body, which left minimal visible marks and was less likely to attract attention. Another gave an account of a prisoner with a black eye who claimed to have tripped over. Certainly, the police and *colaboradores* turned a blind eye to less serious incidences of violence. Until someone was killed or seriously hurt, the governor explained, there was no need to interfere.

No Guards; Prisoners in Charge?

[The turnkey *colaboradores*] take the role of the police, don't they. It's the cat and the rat… But conflict, there isn't… Day to day they have to deal with them, but there's no affection. It isn't good, no. It's necessary to deal with them, that's it. [...] Every cell has a *frente* (front or representative), a leader, you understand? This leader is responsible for the cell, but it doesn't mean he is in charge, that he orders people to get beaten, not at all. It's because there always needs to be someone who organises, a leadership for everything not to get messy. Because there needs to be rules and norms for everything to function well. No one eat someone else's food… have a shower [at the wrong time]… argue… wind each other up… as the saying goes, "he who leaves, shares and does not get the better part, is either crazy or does not understand craft." Someone giving away something… has to make a profit, an advantage, don't they? "Let's make a kitty to buy cleaning products." This one already has a piece in his pocket. And that's the way it is, life is like that. This is Brazil, the *jeitinho brasileiro* (the Brazilian way: see chapter one)… But when power gets to the head of those that are leading, then it gets bad for some. Things end up being done that shouldn't be. (fieldwork interview, *colaborador*, 11 September 2010)

This extended quote helps sum up the most important themes concerning the nature of governance I observed during the time I spent researching Polinter. As noted in the introduction, these relate to issues of order, authority and legitimacy. First, we have seen Polinter did have a functioning, if more habitual or customary than bureaucratic order (cf. Aguirre 2005). The *carceragem* may have been less orderly had the police, CV and Povo de Israel been under different leadership, or had Zaccone not been in overall charge. I explore how much it is possible to generalise from my study of Polinter in the next chapter. For the time being at least, the *carceragem* appeared to have a relatively stable, if provisional order, in which prisoners and officers had pulled together despite its extraordinary levels of deprivation.

Second, I have endeavoured to demonstrate the extent to which Polinter operated under a plural order. Here, our analysis shifts from the fact those that worked at Polinter somehow managed to keep the *carceragem* running, but that they did so despite the fact the *carceragem* was managed without guards. We have seen that through a myriad of duties, inmates were responsible for virtually every aspect of prison work, both on and off the wings, from sweeping corridors and dealing with 200 visitors a day, to providing medicines, clothing and toiletries, even security and systems of alternative dispute resolution. In conditions of under a square metre per prisoner on the wings, even the most basic prison routines—eating; showering; sleeping—would not have been possible were they not coordinated and delivered by prisoners. In the absence of guards, staff-inmate accommodations and tacit agreements, inmate collaboration and self-ordering—co-governance—were not aberrations but defining features of governance at the *carceragem*. Even the policy of transferring troublesome prisoners would have been difficult to implement without the support of their *representantes*. The deputy governor explained that in the case of the *colaboradores*:

> The police cannot be everywhere all the time. You can see there is only one officer on call, or two at the most… If [Polinter] was in the mainstream prison system, to keep 500 inmates it should have 10,000 square meters and at least 20 officers… We fill this gap in relation to the ideal of 20 men by using the *colaboradores*. (fieldwork interview, 10 September 2010)

I have already described the importance the governor attached to the role of *representantes* in managing everyday life on the wings. Here, the deputy governor was more reticent, twice choosing to end my enquiries with the vague words, "there are certain things that are theirs and we don't interfere." Again, not one of my research participants said anything in our conversations or more formal interviews to contradict the point of view of the police, or the *colaborador* quoted at the beginning of this conclusion.

This plurality also had major implications for our understanding of authority at the *carceragem*. It is useful to outline these in some detail.

I have provided a number of illustrations of the extent the current order at the *carceragem* was based not only upon personal relations of trust, but on a hierarchy that included prisoners as well as police. Indeed, we have seen there were no clear divisions between the roles of prison inmates and prison staff. In effect, there were three kinds of guard (prison officer guards, trusty prisoner guards and prisoner representative guards) and two kinds of support staff (trusty prisoner support staff and prisoner representative managed support staff). To summarise and give further detail in places, the police interfered little with the work of the *colaboradores*, who outnumbered them ten to one. Nor, besides the governor, did they leave their posts during work hours, in the office in the case of the deputy governor, and at or nearby the front gate in the case of the two officers that worked as *plantonistas* and the officer that searched female visitors. The governor seldom entered the cell block and rarely spoke to junior *colaboradores* or even their team leaders, choosing instead to communicate through his two head *colaboradores*. Consequently, the police did not supervise all security work, including the end of visit strip searches and the end of day head-count, cell-check and lock-up (the *confere*). Strip-searching was certainly not always supervised. When individual prisoners moved on or off a wing, curtains were drawn across either side of the *gaiola* and they were searched by the turnkey stationed there. I did not notice any police officers the few times I was present in the cell block at the end of visits (I did not enter the visiting rooms themselves). I suspect the *confere* was also overseen by senior *colaboradores* rather than the police. During the *confere* I was usually in the courtyard with the governor watching a team of junior *colaboradores* whose role at this time of the day was to check none of the bars on the outside of the cell block were damaged. The first day I ventured into the cell block at the end of the afternoon (when I witnessed the start of the *confere* on the Povo de Israel wing at a distance), the head turnkey made it clear that for my own safety I was not welcome to stay.

Of particular significance here was the depth of autonomy enjoyed by higher ranking *colaboradores* and *representantes*. We have seen that in certain respects, they exercised more day-to-day authority than the majority of police officers. With the exception of the prisoners involved in clerical work, the only *colaboradores* that were not supervised by other inmates rather than the police were the two head *colaboradores*, who we have seen were responsible only to the governor and, like other senior *colaboradores*, had been transferred with the governor when he took over his current post. Furthermore, we have seen that perhaps half of the senior *colaboradores*, including the head *colaboradores* and the team leader for the turnkeys, registers and receptionists were themselves former police officers.

Similarly, we have seen it was prisoners rather than officers that organised daily routines and managed norms of behaviour on the wings. In fact, *representantes* worked under even less police supervision than senior *colaboradores*. They likewise reported to the governor (despite having worked there for 15 years, the deputy governor was not aware, for instance, that when the new governor had arrived the Povo de Israel had installed a *representante geral*, nor that some of the *colaboradores* the governor brought with him had started as CV). However, their positions were ultimately determined by their relationships to their *coletivos* rather than the police. *Representantes* acted as the intermediaries (the *ligação*) between the *coletivo* and the police, but even this aspect of their work involved little direct contact with the latter. Most of the time they liaised with junior *colaboradores* over relatively mundane matters like calling prisoners with visitors, the delivery of prison meals and packages from families and the purchase of material goods. For more serious matters such as indiscipline and changes to prison routines, they liaised with the senior *colaboradores*. In the three weeks I researched there, I only saw the police enter the cell block on two occasions, both of which previously mentioned. The first was to take me on my first tour of the wings (on the other occasions I entered the wings I was accompanied by one of the head *colaboradores*). The second occurred when the common prisoner assaulted one of the escorts, and the governor entered with his head *colaboradores* to speak with the culprit's *representante*.

There was, then, little to distinguish *colaboradores* and *representantes* from prison officers, not only in terms of function, but also in command. Indeed, one of the most difficult tasks at the beginning of the study was to establish which of the people working there were prisoners and which were police. Once I had confirmed my understanding from my initial visit that those making up the two sides of the *ligação* were all prisoners, I had a little problem distinguishing *representantes* from officers and *colaboradores*. It took longer to distinguish the police from their *colaboradores*, especially the police who were occasionally there to deliver new prisoners or to take existing prisoners to and from judicial hearings. I only realised one of these officers was a policeman the day he took out a gun. We have seen I even found myself being drawn into helping out with prison staff activities. Towards the end of the study, a lawyer with whom I had already spoken a number of times asked me how I had ended up banged up in a Brazilian prison.

The last points that remain to be explored concerning the nature of authority at Polinter relate to the boundary between freedom and incapacitation. This concerns varieties in prisoner confinement and the poverty of prison work.

All of the 464 prisoners that were being held at the time of my research were confined in the sense that they could not officially go beyond the boundaries of the *carceragem*. Likewise, all prisoners faced severe overcrowding. Nevertheless, there was significant variation in the conditions experienced by individual prisoners. This was less so on the wings, where we have seen the only material benefit gained by *representantes* was to leave the cells between 7 a.m. and 7 p.m. to work in the cell block corridors and visiting rooms. The experience of being confined off the wings, on the other hand, varied enormously. We have seen *colaboradores* dressed in their own clothes, ate better than other prisoners held on the wings and slept in more comfort, usually on their own beds or mattresses. However, while the majority were required to sleep where they worked or to share small four to six bed cells, some had their own private rooms. Further, *colaboradores* supposedly had the freedom of the *carceragem* in the few hours of the day they were not working, but there was a clear hierarchy in who could do what. This was particularly noticeable at mealtimes, when lower ranking *colaboradores* would collect their food and return to their posts to eat, but those higher up the *colaborador* hierarchy would eat alongside the police, in the courtyard or kitchen or, we have seen in the case of the most senior *colaboradores*, with the governor. It was also notable at the end of the *confere*, when everyone working at Polinter would rest for a while in the courtyard, but most junior *colaboradores* would congregate away from those that worked closest with the police.

Equally intriguing—and of particular relevance—were the varying conditions of police officer work. Where *colaborador* and *representante* experiences of prison were defined by relative levels of freedom, officer experiences of prison were defined by relative confinement. As previously noted, with the exception of the governor the police effectively had less freedom of movement in their workplace than a number of *colaboradores* and other privileged prisoners. They also spent an extraordinary number of hours at the jail. While the officer that searched visitors worked only Monday to Friday, from 8.30 a.m. to 6.30 p.m., the *plantonistas* worked 12 hours a day, seven days a week. The heaviest burden appeared to fall on the deputy governor, who worked seven days a week, usually until late evening. He likened his situation to having served a long-term sentence in semi-open conditions. The only difference between us, he enjoyed saying to the *colaboradores* working in the office, was that he usually slept at home.

Important for current purposes is that the relative lack of privilege experienced by the majority of officers led to further erosion of everyday police power. What was most striking about the deputy governor's analogy was not so much the solidarity he felt towards the prisoners he worked with, but their mutual experience of being constrained to the office. From this position, we have seen he had little opportunity to influence what went on at the *carceragem*. Nor did he have the necessary knowledge to do so. He depended on senior *colaboradores* and *representantes* to make some of the most important administrative decisions for him, for instance, which cells to allocate new prisoners, and which prisoners to transfer, for bad behaviour or when spaces became available in the *sistema*.

On the other hand, the governor remained in overall charge. We have seen, for example, that the Povo de Israel differed little from the CV in terms of its organisation and rules. This was all of his (and Zaccone's) making. There were no discernible differences in the norms of behaviour that governed day-to-day routines on the two wings, or relations between prisoners and between *representantes*, common prisoners, *colaboradores* and the police. In terms of hierarchy, both had *representantes de cela*, a *representante geral* and a *comissão*. Even the titles were identical. Those with most experience of prison or the longest time at this particular prison were the more likely to become *representantes* on either wing. *Representantes de cela* were chosen among cell mates, and the *representante geral* among the wider cell block *coletivo*. Troublemakers were given over to the police for transfer. Both *representantes geral* would be held to account in other prisons if they failed to keep order at Polinter. Staff-inmate relations were more sober on the CV wing. CV inmates held their hands behind their backs and looked to the floor when, for instance, they went between the visiting rooms and their wing. Different to Povo de Israel prisoners, they were handcuffed when escorted to and from the cell block. However, these were little more than charades. Some CV prisoners seemed to forget what was expected of them and greeted *colaboradores*. We saw in Chapter 1 that the CV leadership shook hands with Zaccone when he met them on their wing. In interview, the CV's *representante geral* said they could count on the police to resolve any issues. Everything was possible through dialogue. We will see in the next chapter that the CV is renowned for being the most organised of Rio de Janeiro's prison gangs. Along with Zaccone, the governor had taught the Povo de Israel how to structure themselves the same way.

Finally, I have highlighted the apparently legitimate, if more de facto than democratic, nature of the governance that I observed at Polinter. In important ways, officers and inmates had come together to adjust to the conditions in which they found themselves working and incarcerated to provide for a number of basic human needs that would not otherwise have been attainable by many prisoners, as well as systems of social control that, if ultimately underpinned by the threat of violence, were intended to apply equally to everyone. (For analysis of the legitimacy afforded by prisoners to the occasional use of violence as a tool of discipline in other prisons in Rio de Janeiro, see Silva 2008a, 2011, covered in Chapter 6). To borrow from Bottoms and Tankebe (2012), we have seen this order was sustained by shared beliefs, common needs and conformity to rules. Many of these beliefs, needs and rules congregated around notions of mutual respect: respect as human beings, respect as people working or doing their time and respect as people having to manage their prison lives with the bare minimum of external resources. Both on and off the wings, prisoners understood disorder and conflict were not in anyone's interest, whether among prisoners held in the cell block or between the *coletivo* and the police. Regarding the latter, they appreciated Zaccone and the police that worked there were making the best of a poor situation. In contrast to many other prisons, their families were treated with dignity. Those held on the wings were confined 24 hours a day in spaces lacking fresh air and natural light, but overcrowding was slowly being reduced. Those that did not settle down or abused their position (the *colaborador* quoted above was referring to the prisoners that formed the Nova Aliança on the *seguro*) were quickly transferred. "In principle, what does an inmate need most?" the deputy governor explained in his assessment of why Polinter was less disorderly than it might have been. "Visits from his family members and transfer when he is sentenced... This we always try to do. And we demand discipline and harmony within the jail. And they collaborate with this" (fieldwork interview, 9 September 2010). The governor praised Zaccone's humanitarian vision. "The consequence of this treatment", he emphasised, "is that you see a prison with 500 inmates but you don't hear anything, as if there were no inmates in there" (fieldwork interview, 17 September 2010).

None of my research participants contradicted the views of the police, including the *representante geral* of the CV wing, who was scathing of the police and prison authorities more generally, but had nothing but praise for the set-up at Polinter: "Any problem we have, we call the *administração*, the *administração* sorts it out... if they sort it out there, we try to correct what is going on inside... we resolve everything through talking (fieldwork interview, 15 September 2010). The CV *representante geral* also refused to countenance the idea there was anything wrong with prisoners working in the place of police officers. It was necessary, he added, "to respect someone who has respected you" (fieldwork interview, 15 September 2010). For their part, most of my *colaborador* participants stressed they were no different to the prisoners still held on the wings.

As the *colaborador* quoted at the start of this conclusion was keen to emphasise, these relations of prisoner and staff-inmate accommodation were regarded by most at the *carceragem* as matters of necessity, of forced rather than affective reciprocity. At the same time, however, their shared interest in order was based on moral as well as instrumental reasoning. This was symbolised by the treatment of prisoners' families, who my participants were quick to emphasise were not to blame for their sons ending up in prison. It also extended, for example, to the emphasis that was put on supporting prisoners who did not have visits, as well as all prisoners in the first days before their families had been registered to start visits, and for released prisoners who needed money for their bus fare home. A few appeared to only grudgingly accept the balance of power and authority—the *ritmo*—at Polinter. This was the case, for example, for one of the *colaboradores* who came to Polinter with the governor, who had spent 14 months on the *seguro* at his previous *carceragem*:

> It's like a religion inside. Those that have the least, that do not have visits, that are ill, the old, they get priority in everything... I am obligated, if I have visits, to share what I have with him... If he comes to ask for an instant noodles, a soup, and I have two and don't give him one, I may pay... I may be beaten by the *coletivo*... the 'Comando de Israel' (the Command of Israel). (fieldwork interview, *colaborador*, 10 September 2010)

Yet even this statement stood in contrast to this *colaboradore*'s overall assessment. Like all other participants, he went on to explain the *seguro* had to be organised, and that its *representantes* worked without privilege for the benefit of prisoners as a whole. The Povo de Israel and the *coletivo*, he emphasised, are one and the same. The authority of the *representantes* was restricted to enforcing the *coletivo*'s established rules.[13]

***

The complexity of inmate and staff-inmate relations that I witnessed at Polinter therefore resonated little with the established sociology of prisons literature associated with the work of Sykes (1956, 1958) and Goffman (1961, 1968), which predicts division and disorder rather than solidarity between prisoners in suffering, puts prison staff and inmates in normative opposition to each other, and treats inmate authority not as an integral feature of prison life, but as a defect in bureaucratic power. I return to the application of these theories in the Brazilian context in the concluding chapter.

Notes

1. As in previous chapters, I have chosen to describe the people held in Brazil's *carceragens* as inmates or prisoners as much as detainees. Although in police custody, they would be held in remand prisons but for the lack of spaces. Most are awaiting trial and sentence rather than charges to be made or dropped. Some remain after until the end of their sentence, sometimes through choice but just as often due to authorities' efforts to keep the prison system less overcrowded than it might be otherwise.
2. The *triagem* at Polinter measured just two or three square metres. It was most likely also used as a holding cell when Polinter was an ordinary police station. In Rio de Janeiro these cells were colloquially referred to as *porquinhos* (little pigs: see, e.g., Soares 2012).
3. In Chapters 3 and 4, I explained that poor, young men affiliated to major gangs like the CV or Primeiro Commando da Capital (PCC) are considered and consider themselves to be criminal due to the fact they make their living through the illicit rather than formal economy. In this sense, we saw the CV might be more appropriately described as an

alliance or organisation of criminals than as a criminal organisation. All qualifying young men are regarded as belonging to the CV. The Povo de Israel is not a criminal gang by this definition. However, this does not mean it is not also involved in organised crime. In the late 2000s, the Povo de Israel became infamous for making money through extortion. Prisoners would phone people's homes pretending to have kidnapped family members and demanding money be immediately deposited into certain bank accounts.

4. The term *faxina* (cleaner or housekeeper) was also used by prisoners held on the wings, but rarely by the trusty prisoners themselves, and never by the police.
5. Here comparison can be made with the compound *pridúrki* of the Soviet gulags, introduced in Chapter 3, many of the most senior of which were likewise former police (Solzhenitsyn 1975). Up to half of all *pridúrki* either started out as prison officers and/or were employed as prison officers at the end of their sentences (Applebaum 2003).
6. I have encountered mechanical workshops serving private clients at two other prison institutions in Brazil: Penitenciária Jair Ferreira de Carvalho, Mato Grosso do Sul (see Chapter 2), and at a voluntary sector day centre for prisoners held in closed units run by the Associação Cultural e de Desenvolvimento do Apenado e Egresso (Cultural Association for the Development of Prisoners and Former Prisoners: ACUDA), Rondônia, covered in Chapter 7. Here, comparison can also be made with the Soviet Union, as well as modern-day Russia, where many prisons continue to rely on the money inmates make from providing services to the local community (Piacentini 2004).
7. At Polinter, arrivals were left to 'dry out' from drink or 'come down' from crack cocaine in the *triagem*. One day, I arrived to find one such crack user sitting in the *triagem* with two other prisoners awaiting transfer. Over the next few hours, the nurse regularly went to check on him before passing him fit to enter the cell block. I also went to speak with him a few times as well as to pass him cigarettes.
8. I only discovered this fact after I had completed the study. One Saturday during the research, the two head *colaboradores* told me they would take me to watch a game of football at Rio de Janeiro's Maracanã stadium the following day. I knew the stadium was closed at the time for renovation but I was apprehensive enough not to turn up at the *carceragem* the following day, much to their amusement on the

Monday morning. I did, however, learn of a rich prisoner, a lawyer who had been arrested for involvement in the smuggling of two tonnes of cocaine, being let out for his birthday. He almost certainly would have paid to do so. Prisoners are reported to have been given such unofficial day release at least one other police jail in the state (see O Globo Rio, 8 November 2011).
9. All prisoners received their right to a weekly visit from their families. In addition, families could pay R$10 (£2.50) to make additional visits. This was one of the reasons many prisoners preferred to serve their pre-trial detention at Polinter than in the *sistema*. R$10 was a lower price for their families to see them a second time in a week than the cost to take public transport to the Gericinó (Bangu) prison complex (introduced in Chapter 2), where they would otherwise be detained.
10. The majority of prisoners held at Polinter who did not work as *colaboradores* or *representantes* were referred to as common prisoners (*presos comuns*).
11. In Chapter 6, I explain that at other prisons in the *sistema* I have encountered *cantinas* operating, inmate representatives sold goods on at a mark up.
12. He most likely also managed the cash involved in the other markets I have referred to in this chapter, for instance in additional visits and places to sleep outside the cell block.
13. In Chapter 3, I noted the same point regarding the authority of the CV. I return to this point in the context of both the CV and PCC in Chapter 6.

References

Aguirre, C. (2005). *The criminals of Lima and their worlds: The prison experience, 1850–1935*. Durham, NC: Duke University.

Applebaum, A. (2003). *Gulag: A history of the Soviet camps*. London: Allen Lane.

Barbosa, A. R. (2005). *Prender e dar fuga biopolítica, sistema penitenciários e tráfico de drogas no Rio de Janeiro*. Ph.D. thesis, Federal University of Rio de Janeiro. http://www.uece.br/labvida/dmdocuments/prender_e_dar_fuga_biopolitica_sistema_penitenciario.pdf. Last accessed 1 May 2017.

Barbosa, A. R. (2007). Um levantamento introdutório das práticas de violência física dentro das cadeias cariocas. In A. C. Marques (Ed.), *Conflitos, política e relações pessoais* (pp. 129–172). Campinas: Pontes.

Bottoms, A., & Tankebe, J. (2012). Beyond procedural justice: A dialogic approach to legitimacy in criminal justice. *Journal of Criminal Law and Criminology, 102*(1), 119–170.

Caldeira, C. (2007). "Povo de Israel": E o milagre da multiplicação do crime. *Insight Inteligência, 38*, 12–18.

Darke, S. (2013). Entangled staff-inmate relations. *Prison Service Journal, 207*, 16–22.

Darke, S. (2014). Managing without guards in a Brazilian police lockup. *Focaal, 68*, 55–67.

Goffman, E. (1961). On the characteristics of total institutions. In D. Cressey (Ed.), *The prison: Studies in institutional organization and change*. New York, NY: Holt, Rinehart and Winston.

Goffman, E. (1968). *Asylums: Essays on the situation of mental patients and other inmates*. London: Penguin. Originally published in 1961.

Goldstein, D. M. (2003). *Laughter out of place: Race, class, violence, and sexuality in a Rio shantytown*. Berkeley: University of California.

Instituto de Defesa do Direito de Defesa. (2018). *Audiências de custódia: Panorama nacional*. Resource document. http://www.iddd.org.br/wp-content/uploads/2017/12/Audiencias-de-Custodia_Panorama-Nacional_Relatorio.pdf. Last accessed 12 January 2018.

Lemgruber, J., & Fernandez, M. (2012). Legal aid and pre-trial prisoners: An experiment in the city of Rio de Janeiro. In C. Foley, C. (Ed.), *Another system is possible: Reforming Brazilian justice* (pp. 31–53). London: International Bar Association.

Marques, A. (2014). *Crime e proceder: Um experimento antropológico*. São Paulo: Alameda.

Ministério da Justiça. (2012). *Sistema integrado de informações penitenciárias: Todas ufs, referência 6/2012*. Brasília: Ministério da Justiça.

Penglase, B. (2009). States of insecurity: Everyday emergencies, public secrets, and drug trafficker power in a Brazilian favela. *PoLAR: Political and Legal Anthropology Review, 32*, 47–63.

Piacentini, L. (2004). *Surviving Russian prisons: Punishment, economy and politics in transition*. Cullompton: Willan.

Silva, A. M. C. (2008a). *Nos braços da lei: O uso da violência negociada no interior das prisões*. Rio de Janeiro: E+A.

Silva, A. M. C. (2008b). A ressocialização da fé: A estigmatização das religiões afro-brasileiras no sistema penal carioca. In E. Albuquerque (Ed.), *Anais do X simpósio da Associação Brasileira de História das Religiões*. http://www.abhr.org.br/?page_id=57. Last accessed 28 December 2012.

Silva, A. M. C. (2011). *Participo que... Desvelando a punição intramuros*. Rio de Janeiro: Publit.

Soares, L. E. (2012). *Tudo ou nada: A história do brasileiro preso em Londres por associação ao tráfico de duas toneladas de cocaina*. Rio de Janeiro: Nova Fronteira.

Solzhenitsyn, A. (1975). *The gulag archipelago: Volume 2*. New York: Harper and Row.

Sykes, G. M. (1956). The corruption of authority and rehabilitation. *Social Forces, 34*(3), 257–262.

Sykes, G. M. (1958). *The society of captives*. Princeton, NY: Princeton University.

Waldram, J. (1998). Anthropology in prison: Negotiating consent and accountability with a "captured population". *Human Organization, 57*(2), 238–244.

Waldram, J. (2009). Challenges of prison ethnography. *Anthropology News, 50*(1), 4–5.

6

Prison Gangs

This chapter picks up directly from where we left off in Chapter 4. It likewise focuses on everyday matters of governance and survival in Brazilian prisons, and interpersonal relations between and among prison inmates and prison staff. In Chapter 4, I charted the various aspects of inmate self-governance and collaboration that have pervaded the experience of imprisonment in Brazil since its first modern prisons were inaugurated in the middle of the nineteenth century. I explored these institutional traditions in the context of what I describe—or more appropriately, Brazilian prisoners describe—as the convivial nature of everyday inmate relations. Or at least in comparison with Northern societies like the USA and UK. I paid most attention to the post-dictatorship period of the 1980s and 1990s, when after a short-lived humanisation agenda, the country's prison systems began to expand in the context of increasing economic inequality, social and spatial exclusion, and the country's embracing of the international war on drugs. We saw the punitive penal politics of the late twentieth century did not have as negative an impact on prison conditions as they did on the severity of sentencing. At the same time, however, Brazilian prisons remained overcrowded, underfunded and unquestionably inhumane. Important for the purpose of my research, in the aftermath of the 1964–1985 dictatorship, Brazil became not only a more divided but also more politically conscious society. The blatant links between poverty, authoritarianism and incarceration were not lost on prisoners, nor on the country's rapidly growing urban poor more generally. There is no Brazilian underclass as the term is understood in the Global North. Today the country is literally torn in two between the haves and have-nots, who rarely cross paths except when the latter services the needs of the former. Sometimes, the poor target the rich as potentially lucrative victims of crime. More often they go to prison for providing the rich with illicit drugs.

I summarised Chapter 4 by drawing attention to three underlying aspects of conviviality and survival in the Brazilian prison climate: those of mutual interest, legitimacy and co-governance. In Chapter 5, I paused my overview of late twentieth century developments in prison governance to present the first of two ethnographic fieldwork studies I have completed in the country, at a police *carceragem* (lock-up; unit of holding cells) in the city of Rio de Janeiro in 2010. The most important and at the time most surprising finding of that study was that the *carceragem* would most likely have been governed quite similarly whether or not its detainees were affiliated to major gangs. We saw one of the gangs—the Povo de Israel—was made up of prisoners considered vulnerable as a result of not being associated or wanting to be associated with organised crime on the outside. Its "members" did not consider themselves criminal. Yet the police had instructed the Povo de Israel how to organise itself as if it were a prison gang. We saw the other gang—the Comando Vermelho (CV)—also worked closely with the governor of the *carceragem*, and also with the coordinator of *carceragens* across the state.

In this chapter, I focus on the emergence of the contemporary Brazilian prison gang. As in Chapter 4, I pay particular attention to the first-hand accounts of those that have worked or been incarcerated in prison. Even more than in Chapter 4, I focus specifically on the Southern states of São Paulo and Rio de Janeiro, as having the two largest and most developed prison systems, in terms of co-governance, as well being the most researched. I refer to other parts of the country mostly in the conclusion, where I return on the question what Brazilian prisoners have to gain from organising themselves into gangs. Besides completing my history of prison governance to the present, my primary objective is to demonstrate the continuing importance of interpersonal relations of reciprocity and trust in the (major) prison gang era. Prison gangs provide opportunity for conflict avoidance as much as conflict generation. Poor relations, I emphasised, are only in the interest of the toughest and most predatory. To say otherwise is to treat prisoners (and staff) as different to the rest of us. As I stated in Chapter 1, the pertinent question is not why Brazilian prisoners get by but under what conditions they manage to do so.

Besides some brief references in the conclusion, I do not include the Povo de Israel in this analysis for the simple reason it remains very little researched. This is a shame. We have seen it is the largest inmate *coletivo* (collective)/prison gang in Rio de Janeiro and symbolises everything that is important in the thesis I have developed in this book with the exception that it does not operate outside prison and so has limited influence over the support structures for prisoners provided by their families and geographical communities. One day I will study the Povo de Israel in more detail.

***

In the second half of Chapter 4, I focused on the inside accounts of Luiz Mendes and Drauzio Varella, the first a former prisoner who served over 30 years in São Paulo prisons, including more than a decade at Latin America's largest ever prison, the Casa de Detenção de São Paulo (Carandiru); the latter a doctor who worked voluntarily at Carandiru in the 1990s and early 2000s and at São Paulo's Penitenciária do Estado (São Paulo State Penitentiary) after Carandiru was deactivated in 2002. Today, Varella continues to dedicate every other Friday to the Penitenciária do Estado, which in the 2000s became Latin America's largest women's prison and was renamed Penitenciária Feminina de Sant'Ana (Sant'Ana Women's Penitentiary). I have referred to my visits to Sant'Ana in previous chapters.

Neither Mendes (2005, 2009, 2012, 2015) nor Varella (2008, 2012) mention the state's predominant gang, the Primeiro Comando da Capital (PCC), operating at Carandiru in the 1990s. Likewise Human Rights Watch (1998), which visited the prison in 1997. However, it is clear from Steinberg and Sacramento's (2004) O Prisioneiro da Grade de

Ferro (The Prisoner of the Iron Bars), also introduced in Chapter 4, that Carandiru's cell block *faxina* (cleaner or housekeeper) system had been taken over by the PCC by the time it was deactivated in 2002. O Prisioneiro da Grade de Ferro is a quite remarkable documentary film shot in Carandiru's final months of operation by prisoners. Besides the interview with the PCC leader previously mentioned, the prisoners recorded PCC symbols in a corridor of cell block nine. They also interviewed a Christian preacher in cell block seven, headquarters of the 1000 strong Assembly of God, who told them he supported the PCC as it had brought an end to "banal violence".

I come back to the birth of the PCC shortly. Instead, I start this chapter with the CV, which by the late 1990s had been operating in Rio de Janeiro's prison system and *favelas* for a generation. Rio de Janeiro, it should be remembered, lies to the east of São Paulo and shares a border of more than 100 kilometres. Several of the PCC's founders served time inside CV prison units in Rio de Janeiro and, before their recent expansion into the North of the country described in Chapter 3, the two criminal organisations reportedly coordinated their drug trafficking operations between them. In the 1990s the original PCC leaders had issued a series of statements of purpose, one of which proclaimed coalition with the CV (Marques 2014). (These statements were later amalgamated into a 16-point *estatuto* [statute]; they are reproduced in Folha de São Paulo, 19 February 2001).

The Red Command

Here, two first-hand accounts of Brazilian prison life are particularly relevant. The first and probably best-known account of imprisonment in Brazil, read by prisoners and public alike, is Ramos' (2015) Memórias do Cárcere (Prison Memories). Ramos was held without charge for ten months as a political prisoner between 1936 and 1937, following a failed communist coup against Brazil's longest serving president, Getúlio Vargas. Ramos spent a brief period in custody in Pernambuco, where he had been arrested, and then at three prisons in Rio de Janeiro, the Casa de Detenção, the high security Instituto Penal Cândido Mendes on the penal colony Ilha Grande (Large Island) and finally the Casa de Correção. In 2013, I followed in Ramos' footsteps on the three to four-hour walk prisoners often took from the Island port to Cândido Mendes. The prison was inaugurated in 1894 and all but demolished in 1994. Besides Memórias do Cárcere, Ramos wrote several best-selling novels. Memórias do Cárcere was later adapted as an award-winning film (Barreto and Santos 1984).

Memórias do Cárcere gained its reputation for being a controversial political text. Ramos' account of his prison experiences is significant here for two reasons: first for what it tells us about the depth to which the trusty (as opposed to cell block) *faxina* system already operated in the early to mid-twentieth century, not only in Rio de Janeiro, but also in the Northern state of Pernambuco, where his journey begins; second for what it tells us about the political origins of the modern day cell block and prison-wide Brazilian gang. Cândido Mendes was used to detain political prisoners throughout much of the twentieth century, including the autocratic republic of 1930–1945 and the military dictatorship of 1964–1985. Most important, it was the birthplace of the CV.

At the time of Ramos' imprisonment, Rio de Janeiro's trusty *faxinas* wore different uniforms to common prisoners (see Fig. 6.1). Ramos' reflections of his time spent at the three prisons in Rio de Janeiro focused as much on his conversations and dealings with *faxinas*, or as he often refers to them, *homens de zebra* (zebra men) or *homens de roupa zebrada* (zebra clothed men), as with guards or other prisoners. Just as Ramalho's (2002), Mendes' (2005), and Varella's (2008) depictions of Carandiru prison half a century later, the prisons at the centre of Ramos' writings clearly could not have operated without the collaboration of their inmates. Besides working in the place of support staff, performing janitorial and administrative duties, the *faxinas* described by Ramos were also the main point of contact for prisoners in the main cell blocks. They also made money from other inmates for themselves and for the prison administration through selling and smuggling items such as cigarettes, toiletries and clothes, and banned items such as playing cards, newspapers and alcohol.

In a particularly vivid account of his dealings with *faxinas*, Ramos described the moment when he arrived at Cândido Mendes and was made to take off his clothes and hand in his private belongings, including photographs of his family, before being given his prison uniform.

Fig. 6.1 Replica prisoner uniforms on display at the Museu do Cárcere (Prison Museum), Ilha Grande, Rio de Janeiro, Brazil. To the viewer's left, a replica of the stripy uniform used by trusty *faxinas* in Rio de Janeiro's prisons up to the 1940s. Photograph taken by the author, 19 April 2013

Although Ramos did not mention *faxinas* carrying keys themselves, they worked closely alongside guards, whose role appeared little more than to lock and unlock cell doors. *Faxinas* would report breaches of prison rules that came to their attention. Some *faxinas* were political prisoners. How could a military man, Ramos (2015: 585) exclaimed, abandon the resistance, pick up a broom and, "serve as a cleaner to the police of a vagabond country." Most, however, had started on common prisoner wings. One had been working as a *faxina* for 15 years. Towards the end of the book, Ramos reflected on the story of a political prisoner who had a heated argument with a *faxina* and was transferred to another prison:

> The complaint of a *malandro* (trickster) had caused the transfer […] Those men were our creation. I laughed through the iron gates. They were a singular creation. They performed crude services and [only] received tips, but they

were numerous and shaped by years of self pity. And we, a hundred or two hundred people, were there in passing, unintentionally breaking the rules. Denunciation by just one of them would cause us difficulties: cautious, the administration was afraid to take a disliking to the old residents of the house. (Ramos 2015: 623, 624–625)

Ramos did not refer to any of the prisons operating systems of cell leadership, although in Chapter 4, we saw everyday prison routines and prison order were partly the responsibility of cell representatives as well as trusty inmates at Rio de Janeiro's Casa de Detenção in the early twentieth century. In place of the traditional cell-level *xerife* (sheriff) system favoured among Rio de Janeiro's common prisoners, Cândido Mendes' political prisoners elected a cell-block-wide *comissão* (committee) of five representatives to maintain discipline and hygiene, organise education classes and negotiate with the prison administration on behalf of the inmate body as a whole. Ramos described this model as a standard one that operated among groups of political prisoners at the time.

Finally, it is worth noting that Ramos (2015) is the earliest account of prison I am aware of that refers to a group of prisoners as a *coletivo*. I explored this concept in detail in Chapter 4, alongside the terms *convivência* (conviviality) and *convívio* (also meaning collective, but used as an abstract rather than concrete noun or adjective). Bassani (2016) also refers to former political prisoners establishing a *coletivo* in Rio Grande do Sul in the early 1970s, as do Coelho (2005) and Lima (1991), discussed below, in their descriptions of the birth of the CV. In possibly the most detailed account of the CV origins, Amorim (1993) describes how political prisoners at Cândido Mendes were motivated by the arrival in 1975 of a political prisoner from Carandiru, whose *coletivo* had used hunger strikes to gain significant improvements in their treatment, including medical care, an ending to cell checks, the right not to wear prison uniform and access to lawyers and journalists. They had even been allowed to run courses, attended by common as well as political prisoners, which they used to focus on developing political and social *conscientização* (critical consciousness). Alongside the term *coletivo*, these accounts suggest the term *conscientização* was also first used in the prison context among communist revolutionaries incarcerated under Brazil's twentieth century dictatorships, and was later taken up by common prisoners interested in organising the wider inmate body.

This is certainly William da Silva Lima's interpretation. Lima, who had been in and out of prison since 1962, played a central role in forming the CV at Cândido Mendes in the 1970s. In Lima (1991), he makes direct reference to the legacy of common prisoners sharing cell blocks with political prisoners in Rio de Janeiro in the 1930s, and the continuing influence of Graciliano Ramos on shaping inmate consciousness. I have already noted Ramos (2015) is a popular read among literate prisoners. Lima's memoirs are worth outlining in some detail.

Following the 1964 coup d'état, common criminals again found themselves serving sentences alongside political prisoners as the new military government passed emergency legislation enabling the imprisonment of military and civilian trade union agitators. Lima writes he was one of many common prisoners in Rio de Janeiro to share political texts with the imprisoned trade unionists. In 1969, the military regime passed another draconian, emergency decree, the Lei de Segurança (Security Law), which introduced sentences of 10–24 years for bank robbery. In the early 1970s, a group of common prisoners held under the law, including Lima, were sent to Cândido Mendes. For a short period, the approximately 90 Security Law prisoners were held on the same wing as a smaller group of middle-class revolutionaries. Political prisoners were slowly being released as the dictatorship was drawing towards a close. Besides these two sets of prisoners, the rest of the prison was populated by inmates divided into rival *falanges* (phalanxes or gangs), created by prison authorities by grouping prisoners according to the area of the city they came from. We have seen this practice continued in the state's *carceragens* until their recent closure. We will see it continues to be common practice in Rio de Janeiro and other parts of the country today.

The Security Law prisoners found themselves locked up 23½ hours a day, four or five to a single cell, and subjected to regular beatings from guards. Lima describes how a number of the prisoners established a *comissão* with the specific aims to increase inmate solidarity and to represent prisoners in dealings with the prison administration.

The group initially referred to itself as the Falange Vermelho (Red Gang). At first, the *comissão* ran a political study group—described by Lima (1991: 48) as "*trabalho de conscientização*" ("consciousness raising work")—to develop prisoners' understanding of state repression and the shortcomings of individualised action, whether directed towards dealings with prison staff or conflict between prisoners. Soon rejected by the middle-class revolutionaries, who demanded to be accommodated separately in a bid to reinforce their own claims to political status and hope to be included in any post-dictatorship amnesty,[1] Lima writes that the *comissão* managed to unite the Security Law prisoners and eventually other men held at the prison under one *coletivo*. It seems the presence of the CV in Rio de Janeiro's prisons led to marked reductions in robbery, sexual and other forms of predatory violence. Systems were also put in place to support those in difficulty. For example, a *cooperativa* (cooperative) was organised to take care of men held on the *isolamento* (segregation unit), while those who received visits were expected to share what was brought in by their families with men that did not receive visits. Through a combination of negotiation, legal action and hunger strikes, Lima concludes, the CV, as the Falange Vermelho was later dubbed by the media and by prison authorities, managed to unify the existing system of inmate *falanges* across the state's prison system, end the use of daytime lockup, and force prison authorities to make available basic provisions such as blankets, toiletries, medical care and legal representation. By the early 1990s, prisoners at Cândido Mendes were not even confined to their cells at night time; some lived outside the prison compound altogether in what came to be known as the CV *favela* (Gay 2015). Lima served several prison sentences and a total of 36 years in prison. He left prison under conditional licence for the last time in 2006.

There is little reason to question the validity of Lima's (1991) account of the political origins and early successes of the CV. Coelho (2005), the only academic researcher to interview prisoners and prison officers at the time, explains the CV initially met much resistance due to the challenge it posed to the norm that prisoners should not take orders from other prisoners, but that prisoners in Rio de Janeiro slowly came to accept its principles of union, equality and collective action. Amorim (1993) cites an interview with one of the political prisoners at Cândido Mendes, who describes how the Security Law prisoners had similarly taken time to acquiesce to the idea of "*um coletivo unido*" ("one united collective") but had later joined them in hunger strike (cited in Shimizu 2011: 119). In a later interview, Lima reiterated the claim the CV had originated as a Marxist organisation with the aim to *conscientizar* (raise awareness among) common prisoners (Batista and Borges 2012). What is left to dispute is the precise influence political prisoners, and in particular the middle-class revolutionaries held at Cândido Mendes in the 1930s and 1970s, had on the birth of the CV. Lima was clearly, maybe rightly angered by the revolutionaries with whom he was imprisoned refusing to cooperate with common prisoners to the extent political prisoners had in the past. In Lima (1991) and Batista and Borges (2012), he dismisses the commonly held understanding that if it had not been for these revolutionaries, the CV might not have emerged at all. Nevertheless, even if it is not the case that middle-class revolutionaries politicised common prisoners at Cândido Mendes in the 1970s, Lima acknowledges they played an important part in common prisoners coming to understanding the importance of collectivity. Lima (1991: 89) concludes that the CV emerged from a coming together of political and common prisoners, and that the former taught the latter, "how to command and function in a more organised way."

In time, the term the CV appears to have acquired from political prisoners—*coletivo*—was also adopted across the state's prison system. As the CV moved beyond the prison system, its original generation (the approximately 100 convicted under the Security Law) continued to make their money through robbing banks (ibid.). As indicated in Chapter 3, however, irrespective of its beginnings, the CV lost much of its initial "Robin Hood mystique" (Perlman 2010: 188) as its original leaders were eventually replaced, and it evolved to regulate local illicit markets, chiefly the sale of cannabis. The CV also lost control of many of Rio de Janeiro's prisons and poor urban areas as it divided into rival splinter groups such as the Terceiro Comando (Third Command: TC) and the Amigos dos Amigos (Friends of Friends: ADA). However, it remains the state's largest and most influential gang. Lima claims that until relatively recently crack cocaine was not sold in CV favelas (Batista and Borges 2012).

Rio de Janeiro's various *comandos* (commands) or *facções* (factions), as Brazil's major gangs are often referred to, have retained a relatively less contentious presence in prison. While the CV is generally considered the most organised of the state's gangs, the following summary of the current situation broadly applies to the TC and ADA as well. First, Rio's *facções* may not have eliminated prison violence to the same extent we will see the PCC has done in São Paulo, but they have certainly played an instrumental part alongside human rights discourses in reducing arbitrary beatings by prison officers, as well as circumventing predatory and expressive violence among prison inmates, including rape and robbery (Barbosa 2007). As in São Paulo (see Chapter 4), prison guard violence continues in the form of punishment beatings, but the parameters surrounding the use of such violence is more often negotiated with inmates (Silva 2008). This applies even on wings and units designated as *seguros* (vulnerable persons units) (ibid.).

Similarly, prison staff continue to accept, even support a certain level of violence on the wings, the difference being they no longer have to rely on individual *xerifes* (sheriffs) (Barbosa 2007). When I asked the Rio de Janeiro guard I spoke with in 2016[2] about inmate violence in his TC remand prison, he suggested inmate-orchestrated punishment beatings were sometimes necessary to maintain discipline, and that officers in his prison did not anyhow have the resources to interfere. Their job was to transfer prisoners to the security wing or to another prison after they had been beaten. We saw a similar set up at the Rio de Janeiro *carceragem* that I researched in 2010. The progressive coordinator of the state's *carceragens* at the time had ended the practice of punishment beatings by officers. However, a certain amount of violence was accepted among the CV and Povo de Israel *coletivos*. So long as no one died, the police were content to leave prisoners to sort out their problems between them.

Rio's contemporary gang era has also largely witnessed an end to the practice of violent disciplinary raids by police special forces. Although a legacy of the dictatorship period, such police incursions were still common in São Paulo until at least the late 1990s (Mendes 2015), but have likewise now all but disappeared.[3] Finally, Rio's major prison gangs gain much of their legitimacy among the *coletivo* through providing goods and services to prisoners, especially those who do not have families to support them, or who are not able to receive *jumbos* (bags of food and other basic goods) from their families, for example while they are held on *isolamentos*. Rio's prison gangs also gain legitimacy from supporting the poorest of inmates' families outside. Again, we will see this is similarly the case in São Paulo.

The First Command of the Capital

I have already emphasised the symbolic importance of the Carandiru massacre to the birth of the PCC. In Chapter 4, I focused in detail on the trusty and later cell block *faxina* systems that predated the PCC at the prison, in part because Carandiru is by far the most written about prison in São Paulo and in part because these writings demonstrate how similar the *faxina* system of the past was with the PCC system of the present. Unfortunately, none of the founders of the PCC have published their prison memoirs as William da Silva Lima did in Rio de Janeiro. All but one died violently in prison by the end of 2006. The other remains in prison. Nor was any ethnographic research on the PCC in prison conducted in the first ten years of its existence. What we do have is the second half of Mendes (2015), which covers the period after he was thrown out of Carandiru in 2000 until his final release from prison in 2004.

Mendes was transferred from Carandiru to Penitenciária Presidente Maurício Henrique Guimarães Pereira (Venceslau II), introduced in Chapter 3. Mendes (2015) describes the prison as a harsh, inhumane place where the governor regularly allowed the police into beat inmates. After his *inclusão* (inclusion), as the time and space prisoners spent their first days at the prison was referred,[4] Mendes was given the opportunity to enter the *seguro*, which held trusty *faxinas*—who he refers to as *faxinas da administração* (administration *faxinas*)—as well as sex offenders and other vulnerable prisoners.

Despite his age, and having in his words become a *humilde* (humble), Mendes refused and moved straight into the *convívio*, where he was held on a wing that still operated under a cell block *faxina* system but also included a number of prisoners affiliated to the PCC.

Shortly after, on 18 February 2001, inmates simultaneously rioted and took over 29 prisons, including Carandiru and the Penitenciária do Estado, in a statewide rebellion orchestrated by the PCC. Between them, the prisons held a third of the state's inmates. Salla (2006) explains the PCC's objective was less to protest against prison conditions as to force the state to acknowledge its arrival—up to that point Brazilian authorities still officially denied its existence; yet a few days prior to the rebellion PCC leaders had been transferred from Carandiru to a maximum security prison—and as a cover for taking control of the prisons from its rivals. In a radical departure from previous prison rebellions, the uprisings occurred on a Sunday, and during visiting hours. This was designed to demonstrate the organisation had grown to the point it included the families of prisoners as well as prisoners themselves (Dias 2013). Besides declaring allegiance with the CV in Rio de Janeiro, points 3 and 13 of the PCC's founding statute proclaimed a "union in the fight against injustice and oppression in prison" in order to increase "respect and solidarity" among prisoners, support prisoners and their families, improve prison conditions and "prevent another massacre similar or worse than that which occurred at [Carandiru]". On the same day, 20 inmates were killed. Like the events witnessed at Anísio Jobim, Monte Cristo and Alcaçuz 16 years later (see Chapter 3), mutilated bodies were put on display. The PCC had taken over the *faxina* on Mendes' wing at Venceslau II a few months previously, and was likewise now in conflict with rival gangs that had consolidated power in other parts of the prison, according to Mendes with the support of the prison administration. Nevertheless, Venceslau II was not one of the prisons to rebel. Still, many inmates on PCC wings, including Mendes, were transferred back to the capital. Years later, Mendes writes, the PCC murdered the judge who had overseen the prison's violent regime.

The final pages of Mendes (2015) are taken up by accounts of the PCC consolidating control in the prisons he completed his sentence. While he continued to experience police violence, Mendes emphasises the prison system was entering a new era. Emboldened by the February 2001 rebellions, "prisoners no longer felt defenceless and at the mercy of guards… [the PCC leaders] did not accept abuse and made the authorities pay for any weaknesses" (Mendes 2015: 355). Mendes recognises that despite the PCC's motto at the time—*paz, justiça* e *liberdade* (peace, justice and liberty)—the group had consolidated power partly through eliminating its rivals. Nevertheless, he concludes:

> I held nothing against this organisation. Quite the opposite. [Its statute was an idealisation] of what should happen in prison. The prisoner, abandoned to their own devises, created cultures, as is natural to all human beings. And in prison this culture could only be a criminal one. It was a culture of abandonment. There were many prisoner-on-prisoner abuses. Rapes committed against the youngest, extortion of the most humble, exploitation of those whose only thought was to complete their sentence. They even abused their companions' visitors. (Mendes 2015: 290)

Mendes' (2015) backing of the PCC should not be read as an apology for prison gangs. The community prison where he currently volunteers (see Chapter 4) does not accept any form of gang affiliation. Like many other progressive former prisoners, Mendes returned to the system as a "professional ex" hoping to use his experience to help steer others away from crime and gang culture. With a university colleague, he has devised and delivers a course that focuses on teaching non-violent forms of conflict management and dispute resolution. Mendes (2015) should be read first and foremost as a text that, like the other first-hand accounts of prison life I have presented here and in Chapter 4, exposes the inhumane conditions of Brazilian incarceration and subsequent pressures towards conflict and oppositional cultures, but at the same time, highlights human capacity to individually and collectively resist.

Since Mendes left prison, the PCC has quietly revolutionised the experience of incarceration and prison work in São Paulo. For a start, there has been a sharp decline in prisoner uprisings since the mega rebellion, as the February 2001 events came to be referred. The 1990s had, on the contrary, been marked by a steep increase in rebellions, as the state's prisoners began to reorganise power between and among themselves and prison staff in the post-Carandiru massacre period (Salla 2006). The number of recorded prison rebellions rose from 11 in 1990 to a peak of 95 in 1997. Seventy-three rebellions were recorded in 2000 (Dias and Salla 2013). Over a four year period, 2002–2005, there were a total of 20 (ibid.). The few rebellions that did occur during this period were linked to continuing conflict between the PCC and its diminishing number of rivals, for instance when prisoners at Sant'Ana took officers hostage in a failed attempt to gain access to two prisoners whose (also) imprisoned husbands had defected from the PCC (Salla 2006).

Salla (2006) concludes his analysis of the aftermath of the 2001 mega rebellion by hinting that prison governors, who by then were already running their establishments with as few as one officer on duty per 200–250 prisoners, were choosing to work with the PCC. As the article went to print, the post-2001 peace in São Paulo's prison system was temporaily but dramatically shattered when, on 11 May 2006, 765 PCC prisoners were transferred without warning to Venceslau II. State authorities had discovered the gang was about to stage a second mass rebellion four days later in an apparent attempt to influence the presidential elections due in October that year, and to protest against the imminent inauguration of Brazil's first federal supermax facility (Miraglia and Salla 2008). PCC leaders were also aggrieved by an operation in which police had secretly recorded telephone calls in order to extort money from their families (Harvard Law School and Justiça Global 2011). In 2005, a group of police officers had also kidnapped and beaten the PCC leader Marcos Willians Herbas Camacho (Marcola)'s son-in-law and demanded a $300,000 (£75,000) ransom for his release (ibid.).

A smaller number of PCC leaders, including Marcola, were temporarily transferred into police custody (Adorno and Dias 2016). A few days later, Marcola was moved to the state's highest security unit, Centro de Reabilitação de Penitenciária Presidente Bernardes, and on 17 May put into Regime Disciplinar Diferenciado (Differentiated Disciplinary Regime: RDD) isolation for 90 days (Adorno and Dias 2016). Over a nine-day period, 12–20 May 2006, inmates at half (74) of the state's prisons rebelled, including two-thirds of its penitentiaries and remand prisons (there were no rebellions in its community prisons). Further rebellions occurred at 10 prisons in the neighbouring states of Paraná and Mato Grosso do Sul. PCC banners were put on display, but this time few if any prisoners from rival groups were killed. São Paulo city was also brought to a standstill as PCC affiliates set buses on fire and exchanged gunfire with the police. In interview, the state Secretary of Public Security at the time of the revolt, Nagashi Furukawa, later explained state authorities had expected such a large prison rebellion—they were aware that the PCC was present in at least 70 prisons—but had not predicted the uprising would also occur outside prison as well (Miraglia and Salla 2008). An estimated 261 people died (Harvard Law School and Justiça Global 2011). This included eight prison officers, 26 police officers and 213 civilians, killed either by uniformed police (129 civilians) or by extermination groups (84 civilians), which like Rio de Janeiro's private militias (see Chapter 2) consist mostly of police officers working off duty. Most of those killed by uniformed police officers were the victims of the special unit ROTA, which we saw in Chapter 1 was also largely responsible for the 1992 Carandiru massacre. One hundred and twenty-two of the May 2006 police killings were most likely extrajudicial executions (ibid.).

According to established opinion, the conflict ended after a meeting at Presidente Bernardes prison between Marcola and a state entourage made up of police as well as government officials on 14 May. The state officials were accompanied by a PCC lawyer who brought a mobile phone for Marcola to let an unidentified PCC member on the outside know he had not been harmed (in the event, Marcola authorised a second prisoner to make the phone call on his behalf). Marcola had also been visited a few days earlier shortly after he arrived in police custody by a group of senior police officers, including the state police chief. At that stage, he had refused to offer any support unless the PCC prisoners who had been transferred were allowed visits the following Sunday (mother's day). Furukawa, who resigned as Secretary of Public Security in the immediate aftermath of the crisis, acknowledged both meetings had taken place and that he had refused Marcola's initial demands made to the police. Importantly, he denied he had ever negotiated or had any direct involvement with the PCC during his tenure (1999–2006). He also claimed to be at the top of a PCC list of planned political assassinations. However, he suggested this might not be the case with other government officials. He had himself needed to resist pressure from within government to negotiate with the PCC. As evidence of current state-PCC collusion, he pointed to the fact Bernardes' RDD regime was full when he left office, but now held only 30 of a maximum capacity of 170 prisoners. Moreover, he was adamant many prison governors had succumbed to the temptation to collaborate with the gang, stating:

> In any human grouping there are leaders. Because of this you always hear among governors and staff a mentality that it is easier, and perhaps more efficient, to maintain peace in a prison unit if the administration works in *sintonia* (tune) with inmate leaders. In this case it is not a matter of corruption but accommodation. (Miraglia and Salla 2008: 31)

Within a month of the 2006 attacks, as these events came to be known, Marcola was questioned by a congressional inquiry into arms trafficking at Bernardes prison for four continuous hours. Marcola was aggressively bombarded with questions from different angles of enquiry in a clear effort to make him contradict himself and admit to the role he was alleged to play in arms and drug trafficking—of which the congressmen were forced by Marcola to admit there was no existing evidence—and in leading the PCC—to which Marcola constantly replied he was no more than a symbolic leader of an organisation that had not had a structured hierarchy since José Márcio Felício dos Santos (also known as Geleião: Big Jelly), one of the PCC's founding members, lost power in late 2002. Alongside the interview with Furukawa, the transcript (Câmara dos Deputados 2008) provides fascinating insight into the relationship between the PCC and the Brazilian state, and the position the PCC had secured among São Paulo's prison population in the years immediately following the 2001 mega rebellion.

Regarding PCC relations with state authorities, Marcola claimed to have met Furukawa four years earlier, shortly before Geleião and other PCC leaders at the time were transferred to the recently inaugurated Presidente Bernardes prison and ejected from the organisation. Geleião had a reputation for violence and authoritarianism, to which

Marcola also claimed to have been opposed. Aware the existing PCC hierarchy was about to be dismantled, Marcola explained Furukawa had visited him to negotiate a reduction in prisoner violence. However, Marcola did not provide any details on the nature of the concessions he claimed Furukawa had made. Nor, as far as I am aware, is there evidence of a face-to-face meeting between the two actually taking place. Nevertheless, it does appear Marcola did at least collaborate with state officials in their investigations into the PCC. Investigative journalists, police and public prosecutors have repeatedly claimed Marcola passed information onto the police in the early 2000s, including mobile phone numbers, which were instrumental in their efforts to gather the evidence required to move Geleião and others into RDD. These claims were most recently repeated in a celebrated book (Christino and Tognolli 2017) co-written by one of São Paulo's most senior public prosecutors, Marcio Christino, and complete with a forward by police chief Ruy Fontes, who Marcola claimed to have met on numerous occasions.

Still, in the year following the change of PCC leadership, the number of registered homicides in São Paulo's prisons fell sharply, from 97 in 2012 to 27 in 2013 (Dias and Salla 2013). There were no prison rebellions in 2013 (ibid.). In important respects, the question whether or not Furukawa or indeed any other local or federal state ministers held meetings with PCC leaders in the years leading up to the May 2006 attacks is largely irrelevant. Both Marcola and Furukawa would have had little if anything to gain. Instead, Marcola's allegations lend support to a consensus among most researchers on Brazilian organised crime that, like the CV in Rio de Janeiro, the PCC was ultimately able to consolidate its position at the turn of the Millennium because of convergences between its own objectives and those of prison and wider political authorities. Marcola's testimony was replete with illustrations of the security and support structures the PCC provides prisoners and their families in the absence of state provision. In Chapter 4, we saw Brazil has historically relied on its prisoners to collaborate and self-govern. I concluded that chapter with the claim that the prison gang phenomenon is best understood as a formalising of these existing practices. I come back to this crucial aspect of my thesis shortly. We saw further that Brazil's major gangs operate in symbiosis with the Brazilian state in providing alternative governance in the country's *favelas* and *quebradas* (broken or ghettos) as well. As such, they do not pose a threat to state authority. They supplement rather than challenge its power. They are an unspoken ally, not an enemy of the Brazilian nation state. Face-to-face meetings are not necessary to coordinate what are in effect governance activities.

Nor, it seems, have senior state government, police or prison officials held meetings with Marcola or other PCC leaders since May 2006 either. Accordingly, it is argued the PCC has stepped into the void in prison governance in the absence of state investment by default rather than by design. Evidence for this interpretation of the existence of the PCC is strong. Those at the top of the PCC hierarchy have certainly been treated favourably in the aftermath of the May 2006 attacks and Furukawa's demoting. As Furukawa emphasised in his interview in Miraglia and Salla (2008), few senior PCC leaders have served much time in isolation, either in federal supermax prisons or in RDD. Bernardes prison remains half empty today. In Chapter 3, I noted that before the rift with the CV in the lead up to the 2017 northern prison massacres, Marcola was only returned to RDD for a brief period in 2014, following the alleged discovery of an escape plan. Nor has there been a major prison rebellion in São Paulo since 2006. Since then, staffing levels have fallen even further and, besides the closure of the state's *carceragens*, there have been little, if any improvements in prison conditions. In Chapter 2, we saw the remand prisons built to replace police detention are themselves severely overcrowded. The state's penitentiaries continue to hold prisoners in multi-occupancy cells. Adorno and Dias (2016) conclude that through its unspoken agreements with the PCC, state authorities have been able to respond to public demands for more imprisonment without having to significantly increase resources, while the PCC—the only actor capable of governing the state's prisoners in the absence of guards—has been left in charge of maintaining inmate discipline and welfare. In Chapter 4, we saw that today São Paulo prison guards are outnumbered by inmates by as many as 300 to one and do not usually maintain a presence in the cell blocks. The threat if not the actual use of RDD, Adorno and Dias add, has also played a part in allowing state authorities to keep the PCC in check, as did the remarkably violent police response to the May 2006 attacks on the streets of the state's towns and cities.

Such analysis of the symbiotic relationship between the PCC, higher state and prison authorities is largely associated with the research of the Núcleo de Estudos de Violençia (Nucleus for the Study of Violence: NEV) at University of São Paulo. In this book, I have dedicated attention to the ethnographic prisons research of Camila Dias (Adorno and Dias 2016; Dias 2013; Dias and Salla 2013), Fernando Salla's historical work on the politics of prison (Adorno and Salla 2007; Alvarez et al. 2013; Miraglia and Salla 2008; Salla 2006, 2007, 2017; Teixeira et al. 2016) and Bruno Paes Manso's research on urban crime and policing (Manso 2012, 2016; Manso and Dias 2017). Each of these authors focuses attention on lower level collusion between local PCC members, police and prison workers in individual police districts and prisons. In doing so, the NEV distances itself, rightly in my view, from aspects of the mafia paradigm utilised by Brazilian government officials to explain the relationship between prison gangs and the 2017 massacres that I critiqued in Chapter 3. From an organised crime perspective, the PCC is of minor significance. We saw that its purported involvement in the international drug trade—and here we might add reason or ability to capture or collude with the high-level state—is exaggerated. To utilise Green and Ward's (2004) typology of organised crime and its relationship to the state, the PCC had not moved beyond a predatory stage of development by 2006. There is little evidence the PCC has progressed any further as a monolithic organisation in the years since. As I concluded in Chapter 4, it might be argued that the exact opposite is the case. Claims occasionally arise in political or media circles of PCC involvement in political corruption, for instance, financing election campaigns (e.g. Junior et al. 2017; Macedo 2014), but these are typically sensationalist and of little substance. The May 2006 attacks demonstrated just how strong a position the PCC had attained over its prison and urban territories, but no more than this.

According to this NEV analysis, the PCC is politically expendable and likely to retain its position vis-à-vis the state only so long as the country's prisons remain under-resourced. This is a stance with which

I broadly concur. Still, Adorno and Dias (2016) emphasise the state of reciprocal accommodation between the Brazilian state and the PCC leadership is fragile and under regular strain. From this position, it might be argued the moment of state-PCC rupture has already arrived. Marcola was put under RDD for the maximum (renewable) allowed period of 360 days in December 2016; he returned to Venceslau II only in December 2017 (see Chapter 3).

Yet there are no signs of conflict in São Paulo's prison system. While Marcola supposedly spent 22 hours a day in isolation, prison life continued as normal for the remainder of the 200,000 or so people held on PCC wings. More significant than the PCC's high-level relationship to federal or state authorities are, as Furukawa emphasised in his 2008 interview, and I have stressed throughout this book, micro-political relations between ordinary prisoners and prison staff, shaped by everyday interactions on the ground.

Three points should be emphasised regarding PCC-prison inmate and PCC-prison staff relations. First, it should be remembered that all local actors have gained from the PCC. The PCC may have replaced rather than increased material provisions to prisoners that in the past were better provided by prison authorities. However, it is also true that São Paulo's prisons have become safer and inmate/staff-inmate relations more predictable. In Chapter 4, we saw homicide rates among São Paulo prisoners were half the rate of homicides on the outside in 2016, and a fifth the rate of homicides across the country as a whole. PCC governance may be more vulnerable to cycles of calm and violence depending on the personalities of individual actors than a more bureaucratic system of state prison governance might potentially be. Nevertheless, it has made São Paulo's prisons less brutal and has saved countless lives. Since the Carandiru massacre, official prison homicide rates in the state have fallen from approximately one per 450 inmates (117 of approximately 53,000 prisoners) in 1999 to one per 4000 inmates (35 of 140,000 prisoners) in 2006 (Dias and Salla 2013), and one per approximately 15,000 inmates today (Biondi 2017a). Troubled and troublesome inmates are less often secluded and beaten by sadistic prison guards, and prisoners no longer experience regular and lethal police incursions (Salla 2006), or the humiliating initiation ritual of passing through a *corredor polonês* (Polish corridor, usually consisting of a line of police officers equipped with batons) when they first arrive. Over the past ten years of research, I have heard many first-hand accounts of serious prison violence.[5] To date, just one concerned a prison, Penitenciária Feminina do Butantã, in the state of São Paulo. An inmate had been judged in a *debate* and found guilty of passing information to prison staff that caused a PCC member to be transferred.

The situation is more complex for prison staff. Everyday prison routines have become easier to manage with just one gang with which to negotiate. However, those deemed "bad officers" (see Chapter 4) remain vulnerable to punishment killings. According to São Paulo prison authorities, 46 guards have been killed outside prison over the past five years (Velasco and Cesar 2018).

Second, the PCC is as reliant on maintaining its legitimacy among prisoners as it is on any higher level, unspoken accommodation with the Brazilian state. The same can be said about its reciprocal negotiations with prison staff. Today, the PCC commands São Paulo's prison population through hegemony rather than force (Dias 2013). Third, to repeat a central tenet of Biondi's (2010, 2014) research first outlined in Chapter 4 and returned to in more detail below, as an organisation the PCC is interpreted differently in each of the prisons and *quebradas* in which it operates. As such, it is shaped less by its official members, its *irmãos* and *irmãs* (brothers and sisters), including its purported leaders, as its relationship (in the prison context) to individual *coletivos*, and in its day-to-day dealings with the lower echelons of the state, that is its relationship to individual prison governors, officers and support staff. From this position, Marcola's denial to the congressional inquiry into arms trafficking (Câmara dos Deputados 2008) that the PCC had operated under a recognised leadership since its original founders were killed or deposed in the early 2000s cannot be so easily dismissed as the organised crime perspective might imply. Indeed, Geleião made the same claim when interrogated by the same inquiry just a few months earlier (Marques 2010). To the contrary, throughout the interrogation Marcola maintained he had been the main author of the PCC dismantling its original hierarchy and that his own position likewise dissipated as Geleião and the other original PCC founders eventually lost their grip on power.[6] Marcola has maintained this position since, including in evidence recently given to an ongoing judicial inquiry into PCC lawyers: the so-called *sintonia dos gravatas* (literally, tuning of neck ties; the word *sintonia* is more commonly used to describe the leadership of the PCC).[7] One aspect of the 2006 attacks rarely mentioned is that after Marcola's supposed intervention it still took several days for the prison rebellions and the violence outside prison to subside. Contrary to established understanding of the attacks, it is equally plausible to claim they were not actually centrally command, and that—like the 2017 northern massacres—what we essentially witnessed was a momentary rupture in ordinary prison governance, a crisis that completed its natural course. The argument to the contrary is not built on solid ground. The only evidence offered by the congressmen to Marcola of his role as PCC leader was a report in the sensationalist news magazine ÉPOCA. No suggestion was made of a PCC instruction—*salve* (communiqué)—being issued at the start of the attacks. It was suggested the attacks were brought to an end by a *salve*, and that this had been written by Marcola, but again the only thing Marcola's accusers had to offer was a report in the tabloid media that had gone viral in the blogosphere. No substantial or substantiated evidence has emerged in the decade since. Nor to this day has either Marcola, Geleião, or indeed any other person associated with the higher PCC hierarchy, succumb to the temptation to claim ownership of the attacks. During his interrogation, Marcola went so far as to lament the rebellion moving beyond prison and onto the streets.

The PCC is not a command but a consensus, Marcola insisted to the congressional inquiry, giving by way of example the ending of the practice of maintaining a *caixinha* (collection box) into which inmates were typically expected to contribute R$20 (£5) a month, the abolition of crack cocaine and sexual violence, and the continued ban on homosexual men living in the *convívio*. A proposal was made to discontinue the latter, but this was opposed by the majority of prisoners. When questioned about the existence of *regras de convivência* (rules of conviviality) among prisoners, Marcola answered that this much was obvious: prisoners anywhere naturally decided on rules of conduct, independent of the existence of any criminal organisation. Brazilian prisoners invariably came from poor, damaged backgrounds. If prisoners did not organise, did not have a nucleus, the violent habitus of the *favela* would be replicated in prison. As we saw in Chapter 1 in the case of the Carandiru massacre, in prison, it is more difficult to prevent conflicts from spiralling out of control. The PCC had facilitated prisoner organisation and removed the authority of the state. Citing Lenin and Mao Zedong, Marcola emphasised the role played by the Brazilian state's violence in politicising prisoners, and the importance of avoiding hierarchy. On these matters, he concluded:

> The people I am talking about were diverse prisoners with diverse ideas. There is no dictator… [What we do have] are enlightened people inside prison who garner the confidence of other prisoners. Why? A prisoner comes along with a problem. You give him a solution, show him logic, show him the way he is being treated and the way it should be. [Our] idealism is one of solidarity. The prisoner knows there is much injustice inside the penitentiary system and that the *cara* (face or man) who is there needs support… (Câmara dos Deputados 2008: 30–31)

After another hour or so of interrogation regarding his role within the PCC, Marcola added the following statement:

> Prisoners support prisoners. *Marginais* (marginals) on the street support *marginais* on the street… Why? Because everyone believes in the fight for justice of the *miseráveis* (miserable) against established power… We will always be *bandidos* (outlaws)… This notion was created… (ibid.: 113)

Marcola may be deluded and he may not have a strong understanding of Marxism-Leninism-Maoism, but there is little in the transcript of his interrogation to suggest he was not being sincere. He avoided directly answering questions about the PCC's involvement in regulating local drug markets, inside and outside prison, but even here he was one step ahead of his accusers. The drug trade, he suggested, was bigger than the PCC.

As for PCC-prison staff relations, Marcola only made two, though important references to prison staff throughout the four hours of questioning. When pressed on why he had been so critical of police corruption but had not mentioned prison guards, Marcola responded:

Because they are of different levels... the guard, he has a miserable life, very similar to that of the prisoner. So the detainee ends up identifying with him, or he with the detainee... Because he also comes from the same *favela*. (Câmara dos Deputados 2008: 130)

A short while after, the senators turned their attention to prison guard violence, which Marcola had suggested was increasingly rare but nonetheless still occurred in some prisons. Marcola explained that some prison governors and guards continued to adhere to "the old, archaic form of working" (Câmara dos Deputados 2008: 142) and that the PCC had forced the issue by resorting to killings. Guards and governors became aware the PCC could reach them outside of prison.

As far as I am aware, no academic analysis has been of the accuracy of Marcola's testimony, whether in support or to question his claims. Marcola's words cannot be taken at face value. At the same time, however, they cannot be treated as fabrication. Evidence has not been offered to the contrary. In any case, a new generation of young, poor criminalised men has been through the state's prison system in the past decade that takes Marcola's messages of inmate solidarity and participatory democracy at face value. Marcola is credited with adding the words *igualdade* (equality) and later *união* (union) to the PCC's original's motto of *paz, justiça* and *liberdade*. Whatever Marcola's intentions, the impact on PCC-prisoner relations has been profound. In a recent interview published in English, a group of former long-term prisoner emphasised that the concept of *igualdade* was quickly understood and taken up inside and outside prison as it built upon a code of behaviour people were already used to in the *quebrada*. One of the interviewees, now a law student and controversial recording artist whose lyrics focus on the PCC, explained:

[We were] born and raised against the oppression that has always existed! [...] [Equality] was already in the ghetto, it's kid street slang. I'll give you an example. We're playing football and Eliezer (one of the other two interviewees) says, "If you play against me I'll kick you down", then I say, "I shall get payback, cause we're equal". So, it's an old thing that became bigger after, like Eliezer said, crime got humanised. It began to be said: "If you wanna kill someone, your equal, if you kill with no explanation, with no reason, you're gonna die too". (Biondi 2017b: 46–47)

In her previously published book (Biondi 2010), the interviewer, Karina Biondi, provides a depth of insight into the power and structure of the PCC as she witnessed it in the years preceding and following Marcola's ascendency. A major part of Biondi's analysis is grounded in her experiences visiting her incarcerated partner over a number of years in PCC prisons. The book was originally written as a master's degree thesis. It was recently translated and published by University of North Carolina Press and won a 2017 American Anthropology Association book prize. Biondi's partner has since been resolved of the criminal charges that were made against him. While developing this early research on the PCC, Biondi studied with Adalton Marques, whose own master's degree thesis on inmate codes in the PCC era was published a few years later as Marques (2014). In Chapter 4 we saw Biondi went on to research the presence of the PCC outside prison.

Alongside Marques (2014), Biondi (2010) is particularly notable for its analysis of the means by which the PCC has come to be regarded as a legitimate form of governance among the majority of São Paulo's prisoners since the departure of its original leaders and apparent dismantling of its vertical hierarchy. I have already mentioned the most important additions the PCC have brought to inmate codes—*éticas*, as they are now referred to in São Paulo's prisons. As well as the more general guiding principles of *paz, justiça, liberdade* and, under Marcola, *igualdade* and *união,* in this chapter, I have already noted a number of specific measures relating to mutual protection, conflict avoidance and resolution, most notably bans on crack cocaine, the carrying of sharp objects, and the use of violence without prior judgment by the accused's peers (through a *debate*).[8] Among other examples of PCC codes aimed at making prisons safer, Biondi draws attention to the positive effect of the PCC prohibiting the sale and consumption of cannabis with prisoners that have fallen into debt.

Regarding mutual aid and the threat of extortion, I have just noted the importance attached by Marcola to the ending of the practice of requiring better off prisoners to make regular contributions to a *caixinha*. The objective of having a *caixinha* may be to provide for prisoners in need. However, it effectively required some prisoners to pay for services and ran the risk of creating divisions. Here Biondi brings to our intention the equally important PCC decision to end the practice of buying and selling cell spaces.

In Chapter 4, I outlined further developments in codes relating to in cell behaviour, including requirements to be silent at night time, to wear flip-flops rather than shoes, and to shower at the end of the working day. I noted that many of these less controversial norms of behaviour, the examples here all taken from Marques (2014), are interpreted differently in different prisons, and are regarded more as recommendations than rules. One PCC norm of in cell behaviour mentioned in Chapter 4 that traverses the distinction between mutual aid and mutual protection and is regarded as a more fundamental rule, concerns the right to move from sleeping on the *praia* (floor) up one of the *beliches* (bunk beds). In PCC prisons, such "privileges" depend simply on the length of time a person has been incarcerated on this occasion. Biondi (2010) explains the previous norm, that "old timers" automatically jumped the queue for a *beliche* when they returned to prison, was a source of much anxiety and conflict.

Under Marcola's premiership, Biondi (2010) concludes her analysis of PCC-inmate relations, São Paulo's prisoners consider themselves to be *junto e misturado* (mixed or blended together). This she contrasts to the position in Rio de Janeiro, where prisoners affiliated to the CV, for instance, are more likely to speak in terms of being *junto e organizado* (organised together). Equally important to São Paulo prisoners' understanding of themselves as equal, and to each of the above examples of the PCC's *éticas*, is Biondi's (2010) and Marques' (2014) analysis of the PCC as a development rather than rupture in existing forms of inmate self-governance (what I distinguish as constituting today's cell block *faxina* system) detailed in Chapter 4.

Finally, concerning PCC-prison staff relations, Biondi (2010) makes numerous references to the role played by *irmãos/irmãs* and *faxinas* in negotiating with governors and guards. Of these, three are particularly noteworthy. I will deal with them briefly. Again we will see each represents more of a continuation than break with the pre-PCC era[9] trusty *faxina* system, also detailed in Chapter 4.

Most intriguing perhaps is the PCC's involvement in receiving new prisoners. Biondi (2010) confirms that the PCC operates its own *triagem* in addition to that operated by prison staff. I have already noted the first cells beyond the entrance to a wing are typically allocated to *faxinas*. Once a prisoner has been allocated to a wing, they will likely spend the first night or more in a *faxina* cell. If the wing *faxina* decide it is not safe for a prisoner to move into the *convívio*, they will hand them back to prison staff. Similarly, it is the PCC rather than prison staff that ultimately decides which cell a prisoner should be allocated. These practices have been described to me at two of the PCC prisons I have visited in São Paulo. Alongside the ban on buying and selling cell spaces, they represent a clear improvement (in terms of inmate safety) on the previous situation in which prison administrators relied on trusty *faxina* and *juizes da xadrez* (cell judges) as their points of contact with the *coletivo*. In Chapter 4, we saw prisoners performing these roles found themselves in the precarious position of being regarded as half prisoner, half guard.

Biondi's (2010) second major illustration of PCC-prison staff negotiations concerns the role played by prison administrators in deciding which PCC affiliates work as *faxinas*. Again this is best understood as a development of previous practices in São Paulo in which *juizes da xadrez* relied on maintaining the confidence of prison staff and their trusty *faxina* as much as the confidence of their cellmates. In Chapter 3, I also noted the relative ambiguity of inmate-staff relations at the Curado prison complex in Pernambuco, where *chaveiros* (key holders) are appointed by prison administrators both to guard the entrances and maintain discipline on the wings. While Biondi does not directly refer to prison governors selecting or deselecting *faxinas*, it is clear they have a de facto power to do so. The PCC is aware prison staff may refuse to work with someone they initially selected, especially those selected to work on the *ligação* (link; as explained in Chapter 3, used to describe the point of contact between prisoners and staff). The prison workers I have spoken with do not necessarily consider this practice controversial. Indeed, they often go on to say they could not work with the majority of prisoners, few of who have the necessary skills of communication. "*Faxinas* work for all of us" is how it is usually explained. In Chapter 5, we saw Rio de Janeiro's police *carceragem* system was co-governed on similar grounds. Prisoners affiliated to the Povo de Israel were taught by the police how to organise themselves along the same lines adopted by the CV. They told the coordinator of the state's 16 *carceragens* he should be the next president of the country. The CV was less keen to be seen cooperating with the police and their trusty *faxinas*, some of who were former police officers themselves, imprisoned for murdering gang affiliates on the street. At the same time, however, they accepted that even their own affiliates might legitimately choose to leave the gang to work in the place of guards. CV affiliates only left their wing with their heads bowed and their hands behind their backs. Yet they allowed trusty *faxinas* to strip-search them and to handcuff them, even those *faxinas* who had themselves started their detention as CV prisoners. As for their relationship to the police, the CV leadership quietly went about their business keeping order and allowing daily prison routines to run as smoothly as possible. In the privacy of their wing, they even shook hands with Zaccone, all the while in the knowledge he would remove any one of them he discovered was a gang leader on the outside.

The third major illustration of advances on the pre-PCC situation focused on in Biondi (2010) is the existence of higher level negotiations between a prison's senior management and an inmate *comissão* (commission). A PCC *comissão* is typically composed of the highest ranking PCC affiliate at the prison, the *piloto de prédio* (literally, building pilot) and the leaders of individual wings (the *pilotos do raio*). In Chapter 3, we saw the CV operates a similar system of prison-wide inmate *conselhos* (councils), and have gone so far as to set up a prison complex-wide *conselho* to represent the interests of the 28,000 prisoners held at the Gericinó (Bangu) prison complex. Among other examples, Biondi notes the role inmate councils have played in São Paulo in forming agreements with prison managers that neither inmates nor officers will come to harm during rebellions. We have seen that a similar tradition existed at Carandiru prison before it became a PCC prison around the turn of the Millennium, but that the cell block *faxina* system of the time did not always guarantee prison guard safety. As the 1992 massacre so tragically illustrated, neither did the old cell block *faxina* system prevent the police from conducting violent punishment raids in the aftermath of prison rebellions.

***

It is clear, then, that the switch in emphasis from the traditional system of in cell inmate governance to a more homogenous, centralised system of cell block, prison and statewide hierarchies in late twentieth century São Paulo was to the advantage of most prison inmates and prison staff. People whose prison experiences traverse the PCC and pre-PCC eras invariably describe the state's prison system as a significantly worse place to be incarcerated or work in the past, as a "lawless land". Rio de Janeiro experienced a broadly similar shift in power dynamics in its prison system during the 1980s and 1990s, the difference being that the position of the *xerife* continued, under a different name, as part of a three-tier hierarchy consisting of cell as well as wing and prison representatives.

First, we have seen that having a more centralised system of informal conflict prevention and resolution made prisons safer for the ordinary inmate. Incidences of violence reduced the more prisoners organised and the more concerted they became in their ability to challenge and revenge abuses of officer power. One important aspect of the reduction in officer violence appears to be the decreasing presence of prison officers on the wings and with it the emerging position of the *ligação*. By maintaining a permanent inmate presence at the entrances to the wings, prisoners emphasise, guards are prevented from entering without prior warning.

I have also noted reductions in inmate on inmate violence. In a survey of 591 prisoners conducted in the late 2000s, Almeida and Paes-Machado (2015) found inmates to be 150 percent more likely to have experienced violence or bullying in Bahia as inmates who participated in a comparable survey in Rio de Janeiro. Bahia's first major prison gang, the Comando do Paz (Peace Command), had emerged less than a decade earlier and had recently divided (Lourenço and Almeida 2013). When I visited the state's largest prison, Lemos Brito, in 2018, however, I discovered its major cell blocks were now under the command of separate gangs and that violence was now decreasing. In Chapter 4, we saw levels of homicide have reduced dramatically at Cadeia Pública de Porto Alegre (Central Prison), Rio Grande do Sul in recent years, from a peak of 70 cases a year in the early 2010s, when cell block gangs were emerging but most of the prison's 11 largest wings were still under the command of more than one gang, to only a handful of confirmed cases since 2013 (since which time the cell blocks have been managed by a total of five gangs). Inmates and prison workers interviewed in Sager and Beto's (2016) documentary gave a second explanation for this dramatic reduction in violence: agreement formed between judicial authorities and gang leaders for the latter to hand over troublesome prisoners for immediate transfer rather than the more common practice of sending them into the *seguro*, where they remained a potential threat. In Chapter 5, we saw a similar agreement in operation at the *carceragem* in which I completed fieldwork in Rio de Janeiro. As for São Paulo, if there were a comparable prison system in the Global North—remember the state has a quarter of a million prisoners—that was free of offensive weapons and crack cocaine as well as predatory and expressive (what Brazilian inmates and prison workers regularly refer to as banal) violence, it would no doubt be internationally celebrated.

Besides regulating prison wings, Brazil's major gangs have also played a part in reducing inmate on inmate violence through their role in receiving and allocating prisoners. I covered this earlier in the context of the PCC in São Paulo. Again this is a practice that exists in other parts of the country as well. In Chapter 5, I also noted practices of inmate involvement in cell allocation in Rio de Janeiro's former *carceragem* system. I had previously observed this practice during my visit to Bangu II prison in Rio de Janeiro too. As I leaving, I met the *representante geral* waiting by the entrance to the cell block for the arrival of a new group of prisoners. His first concern was to check these prisoners were not gang affiliates. He also needed to make sure they were willing to accept the authority of the Povo de Israel, which is largely composed and led by people not generally accepted by other gangs. These, we have seen, include people arrested for sex offences. Under these circumstances, Rio de Janeiro prison authorities have had no choice but to introduce separate wings to accommodate prisoners that are neither prepared to be governed by *facções* or sex offenders. During my fieldwork at the *carceragem* I learned that yet another inmate *coletivo*/gang type had emerged to govern these spaces: referred to as either the Seguro do Seguro (literally, the Insurance of the Insurance) or as the Inimigos dos Inimigos (the Enemies of the Enemies) (cf. Silva 2011).

In Chapter 2, we saw cell doors have been removed to enable inmates to lay mattresses in the corridors of many of the wings at the astonishingly overcrowded Central Prison in Rio Grande do Sul. There it is also cell block hierarchies which manage who sleeps where (Bassani 2016).

As for inmate on officer violence, we have also seen the principle held by prisoners not to harm "good" officers was further reinforced with the emergence of cell-block-wide prison gangs (Biondi 2010; Coelho 2005). To repeat a phrase first used in Chapter 4, the enemy of the *coletivo* is the punitive state, not its servants working on the ground.

Less well known, but just as important, is the role Brazil's prison gangs have played in reducing some of the more serious practices of exploitation. I have briefly mentioned two specific measures in the context of the PCC in São Paulo: the banning of the *caixinha*, and the ending of the market in cell spaces, both of which continue to varying degrees in other parts of the country. Cell spaces are still sold, for instance, at Central Prison (Bassani 2016), as well as in the Curado complex, Pernambuco (Arruda 2015), and at the prisons studied by Lourenço and Almeida (2013) in Bahia, but not in CV prisons in Rio de Janeiro, where we have seen all prisoners are expected to experience the same living conditions, and where the best places to sleep are allocated according to who has been imprisoned longest.

To these we might add a third major example of exploitation, the *cantina* (canteen), through which inmate leaders and prison administrators have traditionally made up for shortages in state provision by selling or informally licensing to local businesses the right to sell products to inmate leaders, who in turn sell the products at a marked up price to other prisoners. In his testimony to the congressional inquiry into the May 2006 attacks (Câmara dos Deputados 2008), Marcola hinted of the PCC's banning of this practice when he told his interrogators that São Paulo's prisoners were no longer required to pay *propinas* (fees or bribes) for anything. In Chapter 5, we saw *propinas* and *cantinas* were major sources of income for the officers running Rio de Janeiro's *carceragens*. Lima (1991) also refers to the CV's taking over of the *cantina* at Cândido Mendes prison as one its first major accomplishments. More recently the practice has been highlighted by Arruda (2015) in the context of Curado, Pernambuco and Bassani (2016) and Sager and Beto

(2016) in the context of Central Prison, Rio Grande do Sul. Besides Central Prison, I have also encountered *cantinas* operating in prisons I have visited in the states of Goiás and Rio Grande do Norte, as well as the faith-based APAC community prisons in Minas Gerais, introduced in Chapter 1. The *cantina* is used mostly as a marketplace for food and toiletries, as well as more luxury items such as confectionaries and cigarettes. For the majority of prisoners (*presos comuns*—common prisoners: prisoners that do not work as trusty or cell block *faxina*), the *cantina* makes up for restrictions on the quantity of such products their families are allowed to include in their weekly *jumbos*. *Cantineiros* (canteen workers) are appointed to purchase these goods on behalf of other inmates. The goods are sold on in makeshift shops on each wing. During my visit to Central Prison in 2016, I read a ledger in a cell dedicated to one of these wing *cantinas* that showed two-litre bottles of soft drink were divided and sold at R$1 (£0.25) per plastic cup on visiting days. Each bottle made 20 cups. The prisoners that run a wing *cantina* at Central Prison are likely to have paid around R$6 (£1.50) per bottle (Bassani 2016). The businesspeople that sell to the prison's *cantineiros* pay approximately R$45,000 (£11,000) a month to the prison for the right to do so (Sager and Beto 2016). At another prison, in Mato Grosso do Sul, I discovered the *cantina* was used partly to raise funds for psychoactive medicines. The prison in question had recently opened a special unit to house prisoners with poor mental health who would previously have been held in the state's antiquated secure psychiatric hospitals. In all cases, it is ultimately prisoners' families that end up paying for the goods purchased from the *cantina*. At Central Prison prisoners' families are allowed to take in as much as R$150 (£35) a week.[10]

More generally, the intensification of prisoner organisation enabled the few officers that continue to work within the cell blocks to allow prisoners more time out of their cells. In the 1970s, prisoners on the third to fifth floors of the main cell blocks of Carandiru (five, eight and nine) spent as little as four and a half hours a day on unlock (Ramalho 2002). In the 1980s (Wolfmann 2000) and 1990s (Mendes 2015; Varella 2008), cells remained open from approximately 8 a.m. to 4 p.m. As the contemporary, one gang per wing, cell block or prison phenomenon spreads beyond Rio de Janeiro and São Paulo, dusk to dawn unlock is increasingly the national norm.

What is less clear is quite why Brazilian prisoners began to organise to the extent that they did from the 1980s. That there was money to be made from the emerging trade in cocaine likely played a part, but to emphasise once again, it is too reductionist to come to the conclusion that cell block *faxinas* took control of prisons on behalf of drug traffickers. This "top-down" interpretation of the economic needs of illicit market forces needs to be supplemented by a "bottom-up" analysis of the needs of prisoners and prison workers for institutional governance. Organised crime continues to play a role in determining what goes on in prison. So too everyday matters of survival. We have seen many people profit from the fallacies of the organised crime perspective. I have already mentioned state interests. When questioned about what needed to be done to break the power of prison gangs, Judge Valois, who helped negotiate the end to the massacre at the Anísio Jobim complex in the state of Amazonas in January 2017, responded (here I translate his words *ad verbatim*):

> It's practically impossible… Brazilian prisons, how they are super overcrowded, that mess, the cell blocks, the wings, have always had inmate leaders. [The state invented prison gangs]. That leader, who used to be a *Zé-ninguém* (nobody), became a leader of organised crime… The police, who arrest the *Zé-ninguém* on the streets… came to arrest the leader of organised crime; and the press who put in the paper "Zé-ninguém was arrested for stealing a mobile", now put "Organised crime leader is arrested by the police". So it's a thing that is good for the prisoner, good for the police, and good for the press. How are we meant to end this? It's really difficult to end these *facções*, today, because it's good for everyone. (Valois and Macaulay 2017: 84–85)[11]

Besides this symbolism, we have seen inmate organisation has also become increasingly important to ordinary prisoners, prison managers and front-line staff. I have given several examples of gangs being created and moulded in recent decades that have at least as much to do with the realities of everyday prison management, including the instructing of Povo de Israel *representantes* and the deselecting of PCC *faxinas*. We have seen the CV emerged in response to a perceived need for mutual aid and protection. Its leaders no doubt benefit from their increased status, but the *coletivos* they represent and to who they are accountable benefit from improvements in prison order.

I have downplayed purported links between increases in inmate governance and reduced levels of prison staffing. In Chapter 4, we saw the ratio of inmates to staff was equally low during the 1960s and 1970s as it is today. Still, a number of things clearly did change from the latter decades of the twentieth century that help to explain the contemporary Brazilian prison gang from the bottom up. These serve to expand on some of the key points I have made in the book so far.

In Chapter 2, I outlined the rapid expansion of the Brazilian prison population since the return to democracy in the 1980s, part due to economic decline (Caldeira 2000) and part due to the drug trade, albeit the criminalisation of the sale of drugs more than the violence and theft associated with the consumption and sale of illicit drugs themselves. This continuing period of mass incarceration has major implications for the experience of prison, of which we have seen three are particularly relevant. First are the biases of drug prohibition policies and practices. Like any other war, the Brazilian war on drugs is a war on people (Karam 2016). This war has intensified rapidly in the new millennium irrespective of changes in drug markets or patterns of drug consumption. In little more than a decade, the number of people in prison for drug sales has tripled as a proportion of all prisoners. When middle- and upper-class offenders get arrested, it is generally for the non-imprisonable offence of consumption. Poor offenders usually get arrested for "trafficking" and usually receive minimum sentences of five years imprisonment. It is not surprising the prison population is comprised mostly of people that did not complete school.

Second, Brazilian prisons began to fill not only with poorer but younger, less experienced and more volatile offenders (Coelho 2005), moreover offenders whose crimes were more often committed as part of a group and/or more often tied to certain geographical areas. As Crewe (2009) and Skarbek (2014) demonstrate in the context of similar changes to the prisoner profile in the UK and the USA, the resulting mix of anomie and "postcode" identity posed a serious challenge to traditional forms of inmate governance.

Yet gang mentality is both quantitatively and qualitatively different in Brazilian prisons. People anywhere are more likely to form reciprocal relationships with people they know and most identify. By separating prisoners according to their area of residence, in other words, Brazilian authorities take advantage of inmates' interpersonal and collective relations and the support networks they have the potential to generate. These relations extend beyond the confines of the prison wall into the *quebrada*, where further support networks emerge to support prisoners' families, who in turn play a vital role in providing for shortages of food, clothing, bedding, medicines and so on in prison.

Last is the matter of class consciousness. The war on drugs is notable not just for its biases, but for the fact these biases are laid bare for all to see. Further, the dictatorship period was marked by extraordinary levels of state violence perpetrated against prisoners. This legacy continues today. Brazilian prison culture was already shaped by class consciousness, in part developed through contact with political prisoners during previous periods of dictatorship. Literate prisoners read Graciliano Ramos as well as Fyodor Dostoevsky. We have seen from Coelho (2005) and Lima (1991) that Brazil's first major prison gang, the CV, emerged in direct resistance to state violence during the 1964–1985 dictatorship and a perceived need to increase prisoner *conscientização*. We saw from Amorim (1993) that these sentiments were shared by prisoners in São Paulo. Mendes (2009) describes numerous incidences of violent military police raids in São Paulo's prison system in the 1970s, perpetrated in response to inmate rebellions. Most of the major gangs that have more recently emerged in other parts of the country similarly started out as quasi-political organisations promising to provide inmates and *favela* residents with alternative systems of governance (in this book, see Arruda 2015 on Pernambuco; Bassani 2016, Sager and Beto 2016 on Rio Grande do Sul; Almeida and Paes-Machado 2015, Lourenço and Almeida 2013 on Bahia).

The process of democratisation also played its own part in facilitating new forms of politicised, collectivist inmate governance. In São Paulo and Rio de Janeiro, the first post-dictatorship state-level authorities instigated prison humanisation agendas (see, inter alia, Alvarez et al. 2013; Coelho 2005; Salla 2007; Shimizu 2011). These turned out to be of little substance in terms of investment in material conditions. At the same time, however, prisons were opened up to lawyers and human rights groups, incentivising prisoners to organise and in some cases get involved in legal proceedings against prison authorities. Prisoners in São Paulo were actively encouraged to elect inmate councils—known as solidarity commissions—to formally liaise with prison managers. At the Penitenciária do Estado, where Luiz Mendes was imprisoned, the inmate council coincided with the prison being managed by a notably progressive governor. During this period, there was a marked reduction in both police and prisoner-on-prisoner violence, both in Rio de Janeiro (Lima 1991) and in São Paulo (Mendes 2005). While the post-dictatorship humanisation agenda and lull in state violence proved to be temporary, the prison gang phenomenon proved to be otherwise. We have seen the PCC was formed just a year after the police massacre at Carandiru. Fortunately for São Paulo's prisoners, this incident spelt the beginning of the end to the practice of violent police incursions into the state's cell blocks, although Mendes (2015) writes of them still occurring, if less frequently, when he finally left prison in 2004. The politicising and organising of prisoners that immediately followed the Carandiru massacre clearly played a major part in this reduction in prison violence. As previously mentioned, the founders of the PCC soon issued a series of statements of purpose (the PCC *estatuto*) declaring, among other things, that the organisation had been established to further solidarity and union among prisoners and to counter state injustice and oppression. The importance of the 1992 massacre and the PCC's origins as a group providing mutual aid and protection was confirmed in evidence given to congressional inquiries both by its current leader, Marcola (Câmara dos Deputados 2008), previously mentioned, and by its most influential founder and leader before Marcola, Geleião (Alvarez et al. 2013).

Notes

1. An amnesty was in fact declared for political prisoners in 1979.
2. See Chapter 3, n. 1.

3. This does not mean the state's self-governing wings and cell blocks are no longer subject to occasional violent raids by special forces. In 2009, São Paulo's Prison Secretariat set up its own rapid response team to perform such operations in place of the police. This force has been criticised for systematically raiding a specific wing at Sant'Ana in the days following prisoners' annual commemoration on 31 August of the birth of the PCC. On each occasion the wing has been occupied by 150 or more officers for up to eight hours while cells are searched and prisoners made to sit in the same position on the floor with their arms crossed behind their heads. Prisoners reported that during the September 2015 raid women who refused to raise their shirts were beaten by the male officers (Mecanismo Nacional de Prevenção e Combate à Tortura 2015).
4. The term *inclusão* is still commonly used in São Paulo today. Another term we have seen that is used across the country is *triagem* (screening).
5. I have already mentioned (in Chapter 4) the 2000–2006 spate of gang-orchestrated murders at Jair Ferreira de Carvalho prison, Mato Grosso do Sul, and (in Chapter 2) an officer at a *carceragem* in the state of Paraná showing off the fact officers used to take inmates into the car park for beatings. Among the most horrific examples of officer violence that have been described to me during my research are of a prison governor in Goiás who had fired his pistol straight into an inmate's face and guards in the state of Minas Gerais shooting through the bars of a cell door into a group of inmates celebrating their football team scoring a goal.
6. Marcola went on to accuse prison and wider state authorities of gaining from his position as a mythical leader. This gave them the chance to be seen to be tough by keeping him in high security RDD. This is an argument I have heard many times in Brazil in the context of prison gangs. In one of the most interesting exchanges, Marcola questioned why authorities had ignored his request to be transferred to another state or the federal prison system. His interrogators immediately switched to another issue altogether. They either failed to understand the significance of the question or more likely chose to completely ignore it.
7. Recording available at Jozino (2017).
8. I paid a certain amount of attention to São Paulo's *debate* system of conflict resolution in Chapter 4. In that chapter I explained that prior to the emergence of the PCC, the prisoners involved in a *debate* would

act as both judge and sentencer. Under the PCC, these roles have been separated in the case of accusations of more serious breaches of inmate code. The gang's system of dispute resolution was described to me in some detail by inmates at Butantã during a class I led at the prison in 2016 (see Chapter 2). They explained how the PCC's *éticas* were generally policed informally among themselves, but that they would take issues they could not resolve to the prison's three PCC *irmãs* (sisters) to convene a more formal *debate*. Sentences for third-time serious offences—defined by blood being drawn, and usually punished through physical beating—were decided through a telephone conference with five other PCC members.

9. I also used the term pre-PCC in Chapter 4. I borrow the term from Brazilian prison ethnographer, Camila Dias, with who I have published (Dias and Darke 2016). Dias coined this phrase in her doctoral research, published as Dias (2013). I have cited this work several times in this chapter. Utilising the classical sociological work of Norbert Elias on processes of civilisation, Dias (2013) differentiates between the pre-PCC and PCC configurations in prison governance, prisoner and staff-inmate relations.
10. In addition to these major examples of corruption, another example might be added that benefits neither prison authorities nor prison gangs, but individuals working in the prison system. As a result of the *propina* charged for gaining contracts to produce and sell prison food, each meal typically costs at least R$20 (£5). In 2017, I visited a prison in Rondônia where I was told prison authorities were currently paying R$27 (£6.50) a meal.
11. Luís Carlos Valois is an executive judge in the state of Amazonas. Valois was present at the prison complex within hours of the massacre. He recently completed a PhD on judicial complicity in the Brazilian state's war on drugs. His doctoral thesis was published as Valois (2016).

References

Adorno, S., & Dias, C. N. (2016). Cronologia doa "ataques de 2006" e a nova configuração de poder nas prisões na última decada. *Revista Brasileira de Segurança Pública, 10*(2), 118–132.

Adorno, S., & Salla, F. (2007). Criminalidade organizada nas prisões e os ataques do PCC. *Estudos Avançados, 21*(61), 7–29.

Almeida, O. L., & Paes-Machado, E. (2015). Sem lugar para corer, nem se esconder: Processos socioorganizacionais de vitimização Prisional. *Espacio Abierto, 24*(3), 69–96.

Alvarez, M. C., Salla, F., & Dias, C. N. (2013). Das comissões de solidariedade ao Primeiro Comando da Capital em São Paulo. *Tempo Social, 25*(1), 61–82.

Amorim, C. R. (1993). *Comando Vermelho: A história segredo do crime organizado* (4th ed.). Rio de Janeiro: Record.

Arruda, R. F. (2015). *Geografia do cárcere: Territorialidades na vida cotidiana carcerária no sistena prisional de Pernambuco.* Ph.D. thesis, University of São Paulo. http://www.teses.usp.br/teses/disponiveis/8/8136/tde-16062015-125328/pt-br.php. Last accessed 3 February 2017.

Barbosa, A. R. (2007). Um levantamento introdutório das práticas de violência física dentro das cadeias cariocas. In A. C. Marques (Ed.), *Conflitos, política e relações pessoais* (pp. 129–172). Campinas: Pontes.

Barreto, L. C., & Santos, N. P. (1984). *Memórias do cárcere*. Film. Brazil: Brentz.

Bassani, F. (2016). *Visita íntima: Sexo, crime e negócios nas prisões*. Porto Alegre: Bestiário.

Batista, N., & Borges, R. (2012). De professor para professor: Entrevista com William da Silva Lima. *Discursos Sediciosos, 17*(19/20), 11–18.

Biondi, K. (2010). *Junto e misturado: Uma etnografia do PCC.* São Paulo: Teirciero Nome. English version: Biondi, K. (2016). *Sharing this walk: An ethnography of prison life and the PCC in Brazil* (J. F. Collins, Trans.). Chapel Hill: University of North Carolina.

Biondi, K. (2014). *Etnografia no movimento: Território, hierarquia e lei no PCC.* Ph.D. thesis, Federal University of São Carlos. https://www.repositorio.ufscar.br/bitstream/handle/ufscar/246/6378.pdf?sequence=1&isAllowed=y. Last accessed 7 April 2017.

Biondi, K. (2017a, January 23). *The extinction of sexual violence in the prisons of São Paulo, Brazil.* http://uncpressblog.com/2017/01/23/karina-biondi-the-extinction-of-sexual-violence-in-the-prisons-of-sao-paulo-brazil. Last accessed 7 March 2017.

Biondi, K. (2017b). 'It was already in the ghetto': Rap, religion and crime in the prison. Interview with Djalma Oliveira Rios, aka 'Cascão'. *Prison Service Journal, 229,* 45–47.

Caldeira, T. (2000). *City of walls: Crime, segregation and citizenship in São Paulo*. Berkeley: University of California.

Câmara dos Deputados. (2008). No title. Resource document. http://www1.folha.uol.com.br/folha/cotidiano/20060708-marcos_camacho.pdf. Last accessed 17 July 2017.

Christino, M. S., & Tognolli, C. (2017). *Laços de sangue: A história secreta do PCC*. São Paulo: Matrix.

Coelho, E. C. (2005). *A oficina do diablo. E outros estudos sobre criminalidade*. Rio de Janeiro: Record.

Crewe, B. (2009). *The prisoner society: Power, adaptation and social life in an English prison*. Oxford: Oxford University.

Dias, C. N. (2013). *PCC: Hegemonia nas prisões e monopólio da violência*. São Paulo: Saraiva.

Dias, C. N., & Darke, S. (2016). From dispersed to monopolized violence: Expansion and consolidation of the Primeiro Comando da Capital's hegemony in São Paulo's prisons. *Crime, Law and Social Change, 65*(3), 213–215.

Dias, C. N., & Salla, F. (2013). Organized crime in Brazilian prisons: The example of the PCC. *International Journal of Criminology and Sociology, 2*, 397–408.

Gay, R. (2015). *Bruno: Conversations with a Brazilian drug dealer*. Durham, NC: Duke University.

Green, P., & Ward, T. (2004). *State Crime: Governments, Violence and Corruption*. London: Sage.

Harvard Law School, & Justiça Global. (2011). *São Paulo sob achaque: Corrupção, crime organizado e violência institucional em maio de 2006*. Resource document. https://harvardhumanrights.files.wordpress.com/2011/05/full-with-cover.pdf. Last accessed 17 July 2017.

Human Rights Watch. (1998). *Behind bars in Brazil*. New York: Human Rights Watch.

Jozino, J. (2017, November 28). *Marcola pede transferência para cadeia de inimigos do PCC*. https://ponte.org/marcola-pede-transferencia-para-cadeia-de-inimigos-do-pcc. Last accessed 2 January 2018.

Junior, A. S., Assis, F. C., & Gadelha, I. (2017, August 21). Há sinais claros da presença do crime organizado na política, diz Gilmar Mendes. *UOL*. https://noticias.uol.com.br/ultimas-noticias/agencia-estado/2017/08/21/ha-sinais-claros-da-presenca-do-crime-organizado-na-politica-diz-gilmar-mendes.htm?cmpid=copiaecola. Last accessed 22 August 2017.

Karam, M. L. (2016). Drogas: Legalizar para garantir direitos humanos fundamentais. *Revista EMERJ, 19*(76), 114–127.

Lima, W. S. (1991). *Quatrocentos contra um: Uma história do Comando Vermelho*. Rio de Janeiro: ISER.

Lourenço, L. C., & Almeida, O. L. (2013). "Quem mantém a ordem, quem cria desordem": Gangues prisionais na Bahia. *Tempo Social, 25*(1), 37–59.
Macedo, F. (2014, June 9). Gilmar Mendes alerta para infiltração do crime em partidos. *EXAME*. http://exame.abril.com.br/brasil/mendes-alerta-para-infiltracao-do-crime-em-partidos. Last accessed 22 August 2017.
Manso, B. P. (2012). *Crescimento e queda dos homicídios em SP entre 1960 e 2010: Uma análise dos mecanismos da escolha homicida e das carreiras no crime*. Ph.D. thesis, University of São Paulo. http://www.teses.usp.br/teses/disponiveis/8/8131/tde-12122012-105928/pt-br.php. Last accessed 13 April 2017.
Manso, B. P. (2016). *Homicide in São Paulo: An examination of trends from 1960–2010*. Cham: Springer.
Manso, B. P., & Dias, C. N. (2017). PCC, sistema prisional e gestão do novo mundo do crime no Brasil. *Revista Brasileira de Segurança Pública, 11*(2), 10–29.
Marques, A. (2010). "Liderança", "proceder" e "igualdade": Uma etnografia das relações políticas no Primeiro Comando da Capital. *Etnográfica, 14*(2), 311–335.
Marques, A. (2014). *Crime e proceder: Um experimento antropológico*. São Paulo: Alameda.
Mecanismo Nacional de Prevenção e Combate à Tortura. (2015). *Relatório de visita a penitenciaria feminina de Sant'ana do estado de São Paulo*. Resource document. http://www.sdh.gov.br/sobre/participacao-social/comite-nacional-de-prevencao-e-combate-a-tortura/representantes/penitenciaria-feminina-de-santana. Last accessed 5 September 2017.
Mendes, L. A. (2005). *Às cegas*. São Paulo: Companhia das Letras.
Mendes, L. A. (2009). *Memórias de um sobrevivente*. São Paulo: Companhia de Bolso.
Mendes, L. A. (2012). *Cela forte*. São Paulo: Global.
Mendes, L. A. (2015). *Confissões de um homen livre*. São Paulo: Companhia das Letras.
Miraglia, P., & Salla, F. (2008). O PCC e a gestão dos presídios em São Paulo: Entrevista com Nagashi Furukawa. *Novos Estudos, 80*, 21–41.
Perlman, J. E. (2010). *Favela: Four decades of living on the edge in Rio de Janeiro*. New York: Oxford University.
Ramalho, J. R. (2002). *Mundo do crime: A ordem pelo avesso* (3rd ed.). Rio de Janeiro: Graal.
Ramos, G. (2015). *Memórias do Cárcere* (49th ed.). Rio de Janeiro: Record.
Sager, T., & Beto, R. (2016). *Central*. Documentary film. Brazil: Panda.

Salla, F. (2006). As rebeliões nas prisões: Novos significados a partir da experiência Brasileira. *Sociologias, 8*(16), 274–307.

Salla, F. (2007). De Montoro a Lembro: As políticas penitenciárias em São Paulo. *Revista Brasileira de Segurança Pública, 1*(1), 72–90.

Salla, F. (2017). Vigiar e punir e os estudos prisionais no Brasil. *DILEMAS*, special edition no. 2, 29–43.

Salla, F., Jesus, M. G. M., & Rocha, T. T. (2012, October). Relato de uma pesquisa sobre a Lei 11.343/2006. *Boletim IBCCRIM, 20*, 10–11.

Shimizu, B. (2011). *Solidariedade e grefarismo nas facções criminosas: Um estudo criminológico à luz da psicologia das massas*. São Paulo: Instituto Brasileiro de Ciências Criminais.

Silva, A. M. C. (2008). *Nos braços da lei: O uso da violência negociada no interior das prisões*. Rio de Janeiro: E+A.

Silva, A. M. C. (2011). *Participo que… Desvelando a punição intramuros*. Rio de Janeiro: Publit.

Skarbek, D. (2014). *The social order of the underworld: How prison gangs govern the American penal system*. New York: Oxford University.

Steinberg, G., & Sacramento, P. (2004). *O prisioneiro da grade de ferro*. Documentary film. Brazil: California Filmes.

Teixeira, A., Salla, F. A., & Marinho, M. G. S. M. C. (2016). Vadiagem e prisões correcionais em São Paulo: Mecanismos de controle no firmamento da República. *Estudos Históricos, 29*(58), 381–400.

Valois, L. C. (2016). *O direito penal da guerra às drogas*. Belo Horizonte: D'Plácido.

Valois, L. C., & Macaulay, F. (2017). O Judiciário e a crise do sistema penitenciário: Luís Carlos Valois, entrevistado por Fiona Macaulay. *Revista Brasileira de Segurança Pública, 11*(2), 78–87.

Varella, D. (2008). *Estação Carandiru*. São Paulo: Companhia das Letras. English edition: Varella, D. (2012). *Lockdown: Inside Brazil's most violent prison* (A. Entrekin, Trans.). London: Simon and Schuster.

Varella, D. (2012). *Carcereiros*. São Paulo: Companhia das Letras.

Velasco, C., & Caesar, G. (2018, February 22). Brasil tem média de 7 presos por agente penitenciário; 19 estados descumprem limite recomendado. *O Globo*. https://g1.globo.com/monitor-da-violencia/noticia/brasil-tem-media-de-7-presos-por-agente-penitenciario-19-estados-descumprem-limite-recomendado.ghtml. Last accessed 25 February 2018.

Wolfmann, L. C. (2000). *Portal do inferno: Mas há esperança*. São Paulo: WVC Gestão Inteligente Com. Ltda.

7

Co-producing Prison Order

The respect [between us and the prison administration] is mutual. […] How are we meant to believe in the state?… The only value a prisoner has for the state is the profit they make from him […] The little that comes to me is shared, the little that goes to him is shared with those that do not have anything. We divide everything, even our space. (Fieldwork interview, Red Command gang leader, Polinter police lock-up, Rio de Janeiro, 15 September 2010)

We're all equal here. (Fieldwork notes, prisoner, ACUDA day centre, Rondônia, 17 May 2017)

Brazilian prison authorities continuously fail to comply with international norms on minimal conditions of incarceration. This is highlighted in one national and international human rights investigation after another. We have seen that even the most humane of Brazil's prisons (the voluntary sector APAC prisons of Minas Gerais) lock up their inmates in shared dormitories containing double or triple bunks lain out side by side. The suffering of the average Brazilian prisoner is rightly brought to attention. In the most comprehensive international exposé of the poverty of Brazilian prisons of the past few decades, Human Rights Watch (1998) uncovered extraordinarily high rates of cell occupancy, understaffing, violence and poor health at most of the prisons its team of researchers visited. The report recommended reduced use of imprisonment, increased investment in infrastructure and services and more investigation into accusations of punishment beatings by riot police and guards. To reduce levels of inmate on inmate violence, it recommended increased levels of staffing, separate prison units for violent and non-violent prisoners, and that "prisoners should never be assigned internal security responsibilities or be placed in positions of power over each other, even informally" (Human Rights Watch 1998: 7). The analysis of inmate collaboration and self-governance I have offered over the preceding chapters would look out of place alongside the last of these policy-focused conclusions. When Human Rights Watch returned to the matter of inmate violence later in the report, it dropped this reference to prison co-governance and instead referred to guards neglecting their duties. It explained:

> The end result of low guard numbers and lax surveillance is a power vacuum. Unsupervised and undisciplined, prisoners in Brazil are left to govern themselves. With the meagre guard presence in many prisons, there is very little to prevent tougher, stronger, richer and more well-connected inmates from threatening, intimidating and sometimes violently abusing their more vulnerable fellows. (Human Rights Watch 1998: 105)

In Chapter 2, we saw Human Rights Watch (1998) was produced at a time when overcrowding was a particular concern, especially for the many thousands of people held illegally in police custody, but that across the country, people are still regularly held in conditions of under a square metre per prisoner today. This was highlighted in Human Rights Watch's more recent (2015) report on Pernambuco, which found the state's largest prisons to be operating with occupancy rates in excess of 300%. As for staffing, Human Rights Watch (2015) included several examples of prisons where its investigators had discovered more than 200 people incarcerated for each guard on duty. Again, there was nothing to dispute in Human Rights Watch's analysis from my own perspective before it came to the question of inmate governance. We saw the report noted the practice of entrusting cell block keys to certain prisoners. The report was given the unfortunate title *The State Let Evil Take Over*. Human Rights Watch gave the following analysis of the connotations of prison administrators delegating powers to inmate *chaveiros* (key holders):

> The keyholders sell drugs, extort payments from fellow prisoners, and require them to pay for places to sleep, according to current and former detainees, family members, and two state officials Human Rights Watch interviewed. They deploy "militias" made up of other inmates to threaten and beat those who do not pay their debts or who question their rule. Prison officials either turn a blind eye or participate in the keyholders' rackets and receive kickbacks, according to several interviewees, including a prison director. (Human Rights Watch 2015: 7)

Not surprisingly, it was this aspect of the report that made the international headlines. Before we explore the policy implications of the alternative interpretation of Brazilian staff-inmate relations developed through this monograph, it is useful to write a chapter by chapter summary.

Chapter 1 (Self-Governing Prison Communities) introduced the reader to the extent to which Brazilian prison order is negotiated between inmates and staff. It started with Varella's (2008, 2012) accounts of working as a doctor at Carandiru prison, and the importance he attached to its cell block *faxina* (cleaner or housekeeper) system and to prisoners adhering to codes of conduct relating to inmate solidarity and dealings with staff. We saw comparable inmate codes and positions of cell block wide authority existed to different and varying degrees in prisons across the country—hence my use of the term prisoner communities in the plural—and that these were the result of locally produced practices.[1] I suggested these varieties in co-produced prison governance were explained in large part by the informal, clientelistic nature of Brazilian social and institutional cultures. However, the extent of co-governance from one prison to another correlated with poor prison conditions on the whole, including but not restricted to shortages in prison staff. As a result of these situational adjustments, most Brazilian prisons contained complex social orders, moreover orders that were not as psychologically damaging as our (predominantly Northern) theories on prison life might lead us to predict. The most important question to explore was not why prison inmates and staff formed reciprocal relations of mutual aid and protection—disorder only served the interests of the most predatory of individuals—but rather the peculiarities of the Brazilian prison environment in which they are able to do so. To achieve this, I emphasised the advantage of adopting an interpretivist framework of analysis. This had allowed me to focus on studying Brazilian prison life in its own terms as much as in comparison with prisons in other places. Interpretivist comparative analysis was also best suited to my position as a research activist. There was little existing published research on Brazilian prisons, in Portuguese let alone in English. If my research were to inform prison policy and practice, it was important I placed myself as near as possible to the phenomena I was studying. Only by immersing myself in the field would I gain a full enough picture to be confident my research would not have the potential to do more harm than good. More specifically, I had utilised a mixed methodology of primary and secondary research that included ethnographic, historical and first-hand, inside accounts.

Still, prison cultures do not develop in a vacuum. They are shaped by staff-inmate conditions of work and incarceration, and by wider sociopolitical conditions on the outside. The former of these background issues was the focus of Chapter 2 (Law and Repression). I commenced this chapter with the observation mass incarceration and inhumane prison conditions were endemic to Brazilian justice and that the few positive aspects of Brazilian prison life (for instance, the relatively larger amount of unlock and family visits in comparison with Western European to Northern American prisons) should be recognised first and foremost as situated responses to inmates' suffering. In the main text of the chapter, I described two key aspects of Brazilian punitivism: its rapidly increasing prison population and its historically high levels of prison overcrowding. I analysed the first of these in the context of the international war on drugs and wider drift towards criminal justice militarisation, and emphasised Brazil should be regarded less a follower as a setter of global punitive trends: in the context of prison, as the principle player in the emergence of a new, Latin American, mass carceral zone.

Regarding overcrowding, I noted the existence of several large penitentiaries where governors had chosen to leave cell doors open rather than squeeze inmates into them at night. At the same time, however, I explained Brazilian punitivism was a historical phenomenon, with roots in Iberian colonial traditions of moral intervention, social exclusion, militarism and authoritarian violence. These were reflected in theories and practices of criminal justice in what had been described as a criminology of apartheid and a never-ending politics of fear and exception. Brazilian prisoners had always experienced inhumane conditions of incarceration. Brazilian prisons had always been institutions of corporal punishment and social defence, never of rehabilitation. The current "crisis" in the penitentiary system, for instance, was largely the result of states closing their police *carceragens* (lock-ups; units of holding cells). As for rates of incarceration, the recent explosion in the prison population should be considered alongside trends in policing and extralegal methods of crime control, both of which were likewise historically characterised by authoritarianism and violence. More generally, I concluded, the war on drugs should be regarded as the latest version of a wider war on the poor, moreover a war whose target populations and excessive violence were blatant and open for all to see. Even more so today than in the past, I suggested, Brazilian prisoners were aware the criminal justice system fundamentally discriminated between the lower and upper classes. Of importance to my research, Brazilian prisoners increasingly understood they had effectively been abandoned to their own devices.

Chapter 3 (The Northern Massacres) explored weaknesses in the Brazilian state's responses to a series of prison gang orchestrated killings in the states of Amazonas, Roraima and Rio Grande do Norte in January 2017, as well as the position taken in much national and international liberal commentary. We saw the federal government came under fire from its liberal critics for not acknowledging poor prison conditions and understaffing were also contributory factors to the massacres, or that major drug trafficking gangs like the Rio de Janeiro's Comando Vermelho (CV) and São Paulo's Primeiro Comando do Capital (PCC) were symptoms rather than causes of mass incarceration and the so-called war on drugs. The government was also accused of promoting a securitisation agenda to deal with such self-professed criminal gangs that was more rhetoric than reality. Besides posing the obvious question why equally violent rebellions had not occurred in similarly overcrowded and understaffed prisons in the country (on the contrary, we saw prison violence had fallen dramatically in some of the country's poorest prisons), I used the northern prison massacres as a case study to demonstrate a need to shift attention away from the purported links between drug trafficking and prison gangs. I promoted a research agenda that instead focused on the historical role played by inmate collectives, gangs as they were often too quickly labelled, in providing inmates with alternative systems of governance and prison staff with informal systems of security, and so studying prison gangs from the bottom up (as emerging from everyday institutional practices, professional, social and interpersonal relations) and from the inside out (gang activity in the country's poor urban areas, including control of the drug trade, depending on what goes on inside prison more than vice versa). Neither should the country's prison gang phenomenon necessarily be regarded as a symptom of international organised crime. For the ordinary prisoner, I explained, gangs operated as ideals as much as physical realities. Even the most advanced of Brazil's prison gangs (the CV and PCC) should be studied as organisations of criminals rather than as criminal organisations, as loose heterogeneous networks of individuals that were just as vulnerable to being corrupted by police and prison authorities as the opposite. They certainly should not be regarded as parallel states (Barbosa 2005; Biondi 2013; Shimizu 2011). Like any other communities, prisoner communities sought institutions of governance to make their members' lives more predictable, to protect them and provide for their material and psychological needs. To the extent prison staff lacked the resources to do so, prison inmates were required to collaborate, organise and self-govern. The northern prison massacres represented a disruption in an increasingly dynamic and institutionalised system of co-produced order, symbolised by the historical figure of the *faxina*, which while fragile and varied, had for decades kept most Brazilian prisons in better order and enabled most Brazilian prisoners to better survive. The immediate cause of the massacres may have been the CV and PCC falling out over their share of the eastern cocaine trail, but for most prisoners that had something to gain from the killings—few of who would ever make serious money from the drug trade—the fight was over territories of informal governance and survival, not territories of commerce.

The following chapters focused more specifically on the Brazilian prison environment and its securitising by inmate organisation and prison gangs. Chapter 4 (Surviving through the *Convívio*) centred on what I refer to as the collective nature of Brazilian prison life. It explored prison routines and staff-inmate relations independently from criminal gangs, and focused mostly on the pre-CV and PCC era. We saw the country's prisons had relied on inmates to collaborate and self-govern since its first modern penitentiaries opened in the mid-nineteenth century. Staff shortages and co-governance, in other words, were defining features of the Brazilian prison system as much as inhumane living conditions. In the absence of guards and prison rules, I explained, inmates had developed codes of conduct that govern relations between and among themselves and their keepers to the tiniest detail. Prisoners referred to these norms of coexistence and co-survival as *regras de convivência* (rules of conviviality), *regras de convívio* (rules of collective living), *regras de proceder* (rules of procedure) or simply as *éticas* (ethics) or *disciplina* (discipline). They referred to themselves in the singular: as one (cell, wing, cell block or prison-wide) *coletivo* (collective). This collective prisoner identity, I argued, was rooted in the everyday realities of living in close proximity to one another, and by prisoners' views of themselves as a repressed group of people in conflict with the law. As a result, the oppositional cultures that arose in Brazilian prisons, and to a lesser extent poor, urban areas, were less destructive than was often assumed. Codes relating to inmate solidarity, for example, invariably included measures aimed at supporting the least fortunate and avoiding conflict not only among common prisoners, but also with *faxinas* and prison staff. Where necessary, inmate codes of conduct were enforced through quasi-legal systems of dispute resolution that, in states with more advanced prison gang systems, invariably aimed to adhere to principles of procedural fairness and substantive justice. Equally significant, prisoners that rose through the ranks of inmate hierarchies were usually those with the most experience of prison and the best skills of communication and negotiation. I provided illustrations of the complexity of Brazilian inmate rules and procedures from states across the country, and from the inside accounts of Varella and others that had formerly worked or been incarcerated in Carandiru prison from the 1970s to the 1990s.

Chapter 5 (Managing without Guards) explored this theoretical framework in the context of an empirical fieldwork study of an overcrowded *carceragem* (pseudonymised in this book as Polinter) in Rio de Janeiro that I completed over three weeks in 2010. It served as a detailed illustration of the futility of studying Brazilian prison order from the top down and from the outside in. We saw the few police officers that worked at the *carceragem* had delegated full responsibility for managing daily routines, prisoner and staff-prisoner relations to teams of trusty prisoners and inmate leaders on the two wings that made up its cell block. Trusty prisoners worked as administrators, janitors and guards. They were headed by former police officers, the most senior of who were referred to by other prisoners as Polinter's *administração* (administration) or *chefia* (management). Together with the wing inmate leaders, these two prisoners answered only to the governor and the general coordinator of Rio's 16 *carceragens*. One of the most impressive things about the means by which Polinter was governed was that almost identical systems of inmate representation operated on both wings, despite the fact prisoners held on the second wing, the *seguro* (insurance or vulnerable persons unit) did not consider themselves career criminals or their *coletivo* (the Povo de Israel: People of Israel) a criminal gang. The senior police officers (the governor and general coordinator) had instructed the Povo de Israel how to operate along the same lines as prisoners held on the other (CV) wing. Both wings had one *representante da cela* (cell representative) per cell and one *representante geral* (general representative). On both wings, prisoners' families contributed to a *caixinha* (collection box), the proceeds of which were used to purchase common goods such as cooking equipment and toiletries. When disputes arose between prisoners held in the cell block or their codes of conduct were broken, *representantes* gathered together as a *comissão* (commission) to adjudicate and pass sentence. When they were unable to control a particular prisoner, *representantes* would inform the police he needed to be transferred to another *carceragem*. On both wings, most prisoners became *representantes* on the basis of how long they had been there rather than the criminal reputation they had arrived with. Nor was there any real difference between the types of people that ended up serving time on the two wings, beside the fact prisoners in the *seguro* tended to be older, most having passed the age where they were expected to earn their living from the illicit economy and to be affiliated to a gang. Prisoners were allocated to the CV wing based on where they lived rather than their being actively involved in gang activity. In the summary to the chapter, I explored a number of key features of the balance of power and authority I had witnessed at the *carceragem* that could be generalised to the wider Brazilian prison system. First, while the senior police officers retained the final word on how Polinter was governed, the *carceragem* effectively operated under a customary rather than legalised order, constructed from informal rules and procedures that had been developed and reproduced in situ. Second, order at the *carceragem* was achieved through a plurality of police officer and (mostly) prisoner roles and responsibilities. Finally, Polinter was not only co-governed by its inmates, but its order was considered legitimate by nearly everyone that worked or was incarcerated there. Of particular importance to this legitimacy, the order achieved at the *carceragem* complied with popular inmate notions of resistance, mutual respect and exchange: to respect in order to be respected, to share in order to share, the CV *representante geral* explained it. These three features, I concluded, stood in contrast to the established sociology of prison life literature associated with the classic work of Gresham Sykes and Erving Goffman. In place of defects in an otherwise bureaucratic power, I had encountered a negotiated order that was broadly to everyone's benefit; and in place of division and disorder among inmates and normative distance between inmates and officers, I had encountered examples of solidarity and reciprocity. Much of this reciprocity was forced in the sense that prisoners and police officers could not manage without it. However, Polinter's order was not just instrumental. It also included moral values, for instance around the treatment of inmates' families.

Chapter 6 (Prison Gangs) centred on the CV and PCC and the phenomenon of the contemporary Brazilian prison gang. In line with the rest of the monograph, however, it explored the significance of the prison gang phenomenon from the bottom up and from the inside out. We saw both gangs emerged from increased levels of prisoner organisation in the wake of the country's 1964–1985 military dictatorship. The CV was founded by a group of bank robbers held under emergency legislation who considered themselves political prisoners. The PCC was formed following the police massacre of more than 100 prisoners at Carandiru prison in 1992. Both gangs explicitly aimed to increase inmate solidarity and collective action, promising to protect prisoners from state brutality and to reduce prison violence and exploitation among prisoners. In time, the two gangs took on responsibility for governing the cell blocks across most of Rio de Janeiro and São Paulo's prisons as well as the poor, urban areas most prisoners came from. In their own words, they "unified" the existing system of *falanges* (postcode gangs created by allocating different wings to people from different areas) under the banner of one statewide *coletivo*, raised prisoners' consciousness (of injustice and oppression), and introduced them to the political ideals of egalitarianism and equality. These ideals had been corrupted to some extent by the lure of the money to be made from illicit markets, especially drugs, but they were far from irrelevant, at least in the eyes of ordinary prisoners who expected them to be delivered. Gang leaders continued to rely on the support of their *coletivos*. Their authority depended on them maintaining legitimacy among other prisoners.

Today, Brazilian prisoners refer to gang leaders as their *representantes*. In chapter 5, we saw prisoners on the *seguro* at Polinter used the words *coletivo* and Povo de Israel interchangeably. Gang leadership regularly changes hands in CV prisons as individuals lose their peers' confidence. In PCC prisons, many wings operate under gang authority despite none of their occupants being gang members. Although children held in administrative detention in São Paulo are not considered gang affiliates, their prison lives are likewise characterised by adherence to inmate codes and collective resistance to state authority (see Vicentin 2005, 2011). In contrast to some other parts of the country (see, e.g., Moore 2017 on Bahia), the same codes and systems of dispute resolution operate in women's as well as men's prisons. As the CV and PCC spread—or more accurately, the ideals of CV and PCC spread—to other parts of the country, horrific displays of power tend to be followed by reductions in prison violence and inmate exploitation. Some prisoners are involved in drug trafficking, and there is money to be made inside as well as outside prison. However, in the last instance, the cell block and statewide prison gang is best regarded as a development—an institutionalising—of existing practices of inmate collaboration, self-governance and the co-production of prison order. As Marques (Biondi and Marques 2010; Marques 2010, 2014) puts it in the context of the PCC, what the contemporary cell block gang in essence represents is a colonising of heterogeneous inmate rules of conviviality. Prisoner organisation continues to serve specific functions. It helps to ensure inmate safety, and it facilitates the work of officers. Prison governors and the few guards that work in the country's cell blocks continue, as always, to negotiate order with inmates, and to employ some of them to work in the place of prison staff. They continue to have a say in which inmates they deal with, that is which inmates work on the gang side of the *ligação* (link). Prison governors are also known to have chosen gang leaders (Gay 2015; Varella 2008). Prisoner organisation also absolves state authorities of their own responsibilities and gives them something else to blame ("gang culture") when things go wrong.

Among the various aspects of prison governance, two core themes stand out from my research: those of informality and variation, and of resistance, conviviality and survival. I have utilised the pioneering work of Karina Biondi (especially Biondi 2010, 2014) to explore the former. My focus in this monograph has been on the latter. We have seen Brazil's major prison gangs have brought a certain level of consistency. Prison gangs operate differently in one prison context to another, but the principles originally formulated by the CV in Rio de Janeiro remain largely the same across the country.

As previously suggested, it is difficult to reconcile these observations with the critique of inmate collaboration and self-governance made by Human Rights Watch (1998, 2015). However, our positions are not as incompatible as they might at first appear. We have seen prison violence was a greater concern in the mid-1990s than it is today. Among the prisons visited, Human Rights Watch (1998) focused most attention on Carandiru and Central Prison, which between them accounted for almost as many homicides in any given year in the 1990s as the total number of violent prison deaths in the two states (São Paulo and Rio Grande do Sul) today. Human Rights Watch (2015) centred on one state, Pernambuco, whose prisons are arguably the most inhumane, and are certainly the most understaffed in the country. Pernambuco is also one of the least advanced states in terms of cell block and prison-wide gangs. Anyhow, universities and human rights organisations serve different purposes. Through its advocacy and prison inspections, Human Rights Watch has done much to improve the position of Brazilian inmates and prison workers. How people negotiate and survive dehumanising and brutalising conditions is not the concern of human rights organisations. They achieve more by focusing public and political attention on the conditions themselves.

Nevertheless, the way we portray Brazilian prisons and staff-inmate relations is important. In this monograph, I have focused on the work of the few Brazilian ethnographers that have spent much time in prison. With so little quality academic research to work with, I have had to supplement this with my own empirical research. To date, my concern has been to gain a deeper understanding of everyday life in Brazilian prisons. This is what has driven me to visit as many prisons as I have, and in as many parts of the country as possible. Although most of these visits have lasted only a few hours, I have nearly always managed to enter the cell blocks as well as the administration areas and talk to prisoners and guards as well as governors. My reading of first-hand accounts has also been important, as have my continuing conversations with prison workers, lawyers and others that have regular access to prisons and prisoners.

Every time a prison death or prison rebellion hits the headlines, the default position is to blame it on the largely fictitious figure of the pathological, rent-seeking gang member or trusty prisoner. When I contact my colleagues on the ground, they invariably give me a more complex account involving individual or small groups of perpetrators.

Quality news corporations are as guilty for getting their facts wrong as any other media source. Of course some gang members and trusty prisoners do sometimes abuse their authority or resort to violence. And of course well-resourced prisons are preferable to self-sustaining prisons. The more established an institution of governance becomes the more able it is to regulate violence and abuse in its territory, by its servants as well as those under its authority. This applies to self-governing prison gangs and self-governing prisons as well as the most bureaucratic institution of governance. The latter is likely to experience longer periods of stability and progression. At the same time, few governance institutions survive in the long term if they continue to rule through authoritarianism and violence, and do not take steps to be accountable to, integrate and provide for the needs of people they govern. Autocracies tend to eventually give way to forms of governance that are regarded as both procedurally and substantively legitimate. In Chapter 6, we saw the PCC provides a classic case of such a trajectory. Initially borrowing from the CV the guiding principles of *paz, justiça* and *liberdade* (peace, justice and liberty), the PCC reached a hegemonic position among São Paulo's prison and urban populations when it became tied to the concepts of *ética* (ethics) and—concepts also originally associated with the CV—*união* (union) and *igualdade* (equality). Even to the extent these might be regarded as distortions, the position has been reached in which prisoners do not feel obliged to take orders that are not contained in or contradict established codes of conduct (Biondi 2010). Even foreign prisoners quickly learn the importance of the phrase *é de igual* (literally, it's equality) (Biondi 2017). São Paulo prisoners rightly identify the move towards *igualdade* as a process of democratisation: "Nobody", they say, "is better than anyone else" (ibid.: 245; see also Dias and Darke 2016). Like most other successful governance institutions, the PCC became more important than its members, including its leaders (Biondi 2010). Today predatory prisoners do not rise up the ranks of the PCC leadership in São Paulo. To be successful, you need to be a good negotiator and to have good self-control (Dias 2013). Above all, you need to be *humilde* (humble) (Biondi 2010; Marques 2014). Even to the extent he was dishonest, Marcola, did not entirely distort the facts when he suggested to the congressional inquiry into the May 2006 attacks (Câmara dos Deputados 2008) that the PCC had chosen him and not the other way round. "Those in powerful positions eventually [became] the main servants of the machine" (Dias and Darke 2016: 219). Marcola has led the PCC for the past 15 years. The more difficult question is what exactly Marcola is the leader of.

To borrow from Pakes (2015), the immediate and long-term aims of my adopting an interpretivist research framework in my research are to explore: (1) how and why everyday prison routines and staff-inmate relations are different in Brazil to other places; (2) how and to what extent changes can and should be made to the Brazilian prison environment; and (3) what, on the other hand, should be regarded as good practices that might possibly be adopted elsewhere. In my research to date, I have focused on the first of these questions. This is not the place to develop a systematic critique of how and why Brazilian prisons need reforming, or how the conclusions I have drawn regarding the dynamics of Brazilian prison order compare with those that have been made about other countries. Nor do I have the required depth of knowledge to do so. Each of these projects would require me to obtain new expertise (on the means and limitations of prison reform; on other countries' prison systems) and to conduct new ethnographic research. What I can provide for now are some broad concluding comments on how the contemporary Brazilian prison environment converges and diverges with global norms and trends. If my research is relevant to people involved in the Brazilian prison reform agenda, it is to serve as a warning to make sure they "get the facts right" before they decide what they should try to change.

***

In observing that mass incarceration and co-governance are defining features of Brazilian and other Latin American prison systems, and are becoming more so in the contemporary context of criminal justice militarisation and securitisation of the prison environment, Maria Lúcia Karam and I have called for the development of nuanced understandings of the usefulness of Northern theories in explaining (and potentially changing or learning from) justice systems on other parts of the world (Darke and Karam 2016). Our focus was on Latin America. Drawing on Cohen's (1988) classic work on the export of Western crime models, we observed many established truths in Northern penology had developed with little reference to other parts of the world. Moreover, Cohen emphasised, the justice systems upon which Northern penology was based emerged during a specific (early nineteenth century) period of industrialisation, urbanisation, democratisation and progressive modernisation, conditions we have seen did not arise for at least another century in Brazil. In Chapter 2, we saw Northern conceptions of democracy and modernity are argued to have not yet reached Brazil. Quite the opposite, I suggested it was more productive to consider Brazil as ahead of the contemporary global race towards exclusionary and repressive social policies, including austere prison conditions as well as punitive sentencing. Brazil, I stressed, is today an exporter as much as an importer of criminal justice policies. In Chapter 1, I introduced Cohen's work with the warning that even the most benign transfer of criminal justice theories and practices developed in one part of the world to another may be problematic if they do not take full account of the local conditions under which they will be understood, translated and implemented. Take zero-tolerance policing (I borrow this example from Aas 2013), which in Brazil has become synonymous with police violence and is justified through discourses of war, not crime control. As we saw in the context of the Police Pacification Unit programme in Rio de Janeiro's *favelas*, community policing has become associated with little more than having a police presence. As for the intensification of drug prohibition policies, we saw that in Brazil, this has meant de facto remanding in custody and five year minimum prison sentences for the possession of even the smallest quantities of weed. The point is that each of these international trends was received quite differently in Brazil than, say, the UK or France. There are major differences between the Global North and Global South (perhaps we in North America and Western Europe are the exceptions here). Brazil has more specific commonalities with Latin, even more so South America. It is also an ex Portuguese colony. Whatever yardstick we use as our point of comparison, positivist research eventually arrives at the same limitation.

To repeat, if the object of research is to understand a certain country, we need to focus our lens of analysis as close to it as possible.

With this warning in mind, I return to Pakes' (2015) framework of interpretivist comparative research and divide the final pages of this monograph into three short sections.

(1) How and why do everyday prison routines and staff-inmate relations differ in Brazil?

That is, what is it like is to be incarcerated or work in a Brazilian prison compared to, for instance, another Latin American prison or a prison in the UK? This has been the main contribution of this monograph to the existing literature. My starting point has been the centrality of inmate collaboration and self-governance. These are global phenomena of both historical and contemporary significance. To introduce (and contrast) the centrality of prison co-governance in other parts of the (Southern) world[2]:

> The administrators of Chinese work camps recruit *zuzhang* (work group chiefs) to monitor production; prisoners with particular skills may be recruited, for instance, as accountants, doctors, scribes or carpenters (Williams and Wu 2004; Wu 1992). In the work camps of North Korea prisoners are likewise divided into small work-teams; one inmate is held responsible for the rest of the group (Hawk 2003). Prisoners are also appointed as foremen in charge of work sites (Harden 2012).
>
> In India at least 10% of prisoners formally work as trusties, many as office clerks or *mate pahara* (convict warders). The roles and powers of these prisoners are defined in statute (Bandyopadhyay 2007, 2010). The origins of the Indian convict warder system can be traced back to nineteenth Century British colonial rule (Bandyopadhyay 2016). It was replicated in neighbouring British colonies, including Burma and the Philippines (Brown 2007; McNair and Baylis 2010; Wintin and Brown 2005). Today many South and Southeast Asian authorities continue to delegate responsibility for managing prison wings to inmate collectives, created by classifying and separating prisoners by class and educational as well as criminal status (Bandyopadhyay 2016). In the Philippines cell block positions of authority include *bosyos* (commanders or elders),

bastoneros (armourers; heads of discipline) and *tiradores* (enforcers or warriors) (Jones et al. 2015; Narag and Jones 2016).

Cell block gangs are also left to take care of inmate discipline in South Africa, although officers maintain a presence in the wing corridors (inmates are locked up in their communal cells for up to 23 hours a day) (Lindegaard and Geer 2014; Steinberg 2004). Recognised systems of trusty inmate and/or in-cell, wing and cell block wide inmate self governance, formally or informally supported by prison governors and guards in other parts of Africa that do not have as developed prison gangs as South Africa include: Zambia (Egelund 2014), Cameroon (Morelle 2014), Nigeria (Jefferson 2010) and Ghana (Akoensi 2014; Ayete-Nyampong 2013, 2014). In Uganda prison authorities formally outsource disciplinary powers to inmate leaders (known as *katikiros*) as an aspect of official policy on developing techniques of dynamic security (Martin 2014a, b). In the Ivory Coast prisoners are allocated numerous cell block positions, including *chief building* (the prisoner in overall charge), *commis aux compte* (accounts clerk: responsible for keeping count of inmate numbers), *porte-clef* (key holder: responsible for locking and unlocking cells), *procureur* (responsible for registering transactions between inmates), *requin* (shark: responsible for enforcing prison rules), *cahier maladie* (sick book: responsible for identifying and registering sick inmates), and *bérêt vert* (green beret: responsible for supervising inmates going to the infirmary). In Rwanda, where there are more than 100 prisoners for each employed guard, inmates are responsible for managing practically every aspect of prison life (Tertsakian 2014). Like the CV and PCC prisons in Rio de Janeiro and São Paulo, one inmate (the *capita général*) is put in overall charge of the prison and one inmate (the *capitas*) in charge of each cell block; the *capita général* is expected to report in writing to the prison governor every morning (ibid.). Ghana has a recognised national prison leader (Akoensi 2014). Like the Ivory Coast, in Sierra Leone prisoners are entrusted with the keys to the cell blocks, wings and individual cells (Jefferson et al. 2014).

Co-governance is also a central theme of prison order across Latin America. Like colonial Asia and Africa, Latin American prison environments have been characterised by reciprocity since the first penitentiaries were built in the nineteenth Century. As Aguirre (2005, 2007) emphasises, staff-inmate relations need to be understood in terms of strategies of survival rather than a dichotomy between resistance and accommodation.

Today traditional systems of (customary and plural) prison order are increasingly institutionalised by the phenomenon of the cell block gang, some of which are involved in the drug trade outside prison and self-identify as criminal organisations, especially in countries on the cocaine trail between the Andes mountains and Northern America (see, inter alia, Cerbini 2017, 2019 and Skarbek 2010 on Bolivia; Carter 2014 and Rivera 2010 on Honduras; Guadalupe 1994 and Postema et al. 2017 on Peru; Weegels 2017, 2019 on Nicaragua; Antillano 2017, 2019, and Duno-Gottberg 2019 on Venezuela; Garces 2010, Núñez and Fleetwood 2017, and Tritton with Fleetwood 2017 on Ecuador; Postema et al. 2017 on Costa Rica and Panama; Salla et al. 2009 on Argentina; Dardel 2013 on Colombia). As in Brazil, in most Latin American countries prisoner participation can be broadly divided between trusty (covering those who formally collaborate and work alongside prison staff) and cell block positions (covering those who informally represent inmate collectives or occupy positions lower down their inmate hierarchy, but usually manage the cell blocks with the support or acquiescence of prison staff). In Honduras, for instance, inmate positions include those of *rondiné* (patroller) *coordinador* (coordinator) and *toro* (bull). Prisoners work as *guias* (guides) and *caporals* (foremen) in Ecuador. Latin American inmate leaders typically coordinate their work through inmate *comités* (committees), as we have seen to be the case in Brazil. Bolivian and Peruvian inmate leaders are referred to as *delegados* (delegates). The closer Latin American prison authorities work with inmate collectives and prison gangs, the weaker the distinction between trusty prisoners and inmate leaders. We have seen this to be increasingly the case in Brazil with the allocating of whole prison units to individual gangs. Inmate collectives naturally want to control what goes on both on and off the wings. The major example I gave was the production and transport of meals. I also referred to a short period following the return to democracy in the mid 1980s when Brazilian prison authorities invited inmate leaders to participate in formal inmate councils. In a moment we will see this model has been adopted in dozens of voluntary sector administered prisons in the country.

The United States also has a history of prison co-governance. In an overview of previous literature, Baker (1964) cites several references to inmate involvement in setting prison rules and adjudicating on breaches from the late eighteenth to the early twentieth centuries, but in his own survey of 44 prisons found only 13 to currently have inmate councils, none of which had been delegated disciplinary powers. Besides inmate councils, 10–20% of prisoners worked formally as trusty prisoners in the post-slavery prison farms of the United States before the mid 1980s, and as warders as well as administrators (see, inter alia, Crouch and Marquart 1989; Marquart and Roebeck 1985; McWhorter 1981). At Mississippi State Penitentiary, the highest ranking trusty prisoners were armed with rifles until as recently as 1972. In the 1960s and 1970s reports emerged of overstretched governors informally employing inmates to maintain order on American prison wings. This included Cook County Jail in the state of Illinois, where inmates were appointed as what were known as barn bosses and tier clerks (Back 2015). Besides these more formalised arrangements, American prison researchers of the mid twentieth Century noted how individual officers also delegated responsibilities to prisoners they came to trust, for instance the inmate runner, described by Sykes (1956: 261) as a prisoner, "formally assigned the tasks of delivering mail, housekeeping duties, and similar jobs", and who might end up taking over guard-like duties, including head counts, cell checks and locking and unlocking internal doors by default. Officers also informally negotiated with inmate leaders, who "[stood] between the inmate system and the formal system" (Cloward 1960: 48), to enforce codes relating to inmate solidarity and hence maintain order on the wings (cf. Clemmer 1940; Cressey 1961; Sykes 1958). Like Brazil's cell block *faxinas*, these prisoners "walked a delicate line between rejection of the officials and cooperation" (Sykes 1958: 125, cited in Crewe 2016: 79). However, the inmate body they hypothetically represented was not as homogenous as the contemporary Brazilian *coletivo*. Most inmates did their own time, especially in the larger prisons where "only a very small group of convicts in any one prison [were] well known enough by enough convicts to constitute their having a role in regard to the prison as a whole" (Irwin 1970: 66). More generally, according to Clemmer (1940: 150), "the prison world [was] not a like-minded, highly integrated collectivity, but [was], on the other hand, a diffuse aggregation wherein interpersonal relations abound, and consensus of a high degree [was] absent due to individuation of most of the personalities involved". Instead, they ultimately worked on behalf of prison staff, who were able to quickly reverse any corruptions of authority when prisoners got out of hand.

From the late twentieth Century America's prison blocks have been increasingly dominated by ethnically segregated gangs that maintain order with little reference to prison rules or negotiation with prison staff (Haslam and Reicher 2012; Skarbek 2014). Today's inmate orderlies (as trusty prisoners are now more commonly known) are not reported to be involved in order maintenance.

As for Europe, most infamous, and comparable only in the sense that individual prisoners collaborated with prison staff (that is, not on behalf or in the interests of other prisoners) was the position of prisoner functionary created by the administrators of the Nazi concentration camps. Levi (1987, 1989) described how as many as one in ten prisoners participated in running the camps, working among other things, as cleaners, cooks, medical staff, messengers, interpreters, clerks, guards, barrack wardens, labour squad leaders, even camp chiefs and most tragically, gas chamber orderlies. These prisoners typically managed to extend their lives by just a few months and gained little in return beyond extra food rations and (in the case of the head prisoner functionaries: the *kapos*) cigarettes and relatively easier work. Levi claimed they made up the majority that survived the holocaust (see also Frankl 2004).

In the gulags of the Soviet period one in four prisoners officially worked as guard, compound or work *pridúrki* (see, inter alia, Applebaum 2003; Solzhenitsyn 1963, 1975). As in the Nazi concentration camps, these prisoners constituted most of those that survived. Many went on to work at the prison in which they were incarcerated after finishing their sentence. The roots of prisoner participation in Russian prisons can be located within the broader national tradition of the worker or community *artel* (guild or cooperative), and traced back to the nineteenth century (Dostoevsky 1956). In the barracks of the Soviet gulags prisoner discipline and welfare was maintained by high-ranking members of organised criminal *artels* known as *vory v zakonye* (thieves-in-law) (Gilinskiy and Kostjukovsky 2004). For a television documentary account of the roles played by *vory v zakonye* in Russian prisons today, see Lambert (2001).

Prior to the Prisons Act 1835 prisoners were legally employed to work in the place of staff in England and Wales, including as turnkeys (Priestly 1985; Thomas 1972). Prisoners continued to work as office clerks until the late 1800s. Today one in six prisoners are registered as working in cleaner or other red band (England and Wales' equivalent to trusty prisoners) positions. Like the United States, they are not involved in guard-like duties. There is little organisation or leadership among English prisoners: "in parallel with citizens at large…., prisoners have become relatively discrete, divided units. Collectively, they are an aggregate rather than a 'community'. The standardisation of their experiences means that they have common interests, but not solidarity as such (Crewe 2009: 455).

The point is that comparable systems of co-produced order not only exist elsewhere, but that prison co-governance appears to be both the historical and contemporary global norm. How, why and to what extent these compare to Brazil is a future research project that will be most effective if it involves collaborative research between people working in/on different countries. The countries they compare and their main points of reference should not be from the exceptional Global North. Some Northern prison systems are deteriorating, as I have demonstrated to be the case in England and Wales. Some would find themselves in deep crisis if prisoners refused to work as cleaners and orderlies. Some Northern prison wings are also governed by gangs. However, I doubt any current prison system beyond the South can be meaningfully compared to Brazil's prison system. Even the relatively recent American trusty inmate and barn boss systems were corruptions, not institutionalisations of ordinary practice. Like the inmate leader and runner described by Sykes (1956, 1958), they were disposed by judicial or prison authorities once they had been exposed or were considered beyond control.

Nor should comparative South–South research start with the assumption that poorly resourced, self-governing prisons are bound to be disorderly. I have described the characteristics of Brazilian prison order in detail. We have seen that Brazilian prisons manage in spite of staff shortages, and that the more developed a prison's gang organisation the more orderly it has the potential to become. Violence is regulated and prisoners are surveyed and disciplined, but by other prisoners more than prison staff, and under inmate rather than prison rules. In Foucauldian terms (Foucault 1977), the judges of institutional normality are an inmate's peers, albeit in negotiation with his or her keepers. As such, prison order does not rely on top-down panoptic surveillance to the extent it does in the better staffed prisons of the North. Similar observations have been made by prison researchers on other parts of Latin America (see, inter alia, Antillano 2019; Cerbini 2017; Núñez and Fleetwood 2017; Salvatore and Aguirre 1996), some of who reject the use of the term panoptic altogether. Regarding San Pedro prison in Bolivia, for instance, Cerbini (2017: 34) writes, "here, on the contrary, official authorities rely on their power to apparently ignore what happens inside the facility, a space to which they prefer not to look".

At the same time, however, Cerbini (2017) suggests inmate collectives (she does not refer to prison gangs) ultimately work on behalf of Bolivian prison administrators. Institutional order, she concludes, depends on how well the power to govern is delegated. I have made the same point regarding Brazilian prison order, including the role played by major gangs. The day the Brazilian state decides to radically overhaul its prison system, it will no longer rely on prisoner organisation, let alone criminal organisations like the CV and PCC. For now, prison order will continue to depend on the willingness of inmates to organise, collaborate and self-govern.

Finally, it is important to reiterate that Brazilian prison order continues to rely on the acquiescence of local actors in the criminal gang era. Even state-level gangs negotiate the parameters of its rules and regulations differently in one prison to another.

I conclude this section with some final reflections on the plurality and de facto legitimacy of Brazilian prison order. I do so through an analysis of Goffman's (1961) concept of the total institution, a concept that also makes limited sense in the Latin American prison context (Birkbeck 2011; Darke and Karam 2016; Sepúlveda and Pojomovsky 2019).

Goffman (1968: 15) defined a total institution as, "symbolized by the barrier to social intercourse with the outside". He was concerned with the ways in which the "total character" of prisons and other such "all encompassing" institutions debilitated inmates. In a classic passage, he explained:

> [The inmate] comes into the establishment with a conception of himself made possible by certain stable arrangements in his home world. Upon entrance, he is immediately stripped of the support provided by these

arrangements. In the accurate language of some of our oldest total institutions, he begins a series of abasements, degradations, humiliations, and profanations of the self. His self is systematically, if often unintentionally, mortified. (Goffman 1968: 24)

The processes of mortification, Goffman continued, had been adequately described by social scientists, for instance in Sykes' (1958) work on the "pains of imprisonment". Goffman was interested in exploring the longer term psychological effects institutions had on inmates, "to help us see the arrangements that ordinary establishments must guarantee if members are to preserve their civilian selves" (Goffman 1968: 24). To do so, he analysed inmate suffering in the context of three broad categories of "curtailment of the self". Each of these related to the traversing or constructing of psychological barriers. For current purposes, it is not necessary to outline these in detail. What is particularly relevant to our understanding of the plural and de facto legitimate nature of Brazilian prison order is Goffman's specific focus on the issue of deference.

Goffman's (1961, 1968) first concern, already mentioned, was the barriers institutions put between inmates and the outside world. Prisons, secure psychiatric hospitals, nunneries and so on were artificial worlds which separated people from their support networks and from their roles as parents, work colleagues, friends etc. The disruption to their "role scheduling" was apparent the moment they arrived, when they were assigned numbers, relieved of their personal possessions and soon found their readiness to obey tested by their keepers. From then on he or she would be regularly forced to defer to the authority of the institution, to the point of being required to beg. Second was the way institutions broke down the barrier between an inmate and their physical and social environment. Inmates "territories of the self" were "contaminated" by their total lack of privacy and personal space brought about by their lack of escape from the company and prising from others. The third was the barrier institutions placed across "the usual relationship between the individual actor and his acts" (Goffman 1968: 41). Here, Goffman gave two major examples. First, the inmate was continually judged. What he or she said or did in one situation would be recorded and always come back to haunt them in another situation. Goffman's second example returned to the significance of deference. In normal life, a person might have no choice but to comply with an affront, but could at least save face and distance themselves from their humiliation by only doing so grudgingly. In a total institution, even the smallest defence of the self would not be accepted.

It is hardly surprising Northern researchers have applied Goffman's (1968) analysis of deferential institutional relations to the relationship between prisoners and prison guards. Guards may be more outnumbered by prisoners than they were when Goffman coined the phrase total institution in the mid-twentieth century—and prisons many have become less orderly as a result—but they have not chosen or have not been forced to reciprocate. In Chapter 3, we saw English prisoners find themselves increasingly locked up in their cells. There has been little collective resistance. Some prison workers retain a humanitarian ethos, but staff-inmate relations continue to be defined by detachment and normative distance on the whole.

Less so in Brazil. Rather than detachment, we have seen it is necessary to consider the effects of fused staff-inmate functions and entangled staff-inmate and prison-community relations. First, while prisoners sleep, work and play in the same place, the starting point of Goffman's analysis, the barriers between prison and community life are generally more permeable than they are in the North. Not only do prisoners have greater contact with their families, but with the growing phenomena of state-wide gangs, they increasingly encounter systems of governance that echo those on the outside, including informal networks of support, and quasi-legal systems of conflict resolution.

Second, and more immediately relevant to institutional order, we have seen power in Brazilian prisons emerges from inmate as well as staff hierarchies. In other words, prisoners are not, as Goffman explained it, governed by a single authority; nor are all their needs cared for by the prison administration. In a survey of 91 prison guards studying sociology classes at the Central University of Belo Horizonte, Minas Gerais, 58 of the participants admitted to having ignored prison rules to benefit an inmate (Lourenço 2010). Prison guards, we have seen, find themselves being "contaminated" by inmate culture.

Returning to my empirical study of the *carceragem* in Rio de Janeiro, we saw that higher ranking trusties and inmate leaders enjoyed greater autonomy than some police officers, including the deputy governor. There was little, I concluded, to distinguish these prisoners from police officers in terms of function or command. The question who was managing and who was being managed was not a straightforward one. Neither was the question who was free and who had lost their liberty. These questions were central to Goffman's analysis of staff-inmate relations and, in the Brazilian prison context, are fundamental to our understanding of everyday relations of power and authority. In circumstances in which, as Birkbeck (2011) describes it in the broader Latin American context, prisons have become little more than institutions of internment, in which guards rely on inmates as much as inmates depend on guards, Brazilian prisons are anything but bureaucratic. The power exercised by prisoners, I have suggested, should be regarded less as corruption, as Sykes (1956, 1958) perceived it in the context of mid-twentieth century North America, as a sharing of authority. As in prisons in other parts of Latin America (Aguirre 2005, 2007), Brazilian staff-inmate relations traverse the boundary between accommodation and resistance. They work together out of necessity, not convenience.

Finally, order is negotiated and authority shared on behalf and with the support of the majority of other prison inmates. It is not unavoidably true, as Sparks et al. (1996: 300) put it in the British context, "that the social order of the prison is imposed and enforced". We saw this to be the case even at the Curado prison complex, where *chaveiros* are appointed with the consent of other prisoners. Nor, again in contrast to the UK, is "the presence of a good screw here or there [seen as] relatively unimportant" (Cohen and Taylor 1972: 119). The cultures that infuse the prison environment and contaminate prison staff are those of solidarity and reciprocity. Brazilian prison gangs have inadvertently if not purposely latched onto historical possesses of institutional conviviality and survival. This has been facilitated by the openly exclusionary and violent practices of the post-dictatorship Brazilian state. Each of these factors was prominent in the narratives of the prisoners I spoke with at Polinter, including the CV leader, who spoke angrily without pause for 45 minutes, yet expressed support for the police and their trusty prisoners, and reserved his denigrations for wider political and prison authorities. I concluded my analysis of Polinter with reference to Bottoms and Tankebe (2012). Legitimate governance, Bottoms and Tankebe emphasised, is premised in shared beliefs, common needs and conformity to rules as well as liberal notions of procedural fairness (see also, Bottoms and Tankebe 2013), each of which we have seen to occupy a central place in Brazilian inmate codes. Among their expected norms of conduct, prisoners place considerable weight on mutual respect, not just between inmates but also between inmates and staff. While Brazilian prisoners are less wedded to liberal notions of electoral democracy, they have historically required their leaders to rule through fair hearings as well as substantive justice. These ideals are not always reflected in practice, but I contend, the average prisoner has become more idealistic and more demanding of their leaders in the democratic era of the cell block prison gang.

(2) **How and to what extent can and should changes be made to the Brazilian prison environment?**

These, I have already indicated, are questions for future research. As a research activist, I have a moral duty to do so. Most of the prisoners I have met along my research journey have been generous with their interest and time. A few, too few have challenged the purpose of my wanting to talk with them or asked how I might help them. In this monograph, I have only mentioned one such instance, when a prisoner held in an overcrowded, windowless cell in Paraná held out his leg to show me an untreated wound. There have been others, always when I was accompanied by a judge or human rights lawyer, no doubt the type of visitor the prisoner believed could make a difference. The people whose lives I access must always be more than participants. To date, my research on the Brazilian prison environment has been unavoidably descriptive. I have maintained contact with a few prisoners and (now) former prisoners via letters and social media, but have not yet given them voice. I have witnessed their strategies of survival, but I have done little to relieve their suffering. I write this with the work of Andrew Jefferson, Tomas Martin and others at the Danish Institute against Torture (DIGNITY) on the implementation of international human rights standards in mind. DIGNITY utilises academic research to inform anti-torture and torture survival projects in urban and detention settings across much of Europe, Asia and Africa. It has produced policy-orientated academic texts on African and Asian prisons (see, e.g., Jefferson and Martin 2014; Jefferson and Gaborit 2015; Jefferson and Jensen 2009; Jefferson et al. 2014).

I am involved in campaigns advocating long-term decarceration and short-term investment in prison conditions, although I leave others with a better understanding of political and legal institutional cultures to engage with the relevant policy makers, prosecutors and judges. I am more hesitant to promote certain reforms inside Brazilian prisons, as I am not convinced the knowledge base exists to do so. Moreover, misplaced reforms or misplaced attempts to reform are potentially more risky in prison. We have seen levels of prison violence vary enormously in Brazil from one place and one time to another. I have a relatively good understanding of inmate culture, but as yet limited understanding of prison officer culture. I could not advise with any degree of confidence, for instance, whether prison guard violence would likely reduce if efforts were made to stop governors and guards from negotiating with gang leaders. It would be irresponsible for me to recommend changes to Brazilian prison rules and routines, prison officer training and so on until I fully appreciate what could go wrong. As Jensen and Jefferson (2009) warn regarding campaigns to reduce state violence:

> Scholars, practitioners and policy makers need to understand how, for instance, state officials make sense of their own violent practices and of human rights interventions. Similarly, we need to understand how intervention practices operate in specific, situated contexts. (Jensen and Jefferson 2009: 1)

What I can do is remind the reader of some of the unintended consequences I have suggested might accompany efforts to dismantle Brazil's tradition of prison co-governance. I referred directly to the potential dangers of such a reform agenda in Chapter 1 in the context of Rio de

Janeiro's former *carceragens*. If the police had been prevented from formally recruiting trusty guards or informally recruiting and working with cell block *faxina*, prisoners would have been more, not less vulnerable to predatory and expressive violence. It would also have been more difficult to prevent hard drugs or weapons from entering the *carceragem*, or to assure the safety of the hundreds of family members that visited each week. I concluded Chapter 6 with an overview of the benefits the PCC has brought to prisoners in São Paulo, including reductions in violence, and also an ending to certain practices of exploitation, for example the selling of cell spaces, food and confectionaries.

An end to prison co-governance is clearly envisaged by the United Nations as well as in the Human Rights Watch (1998, 2016) reports cited earlier. Rule 40 of the recently revised Standard Minimum Rules for the Treatment of Prisoners (United Nations 2016) stipulates:

> No prisoner shall be employed, in the service of the prison, in any disciplinary capacity. This rule shall not, however, impede the proper functioning of systems based on self-government, under which specified social, educational or sports activities or responsibilities are entrusted, under supervision, to prisoners who are formed into groups for the purposes of treatment.

These are possibly the right aspirations. However, they are a long way from reality. Rule 40 should not be implemented in Brazil without a corresponding investment in prison staffing.

(3) What should be regarded as good practices that might be adopted elsewhere?

Two points remain to be addressed in this final section. The first concerns the question whether anything can be learnt from Brazilian prison gangs and the wider phenomenon of co-produced prison order by prison administrators in other parts of the world. The second is more specific. It centres on the recent wave of voluntary sector prisoner and former prisoner managed community prisons previously mentioned.

For reasons explained, the issues I raise should be read as no more than suggestions for future research. Again I can offer only the most cursory of comparative analysis.

As far as I am aware, I am one of only a handful of published prison researchers to question whether gang culture and broader inmate-staff accommodations might sometimes be of benefit to prisoners. Besides the work of Karina Biondi and Adalton Marques on the PCC in Brazil (in particular, Biondi 2010; Marques 2014), I have referred to Skarbek's (2014, 2016) analysis of Californian prison gangs. Among the other papers on prison gangs and co-governance cited in this chapter, only Jones et al. (2015), Narag and Jones (2016), and Postema et al. (2017) directly challenge the consensus of global academic opinion. The first two of these papers were co-written by a former prisoner, now academic criminologist. The papers centred on prison gangs in the Philippines, where Narag was imprisoned for seven years.

However, neither Skarbek (2014, 2016), Jones et al. (2015) nor Narag and Jones (2016) go so far as to promote inmate collaboration and self-governance. Their conclusions are similar to my own. Alternative governance institutions, to paraphrase Skarbek, arise in situations of state neglect, especially in larger prisons where inmates are less able to rely on interpersonal relations. These papers, in other words, are concerned with realities of survival. The systems they describe (both of which, it should be emphasised, the authors claim have made the prisons they studied safer) might provide models that would work in other places, but this is not a matter to which they address their attention.

More applicable here is Postema et al.'s (2017) overview of prison co-governance in Costa Rica, Panama and San Pedro de Lurigancho prison, Peru. Significantly, one of the co-authors, James Cavallaro, was also co-author of Human Rights Watch (1998). He has been a commissioner of the Inter-American Commission on Human Rights since 2014. Postema et al. question whether the principles contained in the 1949 Geneva Convention Relative to the Treatment of Prisoners of War might be extended to ordinary prisoners, and in particular Articles 79–81, which grant inmates the right to elect representatives to liaise with prison authorities and coordinate inmate systems of mutual aid. Postema et al. suggest the recent introduction of peer-elected inmate councils in Costa Rica, Panama and Peru provides models of devolved prison authority that should be further studied and potentially adopted elsewhere. In all three countries, inmate councils have been granted powers to formally propose and monitor prison routines and activities. Specifically relevant to my study of co-governed prison order, the inmate councils in Lurigancho prison include members elected to take responsibility for discipline and order. Prison governors, Postema et al. (2017: 62) conclude, have overseen a major reduction in violence through opting "to work with, rather than against, these structures of inmate organisation."

In the absence of further research, Postema et al. (2017) do not give further details on the means by which Lurigancho's inmate councils maintain discipline in the prison's cell blocks. Nor do they address the important issues of accountability and oversight. For these reasons, I withhold judgement, although I concur with their call for investigation. I conclude my interpretivist analysis of what might potentially be learnt from existing practices of prison co-governance with examples where the power to discipline has arguably been appropriately devolved to prisoners in Brazil. As previously stated, these relate to the many dozens of voluntary sector administered prisons that have been inaugurated in the country since the 1970s. I will focus on three such prison models: the Association for the Protection and Assistance of the Convict (APAC) and Resocialisation Centre (CR) models introduced in Chapter 1, and the Cultural Association for the Development of Prisoners and Former Prisoners (ACUDA) model introduced in Chapter 5. I have visited seven APAC prisons in Minas Gerais, including Franz de Castro (also a pseudonym), where I completed my second intensive three-week empirical study of Brazilian prison order in 2012 (noted in Chapter 1). I have visited two CR prisons in São Paulo, one of which (Centro de Ressocialização de Limeira) on several occasions. I am also in contact with people who work voluntarily at the prison, including the former long-term prisoner Luiz Mendes, who we have seen visits once a week to run an anti-violence project. Finally, I am able to draw upon the work of Fiona Macaulay (2013, 2014, 2015), who studied the CR model in the late 2000s, albeit at a time CR prisons were recovering from the state's 2006 prison uprisings (see Chapter 6). In the aftermath of the uprisings, prison authorities assumed overall control of the CR prison system. There is only one ACUDA prison, in Rondônia. In 2016 it temporarily stopped receiving prisoners following a television news item that exposed its controversial practice of treating inmates with the hallucinogenic drug ayahuasca. For the time being it is operating as a day centre for prisoners held in the neighbouring Complexo Penitenciário Estadual de Porto Velho (Porto Velho State Prison Complex). It has submitted plans to build a new closed prison unit. I spent two days observing and participating in ACUDA's rehabilitation-orientated activities in 2017.

What makes these prisons/centres particularly interesting to an international audience is that they all broadly comply with international human rights standards on the conditions of criminal detention. APAC and ACUDA profess to run therapeutic communities, while CR prisons provide inmates with full-time regimes of work and education. Under these circumstances, they hold the (to date largely unexplored) promise to constructively inform prison policy anywhere in the world. In the coming years, I will address the question what might be learnt from these three alternative models of detention in more detail. This intended research will explore matters of rehabilitation and desistance and as well as institutional order. More specifically, it will explore the models of detention provided by the three prisons/prison movements in the context of Brazil's wider tradition of inmate self-governance, mutual survival and collaboration with prison staff.

For now, some final words on the delegating of order to APAC, ACUDA and CR inmates. I will explore these within one of the most fundamental of human rights issues that is usually denied to prisoners and the one most closely aligned to this future research: the right to democratic participation. We have seen that in the common prison system, Brazilian inmates follow norms of conduct most consider necessary and legitimate but have limited opportunities to shape or enforce.

Neither of the three models fully conform to internationally recognised criteria for a democratic therapeutic community (for activist research on the democratic therapeutic community concept in the UK, see Gosling and Scott 2016; Scott and Gosling 2015). However, each contains elements of democratic participation. APAC prisons place a large degree of responsibility for security and enforcing prison order in the hands of prisoners, but operate under a detailed set of rules written by former rather than current prisoners, moreover rules that apply to each APAC prison in the country. Still, as I explained in Chapter 1 and have described in more detail elsewhere (in Darke 2014), the inmate council at the APAC prison I completed fieldwork played a major role in deciding when and to what extent these rules should be enforced, as well as appropriate sanctions. Furthermore, it had a de facto power to introduce additional "house rules". At the 2012 conference celebrating the 40th anniversary of the first APAC prison referred to in Chapter 1 that I attended, the movement's founder, Mário Ottoboni, alerted prison managers to the risk of prison order becoming over formalised. His view, like many others affiliated to the APAC movement, was that a perpetrator's peers would always know when and how best to sanction. Finally, while APAC inmate councils are not elected by their peers, they serve short six-month terms in office. This way, most prisoners have an opportunity to serve on the council during their term of imprisonment. I have serious reservations about the objectives of the APAC movement (it is fundamentally evangelical and conservative; it regards itself as making up for offenders' lack of socialisation and limits its critique of the common prison system to the way inmates are treated) and its methods of rehabilitation (it holds offenders fully responsible for their actions and for their therapy). However, there is much to learn from its broader approach to human dignity, including for current purposes the responsibility it entrusts in inmates to govern their spaces of confinement.

The other two models have even greater promise from the quasi-prison abolitionist perspective I am adopting here. The ACUDA movement is more concerned with matters of trauma and self-worth (in contrast to the APAC movement's focus on discipline), and with perpetrators of serious predatory violence (in contrast to the APAC movement's focus on early intervention). It is fundamentally religious, although new age spiritualist rather than Christian, but it provides inmates with a full-time regime of work and education, including higher education, as well as therapeutic programmes (the latter of which centre on yoga, peer massage and spiritual healing). Important for current purposes, its rules and regulations are (unlike the APAC system) co-produced by inmates and staff. However, they are enforced by the latter. A prisoner whose company I kept for much of the time I spent there contrasted this favourably with the APAC system, emphasising that inmates were regarded as equals. The majority of the centre's full-time paid employees (like the APAC system) are themselves former prisoners.

Again, my intention is not to promote any existing system of detention. There is also much I could criticise about the ACUDA model from a democratic therapeutic perspective, of its approach to governance (its sanctions, e.g., like those at APAC prisons, are more punitive than restorative or therapeutic) as well as rehabilitation (it likewise emphasises self-help and mutual aid, but less in the interests of emancipatory critical consciousness as understanding of the consequences of one's actions). For now I am merely concerned with identifying the potential policy implications of my study of co-produced institutional order. There is research to be done before I can draw concrete conclusions.

São Paulo's CR model is also relevant to this proposed study for the depth of responsibility it delegates to inmates. This is the last alternative model of detention I wish to explore in future research, and is possibly the most progressive of the three. In Chapter 1, I noted some of the current 22 CR prisons started off as APAC prisons, but lost their APAC status after they were funded by prison authorities from the mid-1990s and legally regulated from 2000. We saw prison authorities also took over responsibility for CR security in 2006. CR prisons are typically larger than APAC prisons (CR de Limeira, e.g., holds around 150 inmates in its closed unit and a further 70 in its semi-open unit). However, they are equally if not more therapeutic. Like APAC and ACUDA prisons/centres, they aim to promote alternative, non-stigmatising institutional cultures, and engagement with inmates' families (Macaulay 2015), but unlike APAC and ACUDA the underlying focus of the voluntary sector organisations that provide for their rehabilitation activities, e.g. Instituto Ação Pela Paz (Action for Peace Institute) is self-esteem and self-understanding rather than spiritual awakening. Although state penitentiary guards are responsible for security, inmates are (like APAC prisons) left in charge of the cell blocks. At CR de

Limeira, cell doors are not locked at night; trusty prisoners are stationed at the entrances to different wings. As for inmate discipline, prison rules are monitored by officers, but like APAC prisons cell representatives and inmate councils are responsible for monitoring wider inmate *regras de convivência*. Prisoners are judged by their peers for infractions. The ultimate sanction is expulsion from your community.

Notes

1. In this monograph, I have provided illustrations of trusty prisoner systems and cell block wide inmate collectives/gangs from 11 of Brazil's 27 states. To these I might have added illustrations from Santa Catarina (Oldoni 2001) and the federal district (Diniz 2015).
2. This list is an updated version of Darke (2013). Many of the additional examples are taken from two special editions of the Prison Service Journal (Darke and Garces 2017; Jefferson and Martin 2014) and a forthcoming book (Garces et al. 2019), two of which I have co-edited with Chris Garces.

References

Aas, K. F. (2013). *Globalization and crime*. London: Sage.

Aguirre, C. (2005). *The criminals of Lima and their worlds: The prison experience, 1850–1935*. Durham, NC: Duke University.

Aguirre, C. (2007). Prisons and prisoners in modernising Latin America. In F. Dikötter & I. Brown (Eds.), *Cultures of confinement: A history of the prison in Africa, Asia, and Latin America*. Ithaca, NY: Cornell University.

Akoensi, T. D. (2014). Governance through power sharing in Ghanaian prisons: A symbiotic relationship between officers and inmates. *Prison Service Journal, 212*, 33–38.

Antillano, A. (2017). When prisoners make the prison: Self-rule in Venezuelan prisons. *Prison Service Journal, 229*, 26–30.

Antillano, A. (2019). When to punish is not to discipline. The self-rule of carceral order in Venezuela. In C. Garces, et al. (Eds.), *Carceral communities:*

Troubling 21st century prison regimes in Latin America. Under contract with University of Pennsylvania.

Applebaum, A. (2003). *Gulag: A history of the Soviet camps.* London: Allen Lane.

Ayete-Nyampong, L. (2013). *Entangled realities and the underlife of a total institution: An ethnography of correctional centres for juvenile and young offenders in Accra, Ghana.* Ph.D. thesis, Wageningen University.

Ayete-Nyampong, L. (2014). Entangled governance practices and the illusion of producing compliant inmates in correctional centres for juvenile and young offenders in Ghana. *Prison Service Journal, 212,* 27–32.

Back, L. (2015). How blue can you get? B.B King, planetary humanism and the blues behind bars. *Theory, Culture & Society, 32*(7–8), 274–285.

Baker, J. E. (1964). Inmate self-government. *Journal of Criminal Law and Criminology, 55*(1), 39–47.

Bandyopadhyay, M. (2007). Reform and everyday practice: Some issues of prison governance. *Contributions to Indian Sociology, 41*(3), 387–416.

Bandyopadhyay, M. (2010). *Everyday life in a prison: Confinement, surveillance, resistance.* New Delhi: Orient BlackSwan.

Bandyopadhyay, M. (2016). Asian prisons. In Y. Jewkes, et al. (Eds.), *Handbook on prisons* (2nd ed., pp. 441–459). Abington: Routledge.

Barbosa, A. R. (2005). *Prender e dar fuga biopolítica, sistema penitenciários e tráfico de drogas no Rio de Janeiro.* Ph.D. thesis, Federal University of Rio de Janeiro. http://www.uece.br/labvida/dmdocuments/prender_e_dar_fuga_biopolitica_sistema_penitenciario.pdf. Last accessed 1 May 2017.

Biondi, K. (2010). *Junto e misturado: Uma etnografia do PCC.* São Paulo: Teirciero Nome. English version: Biondi, K. (2016). *Sharing this walk: An ethnography of prison life and the PCC in Brazil* (J. F. Collins, Trans.). Chapel Hill: University of North Carolina.

Biondi, K. (2013). O PCC: Da organização á ética. In A. R. Barbosa, et al. (Eds.), *Etnografias em uma fronteira difusa* (pp. 23–34). Rio de janeiro: Universidade Federal Fluminense.

Biondi, K. (2014). *Etnografia no movimento: Território, hierarquia e lei no PCC.* Ph.D. thesis, Federal University of São Carlos. https://www.repositorio.ufscar.br/bitstream/handle/ufscar/246/6378.pdf?sequence=1&isAllowed=y. Last accessed 7 April 2017.

Biondi, K. (2017). Prison violence, prison justice: The rise of Brazil's PCC. *NACLA Report on the Americas, 49*(3), 341–346.

Biondi, K., & Marques, A. (2010). Memória e historicidade em dois "comandos" prisionais. *Lua Nova, 79*, 39–70.

Birkbeck, C. (2011). Imprisonment and internment: Comparing penal institutions North and South. *Punishment and Society, 13*(3), 307–332.

Bottoms, A., & Tankebe, J. (2012). Beyond procedural justice: A dialogic approach to legitimacy in criminal justice. *Journal of Criminal Law and Criminology, 102*(1), 119–170.

Bottoms, A., & Tankebe, J. (2013). 'A voice within': Power holders' perspectives on authority and legitimacy. In J. Tankebe & A. Liebling (Eds.), *Legitimacy and criminal justice: An international exploration* (pp. 60–82). Oxford: Oxford University.

Brown, I. (2007). A commissioner calls: Alexander Paterson and Burma's colonial prisons. *Journal of Southeast Asian Studies, 38*(2), 293–308.

Câmara dos Deputados. (2008). No title. Resource document. http://www1.folha.uol.com.br/folha/cotidiano/20060708-marcos_camacho.pdf. Last accessed 17 July 2017.

Carter, J. H. (2014). Gothic sovereignty: Gangs and criminal community in a Honduran prison. *South Atlantic Quarterly, 113*(3), 475–502.

Cerbini, F. (2017). From the panopticon to the anti-panopticon: The 'art of government' in the prison of San Pedro (La Paz, Bolivia). *Prison Service Journal, 229*, 31–34.

Cerbini, F. (2019). "Eat to forget": The dangers of food in San Pedro prison (La Paz, Bolivia). In C. Garces, et al. (Eds.), *Carceral communities: Troubling 21st century prison regimes in Latin America*. Under contract with University of Pennsylvania.

Clemmer, D. (1940). *The prison community*. New York: Holt, Rinehart and Winston.

Cloward, R. A. (1960). Social control in the prison. In R. Cloward, et al. (Eds.), *Theoretical studies in social organization of the prison* (pp. 20–48). New York: Social Science Research Council.

Cohen, S. (1988). *Against criminology*. New Brunswick: Transaction.

Cohen, S., & Taylor, L. (1972). *Psychological survival: The experience of long term imprisonment*. Harmondsworth: Penguin.

Cressey, D. (Ed.). (1961). *The prison: Studies in institutional organization and change*. New York: Holt, Rinehart and Winston.

Crewe, B. (2009). *The prisoner society: Power, adaptation and social life in an English prison*. Oxford: Oxford University.

Crewe, B. (2016). The sociology of imprisonment. In Y. Jewkes, et al. (Eds.), *Handbook on prisons* (2nd ed., pp. 77–100). Abington: Routledge.

Crouch, B., & Marquart, J. (1989). *An appeal to justice: Litigation reform of Texas prisons*. Austin: University of Texas.

Dardel, J. (2013). Resisting 'bare life': Prisoners' agency in the new prison culture era in Colombia. In D. Moran, et al. (Eds.), *Carceral spaces: Mobility and agency in imprisonment and migrant detention*. London: Routledge.

Darke, S. (2013). Entangled staff-inmate relations. *Prison Service Journal, 207*, 16–22.

Darke, S. (2014). Recoverers helping recoverers: Discipline and peer-facilitated reform in Brazilian faith-based prisons. In V. Miller & J. Campbell (Eds.), *Transnational penal cultures: New perspectives on discipline, punishment and desistance* (pp. 217–229). London: Routledge.

Darke, S., & Garces, C. (Eds.). (2017). Informal dynamics of survival in Latin American prisons. *Prison Service Journal, 229*, 1–62.

Darke, S., & Karam, M. L. (2016). Latin American prisons. In Y. Jewkes, et al. (Eds.), *Handbook on prisons* (2nd ed., pp. 460–474). Abington: Routledge. Portuguese version: Karam, M. L., & Darke, S. (2016). Prisões latino americanas (M. L. Karam, Trans.). http://emporiododireito.com.br/leitura/prisoes-latino-americanas-1508702837. Last accessed 17 February 2018. Spanish version: Darke, S., & Karam, M. L. (2017). Las prisiones de América Latina. *Ecuador Debate, 101*, 53–71.

Dias, C. N. (2013). *PCC: Hegemonia nas prisões e monopólio da violência*. São Paulo: Saraiva.

Dias, C. N., & Darke, S. (2016). From dispersed to monopolized violence: Expansion and consolidation of the Primeiro Comando da Capital's hegemony in São Paulo's prisons. *Crime, Law and Social Change, 65*(3), 213–215.

Diniz, D. (2015). *Cadeia: Relatos sobre mulheres*. Rio de Janeiro: Civilização Brasileira.

Dostoevsky, F. (1956). *Memoirs from the house of the dead*. Oxford: Oxford University. Originally published in 1861–1862.

Duno-Gottberg, L. (2019). Spiritual life and the rationalization of violence: The state within the state and evangelical order in a Venezuelan prison. In C. Garces, et al. (Eds.), *Carceral communities: Troubling 21st century prison regimes in Latin America*. Under contract with University of Pennsylvania.

Egelund, A. (2014). Masculinity, sex and survival in Zambian prisons. *Prison Service Journal, 212*, 16–20.

Foucault, M. (1977). *Discipline and punish*. London: Allen Lane.

Frankl, V. E. (2004). *Man's search for meaning*. London: Rider. Originally published in 1947.

Garces, C. (2010). The cross politics of Ecuador's penal state. *Cultural Anthropology, 25*(3), 459–496.

Garces, C., Darke, S., Duno-Gottberg, L., & Antillano, A. (Eds.). (2019). *Carceral communities: Troubling 21st century prison regimes in Latin America*. Under contract with University of Pennsylvania.

Gay, R. (2015). *Bruno: Conversations with a Brazilian drug dealer*. Durham, NC: Duke University.

Gilinskiy, Y., & Kostjukovsky, Y. (2004). From thievish artel to criminal corporation: The history of organised crime in Russia. In C. Fijnaut & P. Letizia (Eds.), *Organised crime in Europe: Concepts, patterns and control policies in the European Union and beyond*. Dordrecht: Springer.

Goffman, E. (1961). On the characteristics of total institutions. In D. Cressey (Ed.), *The prison: Studies in institutional organization and change*. New York: Holt, Rinehart and Winston.

Goffman, E. (1968). *Asylums: Essays on the situation of mental patients and other inmates*. London: Penguin. Originally published in 1961.

Gosling, H. J., & Scott, D. (2016). Otherwise than prisons, not prisons otherwise: Therapeutic communities as non-penal real utopias. In D. Scott (Ed.), *Emancipatory politics and praxis: An anthology of essays written for the European Group for the Study of Deviance and Social Control, 2013–2016* (pp. 181–202). London: EG.

Guadalupe, J. L. P. (1994). *Faites y atorrantes: Una etnografía del penal de Lurigancho*. Lima: Centro de Investigaciones Teológicas.

Harden, B. (2012). *Escape from camp 14*. London: Mantle.

Haslam, S. A., & Reicher, S. D. (2012). When prisoners take over the prison: A social psychology of resistance. *Personality and Social Psychology Review, 16*(2), 154–179.

Hawk, D. (2003). *The hidden gulag: Exposing North Korea's prison camps*. Washington, DC: U.S. Committee for Human Rights in North Korea.

Human Rights Watch. (1998). *Behind bars in Brazil*. New York: Human Rights Watch.

Human Rights Watch. (2015). *The state let evil take over: The prison crisis in the Brazilian state of Pernambuco*. New York: Human Rights Watch.

Human Rights Watch. (2016). *Good cops are afraid: The toll of unchecked police violence in Rio de Janeiro*. New York: Human Rights Watch.

Irwin, J. (1970). *The felon*. Berkeley: University of California.

Jefferson, A. M. (2010). Prison spaces in Nigeria and Honduras. *Prison Service Journal, 187*, 34–39.

Jefferson, A. M., & Gaborit, L. S. (2015). *Human rights in prisons: Comparing institutional encounters in Kosovo, Sierra Leone and the Philippines*. London: Palgrave Macmillan.

Jefferson, A. M., & Jensen, S. (Eds.). (2009). *State violence and human rights: State officials in the South*. Abingdon: Routledge-Cavendish.

Jefferson, A. M., & Martin, T. M. (Eds.). (2014). Everyday prison governance in Africa. *Prison Service Journal, 202*, 1–51.

Jefferson, A. M., Garces, C., & Martin, T. M. (Eds.). (2014). Sensing prison climates: Governance, survival and transition. *Focaal, 68*, 55–67.

Jones, C. R., Narag, R. E., & Morales, R. S. (2015). *Philippine prison gangs: Control or chaos?* (RegNet Research Paper No. 71). Regulatory Institutions Network. Resource document. http://papers.ssrn.com/sol3/papers.cfm?abstract_id=2586912. Last accessed 16 February 2018.

Junior, I. D., Souza, M. T., & Albuquerque, W. M. (2007). O fenômeno da prisionização e seu reflexo na ressocialização do apenado da casa de custódia de Viana. *Revista Preleção, 1*(2), 113–130.

Lambert, A. (2001). *The mark of Cain*. Documentary film. Russian Federation: Go East.

Levi, P. (1987). *If this is a man*. London: Abacus. Originally published in 1947.

Levi, P. (1989). *The drowned and the saved*. London: Abacus. Originally published in 1986.

Lindegaard, M. R., & Geer, S. (2014). Surviving South African prisons. *Focaal, 68*, 35–54.

Lourenço, L. C. (2010). Batendo a tranca: Impactos do encarceramento em agents penitenciários na região metropolitana de Belo Horizonte. *Revista de Estudos de Conflito e Controle Social, 3*(10), 11–31.

Macaulay, F. (2013). Modes of prison administration, control and governmentality in Latin America: Adoption, adaptation and hybridity. *Conflict, Security and Development, 13*(4), 361–392.

Macaulay, F. (2014). Whose prisoners are these anyway? Church, state and society partnerships and co-production of offender resocialization. In V. Miller & J. Campbell (Eds.), *Transnational penal cultures: New perspectives on discipline, punishment and desistance* (pp. 202–216). London: Routledge.

Macaulay, F. (2015, July 28). Os centros de ressocialização no estado de São Paulo. *JOTA*. https://www.jota.info/especiais/os-centros-de-ressocializacao-no-estado-de-sao-paulo-28072015. Last accessed 28 February 2018.

Marquart, J., & Roebeck, J. (1985). Prison guards and "snitches". *British Journal of Criminology, 25*(3), 217–233.

Marques, A. (2010). "Liderança", "proceder" e "igualdade": Uma etnografia das relações políticas no Primeiro Comando da Capital. *Etnográfica, 14*(2), 311–335.

Marques, A. (2014). *Crime e proceder: Um experimento antropológico.* São Paulo: Alameda.

Martin, T. M. (2014a). The importation of human rights by Uganda prison staff. *Prison Service Journal, 212*, 45–51.

Martin, T. M. (2014b). Reasonable caning and the embrace of human rights in Uganda. *Focaal, 68*, 68–82.

McNair, J., & Baylis, W. (2010). *Prisoners their own warders.* Gloucester: Dodo. Originally published in 1899.

McWhorter, W. (1981). *Inmate society: Legs, half-pants and gunmen: A study of inmate guards.* Saratoga, CA: Century Twenty One.

Moore, H. (2017). *Imprisonment and (un)relatedness in northeast Brazil.* Ph.D. thesis, University of Toronto.

Morelle, M. (2014). Power, control and money in prison: The informal governance of the Yaoundé Central Prison. *Prison Service Journal, 212*, 21–26.

Narag, R. E., & Jones, C. R. (2016). Understanding prison management in the Philippines: A case for shared governance. *Prison Journal, 97*(1), 3–26.

Núñez, J., & Fleetwood, J. (2017). The blind panopticon: Prisoners' subversion of the prison in Ecuador, 1875–2014. *Prison Service Journal, 229*, 35–39.

Oldoni, F. (2001). As relações de poder entre os detentos do presídio público de Itajaí (A morte como exteriorizaçaõ maior deste poder). *Novos Estudos Jurídicos, 13*, 115–130.

Pakes, F. (2015). *Comparative criminal justice.* Cullompton: Willan.

Postema, M., Cavallaro, J., & Nagra, R. (2017). Advancing security and human rights by the controlled organisation of inmates. *Prison Service Journal, 229*, 57–62.

Priestly, P. (1985). *Victorian prison lives: English prison biography 1830–1914.* London: Methuen.

Rivera, L. G. (2010). Discipline and punish? Youth gangs' response to 'zero tolerance' policies in Honduras. *Bulletin of Latin American Research, 29*(4), 492–504.

Salla, F., Ballesteros, P., Mavila, O., Mercado, F., Litvachky, P., & Museri, A. (2009). *Democracy, human rights and prison conditions in South America.* São Paulo: University of São Paulo.

Salvatore, R. D., & Aguirre, C. (Eds.). (1996). *The birth of the penitentiary in Latin America: Towards an interpretive social history of prisons.* In R. D. Salvatore & C. Aguirre (Eds.), *The birth of the penitentiary in Latin America* (pp. 1–43). Austin: University of Texas.

Scott, S., & Gosling, H. J. (2015). Thinking beyond the punitive rationale: Promoting therapeutic communities as a radical alternative to prison. *Howard Journal of Criminal Justice, 54*(4), 397–402.

Sepúlveda, C., & Pojomovsky, I. (2019). Carceral order, mediation and representation: Fiction and ethnography in a Venezuelan prison. In C. Garces, et al. (Eds.), *Carceral communities: Troubling 21st century prison regimes in Latin America.* Under contract with University of Pennsylvania.

Skarbek, D. (2010). Self-governance in San Pedro prison. *Independent Review, 14*(2), 569–585.

Shimizu, B. (2011). *Solidariedade e grefarismo nas facções criminosas: Um estudo criminológico à luz da psicologia das massas.* São Paulo: Instituto Brasileiro de Ciências Criminais.

Skarbek, D. (2014). *The social order of the underworld: How prison gangs govern the American penal system.* New York: Oxford University.

Skarbek, D. (2016). Covenants without the Sword? Comparing prison self-governance globally. *American Political Science Review, 110*(4), 845–862.

Solzhenitsyn, A. (1963). *One day in the life of Ivan Denisovich.* London: Penguin.

Solzhenitsyn, A. (1975). *The gulag archipelago* (Vol. 2). New York: Harper and Row.

Sparks, R., Bottoms, A., & Hay, W. (1996). *Prisons and the problem of order.* Oxford: Clarendon.

Steinberg, J. (2004). *The number: One man's search for identity in the Cape underworld and prison gangs.* Cape Town: Jonathan Ball.

Sykes, G. M. (1956). The corruption of authority and rehabilitation. *Social Forces, 34*(3), 257–262.

Sykes, G. M. (1958). *The society of captives.* Princeton, NY: Princeton University.

Tertsakian, C. (2014). 'Some prisons are prisons, and others are like hell': Prison life in Rwanda in the ten years after the genocide. *Prison Service Journal, 212*, 4–10.

Thomas, J. (1972). *The English prison officer since 1850: A study in conflict.* London: Routledge and Kegan Paul.

Tritton, P., & Fleetwood, J. (2017). An insider's view of prison reform in Ecuador. *Prison Service Journal, 229,* 40–45.
United Nations. (2016). *United Nations standard minimum rules for the treatment of prisoners (the Nelson Mandela rules).* A/RES/70/175. Resource document. https://cdn.penalreform.org/wp-content/uploads/1957/06/ENG.pdf. Last accessed 27 February 2018.
Varella, D. (2008). *Estação Carandiru.* São Paulo: Companhia das Letras. English edition: Varella, D. (2012). *Lockdown: Inside Brazil's most violent prison* (A. Entrekin, Trans.). London: Simon and Schuster.
Varella, D. (2012). *Carcereiros.* São Paulo: Companhia das Letras.
Vicentin, M. C. G. (2005). *A vida em rebelião: Jovens em conflito com a lei.* São Paulo: HUCITEC.
Vicentin, M. C. G. (2011). Corpos em rebelião e o sofrimento-resistência: Adolescentes em conflito com a lei. *Tempo Social, 23*(1), 97–113.
Weegels, J. (2017). Prisoner self-governance and survival in a Nicaraguan city police jail. *Prison Service Journal, 229,* 15–19.
Weegels, J. (2019). The 'cemetery of the living': An exploration of disposal, (in)visibility, and change-of-attitude in Nicaraguan prison. In C. Garces, et al. (Eds.), *Carceral communities: Troubling 21st century prison regimes in Latin America.* Under contract with University of Pennsylvania.
Williams, P., & Wu, Y. (2004). *The great wall of confinement: The Chinese prison camp through contemporary fiction and reportage.* Berkeley: University of California.
Wintin, T., & Brown, I. (2005). Colonial Burma's prison: Continuity with its pre-colonial past? *IIAS Newsletter, 39,* 5.
Wu, H. (1992). *Laogai: The Chinese gulag.* Boulder, CO: Westview.

References

Aas, K. F. (2012). The earth is one but the world is not: Criminological theory and its geopolitical divisions. *Theoretical Criminology, 16*(1), 5–20.

Aas, K. F. (2013). *Globalization and crime*. London: Sage.

Acebes, M. C. (2017, January 18). Brazil's correctional houses of horror. *Foreign Affairs*. https://www.foreignaffairs.com/articles/brazil/2017-01-18/brazil-s-correctional-houses-horror. Last accessed 9 March 2017.

Adorno, S. (2013). Democracy in progress in contemporary Brazil: Corruption, organized crime, violence and new paths to the rule of law. *International Journal of Criminology and Sociology, 2,* 409–425.

Adorno, L. (2017, September 1). Com salário de R$7.400, faltam médicos nos presídios de SP; prisões têm 41 mortes por mês. *UOL*. https://noticias.uol.com.br/cotidiano/ultimas-noticias/2017/09/01/em-media-41-presos-morrem-sob-a-custodia-do-estado-de-sp.htm. Last accessed 5 September 2017.

Adorno, S., & Dias, C. N. (2016). Cronologia doa "ataques de 2006" e a nova configuração de poder nas prisões na última decada. *Revista Brasileira de Segurança Pública, 10*(2), 118–132.

Adorno, S., & Salla, F. (2007). Criminalidade organizada nas prisões e os ataques do PCC. *Estudos Avançados, 21*(61), 7–29.

Aguirre, C. (2005). *The criminals of Lima and their worlds: The prison experience, 1850–1935*. Durham, NC: Duke University.

Aguirre, C. (2007). Prisons and prisoners in modernising Latin America. In F. Dikötter & I. Brown (Eds.), *Cultures of confinement: A history of the prison in Africa, Asia, and Latin America*. Ithaca, NY: Cornell University.

Aguirre, C., & Salvatore, R. D. (2001). Writing the history of law, crime, and punishment in Latin America. In R. D. Salvatore, et al. (Eds.), *Crime and punishment in Latin America*. Durham, NC: Duke University.

Akbar, J. (2015, October 27). Inside Brazil's toughest jails where inmates rule. *Mail Online*. http://www.dailymail.co.uk/news/article-3289843/Inside-Brazil-s-toughest-jails-inmates-rule-Prisons-dog-chaveiros-sell-crack-cocaine-charge-taxes-gang-rape-murder-rivals-keys.html#ixzz3qRd9moDE. Last Accessed 3 November 2015.

Akoensi, T. D. (2014). Governance through power sharing in Ghanaian prisons: A symbiotic relationship between officers and inmates. *Prison Service Journal, 212*, 33–38.

Alencastro. L. F. (2007). Brazil in the south Atlantic: 1150–1850 (E. Suari, Trans.). *Mediations, 23*(1), 125–174.

Almeida, O. L., & Paes-Machado, E. (2015). Sem lugar para corer, nem se esconder: Processos socioorganizacionais de vitimização Prisional. *Espacio Abierto, 24*(3), 69–96.

Alvarez, M. C., Salla, F., & Dias, C. N. (2013). Das comissões de solidariedade ao Primeiro Comando da Capital em São Paulo. *Tempo Social, 25*(1), 61–82.

Alves, J. A. (2013). From necropolis to blackpolis: Necropolitical governance and black spatial praxis in São Paulo Brazil. *Antipode, 46*(2), 323–339.

Amora, D., & Cancian, N. (2017, January 4). *Em meio a superlotações, governo federal seca repasses para presídios*. http://www1.folha.uol.com.br/cotidiano/2017/01/1846864-em-meio-a-superlotacoes-governo-federal-seca-repasses-para-presidios.shtml. Last accessed 15 March 2017.

Amorim, C. R. (1993). *Comando Vermelho: A história segredo do crime organizado* (4th ed.). Rio de Janeiro: Record.

Anderson, E. (1999). *Code of the street: Decency, violence and the moral life of the inner city*. New York: W. W. Norton.

Andreoli, S. B., Santos, M. M., Quintana, M. I., Ribeiro, W. S., Blay, S. L., Geraldo, J. V. T., & Mari, J. J. (2014). Prevalence of mental disorders among prisoners in the state of São Paulo, Brazil. *PLoS One, 9*(2). https://doi.org/10.1371/journal.pone.0088836.

Antillano, A. (2017). When prisoners make the prison: Self-rule in Venezuelan prisons. *Prison Service Journal, 229*, 26–30.

Antillano, A. (2019). When to punish is not to discipline. The self-rule of carceral order in Venezuela. In C. Garces, et al. (Eds.), *Carceral communities: Troubling 21st century prison regimes in Latin America*. Under contract with University of Pennsylvania.

Antunes, S. A. (2016). Produção de corpos e categorias de pessoas nos fluxos de uma penitenciária feminina. *Revista Florestan Ferbandes, 3*(1), 63–71.

Antunes, S. A. (2017). Para habitar entre grades: Táticas de [sobre]vida na prisão. *ARACÊ, 4*(4), 116–135.

Apple, C. (2017, May 8). Como o PCC garantiu a segurança do meu marido dentro da prisão. *Vice*. https://www.vice.com/pt_br/article/wnkn7y/pcc-garantiu-seguranca-do-meu-marido-prisao. Last accessed 30 June 2017.

Applebaum, A. (2003). *Gulag: A history of the soviet camps*. London: Allen Lane.

Araújo, C. E. M. (2009). *Cárcares imperiais: Correção do Rio de Janeiro. Seus detentos e o sistema império, 1830–1861*. Ph.D. thesis, State University of Campinas. http://repositorio.unicamp.br/handle/REPOSIP/280976. Last accessed 15 June 2017.

Arcoverde (2016, January 7). A cada mês, 40 detentos morrem nos presídios paulistas. *Fiquem Sabendo*. http://www.fiquemsabendo.com.br/2016/01/a-cada-mes-40-detentos-morrem-nos-presidios-paulistas-2. Last accessed 24 February 2017.

Aresti, A., & Darke, S. (2016). Practicing convict criminology: Lessons learned from British academic activism. *Critical Criminology, 24*(4), 533–547.

Aresti, A., & Darke, S. (Eds.). (2018). Twenty years of convict criminology. Under contract with *Journal of Prisoners on Prison, 27*(2).

Aresti, A., Darke, S., & Manlow, D. (2016). Bridging the gap: Giving public voice to prisoners and former prisoners through research activism. *Prison Service Journal, 224*, 3–13.

Arias, E. D., & Barnes, N. (2016). Crime and plural orders in Rio de Janeiro Brazil. *Current Sociology, 65*(3), 448–465.

Arias, E. D., & Goldstein, D. M. (2010). Violent pluralism: Understanding the new democracies of Latin America. In E. D. Arias & D. M. Goldstein (Eds.), *Violent democracies in Latin America* (pp. 1–34). Durham, NC: Duke University.

Arnold, D. (2005). India: The prisoners revolt. *IIAS Newsletter, 39*, 6.

Arruda, R. F. (2015). *Geografia do cárcere: Territorialidades na vida cotidiana carcerária no sistena prisional de Pernambuco*. Ph.D. thesis, University of São

Paulo. http://www.teses.usp.br/teses/disponiveis/8/8136/tde-16062015-125328/pt-br.php. Last accessed 3 February 2017.

Attanasio, A. (2017, September 9). 'Narcosur': As conexões da máfia italiana com o PCC e os cartéis latino-americanos. *BBC*. http://www.bbc.com/portuguese/internacional-41196027. Last accessed 11 September 2017.

Ayete-Nyampong, L. (2013). *Entangled realities and the underlife of a total institution: An ethnography of correctional centres for juvenile and young offenders in Accra, Ghana*. Ph.D. thesis, Wageningen University.

Ayete-Nyampong, L. (2014). Entangled governance practices and the illusion of producing compliant inmates in correctional centres for juvenile and young offenders in Ghana. *Prison Service Journal, 212*, 27–32.

Azevedo, R. (2006). Crime and criminal justice in Latin America. *Sociologias, 2*, 1517–1522.

Babenco, H., & Kramer, O. (2003). *Carandiru*. Film. Brazil: Globo Filmes.

Babenco, H., Carvalho, W., Gervitz, R., & Faria, M. (2005). *Carandiru: Outros Historias*. Television series. Brazil: Rede Globo.

Back, L. (2015). How blue can you get? B.B King, planetary humanism and the blues behind bars. *Theory, Culture & Society, 32*(7–8), 274–285.

Baker, J. E. (1964). Inmate self-government. *Journal of Criminal law and Criminology, 55*(1), 39–47.

Bandyopadhyay, M. (2007). Reform and everyday practice: Some issues of prison governance. *Contributions to Indian Sociology, 41*(3), 387–416.

Bandyopadhyay, M. (2010). *Everyday life in a prison: Confinement, surveillance, resistance*. New Delhi: Orient BlackSwan.

Bandyopadhyay, M. (2016). Asian prisons. In Y. Jewkes, et al. (Eds.), *Handbook on prisons* (2nd ed., pp. 441–459). Abington: Routledge.

Bandyopadhyay, M., & Jefferson, A. M. (2010, July). *Entangled interactions*. Paper presented at the British Society of Criminology Annual Conference. Unpublished.

Barbosa, A. R. (2005). *Prender e dar fuga biopolítica, sistema penitenciários e tráfico de drogas no Rio de Janeiro*. Ph.D. thesis, Federal University of Rio de Janeiro. http://www.uece.br/labvida/dmdocuments/prender_e_dar_fuga_biopolitica_sistema_penitenciario.pdf. Last accessed 1 May 2017.

Barbosa, A. R. (2006). O baile e a prisão: Onde se juntam as pontas dos segmentos locais que respondem pela dinâmica do tráfico de drogas no Rio de Janeiro. *Cadernos de Ciências Humanas, 9*(15), 119–135.

Barbosa, A. R. (2007). Um levantamento introdutório das práticas de violência física dentro das cadeias cariocas. In A. C. Marques (Ed.), *Conflitos, política e relações pessoais* (pp. 129–172). Campinas: Pontes.

Barrata, A. (2003). Prefácio. In V. M. Batista (Ed.), *Difíceis ganhos fáceis: Drogas e juventude pobre no Rio de Janeiro* (2nd ed., pp. 15–34). Rio de Janeiro: Revan.

Barreto, L. C., & Santos, N. P. (1984). *Memórias do cárcere*. Film. Brazil: Brentz.

Bassani, F. (2016). *Visita íntima: Sexo, crime e negócios nas prisões*. Porto Alegre: Bestiário.

Batista, N. (1996). Fragmentos de uma discurso sedicioso. *Discursos Sediciosos, 1*(1), 69–77.

Batista, N. (1997). A violência do estado e os aparelhos policiais. *Discursos Sediciosos, 2*(4), 145–154.

Batista, N. (2000). *Matrizes ibericas do sistema penal brasileiro*. Rio de Janeiro: Freiras Bastos.

Batista, N., & Borges, R. (2012). De professor para professor: Entrevista com William da Silva Lima. *Discursos Sediciosos, 17*(19/20), 11–18.

Batista, V. M. (2003a). *Difíceis ganhos fáceis: Drogas e juventude pobre no Rio de Janeiro* (2nd ed.). Rio de janeiro: Revan.

Batista, V. M. (2003b). *O medo na cidade do Rio de Janeiro*. Rio de Janeiro: Revan.

Batista, V. M. (2009). Novas funções do cárcere no Brasil contemporâneo. In R. T. Oliveira & V. Mattos (Eds.), *Estudos de execução criminal: Direito e psicologia* (pp. 17–27). Belo Horizonte: Tribunal de Justiça de Minas Gerais.

Batista, V. M. (2011). *Introdução crítica à criminologia brasileira*. Rio de Janeiro: Revan.

Batista, V. M. (2016). *A questão criminal no brasil contemporâneo*. São Paulo: Fundação Bienal de São Paulo.

Batista, V. M. (2018, February 21). O falacioso discurso de segurança pública. *Nova Democracia*. http://anovademocracia.com.br/noticias/8272-exclusivo-professora-vera-malaguti-comenta-a-intervencao-militar-no-rio. Last accessed 28 February 2018.

Beattie, P. M. (2011). The jealous institution: Male nubility, conjugality, sexuality, and discipline on the social margins of imperial Brazil. *Comparative Studies in Society and History, 53*(1), 180–209.

Beattie, P. M. (2015). *Punishment in paradise: Race, slavery, human rights, and a nineteenth-century Brazilian penal colony*. Durham: Duke University.

Bergman, M., & Whitehead, L. (Eds.). (2009). *Criminality, public security, and the challenge to democracy in Latin America*. Notre Dame: University of Notre Dame.

Biondi, K. (2010). *Junto e misturado: Uma etnografia do PCC*. São Paulo: Teirciero Nome. English version: Biondi, K. (2016). *Sharing this walk: An ethnography of prison life and the PCC in Brazil* (J. F. Collins, Trans.). Chapel Hill: University of North Carolina.

Biondi, K. (2013). O PCC: Da organização á ética. In A. R. Barbosa, et al. (Eds.), *Etnografias em uma fronteira difusa* (pp. 23–34). Rio de Janeiro: Universidade Federal Fluminense.

Biondi, K. (2014). *Etnografia no movimento: Território, hierarquia e lei no PCC*. Ph.D. thesis, Federal University of São Carlos. https://www.repositorio.ufscar.br/bitstream/handle/ufscar/246/6378pdf?sequence=1&isAllowed=y. Last accessed 7 April 2017.

Biondi, K. (2016). Author's afterword to the English language edition. In K. Biondi (Ed.), *Sharing this walk: An ethnography of prison life and the PCC in Brazil* (J. F. Collins, Trans.) (pp. 145–176). Chapel Hill: University of North Carolina.

Biondi, K. (2017a, January 23). *The extinction of sexual violence in the prisons of São Paulo, Brazil*. http://uncpressblog.com/2017/01/23/karina-biondi-the-extinction-of-sexual-violence-in-the-prisons-of-sao-paulo-brazil. Last accessed 7 March 2017.

Biondi, K. (2017b). It was already in the ghetto': Rap, religion and crime in the prison. Interview with Djalma Oliveira Rios, aka 'Cascão. *Prison Service Journal, 229*, 45–47.

Biondi, K. (2017c). Movement between and beyond the walls: Micropolitics of incitements and variations among São Paulo's prisoners' movement the 'PCC' and the prison system. *Prison Service Journal, 229*, 23–25.

Biondi, K. (2017d). Prison violence, prison justice: The rise of Brazil's PCC. *NACLA Report on the Americas, 49*(3), 341–346.

Biondi, K. (2019, forthcoming). Facing up to the PCC: Theoretical and methodological strategies to approaching Brazil's largest "prison gang". In C. Garces, et al. (Eds.), *Carceral communities: Troubling 21st century prison regimes in Latin America*. Under contract with University of Pennsylvania.

Biondi, K., & Marques, A. (2010). Memória e historicidade em dois "comandos" prisionais. *Lua Nova, 79*, 39–70.

Birkbeck, C. (2011). Imprisonment and internment: Comparing penal institutions North and South. *Punishment and Society, 13*(3), 307–332.

Blaustein, J. (2016). Exporting criminological innovation abroad: Discursive representation, 'evidence-based crime prevention' and the post-neoliberal development agenda in Latin America. *Theoretical Criminology, 20*(2), 165–184.

Blaustein, J. (2017). Ethical criminologists fly economy: Process-orientated criminological engagement abroad. In S. Armstrong, et al. (Eds.), *Reflexivity and criminal justice: Intersections of policy, practice and research* (pp. 357–379). London: Palgrave Macmillan.

Bochenek, M., & Delgado, F. (2006). Children in custody in Brazil. *Lancet, 367,* 696.

Bortoluci, J. H., & Jansen, R. S. (2013). Toward a postcolonial sociology: The view from Latin America. *Postcolonial Sociology, Political Power and Social Theory, 24,* 199–229.

Bottoms, A., & Tankebe, J. (2012). Beyond procedural justice: A dialogic approach to legitimacy in criminal justice. *Journal of Criminal Law and Criminology, 102*(1), 119–170.

Bottoms, A., & Tankebe, J. (2013). 'A voice within': Power holders' perspectives on authority and legitimacy. In J. Tankebe & A. Liebling (Eds.), *Legitimacy and criminal justice: An international exploration* (pp. 60–82). Oxford: Oxford University.

Boullosa, C., & Wallace, M. (2015). *Narco history: How the United States and Mexico jointly created the Mexican drug war.* New York: Or Books.

Bowcott, O. (2017, April 25). Child locked in cell for more than 23 hours a day at Feltham, high court told. *The Guardian.* https://www.theguardian.com/society/2017/apr/25/single-unlock-prison-regime-breached-youths-rights-court-told?CMP=share_btn_tw. Last accessed 26 April 2017.

Bourgois, P. (1995). *In search of respect: Selling crack in el barrio.* Cambridge: Cambridge University.

Brant, V. C. (1986). *O trabalhador preso no estado de São Paulo: Passado, presente e expectativas.* São Paulo: Cebrap.

Bretas, M. L. (1996). What the eyes can't see: Stories from Rio de Janeiro's prisons. In R. D. Salvatore & C. Aguirre (Eds.), *The birth of the penitentiary in Latin America* (pp. 101–122). Austin: University of Texas.

Brown, I. (2007). A commissioner calls: Alexander Paterson and Burma's colonial prisons. *Journal of Southeast Asian Studies, 38*(2), 293–308.

Cabral, S., & Azevedo, P. F. (2008). The modes of provision of prison services in a comparative perspective. *Brazilian Administrative Review, 5*(1), 53–69.

Caetano, H. (2015, July 20). O juiz e a banalidade do mal. *Justificando.* http://justificando.cartacapital.com.br/2015/07/20/o-juiz-e-a-banalidade-do-mal. Last accessed 3 February 2017.

Cain, M. (2000). Orientalism, occidentalism and the sociology of crime. *British Journal of Criminology, 40,* 239–260.

Caldeira, C. (2003). Bangu 3: Desordem e ordem no quartel-general do Comando Vermelho. *Insight Inteligênçia, 22,* 91–115.

Caldeira, C. (2007). "Povo de Israel": E o milagre da multiplicação do crime. *Insight Inteligênçia, 38,* 12–18.

Caldeira, T. (1996). Fortified enclaves: The new urban segregation. *Public Culture, 8,* 303–328.

Caldeira, T. (2000). *City of walls: Crime, segregation and citizenship in São Paulo.* Berkeley: University of California.

Caldeira, T. (2002). The paradox of police violence in democratic Brazil. *Ethnography, 3,* 235–263.

Câmara dos Deputados. (2008a). *CPI do sistema carcerário.* Resource document. http://bd.camara.leg.br/bd/bitstream/handle/bdcamara/2701/cpi_sistema_carcerario.pdf?sequence=5. Last accessed 10 August 2014.

Câmara dos Deputados. (2008b). No title. Resource document. http://www1.folha.uol.com.br/folha/cotidiano/20060708-marcos_camacho.pdf. Last accessed 17 July 2017.

Cardia, N. (2012). Os direitos humanos segundo a pesquisa 'Atitudes, normas culturais e valores em relação a violação de direitos humanos e violência'. In Núcleo de Estudos da Violência (Ed.), *5º relatório nacional sobre os direitos humanos no Brasil* (pp. 39–49). Resource document. http://www.nevusp.org/downloads/down265.pdf São Paulo: NEV-USP. Last accessed 17 April 2017.

Carlos, J. O. (2015). *Drug policy and incarceration in São Paulo, Brazil.* London: International Drug Policy Consortium.

Carter, J. H. (2014). Gothic sovereignty: Gangs and criminal community in a Honduran prison. *South Atlantic Quarterly, 113*(3), 475–502.

Carter, J. H. (2017). Neoliberal penology and criminal finance in Honduras. *Prison Service Journal, 229,* 10–14.

Carvalho, S. (1996). *A política criminal de drogas no Brasil.* Rio de Janeiro: LUAM.

Carvalho, S., & Freire, C. R. (2007). O regime disciplinar diferenciado: Notas críticas à reforma do sistema punitivo brasileiro. In S. Carvalho (Ed.), *Crítica à execução penal* (2nd ed., pp. 269–281). Rio de janeiro: Lumen Juris.

Carvalho, S. (2013). Theories of punishment in the age of mass incarceration: A closer look at the empirical problem silenced by justificationism (the Brazilian case). *Open Journal of Social Sciences, 1*(4), 1–12.

Carvalho, S., & Rodas, S. (2017, February 20). É absolutamente ilegítimo que o Estado limite o uso de qualquer droga. *Consultor Jurídico.* http://www.conjur.com.br/2017-fev-20/entrevista-salo-carvalho-professor-direito-penal-ufrj. Last accessed 21 February 2017.

Casara, R. (2014). Segurança pública: Facismo e polícia. In R. C. Junior (Ed.), *Criminologia do cotidiano* (pp. 263–280). Rio de Janeiro: Lumens Juris.

Casara, R. (2016, July 9). Na pós-democracia, os direitos e garantias fundamentais também são vistoscomo mercadorias. *Justificando.* http://justificando.cartacapital.com.br/2016/07/09/na-pos-democracia-os-direitos-e-garantias-fundamentais-tambem-sao-vistos-como-mercadorias. Last accessed 21 February 2017.

Casara, R. (2017). *Estado pós-democrático: Neo-obscurantismo e gestão dos indesejáveis.* Rio de Janeiro: Civilização Brasileira.

Castro, L. A. (1987). *Criminologia de la liberacion.* Maracalbo: Universidad del Zulia. Portuguese edition: Castro, L. A. (2005). *Criminologia da libertação* (S. Moretzsohn, Trans.). Rio de Janeiro: Revan.

Castro, L. A. (2000). O trinfo de Lewis Carroll: A nova criminologia latino-americana. *Discursos Sediciosos, 5*(9&10), 129–148.

Cavalcanti, R. P. (2016a). Armed violence and the politics of gun control in Brazil: An analysis of the 2005 referendum. *Bulletin of Latin American Research.* https://doi.org/10.1111/blar.12476.

Cavalcanti, R. P. (2016b). *Over, under and through the walls: The dynamics of public security, police-community relations and the limits of managerialism in crime control in Recife, Brazil.* Ph.D. thesis, University of London. http://westminsterresearch.wmin.ac.uk/18353. Last accessed 7 April 2017.

Cavalcanti, R. P. (2017). Marginalised youth, violence and policing: A qualitative study in Recife, Brazil. *Contemporary Social Science, 12,* 227–241.

Cerbini, F. (2017). From the panopticon to the anti-panopticon: The 'art of government' in the prison of San Pedro (La Paz, Bolivia). *Prison Service Journal, 229,* 31–34.

Cerbini, F. (2019). "Eat to forget": The dangers of food in San Pedro prison (La Paz, Bolivia). In C. Garces, et al. (Eds.), *Carceral communities: Troubling 21st century prison regimes in Latin America.* Under contract with University of Pennsylvania.

César, R. (2016, December 5). Nove presos teriam executado detento em área de isolamento, denuncia Sinsap. *Correio do Estado*. http://www.correiodoestado.com.br/cidades/campo-grande/nove-presos-teriam-executado-detento-em-area-de-isolamento-denuncia/292800. Last accessed 4 October 2017.

Chartoff, R., Winkler, I., & Stallone, S. (1985). *Rocky IV*. Film. Los Angeles: United Artists.

Chazkel, A. (2009). Social life and civic education in the Rio de Janeiro city jail. *Journal of Social History, 42*(3), 697–731.

Cheliotis, L. K. (Ed.). (2014). Prison realities: Views from around the World. *South Atlantic Quarterly, 113*(3), 475–502.

Christie, N. (2000). *Crime control as industry: Towards gulags, western style?* London: Routledge.

Christino, M. S., & Tognolli, C. (2017). *Laços de sangue: A história secreta do PCC*. São Paulo: Matrix.

Clavel, T. (2017, June 29). 'Largest ever' police corruption case unfolds in Brazil's Rio de Janeiro. *InSight Crime*. http://www.insightcrime.org/news-briefs/brazil-largest-ever-police-corruption-case-unfolds-rio-de-janeiro-state. Last accessed 14 July 2017.

Clemmer, D. (1940). *The prison community*. New York: Holt, Rinehart and Winston.

Cloward, R. A. (1960). Social control in the prison. In R. Cloward, et al. (Eds.), *Theoretical studies in social organization of the prison* (pp. 20–48). New York: Social Science Research Council.

Codino, R. (2014). Para uma outra criminologia do terceiro mundo: Perspectivas da criminologia critica no sul (S. Carvalho, Trans.). *Revista Liberdades, 20*, 22–34.

Coelho, E. C. (2005). *A oficina do diablo. E outros estudos sobre criminalidade*. Rio de Janeiro: Record.

Cohen, S. (1985). *Visions of social control*. Cambridge: Polity Press.

Cohen, S. (1988). *Against criminology*. New Brunswick: Transaction.

Cohen, S., & Taylor, L. (1972). *Psychological survival: The experience of long term imprisonment*. Harmondsworth: Penguin.

Comaroff, J., & Comaroff, J. (Eds.). (2006). *Law and disorder in the postcolony*. Chicago: University of Chicago.

Comaroff, J., & Comaroff, J. (2012). *Theories from the south: Or how Euro-America is evolving towards Africa*. London: Paradigm.

Contectas. (2017). *Tortura Blindada: Como as instituições do sistema de justiça perpetuam a violência nas audiências de custódia.* Resource document. http://www.conectas.org/arquivos/editor/files/Relato%CC%81rio%20completo_Tortura%20blindada_Conectas%20Direitos%20Humanos(1).pdf. Last accessed 7 March 2017.

Connell, R. (2006). Northern theory: The political geography of general social theory. *Theoretical Sociology, 35*(2), 237–264.

Connell, R. (2007). *Southern theory: The global dynamics of knowledge in social sciences.* Cambridge: Polity.

Conselho Nacional de Justiça. (2014). *Novo Diagnóstico de Pessoas Presas no Brasil.* Resource document. http://www.cnj.jus.br/images/imprensa/Pessoas_presas_no_Brasil_1.pdf. Last accessed 10 August 2014.

Conselho Nacional de Justiça. (2017). *Reunião especial de jurisdição.* Resource document. http://www.cnj.jus.br/files/conteudo/arquivo/2017/02/b5718a7e7d6f2edee274f93861747304.pdf. Last accessed 3 March 2017.

Conselho Nacional de Política Publica e Penitenciária. (2014). *Relatório de inspeção extraordinária em estabelecimentos penais no estado do Rio de Janeiro.* Resource document. https://www.justica.gov.br/seus-direitos/politica-penal/cnpcp-1/relatorios-de-inspecao-1/relatorios-de-inspecao-2014-1/relatorio-de-inspecao-extraordinaria-rj-jan-21-2014.pdf. Last accessed 25 June 2017.

Coronil, F. (2000). Towards a critique of globalcentrism: Speculations on capitalism's nature. *Public Culture, 12*(2), 351–374.

Coronil, F. (2004). Latin American postcolonial studies and global decolonization. In N. Lazarus (Ed.), *The Cambridge companion to postcolonial literary studies* (pp. 221–240). New York: Cambride University.

Costa, A. T. M. (2011). Police brutality in Brazil: Authoritarian legacy or institutional weakness? (T. Thompson, Trans.). *Latin American Perspectives, 38*(5), 19–32.

Costa, F., & Andrade, V. (n.d.). O poder do crime. *UOL.* https://www.uol/noticias/especiais/marcinho-vp.htm#tematico-1. Last accessed 21 October 2017.

Costa, F., & Bianchi, P. (2017). "Massacre silencioso": Doenças tratáveis matam mais que violência nas prisões brasileira. *UOL.* https://noticias.uol.com.br/cotidiano/ultimas-noticias/2017/08/14/massacre-silencioso-mortes-por-doencas-trataveis-superam-mortes-violentas-nas-prisoes-brasileiras.htm. Last accessed 8 September 2017.

Count the Costs. (n.d.). *The war on drugs: Wasting billions and undermining economies.* Resource document. http://www.countthecosts.org/sites/default/files/Economics-briefing.pdf. Last accessed 17 August 2017.

Cowie, S. (2017, March 27). Brazil's prisons: A battleground in the drug wars. *Al Jazeera*. http://www.aljazeera.com/indepth/features/2017/02/brazil-prisons-battleground-drug-wars-170219053354497.html. Last accessed 5 April 2017.

Coyle, A., Fair, H., Jacobson, J., & Walmsley, R. (2016). *Imprisonment worldwide: The current situation and an alternative future*. Bristol: Policy.

Council of Europe. (2017). *Report to the government of the United Kingdom on the visit to the United Kingdom carried out by the European Committee for the prevention of torture and inhuman or degrading treatment or punishment (CPT) from 30 March to 12 April 2016. CPT/Inf (2017) (Roman)*. Resource document. https://rm.coe.int/CoERMPublicCommonSearchServices/DisplayDCTMContent?documentId=090000168070a773. Last accessed 18 April 2017.

Cressey, D. (Ed.). (1961). *The prison: Studies in institutional organization and change*. New York: Holt, Rinehart and Winston.

Crewe, B. (2009). *The prisoner society: Power, adaptation and social life in an English prison*. Oxford: Oxford University.

Crewe, B. (2016). The sociology of imprisonment. In Y. Jewkes, et al. (Eds.), *Handbook on prisons* (2nd ed., pp. 77–100). Abington: Routledge.

Crouch, B., & Marquart, J. (1989). *An appeal to justice: Litigation reform of Texas prisons*. Austin: University of Texas.

Dantas, H. S., Silveira, C. M., & Rovaron, M. (2016). Adolescências inscritas na ilegalidade. A Lei 11.343/2006 e os adolescentes em cumprimento de medida socioeducativa. *Boletim IBCCRIM, 24,* 15–17.

Dardel, J. (2013). Resisting 'bare life': Prisoners' agency in the new prison culture era in Colombia. In D. Moran, et al. (Eds.), *Carceral spaces: Mobility and agency in imprisonment and migrant detention*. London: Routledge.

Darke, S. (2012). Estação Carandiru. *Prison Service Journal, 199,* 26–28.

Darke, S. (2013a). Entangled staff-inmate relations. *Prison Service Journal, 207,* 16–22.

Darke, S. (2013b). Inmate governance in Brazilian prisons. *Howard Journal of Criminal Justice, 52*(3), 272–284.

Darke, S. (2014a). Managing without guards in a Brazilian police lockup. *Focaal, 68,* 55–67.

Darke, S. (2014b). Recoverers helping recoverers: Discipline and peer-facilitated reform in Brazilian faith-based prisons. In V. Miller & J. Campbell (Eds.), *Transnational penal cultures: New perspectives on discipline, punishment and desistance* (pp. 217–229). London: Routledge.

Darke, S. (2017, January 26). Who is really in control of Brazil's prisons? *The conversation*. https://theconversation.com/who-is-really-in-control-of-brazils-prisons-71391. Last accessed 23 June 2017.

Darke, S., & Garces, C. (2017a). Surviving in the new mass carceral zone. *Prison Service Journal, 229*, 2–9.

Darke, S., & Garces, C. (2017b, January 9). What's causing Brazil's prison massacres? *Centre for Crime and Justice Studies*. https://www.crimeandjustice.org.uk/resources/whats-causing-brazils-prison-massacres. Last accessed 23 June 2017.

Darke, S., & Garces, C. (Eds.). (2017c). Informal dynamics of survival in Latin American prisons. *Prison Service Journal, 229*, 1–62.

Darke, S., & Karam, M. L. (2016). Latin American prisons. In Y. Jewkes, et al. (Eds.), *Handbook on prisons* (2nd ed., pp. 460–474). Abington: Routledge. Portuguese version: Karam, M. L., & Darke, S. (2016). *Prisões latino americanas* (M. L. Karam, Trans.). http://emporiododireito.com.br/leitura/prisoes-latino-americanas-1508702837. Last accessed 17 February 2018. Spanish version: Darke, S., & Karam, M. L. (2017). Las prisiones de América Latina. *Ecuador Debate, 101*, 53–71.

Davis, M. (2007). *Planet of slums*. London: Verso.

Department of Health. (2009). *The bradley report*. Resource document. http://www.rcpsych.ac.uk/pdf/Bradley%20Report11.pdf. Last accessed 27 June 2017.

Dias, C. N. (2013). *PCC: Hegemonia nas prisões e monopólio da violência*. São Paulo: Saraiva.

Dias, C. N., & Darke, S. (2016). From dispersed to monopolized violence: Expansion and consolidation of the Primeiro Comando da Capital's hegemony in São Paulo's prisons. *Crime, Law and Social Change, 65*(3), 213–215.

Dias, C. N., & Salla, F. (2013). Organized crime in Brazilian prisons: The example of the PCC. *International Journal of Criminology and Sociology, 2*, 397–408.

Dias, C. N., & Salla, F. (2017). Formal and informal controls and punishment: The production of order in the prisons of São Paulo. *Prison Service Journal, 229*, 19–22.

Dieter, M. S. (2013). *Política criminal actuarial: A criminologia do fim da história*. Rio de Janeiro: Revan.

Dikötter, F. (2007). The prison in the world. In F. Dikötter & I. Brown (Eds.), *Cultures of confinement: A history of the prison in Africa, Asia, and Latin America* (pp. 1–14). Ithaca, NY: Cornell University.

Dikötter, F., & Brown, I. (Eds.). (2007). *Cultures of confinement: A history of the prison in Africa, Asia, and Latin America*. Ithaca, NY: Cornell University.

Diniz, D. (2015a). Cadeia de papel: Nome de horror. *Revista Liberdades, 20*, 234–244.

Diniz, D. (2015b). *Cadeia: Relatos sobre mulheres*. Rio de Janeiro: Civilização Brasileira.

Diniz, D. (2015c). Cadeia de papel: Nome de horror. *Revista Liberdades, 20*, 234–244.

Dostoevsky, F. (1956). *Memoirs from the house of the dead*. Oxford: Oxford University. Originally published in 1861–1862.

Dreisinger, B. (2016). *Incarceration nations: A journey to justice in prisons around the world*. New York: Other.

Drybread, K. (2014). Murder and the making of man-subjects in a Brazilian juvenile prison. *American Anthropologist, 116*(4), 752–764.

Dudley, S., & Bargent, J. (2017, January 19). The prison dilemma: Latin America's incubators of organized crime. *InSight Crime*. http://www.insight-crime.org/investigations/prison-dilemma-latin-america-incubators-organized-crime. Last accessed 15 June 2017.

Duno-Gottberg, L. (2019). Spiritual life and the rationalization of violence: The state within the state and evangelical order in a Venezuelan prison. In C. Garces, et al. (Eds.), *Carceral communities: Troubling 21st century prison regimes in Latin America*. Under contract with University of Pennsylvania.

Dwyer, T. (2012). On the internationalization of Brazilian academic sociology. In A. L. Bialakowsky, et al. (Eds.), *Latin American critical thought: Theory and practice* (pp. 84–104). Buenos Aires: CLASCO.

Egelund, A. (2014). Masculinity, sex and survival in Zambian prisons. *Prison Service Journal, 212*, 16–20.

Fassin, D. (2017). *Prison worlds: An ethnography of the carceral condition*. Cambridge: Polity.

Fraternidade Brasileira de Assistência aos Condenados. (2014). *Regulamento Disciplinar APAC*. Resource document. http://www.criminal.mppr.mp.br/arquivos/File/ExecucaoPenal/Mateiral_de_Apoio/APAC/Regulamento_Disciplinar_APACs.pdf. Last accessed 30 December 2017.

Feeley, M., & Simon, J. (1992). The new penology: Notes on the emerging strategy of corrections and its implications. *Criminology, 30*, 449–474.

Feltran, G. S. (2010). The management of violence on the São Paulo periphery: The repertoire of normative apparatus in the PCC era. *Vibrant, 7*(2), 109–134.

Feltran, G. S. (2011). *Fronteiras de tensão: Política e violência nas periferias de São Paulo*. São Paulo: Unesp.

Feltran, G. S. (2012). Governo que produz crime, crime que produz governo: Políticas estatais e políticas criminais na gestão do homicídio em São Paulo. *Revista Brasileira de Segurança Pública, 6*(2), 232–255.

Ferreira, V. A. (2016). *Juntando cacos, resgatando vidas: Valorização humana – base do método APAC e a viagem ao mundo interior do prisioneiro – psicologia do preso*. Belo Horizonte: Gráfica o Lutador.

Filho, J. J. (2013). The rise of the supermax in Brazil. In J. I. Ross (Ed.), *The globalization of supermax prisons* (pp. 129–144). New Brunswick, NJ: Rutgers University.

Filho, J. J. (2017). *Administração Penitenciária: O controle da população carcerária a partir da gestão partilhada entre diretores, judiciário e facções*. Ph.D. thesis, Fundação Getulio Vargas. http://bibliotecadigital.fgv.br/dspace/handle/10438/18432. Last accessed 10 July 2017.

Foley, C. (2012). The Mutirão Carcerário. In C. Foley (Ed.), *Another system is possible: Reforming Brazilian justice* (pp. 13–29). London: International Bar Association.

Foley, C. (2013). *Protecting Brazilians from torture: A manual for judges, prosecutors, public defenders and lawyers* (2nd ed.). Resource document. International Bar Association. http://www.conectas.org/arquivos/editor/files/Relato%CC%81rio%20completo_Tortura%20blindada_Conectas%20Direitos%20Humanos(1).pdf. Last accessed 6 July 2017.

Fonseca, D. S. (2018). Reimagining the sociology of punishment through the global-south: Postcolonial social control and modernization discontents. *Punishment & Society, 20*(1), 8–33.

Fórum Brasileiro de Segurança Pública. (2015). *Anuário brasileiro de segurança pública*. São Paulo: Fórum Brasileiro de Segurança Pública.

Fórum Brasileiro de Segurança Pública. (2016). *Anuário brasileiro de segurança pública*. São Paulo: Fórum Brasileiro de Segurança Pública.

Fórum Brasileiro de Segurança Pública. (2017). *Anuário brasileiro de segurança pública*. São Paulo: Fórum Brasileiro de Segurança Pública.

Foucault, M. (1977). *Discipline and punish*. London: Allen Lane.

França, L. A., Neto, A. S., & Artuso, A. R. (2016). *As marcas do cárcere*. Curitiba: IEA.

Frankl, V. E. (2004). *Man's search for meaning*. London: Rider. Originally published in 1947.

Fundação AVSI. (2012). *Um novo olhar além dos muros: O potencial gestão no fortalecimento das APACs de Minas Gerais*. Belo Horizonte: Fundação AVSI.

Gambetta, D. (2009). *Codes of the underworld: How criminals communicate*. Princeton: Princeton University.

Garces, C. (2010). The cross politics of Ecuador's penal state. *Cultural Anthropology, 25*(3), 459–496.

Garces, C. (2014). Denuding surveillance at the carceral boundary. *South Atlantic Quarterly, 113*(3), 447–473.

Garces, C., Darke, S., Duno-Gottberg, L., & Antillano, A. (Eds.). (2019). *Carceral communities: Troubling 21st century prison regimes in Latin America*. Under contract with University of Pennsylvania.

Garces, C., Martin, T., & Darke, S. (2013). Informal prison dynamics in Africa and Latin America. *Criminal Justice Matters, 91*(1), 26–27.

Garfield, S. (2010). The environment of wartime migration: Labor transfers from the Brazilian Northeast to the Amazon during World War II. *Journal of Social History, 42*(3), 989–1019.

Garland, D. (1990). *Punishment and modern society: A study in social theory*. Oxford: Clarendon.

Garland, D. (2002). *The culture of control: Crime and social order in contemporary society*. Oxford: Oxford University.

Garmany, J. (2009). The embodied state: Governmentality in a Brazilian favela. *Social and Cultural Geography, 10*(7), 721–739.

Gay, R. (2009). From popular movements to drugs gangs to militaries: An anatomy of violence in Rio de Janeiro. In K. Koonings & D. Kruijt (Eds.), *Megacities: The politics of urban exclusion and violence in the global south* (pp. 29–51). London: Zed.

Gay, R. (2015). *Bruno: Conversations with a Brazilian drug dealer*. Durham, NC: Duke University.

Gilinskiy, Y., & Kostjukovsky, Y. (2004). From thievish artel to criminal corporation: The history of organised crime in Russia. In C. Fijnaut & P. Letizia (Eds.), *Organised crime in Europe: Concepts, patterns and control policies in the European Union and beyond*. Dordrecht: Springer.

Gledhill, J. (2015). *The new war on the poor*. London: Zed.

Globo. (2014). *Domingo Espetacular revela rotina de um presídio de segurança maxima*. Television documentary. https://www.youtube.com/watch?v=XAziwMDOCnE. Last accessed 19 January 2018.

Godoi, R. (2015). *Fluxos em cadeias: As prisões em São paulo na virada dos tempos*. Ph.D. thesis, University of São Paulo. http://www.teses.usp.br/teses/

disponiveis/8/8132/tde-05082015-161338/pt-br.php. Last accessed 3 July 2017.

Godoi, R. (2016). Intimacy and power: Body searches and intimate visits in the prison system of São Paulo. *Chámp Penal, XIII.* https://doi.org/10.4000/champpenal.9386.

Goffman, E. (1961). On the characteristics of total institutions. In D. Cressey (Ed.), *The prison: Studies in institutional organization and change.* New York: Holt, Rinehart and Winston.

Goffman, E. (1968). *Asylums: Essays on the situation of mental patients and other inmates.* London: Penguin. Originally published in 1961.

Goifman, K. (2002). Killing time in the Brazilian slammer. *Ethnography, 3*(4), 435–441.

Goldstein, D. M. (2003). *Laughter out of place: Race, class, violence, and sexuality in a Rio shantytown.* Berkeley: University of California.

Gosling, H. J., & Scott, D. (2016). Otherwise than prisons, not prisons otherwise: Therapeutic communities as non-penal real utopias. In D. Scott (Ed.), *Emancipatory politics and praxis: An anthology of essays written for the European Group for the Study of Deviance and Social Control, 2013–2016* (pp. 181–202). London: EG.

Green, P., & Ward, T. (2004). *State crime: Governments, violence and corruption.* London: Sage.

Green, P., & Ward, T. (2009). Violence and the state. In R. Coleman, et al. (Eds.), *State, power, crime* (pp. 116–128). London: Sage.

Gregory, P. R. (2008). *Lenin's brain and other tales from the secret Soviet archives.* Stanford: Hoover International.

Griffin, J. (2017, March 3). Is brutal treatment of young offenders fuelling crime rates in Brazil? *The Guardian.* https://www.theguardian.com/global-development/2017/mar/03/brazil-crime-rates-brutal-treatment-young-offenders. Last accessed 8 March 2017.

Guadalupe, J. L. P. (1994). *Faites y atorrantes: Una etnografía del penal de Lurigancho.* Lima: Centro de Investigaciones Teológicas.

Hadler, O. H., Guareschi, N. M. F., & Scisleski, A. C. C. (2017). Observances: Psychology, public security policies and incarcerated youth. *Pesquisas e Práticas Pscicossociais, 12*(4), e2271.

Harden, B. (2012). *Escape from camp 14.* London: Mantle.

Hathazy, P., & Müller, M. M. (Eds.). (2016). The rebirth of the prison in Latin America: Variations, changes and continuities. *Crime, Law and Social Change, 65*(3), 114–285.

Hall, S. (1991). The local and the global: Globalization and ethnicity. In A. King (Ed.), *Culture, globalization and the world-system* (pp. 19–39). London: Macmillan.

Harvard Law School, & Justiça Global. (2011). *São Paulo sob achaque: Corrupção, crime organizado e violência institucional em maio de 2006.* Resource document. https://harvardhumanrights.files.wordpress.com/2011/05/full-with-cover.pdf. Last accessed 17 July 2017.

Haslam, S. A., & Reicher, S. D. (2012). When prisoners take over the prison: A social psychology of resistance. *Personality and Social Psychology Review, 16*(2), 154–179.

Hawk, D. (2003). *The hidden gulag: Exposing North Korea's prison camps.* Washington, DC: U.S. Committee for Human Rights in North Korea.

Heiskanen, S. (2010). Trends in police-recorded crime. In S. Harrendorf, et al. (Eds.), *International statistics on crime and justice* (pp. 21–48). Helsinki: European Institute for Crime Prevention and Control.

Hess, D. J. (1995). Introduction. In D. J. Hess & R. Matta (Eds.), *The Brazilian puzzle: Culture in the borderlands of the western world* (pp. 1–30). New York: Columbia University.

Hirata, D. V. (2010). *Sobreviver na universidade: Entre o mercado e a vida.* Ph.D. thesis, University of São Paulo. http://www.teses.usp.br/teses/disponiveis/8/8132/tde-03032011-122251/pt-br.php. Last accessed 13 April 2017.

HM Inspectorate of Prisons. (2017). *Life in prison: Living conditions.* Resource document. http://www.justiceinspectorates.gov.uk/hmiprisons/wp-content/uploads/sites/4/2017/10/Findings-paper-Living-conditions-FINAL-.pdf. Last accessed 11 October 2017.

Holsback, L. (2017, September 22). Preso é assassinado em pavilhão de isolamento da Máxima. *Capital News.* http://www.capitalnews.com.br/policia/preso-e-assassinado-em-pavilhao-de-isolamento-da-maxima/309277. Last accessed 4 October 2017.

Holston, J. (2008). *Insurgent citizenship: Disjunctions of democracy and modernity in Brazil.* Princeton: Princeton University.

Huggins, M. K. (1985). *From slavery to vagrancy in Brazil.* New York: Rutgers University.

Huggins, M. K. (2000). Urban violence and police privatization in Brazil: Blended invisibility. *Social Justice, 27*(2), 113–134.

Huggins, M. K., & Mesquita, M. (1995). Scapegoating outsiders: The murders of street youth in modern Brazil. *Policing and Society, 5,* 265–280.

Human Rights Watch. (1998). *Behind bars in Brazil*. New York: Human Rights Watch.
Human Rights Watch. (2009). *Lethal force: Police violence and public security in Rio de Janeiro and São Paulo*. New York: Human Rights Watch.
Human Rights Watch. (2015a). *Brazil: Prison crisis spurs rights reform*. São Paulo: Human Rights Watch.
Human Rights Watch. (2015b). *The state let evil take over: The prison crisis in the Brazilian state of Pernambuco*. New York: Human Rights Watch.
Human Rights Watch. (2016). *Good cops are afraid: The toll of unchecked police violence in Rio de Janeiro*. New York: Human Rights Watch.
Human Rights Watch. (2018). *World Report 2018*. New York: Human Rights Watch.
Hutton, M. (2016). Visiting time: A tale of two prisons. *Probation Journal, 63*(3), 347–361.
INQUEST. (2018). *Deaths in prison*. http://www.inquest.org.uk/statistics/deaths-in-prison. Last accessed 19 January 2018.
Instituto de Defesa do Direito de Defesa. (2018). *Audiências de custódia: Panorama nacional*. Resource document. http://www.iddd.org.br/wp-content/uploads/2017/12/Audiencias-de-Custodia_Panorama-Nacional_Relatorio.pdf. Last accessed 12 January 2018.
Instituto de Segurança Pública. (2016). *Panorama das apreensões de drogas no Rio de Janeiro 2010–2016*. Resource document. http://arquivos.proderj.rj.gov.br/isp_imagens/uploads/RelatorioDrogas2016.pdf. Last accessed 16 February 2017.
Instituto Sou da Paz. (2016). *Panorama dos dados divulgados pela Secretaria da Segurança Pública de São Paulo*. Resource document. http://www.soudapaz.org/noticia/sou-da-paz-lanca-panorama-2015-dos-dados-divulgados-pela-secretaria-da-seguranca-publica-de-sao-paulo. Last accessed 18 May 2016.
International Centre for Prison Studies. (2017). *World prison brief*. http://www.prisonstudies.org/world-prison-brief. Last accessed 21 December 2017.
Inter-American Commission on Human Rights. (2011). *Report on the human rights of persons deprived of liberty in the Americas*. Resource document. http://www.oas.org/en/iachr/pdl/docs/pdf/PPL2011eng.pdf. Last accessed 10 August 2014.
Inter-American Court of Human Rights. (2013, December 30). *Precautionary measure no. 8–13. Matter of persons deprived of liberty at the central penitentiary of Porto Alegre regarding Brazil*. Resource document. https://www.oas.

org/en/iachr/decisions/pdf/Resolution14-13(MC-8-13).pdf. Last accessed 17 April 2017.

Inter-American Court of Human Rights. (2014, May 22). *Order of the Inter-American Court of Human Rights*. Provisional measures regarding Brazil. Matter of the penitentiary complex of Curado. Resource document. http://www.corteidh.or.cr/docs/medidas/curado_se_01_ing.pdf. Last accessed 6 May 2016.

Inter-American Court of Human Rights. (2016). *Medidas provisórias a respeito do brasil. Assunto do compexo penitenciário de Curado de 23 de Novembro 2016*. Resource document. http://www.corteidh.or.cr/docs/medidas/curado_se_04_por.pdf. Last accessed 17 April 2017.

International Bar Association (2010). *1 in 5: The crisis in Brazil's prisons and criminal justice system*. Resource document. http://www.ibanet.org/Article/Detail.aspx?ArticleUid=9a841b12-4a44-41db-a4bd-4433e694e2ba. Last accessed 10 August 2014.

Irwin, J. (1970). *The felon*. Berkeley: University of California.

Iturralde, M. (2012). O governo neoliberal de ainsegurança social na América Latina: Semelhanças e diferenças com o Norte Global. In V. M. Batista (Ed.), *Loïc Wacquant e a questão penal no capitalism neoliberal* (pp. 169–191). Rio de Janeiro: Revan.

Jefferson, A. M. (2010). Prison spaces in Nigeria and Honduras. *Prison Service Journal, 187,* 34–39.

Jefferson, A. M. (2013). The situated production of legitimacy: Perspectives from the global South. In J. Tankebe & A. Liebling (Eds.), *Legitimacy and criminal justice: An international exploration* (pp. 248–266). Oxford: Oxford University.

Jefferson, A. M., & Gaborit, L. S. (2015). *Human rights in prisons: Comparing institutional encounters in Kosovo, Sierra Leone and the Philippines*. London: Palgrave Macmillan.

Jefferson, A. M., & Jensen, S. (Eds.). (2009). *State violence and human rights: State officials in the South*. Abingdon: Routledge-Cavendish.

Jefferson, A. M., & Martin, T. M. (Eds.). (2014). Everyday prison governance in Africa. *Prison Service Journal, 202,* 1–51.

Jefferson, A. M., Feika, M. C., & Jalloh, A. S. (2014). Prison officers in Sierra Leone: Paradoxical puzzles. *Prison Service Journal, 212,* 39–44.

Jefferson, A. M., Garces, C., & Martin, T. M. (Eds.). (2014). Sensing prison climates: Governance, survival and transition. *Focaal, 68*, 55–67.

João do Rio. (1905). *O memento literário*. Paris: Garnier.

Jones, G., & Rodgers, D. (Eds.). (2009). *Youth violence in Latin America: Gangs and juvenile justice in perspective*. New York: Palgrave Macmillan.

Jones, C. R., Narag, R. E., & Morales, R. S. (2015). *Philippine prison gangs: Control or chaos?* (RegNet Research Paper No. 71). Regulatory Institutions Network. Resource document. http://papers.ssrn.com/sol3/papers.cfm?abstract_id=2586912. Last accessed 16 February 2018.

Jozino, J. (2017, November 28). *Marcola pede transferência para cadeia de inimigos do PCC*. https://ponte.org/marcola-pede-transferencia-para-cadeia-de-inimigos-do-pcc. Last accessed 2 January 2018.

Junior, A. S., Assis, F. C., & Gadelha, I. (2017, August 21). Há sinais claros da presença do crime organizado na política, diz Gilmar Mendes. *UOL*. https://noticias.uol.com.br/ultimas-noticias/agencia-estado/2017/08/21/ha-sinais-claros-da-presenca-do-crime-organizado-na-politica-diz-gilmar-mendes.htm?cmpid=copiaecola. Last accessed 22 August 2017.

Justiça Global. (2001). *Massacre at Carandiru*. Resource document. http://www.observatoriodeseguranca.org/files/Carandiru%20Prison%20Massacre.PDF. Last accessed 27 October 2015.

Kaminski, M. M. (2004). *Games prisoners play: The tragic worlds of Polish prisoners*. Princeton: Princeton University.

Karam, M. L. (1996). *A esquerda punitiva. Discursos Sediciosos, 1*(1), 79–92.

Karam, M. L. (2009). Estado penal, novo inimigo interno e totalitarismo. In R. T. Oliveira & V. Mattos (Eds.), *Estudos de execução criminal: Direito e psicologia* (pp. 127–133). Belo Horizonte: Tribunal de Justiça de Minas Gerais.

Karam, M. L. (2015, December 24). Mulheres presas. *Empório do Direito*.http://emporiododireito.com.br/mulheres-presas-por-maria-lucia-karam. *Last accessed 24 June 2017.*

Karam, M. L. (2016). Drogas: Legalizar para garantir direitos humanos fundamentais. *Revista EMERJ, 19*(76), 114–127.

Karam, M. L. (2018, February 22). O uso indevido das forças armadas em atividades de segurança pública. *Cunsultor Jurídico*. https://www.conjur.com.br/2018-fev-22/maria-lucia-karam-uso-indevido-militares-seguranca-publica. Last accessed 28 February 2018.

Karam, M. L., & Saraiva, H. R. (2017). Ouvindo as vozes de carcereiros brasileiros. Unpublished. English version: Hearing the voices of Brazilian correction officers (M. L. Karam, Trans.). *Prison Service Journal, 229*, 48–50.

Karstedt, S. (2001). Comparing cultures, comparing crime: Challenges, prospects and problems for a global criminology. *Crime, Law and Social Change, 36*(3), 285–308.

Keefe, P. R. (2012, June 15). Cocaine incorporated. *The New York Times Magazine*. http://www.nytimes.com/2012/06/17/magazine/how-a-mexican-drug-cartel-makes-its-billions.html. Last accessed 5 July 2017.

Koerner, A. (2006). Punição, disciplina e pensamento penal no brasil do século xix. *Lua Nova, 68*, 205–242.

Koonings, K., & Kruijt, D. (Eds.). (2009). *MegaCities: The politics of urban exclusion and violence in the Global South*. London: Zed.

Lambert, A. (2001). *The mark of Cain*. Documentary film. Russian Federation: Go East.

Lee, M., & Laidler, K. J. (2013). Doing criminology from the periphery: Crime and punishment in Asia. *Theoretical Criminology, 17*(2), 141–157.

Leeds, E. (1996). Cocaine and parallel politics in the Brazilian urban periphery. *Latin American Research Review, 31*, 47–85.

Leeds, E. (2016). *The Brazilian prison system: Challenges and prospects for reform*. WOLA: Advocacy for Human Rights in the Americas. Resource document. http://www.psych.org/edu/other_res/lib_archives/archives/200604.pdf. Last accessed 18 January 2017.

Lemgruber, J. (2005). *The Brazilian prison system: A brief diagnosis*. Eugene, OR: University of Oregon.

Lemgruber, J., & Fernandez, M. (2011). *Impacto da assistência jurídical a presos provisóriso: Um experiment na cidade de Rio de Janeiro*. Rio de Janeiro: Associação pela Reforma Prisional and Centro de Estudos de Segurança e Cidadania. English version: Lemgruber, J., & Fernandez, M. (2012). Legal aid and pre-trial prisoners: An experiment in the city of Rio de Janeiro. In C. Foley, C. (Ed.), *Another system is possible: Reforming Brazilian justice* (pp. 31–53). London: International Bar Association.

Lemgruber, J., Fernandes, M., Cano, I., & Musumeci, L. (2013). *Usos e Abusos da Prisão Provisória no Rio de Janeiro*. Rio de Janeiro: Associação pela Reforma Prisional and Centro de Estudos de Segurança e Cidadania.

Lessing, B. (2016). *Inside out: The challenge of prison-based criminal organizations*. Resource document. The Brookings Institution. https://www.brookings.edu/wp-content/uploads/2016/09/fp_20160927_prison_based_organizations.pdf. Last accessed 19 April 2017.

Levi, P. (1987). *If this is a man*. London: Abacus. Originally published in 1947.

Levi, P. (1989). *The drowned and the saved*. London: Abacus. Originally published in 1986.

Lima, W. S. (1991). *Quatrocentos contra um: Uma história do Comando Vermelho*. Rio de Janeiro: ISER.

Lindegaard, M. R., & Geer, S. (2014). Surviving South African prisons. *Focaal, 68*, 35–54.

Lins e Silva, T., & Rodas, S. (2017, February 21). Mesmo sem provas, acusado de tráfico e furto começa o processo condenado. *Consultor Jurídico.*. http://www.conjur.com.br/2017-fev-20/entrevista-salo-carvalho-professor-direito-penal-ufrj. Last accessed 22 February 2017.

Lourenço, L. C. (2010). Batendo a tranca: Impactos do encarceramento em agentes penitenciários na região metropolitana de Belo Horizonte. *Revista de Estudos de Conflito e Controle Social, 3*(10), 11–31.

Lourenço, L. C., & Almeida, O. L. (2013). "Quem mantém a ordem, quem cria desordem": Gangues prisionais na Bahia. *Tempo Social, 25*(1), 37–59.

Macaulay, F. (2007). Knowledge production, framing and criminal justice reform in Latin America. *Journal of Latin American Studies, 39*, 627–651.

Macaulay, F. (2013). Modes of prison administration, control and governmentality in Latin America: Adoption, adaptation and hybridity. *Conflict, Security and Development, 13*(4), 361–392.

Macaulay, F. (2014). Whose prisoners are these anyway? Church, state and society partnerships and co-production of offender resocialization. In V. Miller & J. Campbell (Eds.), *Transnational penal cultures: New perspectives on discipline, punishment and desistance* (pp. 202–216). London: Routledge.

Macaulay, F. (2015, July 28). Os centros de ressocialização no estado de São Paulo. *JOTA*. https://www.jota.info/especiais/os-centros-de-ressocializacao-no-estado-de-sao-paulo-28072015. Last accessed 28 February 2018.

Macedo, F. (2014, June 9). Gilmar Mendes alerta para infiltração do crime em partidos. *EXAME*. http://exame.abril.com.br/brasil/mendes-alerta-para-infiltracao-do-crime-em-partidos. Last accessed 22 August 2017.

Madeira, L. M. (2008). *Trajetórias de homens infames: Políticas públicas penais e programas de apoio a egressos do sistema penitenciário no brasil*. Ph.D. thesis, Federal University of Rio Grande do Sul. http://www.lume.ufrgs.br/handle/10183/15656. Last accessed 11 February 2018.

Madeiro, C. (2017, January 22). Em Alcaçuz, presos controlam chave de pavilhões e até entrada de comida. *Amigos de Plantão*. http://marechalonline.net/noticia/em-alcacuz-presos-controlam-chave-de-pavilhoes-e-ate-entrada-de-comida/11317. Last accessed 23 January 2017.

Maisonave, F. (2018, January 11). Até mutirão de Cármen Lúcia empaca, e prisões seguem superlotadas no país. *Folha de São Paulo*. http://www1.folha.

uol.com.br/cotidiano/2018/01/1949577-ate-mutirao-de-carmen-lucia-em-paca-e-prisoes-seguem-superlotadas-no-pais.shtml. Last accessed 18 January 2018.

Malby, S. (2010). Homicide. In S. Harrendorf, et al. (Eds.), *International statistics on crime and justice* (pp. 7–20). Helsinki: European Institute for Crime Prevention and Control.

Manso, B. P. (2012). *Crescimento e queda dos homicídios em SP entre 1960 e 2010: Uma análise dos mecanismos da escolha homicida e das carreiras no crime.* Ph.D. thesis, University of São Paulo. http://www.teses.usp.br/teses/disponiveis/8/8131/tde-12122012-105928/pt-br.php. Last accessed 13 April 2017.

Manso, B. P. (2016). *Homicide in São Paulo: An examination of trends from 1960–2010.* Cham: Springer.

Manso, B. P., & Dias, C. N. (2017). PCC, sistema prisional e gestão do novo mundo do crime no Brasil. *Revista Brasileira de Segurança Pública, 11*(2), 10–29.

Marcis, F. (2014). Everyday prison governance in Abidjan, Ivory Coast. *Prison Service Journal, 212,* 11–15.

Marquart, J., & Roebeck, J. (1985). Prison guards and "snitches". *British Journal of Criminology, 25*(3), 217–233.

Marques, A. (2010a, August 1–4). *Um "debate" sobre o estado de "isento" no Primeiro Comando da Capital.* Paper presented at the 27th Brazilian Anthropology Reunion. Unpublished.

Marques, A. (2010b). "Liderança", "proceder" e "igualdade": Uma etnografia das relações políticas no Primeiro Comando da Capital. *Etnográfica, 14*(2), 311–335.

Marques, A. (2014). *Crime e proceder: Um experimento antropológico.* São Paulo: Alameda.

Martin, T. M. (2014a). The importation of human rights by Uganda prison staff. *Prison Service Journal, 212,* 45–51.

Martin, T. M. (2014b). Reasonable caning and the embrace of human rights in Uganda. *Focaal, 68,* 68–82.

Mascareño, A., & Chernilo, D. (2009). Obstacles and perspectives of Latin American sociology: Normative universalism and functional differentiation. *Soziale Systeme, 15*(1), 72–96.

Mathiesen, T. (1965). *The defences of the weak: A study of a Norwegian correctional institution.* London: Tavistock.

Mathiesen, T. (2012). Scandinavian exceptionalism in penal matters: Reality or wishful thinking? In T. Ugelvik & J. Dullum (Eds.), *Penal exceptionalism? Nordic prison policy and practice* (pp. 13–37). London: Routledge.

Mattos, V. (2010). *De uniforme diferente: O livro das agentes*. Belo Horizonte: Fundação MDC.

McNair, J., & Baylis, W. (2010). *Prisoners their own warders*. Gloucester: Dodo. Originally published in 1899.

McWhorter, W. (1981). *Inmate society: Legs, half-pants and gunmen: A study of inmate guards*. Saratoga, CA: Century Twenty One.

Mecanismo Nacional de Prevenção e Combate à Tortura. (2015). *Relatório de visita ao presidio central de Porto Alegre, Rio Grande do Sul*. http://www.sdh.gov.br/sobre/participacao-social/comite-nacional-de-prevencao-e-combate-a-tortura/representantes/presidio-central-de-porto-alegre. Last accessed 5 September 2017.

Mecanismo Nacional de Prevenção e Combate à Tortura. (2016). *Relatório devisita a unidades prisionais de Manaus – Amazonas*. Resource document. http://www.sdh.gov.br/sobre/participacao-social/sistema-nacional-de-prevencao-e-combate-a-tortura-snpct/mecanismo/Unidades_Prisionais_de_Manaus___AM.pdf. Last accessed 5 September 2017.

Mecanismo Nacional de Prevenção e Combate à Tortura. (2017). *Relatório anual 2016–2017*. Resource document. http://www.sdh.gov.br/noticias/pdf/mecanismo-nacional-de-prevencao-e-combate-a-tortura-lanca-relatorio-anual-2016-2017-2. Last accessed 28 June 2017.

Melo, J. G., & Rodrigues, R. (2017). Notícias de uma massacre anunciado e em andamento: O poder de matar e deixar morrer à luz do massacre no presidio de Alcaçus, RN. *Revista Brasileira de Segurança Pública, 11*(2), 48–62.

Mendes, L. A. (2005). *Às cegas*. São Paulo: Companhia das Letras.

Mendes, L. A. (2009). *Memórias de um sobrevivente*. São Paulo: Companhia de Bolso.

Mendes, L. A. (2012). *Cela forte*. São Paulo: Global.

Mendes, L. A. (2015). *Confissões de um homen livre*. São Paulo: Companhia das Letras.

Mendonça, M. (2017, May 22). Três fogem do Presídio de Segurança Máxima da Capital. *Correio do Estado*. http://www.correiodoestado.com.br/cidades/campo-grande/tres-fogem-do-presidio-de-seguranca-da-maxima-da-capital/304389. Last accessed 21 June 2017.

Menegat, M. (2012). *Estudos sobre ruínas*. Rio de Janeiro: Instituto Carioca de Criminologia.

Ministério da Justiça. (2005). *Diretrizes básicas para construção, ampliação e reforma de estabelecimentos penais*. Resource document. http://www.justica.gov.br/seus-direitos/politica-penal/transparencia-institucional/biblioteca-on-line-2/biblioteca-on-line-manuais/manual-diretrizes-basicas-construcao-2005.pdf. Last accessed 15 December 2015.

Ministério da Justiça. (2010). *Sistema integrado de informações penitenciárias: Rio de Janeiro, referência 6/2010*. Brasília: Ministério da Justiça.

Ministério da Justiça. (2012). *Sistema integrado de informações penitenciárias: Todas ufs, referência 6/2012*. Brasília: Ministério da Justiça.

Ministério da Justiça. (2015). *Levantamento nacional de informações penitenciárias infopen, junho de 2014*. Resource document. http://www.justica.gov.br/seus-direitos/politica-penal/relatorio-depen-versao-web.pdf. Last accessed 15 December 2015.

Ministério da Justiça. (2016a). *Implementação das audiências de custódia no brasil: análise de experiências e recomendações de aprimoramento*. Resource document. http://www.justica.gov.br/seus-direitos/politica-penal/politicas-2/alternativas-penais-1/arquivos/implementacao-das-audiencias-de-custodia-no-brasil-analise-de-experiencias-e-recomendacoes-de-aprimoramento-1.pdf. Last accessed 11 October 2016.

Ministério da Justiça. (2016b). *Levantamento nacional de informações penitenciárias infopen, dezembro de 2014*. Resource document. http://www.justica.gov.br/seus-direitos/politica-penal/infopen_dez14.pdf. Last accessed 24 October 2016.

Ministry of Justice. (2017a). *National Offender Management Service workforce statistics bulletin, 30 September 2016*. Resource document. https://www.gov.uk/government/uploads/system/uploads/attachment_data/file/567178/noms-workforce-statistics-30-September-2016.pdf. Last accessed 22 March 2017.

Ministry of Justice. (2017b). *Offender management statistics quarterly: October to December 2016*. Resource document. https://www.gov.uk/government/statistics/offender-management-statistics-quarterly-october-to-december-2016. Last accessed 4 June 2017.

Ministry of Justice. (2017c). *Safety in custody quarterly bulletin: December 2016*. Resource document. https://www.gov.uk/government/statistics/safety-in-custody-quarterly-update-to-december-2016--2. Last accessed 4 June 2017.

Ministério da Justiça e Cidadania. (2017). *Plano nacional de segurança pública*. Resource document. http://www.justica.gov.br/noticias/plano-nacional-de-seguranca-preve-integracao-entre-poder-publico-e-sociedade/pnsp-06jan17.pdf. Last accessed 5 March 2017.

Ministério da Justiça e Segurança Pública. (2017). *Levantamento nacional de informações penitenciárias: Atualização - Junho de 2016*. Resource document. http://www.justica.gov.br/news/ha-726-712-pessoas-presas-no-brasil/relatorio_2016_junho.pdf. Last accessed 21 December 2017.

Ministério Público do Ceará. (2009). *Justiça interdita Colônia Agropastoril do Amanari*. http://www.mpce.mp.br/servicos/asscom/releases.asp?icodigo=893. Last accessed 7 January 2016.

Miraglia, P., & Salla, F. (2008). O PCC e a gestão dos presídios em São Paulo: Entrevista com Nagashi Furukawa. *Novos Estudos, 80*, 21–41.

Misse, M. (2007). Illegal markets, protection rackets and organized crime in Rio de Janeiro. *Estudos Avançados, 61*, 139–157.

Misse, M., & Vargas, J. D. (2010). Drug use and trafficking in Rio de Janeiro. *Vibrant, 7*(2), 88–108.

Moore, H. (2017). *Imprisonment and (un)relatedness in northeast Brazil*. Ph.D. thesis, University of Toronto.

Moore, H. (2019). The Mata Escura penal compound: An analysis of the prison-neighbourhood nexus in Northeast Brazil. In C. Garces, et al. (Eds.), *Carceral communities: Troubling 21st Century prison regimes in Latin America*. Under contract with University of Pennsylvania.

Moraes, P. R. B. (2005). *Punição, encarceramento e construção de identidade professional entre agents penitenciários*. São Paulo: Instituto Brasileiro de Ciências Criminais.

Morelle, M. (2014). Power, control and money in prison: The Informal Governance of the Yaoundé Central Prison. *Prison Service Journal, 212*, 21–26.

Muñoz, C. (2015, October 20). A privatização perversa das prisões. *Folha de São Paulo*. http://www1.folha.uol.com.br/opiniao/2015/10/1695836-a-privatizacao-perversa-das-prisoes.shtml. Last accessed 3 February 2017.

Narag, R. E., & Jones, C. R. (2016). Understanding prison management in the Philippines: A case for shared governance. *Prison Journal, 97*(1), 3–26.

Neder, G. (1996). *Absolutismo e punição*. Discursos Sediciosos, *1*(1), 191–206.

Negrelli, A. M. (2006). *Suicídio no sistema carcerário: Análise a partir do perfil biopsicossocial nas instituições prisionais no Rio Grande do Sul*. Master's degree dissertation, Pontifical Catholic University, Rio Grande do Sul. http://tede.pucrs.br/tde_busca/arquivo.php?codArquivo=510. Last accessed 27 June 2017.

Nelken, D. (2010). *Comparative criminal justice: Making sense of difference*. London: Sage.

Nelken, D. (2012). Comparing criminal justice. In M. Maguire, et al. (Eds.), *The Oxford handbook of criminology* (6th edn.) (pp. 138–157). Oxford: Oxford University.

Nunes, R. M. (2015). The politics of sentencing reform in Brazil: Autonomous bureaucrats, constrained politicians and gradual policy change. *Journal of Latin American Studies, 47*(1), 121–148.

Núñez, J., & Fleetwood, J. (2017). The blind panopticon: Prisoners' subversion of the prison in Ecuador, 1875–2014. *Prison Service Journal, 229*, 35–39.

O'Day, P., & O'Connor, T. (2013). Supermaxes south of the border. In J. I. Ross (Ed.), *The globalization of supermax prisons* (pp. 35–48). New Brunswick, NJ: Rutgers University.

O'Donnell, G. (1998). *Polyarchies and the (un)rule of law in Latin America*. Resource document. Kellogg Institute. http://kellogg.nd.edu/publications/workingpapers/WPS/254.pdf. Last accessed 20 April 2017.

Oldoni, F. (2001). As relações de poder entre os detentos do presídio público de Itajaí (A morte como exteriorizaçaõ maior deste poder). *Novos Estudos Jurídicos, 13*, 115–130.

Oliveira, H. (2017, September 5). *Rafael Braga com tuberculose: A contradição da lei antidrogas que zela pela saúde pública. Justificando.* https://portal-justificando.jusbrasil.com.br/noticias/495868237/rafael-braga-com-tuberculose-a-contradicao-da-lei-antidrogas-que-zela-pela-saude-publica. Last accessed 7 September 2017.

Olmo, R. (1981). *America latina y su criminologia*. Delegación Coyoacán: Siglo Ventiuno.

Olmo, R. (1999). The development of criminology in Latin America. *Social Justice, 26*(2), 19–45.

Ottoboni, M. (2006). *Vamos matar o criminoso? Método APAC*. São Paulo: Paulinas.

Padilha, J., & Prado, M. (2007). *Tropa de elite*. Film. Brazil: Zazen.

Pakes, F. (2015). *Comparative criminal justice*. Cullompton: Willan.

Pastoral Carcerária. (2016). *Tortura em tempos de encarceramento em massa*. Resource document. http://carceraria.org.br/wp-content/uploads/2016/10/tortura_web.pdf. Last accessed 22 November 2016.

Pastoral Carcerária (2017a, December 21). Como uma nomeação pode colocar as audiências de custódia em xeque. http://carceraria.org.br/como-uma-nomeacao-pode-colocar-as-audiencias-de-custodia-em-xeque.html. Last accessed 18 January 2018.

Pastoral Carcerária (2017b, August 17). *Pastoral Carcerária pede MP apure suicídios em presídio feminino em SP.* http://carceraria.org.br/pastoral-carceraria-pede-que-mp-apure-suicidios-em-presidio-feminino.html. Last accessed 5 September 2017.

Pastoral Carcerária/PE, Serviço Ecumênico de Militância nas Prisões, Pastoral Carcerária Nacional, Justiça Global and Harvard Law School. (2014). *4⁰ contrainforme dos representantes dos beneficiários, MC 199-11: Pessoas privadas da liberdade no Presídio Professor Aníbal Bruno e outros, estado de Pernambuco, Brasil.* Resource document. http://arquivoanibal.weebly.com/uploads/4/7/4/9/47496497/19_-_2014_02_18_-_4o_contrainforme_dos_representantes_-_mc_199-11_-pub.pdf. Last accessed 16 December 2015.

Pavarini, M., & Giamberardino, A. (2011). *Teoria da pena e execução penal: Uma introdução crítica.* Rio de Janeiro: Lumen Juris.

Penglase, B. (2009). States of insecurity: Everyday emergencies, public secrets, and drug trafficker power in a Brazilian favela. *PoLAR: Political and Legal Anthropology Review, 32,* 47–63.

Penglase, B. (2010). The owner of the hill: Masculinity and drug-trafficking in Rio de Janeiro, Brazil. *Journal of Latin American and Caribbean Anthropology, 15*(2), 317–337.

Perlman, J. E. (2009). Megacity's violence and its consequences in Rio de Janeiro. In K. Koonings & D. Kruijt (Eds.), *Megacities: The politics of urban exclusion and violence in the global south* (pp. 52–68). London: Zed.

Perlman, J. E. (2010). *Favela: Four decades of living on the edge in Rio de Janeiro.* New York: Oxford University.

Pereira, A. (1997). *Elitist liberalism: Citizenship, state violence, and the rule of law in Brazil.* Paper presented at the XX International Congress of the Latin American Studies Association, April, Guadalajara, Mexico.

Pereira, J. (2015). Narrativas silenciadas: Memórias que a morte não apaga. In M. R. Machado & M. R. A. Machado (Eds.), *Carandiru não é coisa do passado* (pp. 159–178). FGV Direito SP.

Peres, M. F. T., Almeida, J. F., Vicentin, D., Cerda, M., Cardia, N., & Adorno, S. (2011). Queda dos homicídios no Município de São Paulo: Uma análise exploratória de possíveis condicionantes. *Revista Brasileira Epidemiol, 14*(4), 709–721.

Pessoa, G. T. A. (2014a, August 18). *Casa de Correção.* http://linux.an.gov.br/mapa/?p=6333. Last accessed 9 March 2017.

Pessoa, G. T. A. (2014b, December 15). *Casa de Detenção.* http://linux.an.gov.br/mapa/?p=7400. Last accessed 9 March 2017.

Phillips, D. (2015, June 16). Brazil divided over how to deal with its teenage criminals. *The Guardian.* https://www.theguardian.com/world/2015/jun/16/brazil-teenage-criminals-juvenile-rehabilitation. Last accessed 8 March 2017.

Piacentini, L. (2004). *Surviving Russian prisons: Punishment, economy and politics in transition.* Cullompton: Willan.

Postema, M., Cavallaro, J., & Nagra, R. (2017). Advancing security and human rights by the controlled organisation of inmates. *Prison Service Journal, 229,* 57–62.

Prado Júnior, C. (1961). *Formação do brasil contemporâneo (colônia)* (6th ed.). São Paulo: Editôra Brasiliense.

Priestly, P. (1985). *Victorian prison lives: English prison biography 1830–1914.* London: Methuen.

Prison Reform Trust. (n.d.). *Bromley briefings prison fact file: Autumn 2016.* Resource document. http://www.prisonreformtrust.org.uk/Portals/0/Documents/Bromley%20Briefings/Autumn%202016%20Factfile.pdf. Last accessed 21 March 2017.

Prison Reform Trust, & INQUEST. (2012). *Fatally flawed: Has the state learned lessons from the deaths of children and young people in prison?* Resource document. http://inquest.org.uk/pdf/reports/Fatally_Flawed.pdf. Last accessed 17 August 2017.

Ramalho, J. R. (2002). *Mundo do crime: A ordem pelo avesso* (3rd ed.). Rio de Janeiro: Graal.

Ramos, G. (2015). *Memórias do Cárcere* (49th ed.). Rio de Janeiro: Record.

Ramos, H. (2003). *Pavilhão 9: Paixão e morte no Carandiru* (4th ed.). Paris: Gallimard.

Ramsay, G. (2014, June 27). A closer look at Brazil-bound drug networks. *Insight Crime.* http://www.insightcrime.org/news-analysis/a-closer-look-at-brazil-bound-drug-networks. Last accessed 6 July 2017.

Rap, A., & Zeni, B. (2002). *Sobrevivente André du Rap (do Massacre do Carandiru).* São Paulo: Labortexto.

Reis, V. (2017, August 30). MP analisa denúncia de 'suicídios em série' em penitenciária feminina de SP. *O globo.* http://g1.globo.com/sao-paulo/noticia/mp-analisa-denuncia-de-suicidios-em-serie-em-penitenciaria-feminina-de-sp.ghtml#. Last accessed 5 September 2017.

Ribeiro, L. (2017, May 17). Agente penitenciário encontra detento morto em presídio de segurança maxima. *Capital news.* http://www.capitalnews.com.br/policia/agente-penitenciario-encontra-detento-morto-em-presidio-de-seguranca-maxima/304806. Last accessed 21 June 2017.

Ribeiro, A., Corrêa, H., & Fonseca, H. (2016, October 25). As rebeliões em presídios são um aviso: A selvageria está à solta. *ÉPOCA*. http://epoca.globo.com/tempo/noticia/2016/10/o-crime-esta-em-guerra-maiores-faccoes-brasileiras-romperam.html. Last accessed 28 February 2017.

Rivera, L. G. (2010). Discipline and punish? Youth gangs' response to 'zero tolerance' policies in Honduras. *Bulletin of Latin American Research, 29*(4), 492–504.

Roig, R. D. E. (2005). *Direito e prática histórica da execução penal no brasil*. Rio de Janeiro: Revan.

Rolim, M. (2007). Prisão e ideologia: Limites e possibilidades para a reforma prisional no brasil. In S. Carvalho (Ed.), *Crítica à execução penal* (2nd ed., pp. 77–115). Rio de Janeiro: Lumen Juris.

Rosa, M. C. (2014). Theories of the South: Limits and perspectives of an emergent movement in social sciences. *Current Sociology, 62*(6), 851–867.

Ross, J. I. (2013). Invention of the American supermax prison. In J. I. Ross (Ed.), *The globalization of supermax prisons* (pp. 10–24). New Brunswick, NJ: Rutgers University.

Ross, J. I., Darke, S., Aresti, A., Newbold, G., & Earle, R. (2014). Developing convict criminology beyond North America. *International Criminal Justice Review, 24*(2), 121–133.

Said, E. (1978). *Orientalism*. New York: Pantheon.

Sager, T., & Beto, R. (2016). *Central*. Documentary film. Brazil: Panda.

Salla, F. (2006). As rebeliões nas prisões: Novos significados a partir da experiência Brasileira. *Sociologias, 8*(16), 274–307.

Salla, F. (2007). De Montoro a Lembro: As políticas penitenciárias em São Paulo. *Revista Brasileira de Segurança Pública, 1*(1), 72–90.

Salla, F. (2015). Rebelião na Ilha Anchieta em 1952 e a primeira grande crise na segurança pública paulista. *DILEMAS, 8*(4), 633–658.

Salla, F. (2017). Vigiar e punir e os estudos prisionais no Brasil. *DILEMAS*, special edition no. 2, 29–43.

Salla, F., Gauto, M., & Alvarez, M. C. (2006). A contribuição de David Garland: A sociologia da punição. *Tempo Social, 15*(1), 329–350.

Salla, F., & Ballesteros, P. (2008). *Democracy, human rights and prison conditions in South America*. Paper prepared for the Research Project of Geneva Academy of International Humanitarian Law and Human Rights. Resource document. University of São Paulo. http://www.nevusp.org/downloads/down227.pdf. Last accessed 16 February 2017.

Salla, F., Ballesteros, P., Mavila, O., Mercado, F., Litvachky, P., & Museri, A. (2009). *Democracy, human rights and prison conditions in South America*. São Paulo: University of São Paulo.

Salla, F., Jesus, M. G. M., & Rocha, T. T. (2012, October). Relato de uma pesquisa sobre a Lei 11.343/2006. *Boletim IBCCRIM, 20*, 10–11.

Salvadori, F., & Dias, C. N. (2016, June 3). Quem disse que a bandidagem não tolera estuprador? *Ponte*. https://ponte.org/crime-organizado-estupro. Last accessed 15 June 2017.

Salvatore, R. D. (1996). Penitentiaries, visions of class, and export economies: Brazil and Argentina compared. In R. D. Salvatore & C. Aguirre (Eds.), *The birth of the penitentiary in Latin America* (pp. 194–223). Austin: University of Texas.

Salvatore, R. D., & Aguirre, C. (Eds.). (1996). The birth of the penitentiary in Latin America: Towards an interpretive social history of prisons. In R. D. Salvatore & C. Aguirre (Eds.), *The birth of the penitentiary in Latin America* (pp. 1–43). Austin: University of Texas.

Santos, B. S. (2002). *Towards a new legal common sense: Law, globalization and emancipation* (2nd ed.). London: Lexis Nexis Butterworths.

Santos, B. S. (2007). Human rights as emancipatory script? Cultural and political conditions. In B. S. Santos (Ed.), *Another knowledge is possible: Beyond northern epistemologies* (pp. 3–40). London: Verso.

Santos, B. S., Nunes, J. A., & Meneses, M. P. (2007). Opening up the canon of knowledge and recognition of difference. In B. S. Santos (Ed.), *Another knowledge is possible: Beyond northern epistemologies* (pp. ix–lxii). London: Verso.

Santos, J. V. T. (2010). The dialogue between criminology and the south's sociology of violence: The policing crisis and alternatives. In M. Burawoy, et al. (Eds.), *Facing an unequal world: Challenges for a global sociology* (pp. 105–125). Taiwan: Institute of Sociology, Academia Sinica.

Santos, J. V. T. (2012). Contemporary Latin American sociology and the challenges for an international dialogue. In A. L. Bialakowsky, et al. (Eds.), *Latin American critical thought: Theory and practice* (pp. 237–271). Buenos Aires: CLASCO.

Saviano, R. (2015). *Zero, zero, zero*. London: Allen Lane.

Scott, D., & Codd, H. (2010). *Controversial issues in prison*. Maidenhead: Open University.

Scott, S., & Gosling, H. J. (2015). Thinking beyond the punitive rationale: Promoting therapeutic communities as a radical alternative to prison. *Howard Journal of Criminal Justice, 54*(4), 397–402.

Secretaria de Administração Penitenciária do Estado de São Paulo. (n.d.). *168 unidades prisionais*. http://www.sap.sp.gov.br/uni-prisionais/cdp.html. Last accessed 12 January 2016.

Secretaria de Administração Penitenciária do Estado de São Paulo. (2015). *Levantamento presos X delitos*. Resource document. http://www.sap.sp.gov.br/download_files/pdf_files/levantamento_presosxdelitos.pdf. Last accessed 19 November 2015.

Semer, M. (2014). A serpente que só pica os pés descalços: Desigualdade e direito penal. In R. C. Junior (Ed.), *Criminologia do cotidiano* (pp. 185–199). Rio de Janeiro: Lumens Juris.

Sepúlveda, C., & Pojomovsky, I. (2019). Carceral order, mediation and representation: Fiction and ethnography in a Venezuelan prison. In C. Garces, et al. (Eds.), *Carceral communities: Troubling 21st century prison regimes in Latin America*. Under contract with University of Pennsylvania.

Shimizu, B. (2011). *Solidariedade e grefarismo nas facções criminosas: Um estudo criminológico à luz da psicologia das massas*. São Paulo: Instituto Brasileiro de Ciências Criminais.

Shimizu, B., & Cacicedo, P. (2016). Crítica à estipulação de critérios quantitativos objetivos para diferenciação entre traficantes e usuários de drogas: Reflexões a partir da perversidade do sistema penal em uma realidade margina. *Boletim IBCCRIM, 24*, 8–9.

Silva, A. M. C. (2008a). *Nos braços da lei: O uso da violência negociada no interior das prisões*. Rio de Janeiro: E+A.

Silva, A. M. C. (2008b). A ressocialização da fé: A estigmatização das religiões afro-brasileiras no sistema penal carioca. In E. Albuquerque (Ed.), *Anais do X simpósio da Associação Brasileira de História das Religiões*. http://www.abhr.org.br/?page_id=57. Last accessed 28 December 2012.

Silva, A. M. C. (2011). *Participo que... Desvelando a punição intramuros*. Rio de Janeiro: Publit.

Silva, E. S. (2017). *A ocupação da Maré pelo exército brasileiro: Percepção de moradores sobre a ocupação das forças armadas na Maré*. Rio de Janeiro: Redes da Maré.

Singleton, N., Meltzer, H., & Gatward, R. (1998). *Psychiatric morbidity among prisoners in England and Wales*. London: Office for National Statistics.

Singleton, N., Bumpstead, R., O'Brien, M., Lee, A., & Meltzer, H. (2000). *Psychiatric morbidity among adults living in private households, 2000.* London: Office for National Statistics.

Skarbek, D. (2010). Self-governance in San Pedro prison. *Independent Review, 14*(2), 569–585.

Skarbek, D. (2014). *The social order of the underworld: How prison gangs govern the American penal system.* New York: Oxford University.

Skarbek, D. (2016). Covenants without the sword? Comparing prison self-governance globally. *American Political Science Review, 110*(4), 845–862.

Soares, L. E. (2012). *Tudo ou nada: A história do brasileiro preso em Londres por associação ao tráfico de duas toneladas de cocaína.* Rio de Janeiro: Nova Fronteira.

Solzhenitsyn, A. (1963). *One day in the life of Ivan Denisovich.* London: Penguin.

Solzhenitsyn, A. (1975). *The gulag archipelago* (Vol. 2). New York: Harper and Row.

Souza, F. (2017, September 1). Polícia diz que agentes facilitaram massacre de presos em Manaus e indicia 210 detentos. *BBC.* http://www.bbc.com/portuguese/brasil-41118908. Last accessed 6 September 2017.

Sozzo, M. (2006). 'Traduttore traditore': Tradución, importación cultural e historia del presente de la criminología en América Latina. *Cuadernos de Doctrina y Jusrisprudencia Penal, 7,* 354–430.

Sozzo, M. (Ed.). (2017). *Pós-neoliberalismo e penalidade na américa do sul.* São Paulo: Fundação Perseu Abramo.

Sparks, R., Bottoms, A., & Hay, W. (1996). *Prisons and the problem of order.* Oxford: Clarendon.

Steinberg, G., & Sacramento, P. (2004). *O prisioneiro da grade de ferro.* Documentary film. Brazil: California Filmes.

Steinberg, J. (2004). *The number: One man's search for identity in the cape underworld and prison gangs.* Cape Town: Jonathan Ball.

Steinberg, J. (2016). How well does theory travel? David Garland in the global south. *Howard Journal of Criminal Justice, 55*(4), 514–531.

Stern, V. (2006). *Creating criminals: Prisons and people in a market society.* London: Zed Books.

Supervielle, M. (2012). Revitalizing the sociological view in Latin America. In M. Burawoy, et al. (Eds.), *Facing an unequal world: Challenges for a global sociology* (pp. 63–84). Taiwan: Institute of Sociology, Academia Sinica.

Süssekind, E. (2014). *Estratégias de sobrevivência e de convivência nas prisões do Rio de Janeiro*. Ph.D. thesis, Fundação Getulio Vargas. http://bibliotecadigital.fgv.br/dspace/handle/10438/13390. Last accessed 15 June 2017.

Sykes, G. M. (1956). The corruption of authority and rehabilitation. *Social Forces, 34*(3), 257–262.

Sykes, G. M. (1958). *The society of captives*. Princeton: Princeton University.

Teixeira, A., Salla, F. A., & Marinho, M. G. S. M. C. (2016). Vadiagem e prisões correcionais em São Paulo: Mecanismos de controle no firmamento da República. *Estudos Históricos, 29*(58), 381–400.

Tertsakian, C. (2014). 'Some prisons are prisons, and others are like hell': Prison life in Rwanda in the ten years after the genocide. *Prison Service Journal, 212*, 4–10.

Thomas, J. (1972). *The English prison officer since 1850: A study in conflict*. London: Routledge and Kegan Paul.

Travis, A. (2017, July 4). Prolonged solitary confinement of boy at Feltham YOI 'breached human rights'. *The Guardian*. https://www.theguardian.com/society/2017/jul/04/feltham-yoi-high-court-human-rights. Last accessed 5 July 2017.

Tritton, P., & Fleetwood, J. (2017). An insider's view of prison reform in Ecuador. *Prison Service Journal, 229*, 40–45.

Tuhiwai Smith, L. (2012). *Decolonizing methodologies: Research and indigenous People* (2nd ed.). London: Zed.

Ungar, M. (2003). Prisons and politics in contemporary Latin America. *Human Rights Quarterly, 25*(4), 909–934.

Ungar, M., & Magaloni, A. L. (2009). Latin America's prisons: A crisis of criminal policy and democratic rule. In M. Bergman & L. Whitehead (Eds.), *Criminality, public security, and the challenge to democracy in Latin America* (pp. 223–249). Notre Dame: University of Notre Dame.

Ugelvik, T. (2016). Prisons as welfare institutions? Punishment and the Nordic model. In Y. Jewkes, et al. (Eds.), *Handbook on prisons* (2nd ed., pp. 388–402). Abington: Routledge.

United Nations. (2008). *Report on Brazil*. CAT/C/39/2. Resource document. http://www2.ohchr.org/english/bodies/cat/docs/AdvanceVersions/cat.c.39.2.doc. Last accessed 27 February 2018.

United Nations. (2012). *Report on the visit of the subcommittee on prevention of torture and other cruel, inhuman or degrading treatment or punishment to Brazil*. CAT/OP/BRA/1. Resource document. http://www2.ohchr.org/

english/bodies/cat/opcat/docs/CAT-OP-BRA-1_en.pdf. Last accessed 27 February 2018.
United Nations (2014). *Report of the working group on arbitrary detention: Mission to Brazil*. A/HRC/27/48/Add.3. Resource document. http://www.ohchr.org/EN/HRBodies/HRC/RegularSessions/Session27/Documents/A_HRC_27_48_Add_3_ENG.doc. Last accessed 27 February 2018.
United Nations. (2016). *United Nations standard minimum rules for the treatment of prisoners (the Nelson Mandela rules)*. A/RES/70/175. Resource document. https://cdn.penalreform.org/wp-content/uploads/1957/06/ENG.pdf. Last accessed 27 February 2018.
Valois, L. C. (2016). *O direito penal da guerra às drogas*. Belo Horizonte: D'Plácido.
Valois, L. C., & Macaulay, F. (2017). O Judiciário e a crise do sistema penitenciário: Luís Carlos Valois, entrevistado por Fiona Macaulay. *Revista Brasileira de Segurança Pública, 11*(2), 78–87.
Velasco, C., & Caesar, G. (2018, February 22). Brasil tem média de 7 presos por agente penitenciário; 19 estados descumprem limite recomendado. *O globo*. https://g1.globo.com/monitor-da-violencia/noticia/brasil-tem-media-de-7-presos-por-agente-penitenciario-19-estados-descumprem-limite-recomendado.ghtml. Last accessed 25 February 2018.
Varella, D. (2004). Carandiru. *Lancet, 364,* 32–33.
Varella, D. (2008). *Estação Carandiru*. São Paulo: Companhia das Letras. English edition: Varella, D. (2012). *Lockdown: Inside Brazil's most violent prison* (A. Entrekin, Trans.). London: Simon & Schuster.
Varella, D. (2012). *Carcereiros*. São Paulo: Companhia das Letras.
Varella, D. (2017). *Prisioneiras*. São Paulo: Companhia das Letras.
Vicentin, M. C. G. (2005). *A vida em rebelião: Jovens em conflito com a lei*. São Paulo: HUCITEC.
Vicentin, M. C. G. (2011). Corpos em rebelião e o sofrimento-resistência: Adolescentes em conflito com a lei. *Tempo Social, 23*(1), 97–113.
Wacquant, L. (2003). Towards a dictatorship over the poor: Notes on the penalization of poverty in Brazil. *Punishment and Society, 5*(2), 197–205.
Wacquant, L. (2008). The militarization of urban marginality: Lessons from the Brazilian metropolis. *International Political Sociology, 2,* 56–74.
Waldram, J. (1998). Anthropology in prison: Negotiating consent and accountability with a "captured population". *Human Organization, 57*(2), 238–244.

Waldram, J. (2009). Challenges of prison ethnography. *Anthropology News, 50*(1), 4–5.

Walmsley, R. (1999). *World prison population list.* London: Home Office.

Walmsley, R. (2010). Trends in world prison population. In S. Harrendorf, et al. (Eds.), *International statistics on crime and justice* (pp. 153–166). Helsinki: European Institute for Crime Prevention and Control.

Walmsley, R. (2015). *World prison population list* (11th ed.). London: International Centre for Prison Studies.

Weegels, J. (2017). Prisoner self-governance and survival in a Nicaraguan city police jail. *Prison Service Journal, 229,* 15–19.

Weegels, J. (2019). The 'cemetery of the living': An exploration of disposal, (in)visibility, and change-of-attitude in Nicaraguan prison. In C. Garces, et al. (Eds.), *Carceral communities: Troubling 21st century prison regimes in Latin America.* Under contract with University of Pennsylvania.

Williams, P., & Wu, Y. (2004). *The great wall of confinement: The Chinese prison camp through contemporary fiction and reportage.* Berkeley: University of California.

Willis, G. D. (2009). Deadly symbiosis? The PCC, the state, and the institutionalization of violence in São Paulo, Brazil. In G. Jones & D. Rodgers (Eds.), *Youth violence in Latin America: Gangs and juvenile justice in perspective* (pp. 167–182). New York: Palgrave Macmillan.

Willis, G. D. (2015). *The killing consensus: Police, organized crime, and the regulation of life and death in urban Brazil.* Oakland: University of California.

Willis, G. D. (2016). Before the body count: Homicide statistics and everyday security in Latin America. *Journal of Latin American Studies, 49,* 29–54.

Willys, J. (2015). Os corpos do delito e os delitos do corpo. In M. R. Machado & M. R. A. Machado (Eds.), *Carandiru não é coisa do passado* (pp. 115–133). FGV Direito SP.

Wintin, T., & Brown, I. (2005). Colonial Burma's prison: Continuity with its pre-colonial past? *IIAS Newsletter, 39,* 5.

Woodiwiss, M., & Hobbs, D. (2009). Organized evil and the Atlantic alliance: Moral panics and the rhetoric of organized crime policing in America and Britain. *British Journal of Criminology, 49*(1), 106–112.

Wolfmann, L. C. (2000). *Portal do inferno: Mas há esperança.* São Paulo: WVC Gestão Inteligente Com. Ltda.

World Health Organisation. (2017). *Suicide rates, age standardized.* http://www.who.int/gho/mental_health/suicide_rates/en/. Last accessed 12 June 2017.

Wu, H. (1992). *Laogai: The Chinese gulag*. Boulder, CO: Westview.
Zaccone, O. (2007). *Acionistas do Nada: Quem são os traficantes de drogas*. Rio de Janeiro: Revan.
Zaccone, O. (2015). *Indignos de vida. A forma juridical da política de extermínio de inimigos na cidade de Rio de Janeiro*. Rio de Janeiro: Revan.
Zaffaroni, E. R. (1989). *En busca de las penas perdidas*. Buenos Aires: Editar Sociedad Anónima. Portuguese version: Zaffaroni, E. R. (1991). *Em busca das penas perdidas* (V. R. Pedrosa & A. L. Conceição, Trans.). Rio de Janeiro: Revan.
Zaffaroni, E. R. (1996). "Crime Organizado": Uma categoricação frustrada. *Discursos Sediciosos, 1*(1), 45–67.
Zaffaroni, E. R. (2006). *El enemigo en el derecho penal*. Madrid: Dykinson.
Zaffaroni, E. R., Batista, N., Alagia, A., & Slokar, A. (2003). *Direito Pena Brasileiro – Primeiro volume*. Rio de Janeiro: Revan.
Zaluar, A. (1994). *Condomínio do diablo*. Rio de Janeiro: Revan.
Zapater, M. (2017, February 3). Prisão com ala VIP: Qual a necessidade de cela especial? *Justificando*. http://justificando.cartacapital.com.br/2017/02/03/prisao-com-ala-vip-qual-necessidade-de-cela-especial. Last accessed 24 February 2017.
Zauli, F. (2017, January 20). Presos interrompem rebelião em presídio do RN para culto evangélico. *O globo*. http://g1.globo.com/rn/rio-grande-do-norte/noticia/2017/01/presos-interrompem-rebeliao-em-presidio-do-rn-para-culto-evangelico.html. Last accessed 28 February 2017.